Australia and the Antarctic Treaty System

50 Years of Influence

Edited by Marcus Haward
Tom Griffiths

Copyright Page from the Original Book

A UNSW Press book

Published by
University of New South Wales Press Ltd
University of New South Wales
Sydney NSW 2052
AUSTRALIA
www.unswpress.com.au

First published 2011

10 9 8 7 6 5 4 3 2 1

National Library of Australia
Cataloguing-in-Publication entry
Title: Australia and the Antarctic Treaty system: 50 years of influence/edited by Marcus Haward and Tom Griffiths.
ISBN: 978 174223 223 2 (hbk.)
Subjects: Australia. Antarctic Division – History.
        Antarctic Treaty system – History.
        Antarctica – International status – History.
Other Authors/Contributors: Griffiths, Tom, 1957–
        Haward, M. G. (Marcus G.)
Dewey Number: 341.290994

Design Josephine Pajor-Markus
Cover photos © Kristin Yates and Chris Wilson/Australian Antarctic Division
Printer Everbest

Front endpaper Map of Antarctica, produced by the Department of the Interior, Property and Survey Branch, Commonwealth of Australia 1939 [NLA 331525]. A facsimile map was published by the Australian Antarctic Division in November 2008 to celebrate the 75th anniversary of the Royal-Order-in-Council issued in February 1933 placing Antarctic territory under the control of the Commonwealth of Australia.

Back endpaper Australia's maritime jurisdiction, 2008. Map by Geoscience Australia.

Colour map Antarctica and the Southern Ocean: Oceanographic features and territorial claims. Map by Australian Antarctic Division, Copyright Commonwealth of Australia.

This book is printed on paper using fibre supplied from plantation or sustainably managed forests.

This optimized ReadHowYouWant edition contains the complete, unabridged text of the original publisher's edition. Other aspects of the book may vary from the original edition.

Copyright © 2010 Accessible Publishing Systems PTY, Ltd.
ACN 085 119 953

The text in this edition has been formatted and typeset to make reading easier and more enjoyable for ALL kinds of readers. In addition the text has been formatted to the specifications indicated on the title page. The formatting of this edition is the copyright of Accessible Publishing Systems Pty Ltd.

Set in 16 pt. Verdana

TABLE OF CONTENTS

List of contributors

ALESSANDRO ANTONELLO is a PhD candidate in the School of History in the Australian National University's Research School of Social Sciences. His research investigates scientific, environmental and diplomatic aspects of Antarctic history after the Second World War.

RACHEL BAIRD has a long-standing interest in Antarctica, particularly the history of the great expeditions of Shackleton and Amundsen. Rachel's PhD examined IUU fishing in the Southern Ocean and since then she has moved into fisheries and marine governance more generally. Recent publications include a chapter on fisheries enforcement in *Marine resources management* (Butterworths, 2011) and a forthcoming edited text with Don Rothwell on Australian coastal and marine law. Rachel is a consultant in the Environment and Planning section of the Brisbane office of Clayton Utz lawyers, and an adjunct associate professor at Queensland University Faculty of Law.

TIM BOWDEN AM is a Tasmanian-born writer and broadcaster with the Australian Broadcasting Corporation. He is the author of two books on Antarctica: *Antarctica and back in sixty days* (ABC Enterprises, 1991) and *The silence calling – Australians in Antarctica 1947–97* (Allen & Unwin, 1997).

EMERITUS PROFESSOR PETER BOYCE AO has held the Chair of Political Science at the universities of Queensland and Western Australia and served for eleven years as Vice-Chancellor of Murdoch University. He has researched and published in the field of Australian foreign relations and is currently an honorary research fellow in the University of Tasmania's School of Government.

DR LYNETTE FINCH is a historian whose publications include books on propaganda, urban childhood and urban health. In 2007 she travelled to Antarctica with the Australian Antarctic Division as an Arts Fellow to research a biography of Syd Kirkby, which she is presently writing.

SIR GUY GREEN, a former governor of Tasmania, has a particular interest in the Antarctic, sub-Antarctic and Southern Ocean region and Tasmania's role in it. He has given many Antarctic-related papers and addresses, including the inaugural Phillip Law Lecture. Current appointments include Chairman of Trustees, Tasmanian Museum and Art Gallery, Honorary Antarctic Ambassador for Tasmania and Chairman of the International Forum on the Sub-Antarctic.

TOM GRIFFITHS is the W K Hancock Professor of History at the Australian National University and author of *Slicing the Silence: voyaging to Antarctica* (UNSW Press, 2007), which was a co-winner of the Prime Minister's Prize for Australian History. In the summer of 2002/03 he travelled to Antarctica as a Humanities Fellow with the Australian Antarctic Division.

DR ROB HALL is Senior Lecturer in the School of Government at the University of Tasmania. His main research areas are the international politics of Antarctica, political leadership and the politics of bird conservation. His PhD was based on archival research conducted in Australia, the United States and the United Kingdom on the origins of the Antarctic Treaty.

MARCUS HAWARD is Associate Professor in the School of Government and the Antarctic Climate and Ecosystems Cooperative Research Centre, University of Tasmania, Hobart. Marcus has visited Macquarie Island as part of an Australian National Antarctic Research Expedition voyage and has been a member of Australian delegations to the Antarctic Treaty Consultative Meeting and CCAMLR. He is a member of the Australian Antarctic Division's CCAMLR Consultative Forum.

DR ALAN D HEMMINGS works on Antarctic governance and environmental management. As an independent consultant, Adjunct Associate Professor at Gateway Antarctica at New Zealand's University of Canterbury, and Research Associate at the University of Tasmania's Institute for Marine and Antarctic Studies, he is currently focused on the effects of globalisation and the erosion of Antarctica's historical, physical and political isolation. He is co-editor of *Antarctic security in the twenty-first century,* to be published by Routledge in 2011.

DR JULIA JABOUR is a senior lecturer and Program Leader – Ocean and Antarctic Policy, at the Institute for Marine and Antarctic Studies at the University of Tasmania. Her doctoral research investigated the changing nature of sovereignty in the Arctic and Antarctic in response to global environmental interdependence, and she has been writing and lecturing on Antarctic law and policy for nearly 20 years. Julia has visited Antarctica five times and has twice attended Antarctic Treaty Consultative Meetings.

ANDREW JACKSON'S career with the Australian Antarctic Division included over 20 years leading the policy functions. This took him to multiple Antarctic Treaty forums to pursue Australian initiatives as a delegation member during important developments in the Treaty system. He lurched across the Southern Ocean many times, visiting Antarctica and the sub-Antarctic with the Australian program. He now free-lances on Antarctic issues, including as an Honorary Fellow at the Antarctic Climate and Ecosystems Cooperative Research Centre in Hobart.

MICHAEL JOHNSON is a principal legal officer in the Australian Commonwealth Attorney-General's Department, where he has worked on international law and Antarctic issues. He has represented Australia at various Antarctic Treaty System meetings, including Antarctic Treaty Consultative Meetings. He holds a Master of Laws (International Law) degree from the University of Cambridge. The views expressed in his chapter are his own and do not necessarily represent the views of the Australian Government.

MARIE KAWAJA is an ARC Post-Doctoral Fellow, Australian National University, researching the history of the politics and diplomacy of the Australian

Antarctic. Her interest in the Australian Antarctic Territory resulted from her placement as an Antarctic desk officer in the Department of Foreign Affairs and Trade during the period of the Australian-French environmental initiative that led to the Environmental Protocol to the Antarctic Treaty in 1991. She edited the Antarctic Treaty Consultative Meeting documents from the 1960s to the 1980s.

STUART KAYE is Dean and Winthrop Professor of Law at the University of Western Australia. He has written extensively on international law, including *The Torres Strait, Australia's maritime boundaries, International fisheries management* and *Maritime claims in the Indian and Western Pacific oceans.* He was appointed to the List of Arbitrators under the Environmental Protocol to the Antarctic Treaty in 2000 and is a Fellow of the Royal Geographical Society.

DR LORNE KRIWOKEN is an environmental scientist in the School of Geography and Environmental Studies and a Research Associate with the Antarctic Climate and Ecosystems Cooperative Research Centre, University of Tasmania. His research interests are interdisciplinary and include biodiversity protection, environmental management and ocean and coastal governance. He has degrees in environmental science from Simon Fraser University, Dalhousie University and a PhD from University of Tasmania. He is co-editor of *Looking south: Australia's Antarctic agenda* (Federation Press, 2007).

TOM MAGGS joined ANARE in 1976. His roles in the Australian Antarctic Division over the following 35 years included Station Leader, Environment Manager and General Manager of the Strategies Branch. Tom's career includes a unique blend of Antarctic, operational and policy-related work, culminating with helping to set the vision for the next 25 years of Australia's engagement in Antarctic affairs. He represented Australia in many Antarctic Treaty Consultative Meetings, the CEP and associated forums.

DAVID MASON is Director of Treaties, Department of Foreign Affairs and Trade. He is a career diplomat who, after a first posting to Washington, became Head of Antarctica Section in 1979 and has retained his involvement in Antarctic affairs since then. He has held senior diplomatic positions in Dhaka, Seoul, London, Kuala Lumpur and most recently Vienna. David holds BA and LLB (Melb) degrees, and an ANU Master of International Law. He is currently completing a PhD thesis on treaties at the ANU.

DR CARL MURRAY is a Research Fellow in the School of Government at the University of Tasmania and an Honorary Fellow in the Antarctic Cooperative Research Centre. A wandering mind, a preference for cold climates, and visits to Antarctica with Russian and Chilean expeditions led to an academic interest in Antarctica. He has published on Antarctic adventure tourism, pre-discovery Antarctic mapping, and the story of Scott of the Antarctic.

DR TONY PRESS is the CEO of the Antarctic Climate and Ecosystems Cooperative Research Centre based at the University of Tasmania. From 1998 to 2008 he was the Director of the Australian Antarctic Division. Tony chaired the Antarctic Treaty's Committee for Environmental Protection from 2002 to 2006. He was Australia's representative to the CEP and Alternative Representative to the Antarctic Treaty Consultative Meetings from 1999 to 2008 and Australia's CCAMLR Commissioner from 1998 to 2008.

DONALD R ROTHWELL is Professor of International Law at the ANU College of Law, Australian National University. His research addresses many overlapping areas of international law with a specific focus on law of the sea, law of the polar regions, and implementation of international law within Australia. He is presently working on projects assessing Antarctic security, and a second edition of his book *The polar regions and the development of international law* (Cambridge, 1996).

SHIRLEY SCOTT is Associate Professor of International Relations and Director of Learning and Teaching in the Faculty of Arts and Social Sciences, UNSW. Her research lies at the intersection of international law, international relations and history. Publications on Antarctica include articles in *Polar Record* and *The International and Comparative Law Quarterly* and *The political interpretation of multilateral treaties* (Martinus Nijhoff, 2004). Shirley attributes her longstanding interest in Antarctic affairs to her Hobart upbringing.

MICHAEL STODDART is Chair of the Institute for Marine and Antarctic Studies at the University of Tasmania and a former Chief Scientist at the Australian Antarctic Division. He studied zoology at Aberdeen and Oxford Universities before teaching at London University prior to emigrating to Australia in 1985. He has written over 130 papers and book chapters, and three single-authored books on the olfactory biology of vertebrates.

Foreword

Richard Woolcott AC

Australia has a significant and continuing commitment to Antarctica and to the Antarctic Treaty System, yet the extent of our involvement is not as well known as it should be. This major work, *Australia and the Antarctic Treaty System: 50 years of influence,* is a well-researched, wide-ranging and valuable account of the nation's role on the continent and in the development of the highly successful Antarctic Treaty. The Treaty has served Australian interests by maintaining the conditions for peace and scientific research, protecting the continent's pristine environment, and preserving our sovereignty claim over the Australian Antarctic Territory, including our rights over adjacent waters. Importantly, throughout the Cold War, the Treaty maintained Antarctica as demilitarised and free from nuclear testing, providing one forum in which the United States and the Soviet Union were able to cooperate closely. This remains the case for all nations in Antarctica today.

Vast, frozen, remote and without permanent inhabitants, Antarctica fascinated me even as a child. At school I had studied James Cook's voyages and noted his comment in his journal in 1773 that 'no man will ever venture further south than I have done and the land which may lie to the south will never be explored'. Cook could not have imagined that in less than two centuries seven countries would have claimed sovereignty over parts of this last continent to be discovered and that a major treaty would have been negotiated to regulate international activity there. At school I had also read Douglas Stewart's epic verse play *The fire on the snow,* describing Scott's last days before he perished on the way back from the South Pole. Stewart wrote of the 'wide, white land' with 'ice breaking under foot like glass' and snow drifts forming white 'waves of iron'.

So I was delighted when Antarctica came to occupy an important place in my career in the Department of Foreign Affairs and Trade, first at the United Nations between 1983 and 1988 and then in Canberra between 1989 and 1991, when we were developing the Madrid Protocol. I visited Antarctica, including the South Pole, for a week in January 1985. Nothing I had read had so impressed upon me the pristine beauty of this awesome continent. I was closely involved in the Australian Government's defence of the legitimacy of the Antarctic Treaty, which was challenged by Malaysia and a number of other countries during the 1980s. The Treaty emerged from the test strengthened rather than weakened and, so long as the parties remain united in their approach, I believe it is now unassailable. After I became Head of the Department of Foreign Affairs and Trade, I was involved in the dramatic change in policy when, in May 1989, the Hawke government decided to reject the Convention on the Regulation of Antarctic Mineral Resource

Activities (CRAMRA). Australia had made a significant contribution to the development of CRAMRA but we were now to take the lead in undoing it and securing instead the agreement of the Treaty parties to the Madrid Protocol. This was finally achieved in October 1991 in the face of strong opposition from a number of other Treaty parties, including some with which we had long had close ties. It was one of the most successful exercises in Australian diplomacy that I can recall. That process and the defence of the Treaty in New York are well described in chapters 9, 11 and 12. The book also highlights our great and enduring interest in scientific research in Antarctica, especially relating to global oceanic and atmospheric circulation, climate change and glaciation, all of which can have important impacts on the southern region of the world and on our economy.

Given the scope of the activities described in this volume, Australia's enduring contribution to the success of the Antarctic Treaty System should be better known. I hope this book will make a significant contribution to increasing public understanding of Australia's influence in this vital international regime.

Acknowledgments

We gratefully acknowledge the contributors to this book. A collaborative project such as this generates its own challenges and we thank our authors for their commitment to the common endeavour and for their forbearance in coping with editorial demands. We hope that they have enjoyed the 'expedition'. Any expedition needs a calm hand on the helm; we wish to record our thanks to Carl Murray, an Antarctic scholar in his own right, who has provided ongoing editorial assistance and project support. Carl has been a very able project coordinator and we owe him a great debt.

The book was strengthened immensely by the generous contribution of Andrew Jackson, whose knowledge of Antarctic history and policy is unsurpassed. Professor Peter Boyce AO contributed his substantial insights into Australian diplomacy and also provided exemplary guidance as chair of the project's steering committee, which included Andrew Jackson, Tom Maggs and Rob Hall. We thank, too, Bernadette Hince, another esteemed Antarctic scholar, for her work on the manuscript and preparation of the notes and bibliography. We were gratified by interest in the project from current and former members of the Department of Foreign Affairs and Trade.

We acknowledge the support for this project from the Australian Government's Australian Antarctic Division within the Department of Sustainability, Environment, Water, Population and Communities. This enabled us to provide opportunities for public engagement in the course of our research, including a public seminar at Old Parliament House, Canberra on 1 December 2009 on the occasion of the 50th anniversary of the signing of the Antarctic Treaty. We also wish to recognise the support of the Australian Research Council through the award of a Discovery Grant 2010-12 (DP1094742 *Australia and the Antarctic Treaty System – a historical investigation*) that has enabled the project to be completed expeditiously. We gratefully acknowledge the Rockefeller Foundation Bellagio Center for its award of a Scholarly Residency to one of the project editors. Bellagio provided an inspiring environment for thinking about the creative tension between nationalism and global citizenship. We also note with thanks the support from the University of Tasmania, the Australian National University and the Antarctic Climate and Ecosystems Cooperative Research Centre.

Marcus Haward and Tom Griffiths

Introduction

Marcus Haward and Tom Griffiths

The Antarctic Treaty, which entered into force in 1961, is at the centre of an extensive and continually evolving regime governing Antarctica and the Southern Ocean. The Treaty represents a remarkable agreement that provides the basis for peaceful cooperation in that area of Earth south of 60º. It enables freedom of scientific investigation, facilitates free exchange of information between parties to the Treaty, and sets aside differences of view over sovereignty. From the nucleus of the Treaty has grown the Antarctic Treaty System (ATS), which comprises instruments to regulate activities in the region and institutions that allow Treaty parties to consult with each other and find agreement. As an original signatory to the Antarctic Treaty and a country with a substantial investment in a region immediately to its south, Australia has a strong interest in maintaining the Treaty and developing the ATS.

The year 2011 marks the centenary of Douglas Mawson's 1911–14 Australasian Antarctic Expedition (AAE), the 75th anniversary of the proclamation of the Australian Antarctic Territory and the 50th anniversary of the entry into force of the Antarctic Treaty. Anniversaries are appropriate times to reflect on the past, assess achievements and identify opportunities for the future. This book considers Australia's engagement with, and influence in, the ATS since its foundation.

Richard Casey, Australia's Minister for External Affairs from 1951 to 1960, welcomed the signing of the Antarctic Treaty on 1 December 1959 and asserted that its entry into force would represent:

> both a practical settlement of potentially difficult issues in an area of close and immediate concern to Australia, and a hopeful example of cooperation between East and West which might help to restore the confidence so sadly lacking in the post-war international scene.[1]

The ATS, while robust and arguably one of the most successful international regimes of the past half century, has faced a number of challenges. The Treaty itself was developed during the Cold War between the Soviet Union and the United States of America and provided a contrast to – and is also a remarkable product of – the tensions of that era. Its negotiation was a significant diplomatic effort, balancing the aspirations and interests of a number of countries, both claimants and non-claimants.

When delegates from the 12 nations that had participated in the International Geophysical Year (1957–58) in Antarctica met to discuss the potential treaty in Washington in October and November 1959, there was still uncertainty in the air. It was not simple. The result of their deliberations is a relatively brief, eloquent document – but it took the experience of working together in Antarctica, the momentum and euphoria of the International Geophysical Year, 18 months of working party meetings, and finally six weeks of demanding, cooperative negotiation in Washington to create it. It required courage and goodwill – and some planetary consciousness – from all parties. Participants were walking a kind of tightrope. The leader of the French delegation explained that 'each day that went by could bring about the failure of the Conference, but each day that passed brought to us a strengthened hope of success'. And there was indeed hope and optimism in the air – and a sense of history too. Antarctic history itself was an inspiration. Delegates to the Washington conference felt a humble continuity with the courage of explorers past. A Norwegian delegate declared that 'the thrilling saga of Antarctica has inspired men everywhere with its emphasis on basic human values – courage, patience and willingness to work together towards a common goal'. The conference, he said, was imbued with 'the spirit of mutual understanding, goodwill and, I shall even say friendship'.[2] This spirit has endured.

This book examines Australia's actions and influence, past and present, within the ATS. Antarctica constitutes a significant gap in Australian foreign policy history. Australia has made vital contributions to international debates about Antarctic policy, yet this influential dimension of foreign policy has been insufficiently studied through detailed historical research of Australian government archives. It is this book's investment in sustained historical research in the files of the National Archives of Australia that, in part, distinguishes it from the two excellent Australian Antarctic policy reviews of Harris in 1984 and Kriwoken, Jabour and Hemmings in 2007.[3] A serious effect of the underuse of Australian archival sources has been that Australia's contribution to British imperial policy in the Antarctic has been underestimated.[4]

Although Australian interest in Antarctica was strong even before Federation in 1901, the nation's official exploration of the southern continent effectively dates from Douglas Mawson's Australasian Antarctic Expedition (AAE) of 1911–14. Throughout the 1920s and 1930s, energetic Australian diplomacy was instrumental in expanding the frontiers of the British Empire into the Antarctic. Australia was no 'passive witness' to imperial events but acted according to its own clear and distinctive views and its material self-interest in Antarctic affairs.[5] This Antarctic perspective adds a new dimension to understandings of 'Australia's Empire' in this period, to use the title of the recent stimulating companion volume in the Oxford History of the British Empire series.[6] Mawson continued to promote Antarctic exploration and himself led the 1929–31 British, Australian and New Zealand Antarctic Research Expedition (BANZARE), which resulted in the formalisation in 1933 of Australia's claim to 42 per cent of the continent.

In an important commentary in 1984, diplomat John Brook noted that Australia's policy interests down south included sovereignty, neutrality, protection of the Antarctic environment, Antarctic science, involvement in Antarctica and national benefit.[7] Territorial and sovereignty interests were significant drivers for initial Australian activities, but so too was the need to understand Antarctica's influence on Australian (and later global) weather and climate. This has meant that science, which figured prominently in Mawson's AAE, has always been central to Australia's involvement in Antarctica. Security has been another enduring Australian interest in Antarctic affairs, with the government expressing concern at the Antarctic Conference of 1959 about the potential for superpower rivalry in the continent, militarisation and the use of the continent for nuclear testing or storage of nuclear waste.

This volume's main focus is the 50-year period of operation of the ATS, but the contributors also glance backwards to the antecedents of the regime and look forward to identify emerging issues. We have organised the book to provide an opportunity to explore the diplomatic history of Australian engagement, leadership and influence in the ATS and at the same time to allow consideration of key thematic topics in greater depth. The thematic chapters are placed adjacent to the historical chapters for which they have special relevance, but they also range across the entire timeframe of the ATS. This approach allows the subject of the book to be simultaneously surveyed from a variety of different vantage points with the aim of producing fresh insights and connections. By combining the perspectives of academics with those of practitioners, the book provides a unique view of its subject from both inside and outside the Antarctic Treaty forums. It is an unashamedly Australian view.

The book's subject is the evolution of Australia's long engagement with the continent of ice and the influence this nation has had on specific areas of science, policy and culture. Aspects of both continuity and change are identified and explored. The Australian Antarctic Division administers three permanent research stations on the continent, one of them the longest continuously operating station south of the Antarctic Circle; but while Australia's efforts down south have been persistent, they have not always been of the same intensity. In addition, Australia has both initiated change within the ATS and responded to changed external circumstances. In the late 1970s Australian engagement in the ATS centred on negotiations over what became the Convention on the Conservation of Antarctic Marine Living Resources (CCAMLR). CCAMLR introduced an ecosystem-based policy into the management of living resources, an approach that became incorporated more widely in other international instruments in the 1990s. Australia acts as Depositary State for CCAMLR and hosts its secretariat in Hobart. In the early 1980s, Australia played a central role in addressing the 'Question of Antarctica', a challenge to the ATS mounted by a group of third-world countries led by Malaysia. In the late 1980s, Australia itself challenged consensus within the ATS. Although it had taken an active part in the negotiation of the Convention on the Regulation of Antarctic Mineral Resource Activities (CRAMRA) between 1982 and 1988, Australia decided in 1989 not to sign the agreement. External criticism over this decision was matched by initial internal differences within government, but Australia's concerns about the convention, supported by France, were eventually pivotal in initiating a new round of negotiations that led to the development of the Protocol on Environmental Protection to the Antarctic Treaty that supplanted CRAMRA. Australia has also led approaches to managing fishing in the Southern Ocean, and set precedents for Antarctica's interface with the Law of the Sea.

While we explicitly focus on Australia and have explored the breadth, extent and impact of Australian engagement with the Antarctic Treaty and the broader ATS, collaboration with other Treaty parties has been crucial in the exercise of Australian influence. At all times Australia has remained committed to working through the principles and norms of the ATS, but this does not mean that it has avoided opportunities to challenge other parties to consider alternative approaches on some issues. Australian engagement has involved active participation. It has taken the lead on numerous issues, including some that initially lacked broad consensus or support. To use a sporting metaphor, Australia has not been afraid of going for the hard ball, of taking the game forward, even if it at times it has appeared offside with other parties.

By pursuing difficult issues and by deepening policy discussions, Australia and like-minded parties have contributed to ensuring the viability and relevance of the ATS.

Longstanding and bipartisan domestic political support exists for Australia's active engagement in the ATS and, together with a strong commitment to maintaining the Australian Antarctic Territory, underpins the nation's influence within the ATS. The key interests that drive that domestic political commitment have remained relatively stable, even as they have also developed and evolved. Current Australian government goals for the Australian Antarctic Program are:

- to maintain the Antarctic Treaty System and enhance Australia's influence within it;
- to protect the Antarctic environment;
- to understand the role of Antarctica in the global climate system; and
- to undertake scientific work of practical, economic and national significance.[8]

Antarctica itself continues to humble and educate those who have the privilege to visit or to work there. Marshall Green, the US State Department's leading expert on East Asia (who became the American Ambassador to Australia in 1973–75) visited Antarctica for six days in late December 1974 at the invitation of the US National Science Foundation. In the late 1950s, he had opposed the Antarctic Treaty. But his 1974 visit to McMurdo, the Dry Valleys and the South

Pole confirmed in his mind that he had been wrong to do so. He came to believe strongly that 'the unique international framework' under which science flourished in Antarctica 'should be as well known to diplomats as other important developments on this globe'. Impressed as he was by the scientific work, he was impressed even more 'by the avid spirit of unfettered cooperation among the scientists of all nationalities involved and the remarkable wisdom and foresight underlying the Antarctic Treaty of 1961'.[9]

At an evening discussion at McMurdo, which included the leader from New Zealand's nearby Scott Base, Green 'advanced the thought that perhaps in the long run the most important contribution of Antarctica to mankind might be in the fact that this Antarctic experiment in international cooperation is actually succeeding, unlike virtually all other international cooperative efforts'. He continued his account in his diary:

> In sum, it seemed to me that Antarctica, the last discovered, most remote and only uninhabited continent, could achieve great significance in an age when international cooperation is an absolute imperative. If we can resist the pressures of narrow national advantage, be it in terms of fisheries or minerals or military power, and continue on the present path of pure Antarctic cooperation, then it could be the model for the future ... Were that great Antarctic experiment in inter-

national cooperation to succeed, then perhaps there is hope for other forms of global cooperation as well; if it fails, then what international cooperation could succeed?

Surely the Antarctic Treaty signed in 1959 is an extraordinarily farsighted, wise document and it is to my lasting shame that, in the cold war atmosphere dominating the Far East in 1957–59, I opposed the Treaty.[10]

Green prefaced the diary of his visit, which is now preserved in the National Archives of Australia, with the observation: 'It is ironic, as I note in this journal, that the UN flag centered on the North Pole cannot properly depict the one continent where international cooperation has triumphed so successfully over narrow nationalism.'[11]

The annual Antarctic Treaty Consultative Meeting (ATCM) is the international forum for all significant decisions regarding the management of Antarctica, through the processes of consensus and collaboration saluted by Marshall Green. Australia hosted the first ATCM, in Canberra in 1961. In 2012 Australia again hosts the ATCM, this time in Hobart, Australia's Antarctic gateway. This meeting, together with the anniversaries of Australian engagement with Antarctica, will provide further opportunities for reflection on the achievements and future of the ATS. We hope that this book will contribute to such discussions.

We will let Richard Casey have the last word. His lifelong enthusiasm for Antarctica was expressed in his parliamentary speeches. In 1953, as plans to establish Mawson Station were underway, Casey declared:

> The present generation is the trustee for an Australian posterity. For us to neglect the Antarctic would be as serious as if our forefathers had confined themselves to a small strip of coastal settlement in Australia. Today the Antarctic is a challenge, which cannot be ignored, to Australian courage and imagination.

Later that decade, Casey attended the 1959 Washington Conference and worked strenuously for an international treaty, which he described as 'one of the most promising developments in recent history'. He understood the indissoluble connection between Australia's Antarctic interest and the health of the Antarctic Treaty System.

Notes

[1]   Casey (1959) 667.
[2]   United States Government (1960) 47, 50.
[3]   Harris (1984) and Kriwoken, Jabour and Hemmings (2007).
[4]   Beck (1983b); Beck (1986a); Dodds (1997).
[5]   See chapter 1, and Kawaja (2010).
[6]   Schreuder and Ward (2008).
[7]   Brook (1984) 256–59. Also Haward, Rothwell et al (2006).
[8]   Australian Antarctic Division (2002).
[9]   Green (1974).

[10]   Green (1974).
[11]   Green (1974).

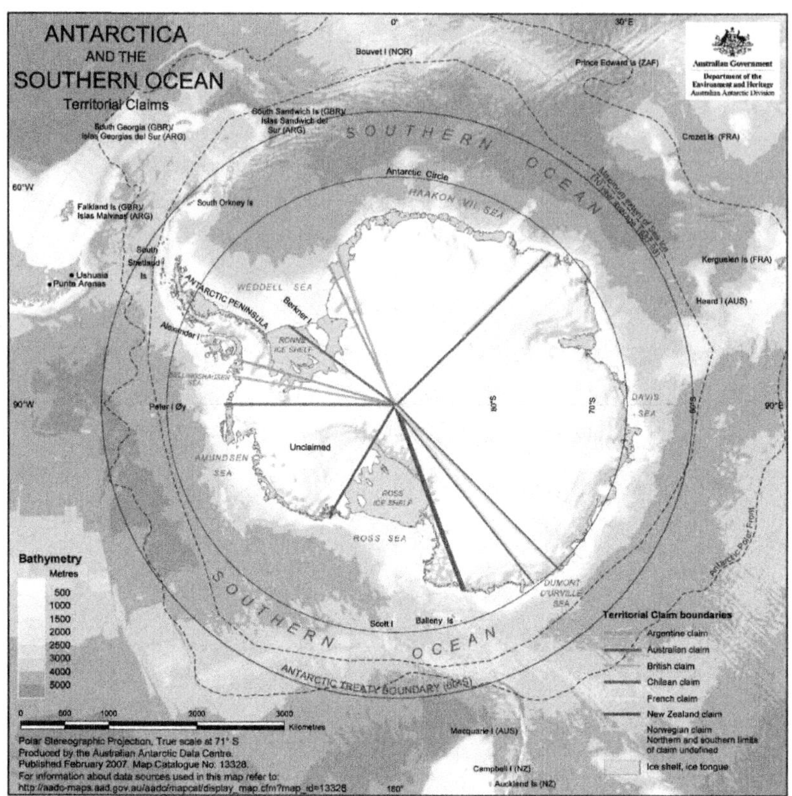

ANTARCTICA
AND THE
SOUTHERN OCEAN
Territorial Claims
Australian Government
Department of the
Environment and Heritage
Australian Antarctic Division
SOUTHERN OCEAN
SOUTHERN OCEAN
Bouvet I (NOR)
Prince Edward Is (ZAF)
Crozet Is (FRA)
Kerguelen Is (FRA)
Heard I (AUS)
South Sandwich Is (GBR)
Islas Sandwich del Sur (ARG)
South Georgia (GBR)
Islas Georgias del Sur (ARG)
Antarctic Circle
HAAKON VII SEA
Falkland Is (GBR)
Islas Malvinas (ARG)
South Orkney Is
South Shetland Is
ANTARCTIC PENINSULA
WEDDELL SEA
Berkner I
Ushuaia
Punta Arenas
Alexander I
RONNE ICE SHELF
Peter I Øy
DAVIS SEA
90°W
90°E
90°S
70°S
AMUNDSEN SEA
Unclaimed
ROSS ICE SHELF
ROSS SEA
DUMONT D'URVILLE SEA
Scott I
Balleny Is
SOUTHERN OCEAN
ANTARCTIC TREATY BOUNDARY (60°S)
Macquarie I (AUS)
Campbell I (NZ)
Auckland Is (NZ)
60°W
0°
30°E
180°
Bathymetry
Metres
500
1000
1500
2000
2500
3000
4000
5000
0   500   1000   2000   3000
Kilometres
Polar Stereographic Projection, True scale at 71° S
Produced by the Australian Antarctic Data Centre.
Published February 2007. Map Catalogue No: 13328.
For information about data sources used in this map refer to:
http://aadc-maps.aad.gov.au/aadc/mapcat/display_map.cfm?map_id=13328
Territorial Claim boundaries
Argentine claim
Australian claim
British claim
Chilean claim
French claim
New Zealand claim
Norwegian claim
Northern and southern limits
of claim undefined
Ice shelf, ice tongue

1

'Our great frozen neighbour': Australia and Antarctica before the Treaty, 1880–1945

Marie Kawaja and Tom Griffiths

The Antarctic has been embedded in Australian consciousness from colonial times. Voyagers, sealers and whalers headed south from colonial ports and from the 1880s the colonists themselves began to turn an imperial gaze towards the ice. Exploring Antarctica became a proud initiative of the newly federated nation in the early twentieth century. After the Great War, Australia exerted strong pressure on Britain to secure sovereignty over the vast region of Antarctica south of Australia. It was as close to Australia as Hobart was to Fremantle. Australians felt a growing affinity with, and responsibility for, their 'Great Frozen Neighbour'.[1]

During the first half of the twentieth century, Antarctica evolved from a heroic destination for the adventurous explorer into an imperial 'question' and national challenge, and finally into an international 'problem'. This chapter summarises the scientific, political and diplomatic events that led to Australia becoming Antarctica's major claimant state through the creation of the Australian Antarctic Territory (AAT) in 1933. An analysis of Australia's role in developing the British Empire's Antarctic policy, particularly in the interwar period, offers a distinctive view of the Anglo-Australian relationship and reveals an assertive Australian government wishing to be the controlling power in the region to Australia's south. The government's Antarctic goal drew strength from popular domestic support for Antarctic endeavour and also from a confident and enthusiastic Australian scientific community which offered its expertise in developing Antarctic policy.[2]

Great South Lands

The search for the mythical Great South Land had long stimulated exploration of high southern latitudes. Australia and Antarctica – once linked in deep geological time – became united again in the European geographical imagination. But neither was to satisfy the northern hemisphere expectation of a vast, rich continent spanning the Southern Ocean. Captain James Cook voyaged adventurously through seas 'pestered with ice' in 1772–75 and circumnavigated Antarctica without ever quite being sure it was there. From his vantage point as the first human to cross the Antarctic Circle, he gazed further south with foreboding and intuition. He was convinced by the character of the ice that there was a nucleus of land at the pole. But if it was there, it held no promise: 'If any one go further south than I have been,' declared Cook, 'I shall not envy him the honour of the discovery.'[3]

In January 1820, Admiral Fabian Gottlieb Bellingshausen of the Imperial Russian Navy became the first since Cook to cross the Antarctic Circle, and he may also have sighted the continent. The following decade, John Biscoe, a captain of the British Enderby mercantile firm, reported on arrival in Hobart Town that he had managed 'intermittent views of the Antarctic continent'.[4] Australian explorer Douglas Mawson later credited Biscoe with the discovery of the region that became the Australian Antarctic Territory.[5] But most of the ships nosing around Antarctic and sub-Antarctic seas were those of sealers making a living at the edge of the known world. Sealing took off in the far south in the wake of Cook's reports of island colonies of glistening creatures, and it was sealers who became the incidental (and sometimes secretive) explorers of the Antarctic and sub-Antarctic coastlines. The history of sealing and whaling in the Southern Ocean offers a stunning, repeated pattern of discovery, over-exploitation and rapid decline, as new islands and oceans were invaded and swiftly exhausted. Remarkably quickly, and with ruthless efficiency, British and American sealing ships stripped the rocks and beaches bare of the animals, slaughtering fur seals for their pelts and elephant seals for their blubber oil (see chapter 10).

In the mid-nineteenth century, the desire to understand and map terrestrial magnetism brought voyagers face to face with great ramparts of ice. Following the location of the North Magnetic Pole by the British naval officer James Clark Ross in 1831, there was a competitive quest to locate the South Magnetic Pole in the years 1837–43. Australian colonial ports provided stepping stones to the Antarctic and safe havens for the returning battered ships and men, while the Sydney and Hobart newspapers carried accounts of their discoveries. Three official expeditions voyaged south, taking magnetic readings in the Antarctic region – they were led by Jules Sébastien César Dumont d'Urville of France, Charles Wilkes of the American South Seas Exploring Expedition, and James Clark Ross in his British ships, *Erebus* and *Terror.* All reported sightings of the perceived Antarctic continent. After landing on a rocky island Dumont d'Urville took possession for France of the coastline he sighted, which was due south of Van Diemen's Land, and named it Adélie Land after his fiancée, while Ross happened upon the huge embayment that came to bear his name (the Ross Sea) and named his territorial discovery Victoria Land after his Queen.[6]

The voyagers found it difficult to distinguish land from clouds, land from ice, and land from islands. Rocks were of more than scientific interest; they were crucial geopolitical footholds. But the existence of a continent under the ice was not confirmed until the

1930s and the great depth of the ice cap was discovered only in the 1950s.

To Europeans, Russians and North Americans, the Antarctic continent was at the other end of their universe, an exotic destination for heroic exploration. To Australians, Antarctica was both their neighbour and their natural inheritance. In the second half of the nineteenth century, colonial Australians became increasingly aware of the icy world to their south. Experiencing the west winds of the Roaring Forties and Furious Fifties was like an initiation ritual for Australian-bound immigrants. From the 1850s, the Great Circle route to Australia was pioneered and promoted, and captains began arcing down to higher latitudes to save a thousand miles. Icebergs – glistening emissaries of the polar continent – sometimes strayed across their bows. Sailors and scientists analysed the sea, ice and wind as indirect evidence of the character of Antarctica. Writing in 1859, the American oceanographer Matthew Maury hoped that one day meteorological stations would be established on Heard Island and other points in the region of the 'brave west winds ... I know of no enterprise in the meteorological way that ... gives promise of richer rewards than this does, both practically to the mariner and scientifically to the philosopher'.[7] Australian colonists trying to come to terms with their land of drought began to wonder about the effect of the southern distribution of ice on the country's climate. Colonial learned societies pondered Antarctica's mysteries and wished to be part of the global campaign to reveal them (see chapter 6).

The Australian Antarctic Exploration Committee

In 1886, an Australian Antarctic Exploration Committee was formed in Melbourne. Its purpose was to look to the Antarctic region for the 'grandest results' in geographical science.[8] Cartographer E F Du Faur, who had been Chief Draftsman at the Crown Lands Office in Sydney, together with Baron Ferdinand von Mueller, the Victorian Government Botanist, believed that Antarctic scientific research was necessary because the Australian climate was affected by Antarctica.[9] Charles Sprent, Tasmanian Deputy Surveyor-General and a member of the Geographical Society of Australasia, went further by suggesting it was Australia's responsibility to explore the Antarctic regions because 'we aspire to be the leading power in these Southern Seas, we are gradually setting up a Monroe Doctrine of our own'.[10] The Monroe Doctrine was a policy articulated by the United States in the 1820s which asserted that its own region of the world was not to be further colonised by European countries. Sprent's model for an Australian Monroe Doctrine did not exclude the prospect of Australians joining with other 'Geographical Societies of England, Germany,

Italy and Denmark' to undertake work in Antarctica.[11]

If the Antarctic Exploration Committee wished to translate its desire into reality, it had to find funds to equip an expedition. Victoria was the first colonial government to promise funds in its budget estimates, provided other colonies also contributed.[12] If such support were forthcoming, an expedition could be ready to sail from Melbourne in October 1887.[13] The Premier of Tasmania, P O Fysh, who would become part of the Federation movement of the 1890s, suggested that such a venture would help the Australian colonies to develop a 'federal spirit'.[14] G S Griffiths, one of the organisers of the committee, argued that 'the exploration of these regions is a task which, by our geographical position and our wealth, is thrown on Australia as a duty which we cannot evade if we have any adequate conception of our great position in the southern seas'.[15] Exploring Antarctica was Australia's duty, Australia's 'preserve', Australia's destiny.

The exploration committee also hoped to gain the support of the Antarctic Committee of the British Association for the Advancement of Science, and of other influential persons in London.[16] The Australian plan attracted attention from commercial interests in England, Scotland and Norway, especially if science could be combined with a business venture such as whaling.[17] In London, the reception was mixed. Naval officer and Arctic explorer Sir Erasmus

Ommanney, secretary to the Antarctic Committee of the association, was sympathetic but remained 'strongly of opinion that the mother country only can adequately equip and conduct a suitable scientific expedition, which *must* be naval'.[18]

The negative response forced the Australians to turn elsewhere. In 1890, Baron Oscar Dickson, a Swedish industrialist, offered to defray half of the costs of an expedition 'provided that the other half, not exceeding £5,000' came from the colonies. The expedition would be under the command of Baron Adolf Erik Nordenskiöld.[19] Without hesitation, the Royal Society of Victoria and the Royal Geographical Society of Victoria expressed satisfaction and delight in the prospect that the 'red cross of Sweden and the starry cross of Australia planted side by side will at some future but not far distant day open their folds to the Antarctic breezes'.[20] The Anglican Bishop of Hobart, Bishop Montgomery, exclaimed that 'he might yet have the South Pole in his diocese'.[21]

By mid-1891 the prospect of an Australian Antarctic expedition had gained further momentum as various colonial governments pledged funds.[22] But within a few years, the economic bust of the 1890s intervened. Expedition funds had been placed in a 'boom bank and were lost'.[23] It is intriguing to speculate that, had a joint expedition with Sweden taken place in the late nineteenth century, Australia's external relations might well have been exercised more boldly at a future time.

The heroic age

The terms 'heroic age' and 'heroic era' refer to the two decades when Antarctica became the focus of intense private and patriotic endeavour, from the final years of the nineteenth century until the Great War. At the Sixth International Geographical Congress in London in 1895, scientists resolved that 'the exploration of the Antarctic regions is the greatest piece of geographical exploration still to be undertaken'. Belgium, Britain, Germany, Sweden, Scotland, Argentina, France, Norway, Japan and Australia launched scientific expeditions south, and there was a simultaneous quest for the northern pole. Funded more from private than government sources, these expeditions were nevertheless inspired by nationalism. The age was heroic not only because it generated tales of extraordinary individual achievement and sacrifice, but also because the explorers raced one another not so much to secure territory as to establish national pride and personal honour on the world stage.

Australians joined British expeditions led by Carsten Egeberg Borchgrevink (1898–1900), Robert Falcon Scott (1901–04 and 1910–13) and Ernest Shackleton (1907–09). There had been a few landfalls on the Antarctic Peninsula earlier in the nineteenth century, but the first recorded landing in eastern Antarctica took place in 1895 when several members of a whaling expedition stumbled ashore at Cape

Adare in today's Ross Dependency. One of those men was Borchgrevink, a Norwegian colonist of Australia who within a few years took his own ship, the *Southern Cross,* back to this region. In 1899, the men of the *Southern Cross* became the first humans to winter on the continent.[24] Expedition member and Tasmanian physicist Louis Bernacchi collected meteorological and magnetic records for a whole year.[25] The state of knowledge about Antarctica was poor. Was it a continent or just an archipelago of islands connected by ice sheets? What kinds of animals might they find? The *Southern Cross,* just 45 metres long, was equipped with shotguns and ammunition to deal with polar bears or other threatening land animals.[26] The Hobart *Mercury,* in explaining to its readers the need for Borchgrevink's expedition, speculated that 'there is reason to believe that the two Poles of the earth do not correspond'.[27]

In 1901, Sir Henry Copeland, the Agent-General for New South Wales in London, sought to convince Edmund Barton, the first prime minister of the newly federated Commonwealth of Australia, to purchase sub-Antarctic Kerguelen Island from France. Copeland believed that Kerguelen's location in the southern Indian Ocean between Australia and Africa gave it strategic value in protecting Australia's trade routes.[28] Although Barton was attracted to the idea, the British Admiralty rejected it outright, holding that the risk to shipping was too great in the turbulent waters of the region.[29] Apart from its political advance on Kerguelen Island, the Barton government showed little enthusiasm to join in the international effort to explore and map Antarctica. Barton was sympathetic to scientific collaboration, but he felt unable to promise any financial assistance to Scott's first expedition because of budgetary concerns in the year of Federation.[30]

Six years later, in 1907, the question of Australian participation in Antarctic exploration occupied the attention of another Australian prime minister, Alfred Deakin. When Ernest Shackleton began organising his own Antarctic expedition to the Ross Sea in the *Nimrod* (1907–09), he hoped to raise funds in both Australia and New Zealand.[31] He invited the professor of geology at Sydney University, Tannatt William Edgeworth David, and Edgeworth David's young protégé, Douglas Mawson, to accompany him.[32] With Edgeworth David's help, Shackleton was able to attract financial support from the Australian Government, convincing Deakin that both Australia and New Zealand 'are affected by weather conditions that have their origin in the Antarctic'.[33] Members of parliament from all parties supported the government's £5000 contribution. In the words of Joseph Cook, a future prime minister of the Common-wealth, 'it is our obligation to do what we can to make known all that lies hidden in that mysterious land'.[34]

Shackleton's ambition was the conquest of the Geographic South Pole. Deakin, on the other hand, was keen to see Australia participate in the emerging field of Antarctic science. In 1908, Shackleton failed to reach the pole, falling short of his destination by only 155 kilometres through lack of food.[35]

Edgeworth David's expedition to the South Magnetic Pole had more success. With Mawson and Scottish surgeon Alistair Mackay, Edgeworth David reached the vicinity of the South Magnetic Pole, hoisted the Union Jack and took possession of the area for the British Empire on the afternoon of 16 January 1909.[36] This trio's 2030-kilometre trek was the longest unsupported manhaul sledging journey of the heroic era.

While the Shackleton expedition was exploring in the Ross Sea in 1908, Britain declared sovereignty over the Falkland Islands Dependencies.[37] In addition to sub-Antarctic islands, the Dependencies included Graham Land, part of the Antarctic Peninsula, and Coats Land, although Coats Land was not named in the Letters Patent in which sovereignty was declared.[38] Through this act, the British Empire became the first power not only to assert legal title to sub-Antarctic islands and the seas around them but to extend sovereignty to Antarctica itself.[39] The British Government had always considered the sub-Antarctic islands around the Falkland Islands as British dependencies and had issued sealing and whaling licences to commercial enterprises, both British and foreign.[40] The area was south of Chile and Argentina, but neither country protested Britain's sovereignty claims at the time, although both had wished to incorporate these islands into their own territories.[41] The British declaration halted South American ambitions, but only temporarily, as disputes over legal title began to surface during World War II (see chapter 3).

The two most famous heroic-era expeditions were noble tragedies. Robert Falcon Scott and his four companions died in early 1912 after manhauling their sledges to the South Pole and most of the way back – but the Norwegian Roald Amundsen and his four companions had beaten them to the pole by five weeks. Scott's inspiring letters and diary entries, written from the tent that would become his tomb, have become sacred texts of Antarctic history. In 1914–15, Ernest Shackleton's attempt to cross the Antarctic ice cap from the Weddell Sea to the Ross Sea foundered when his ship, the *Endurance,* was trapped and crushed in the ice of the Weddell Sea. The story of how Shackleton and his men rescued themselves – and then rescued most of the marooned party waiting for them on the other side of the continent – is a tale of tenacity and hardship. The central icon of that saga is a small whaling boat, the *James Caird,* which carried Shackleton and five men across 1300 kilometres of stormy Southern Ocean to the whaling communities of South Georgia. As the explorers stumbled into Stromness, the first human sound they heard was a factory whistle. Industry was already well entrenched in Antarctica's backyard.[42]

Steam Yacht Aurora at the edge of the ice shelf off Queen Mary Land in 1911, during the Australasian Antarctic Expedition. National Archives of Australia: M584, 2

Douglas Mawson's Australasian Antarctic Expedition, 1911–14

The most adventurously scientific expedition of the heroic era, and one that put geographical exploration ahead of the race to the pole, was the Australasian Antarctic Expedition (AAE) led by Douglas Mawson in 1911–14.[43] When Mawson returned from the Shackleton expedition, he was convinced that the Australian Government should take the lead in asserting control over the sector of Antarctica to the south of Australia. In 1910 he and other members of the scientific community began preparing for an Antarctic expedition which they hoped would lead to control of the region that 'seems to belong to Australia' and which was referred to as the 'Australian

Quadrant, geographically'.[44] This vast sector had not been visited since the great expeditions of the 1840s and remained relatively unknown.

In February 1910, Mawson travelled to London to discuss with both Scott and Shackleton his plans for exploration. Scott offered Mawson a place on his own 1910 expedition and even promised him membership of the polar party.[45] Mawson declined, stating that his interests lay in exploring the uncharted coastline south of Australia.[46] (Two other Australians, Griffith Taylor and Frank Debenham, accompanied Scott south in 1910.[47]) Shackleton 'was warmly enthusiastic' when Mawson laid his plans before him, but declined to lead the expedition. Instead he encouraged Mawson, and promised his support.[48] The Melbourne *Argus* declared without reservation that Australians should financially support the expedition, which it understood would be 'scientific and economic' and would 'not make any dash for the Pole'.[49] The anticipated cost was £40,000.

The Australasian Association for the Advancement of Science wished to involve the government in this 'Australian expedition'.[50] In January 1911, the association proposed to G F Pearce, Minister for Defence, that a planning committee be appointed that 'would be modified if the Commonwealth Government came in, otherwise the expedition would be free from any other control whatever'.[51] Mawson promoted the expedition to the minister as an investment in Australia's long-term prosperity. He argued that the

Australian Quadrant had untapped marine and mineral wealth which would lead to its eventual colonisation, for it was easier to reach than the Klondike.[52] Mawson also anticipated that sealing alone would result in a bustling shipping trade, while a sanatorium could be built for those wishing a healthy holiday where the climate was bracing and the scenery gorgeous.[53] Mawson's marketing pitch convinced the minister, who discussed a permanent settlement and minerals exploration.[54]

Although the minister's enthusiasm did not translate into complete financial support, Prime Minister Andrew Fisher joined Leader of the Opposition Alfred Deakin and Governor-General Lord Denman at a Melbourne Town Hall meeting to encourage private donations for the first Australian expedition to Antarctica.[55] The scientists were asking for at least £20,000 from the government, a daunting sum – but still only half the amount needed.[56] The government voted the sum of £5000 (it had given a similar amount to Shackleton four years earlier).[57] Together with donations from some of the state governments, the expedition received £23,500 in official funds. The rest was made up from private donations.[58]

Mawson went south armed with flags. The Shackleton expedition had not taken enough, and David's party to the South Magnetic Pole had needed to sew up a Union Jack in their quarters. Mawson wanted his expedition to take possession for Australia and the Empire of any territory he discovered and thus sought

Colonial Office permission to formalise his proclamations.[59] He was not given the official authority he requested – but nor did the Colonial Office discourage him from raising the flag.[60] In anticipation of questions about the status of Dumont d'Urville's claim, Mawson assumed that France had abandoned the claim, as Adélie Land had not been revisited by a French explorer since 1840.[61]

The Australasian Antarctic Expedition (AAE) raising the Union Jack after the completion of their hut at Cape Denison, Commonwealth Bay, in 1912. James Francis (Frank) Hurley, State Library of NSW

At the end of 1911, Mawson established a base on the edge of the East Antarctic ice cap at Commonwealth Bay and launched a comprehensive scientific program in new territory. His expedition discovered and mapped most of the Australian Quadrant from approximately 160° to 90° East and, after receiving Royal approval, named two large separate tracts of land King George V Land and Queen Mary Land. Apart from land discoveries, the AAE pioneered the use of wireless telegraphy, allowing the expedition to communicate with Australia and London. A priority of Mawson's AAE was also to establish a weather station at Macquarie Island, and it was achieved with the strong support of Henry Hunt, the Commonwealth Meteorologist, who lent one of his officers, George Ainsworth, to lead the party. A wireless mast was erected on the island and daily weather readings were broadcast to Australia and New Zealand.[62]

In the summer of 1912–13, Mawson survived a traumatic sledging journey during which he lost both his companions, Belgrave Ninnis and Xavier Mertz. Ninnis was swallowed by a crevasse and disappeared with most of the food, forcing Mawson and Mertz to begin a desperate journey back to base. Mertz died of malnutrition and vitamin A poisoning from eating the livers of the sledge dogs, and Mawson nursed him to the last.

Alone and with still more than 160 kilometres to go, Mawson battled on, falling down crevasses and hauling himself out again with a rope ladder that tied him to his sledge. On 8 February 1913, he picked his way down the final, steep, slippery slope to the hut in time to glimpse his ship, the *Aurora,* steaming out of Commonwealth Bay. To Mawson's untold relief, six men had stayed behind for another whole year in case their leader returned. He had staggered back to the hut just three days before the story of Scott's death broke upon the world.[63]

Playing imperial politics

The AAE laid strong foundations for continuing joint action between the Australian scientific community and the federal government on Antarctic matters. During the Great War, Mawson began lobbying both the Australian and British governments to formalise the claims he had made for Australia and the British Empire. In 1916 he urged Australian Prime Minister W M Hughes to put Antarctica on the international agenda for post-war territorial settlement, arguing that 'all unclaimed territories of the world should be allocated, for better or for worse, to specific nations'. Antarctica, he suggested, was the only land of this kind remaining.[64] Mawson believed that the Antarctic continent should be divided into geographical sectors and that these should be allocated to the nations that had undertaken the most significant exploration and research.[65] If the Australian Quadrant were brought under Australian control, the new Commonwealth 'would then stretch from Pole to Equator'.[66]

Since colonial times 'the vitally important subject of "Droughts, their Cause, Effect, and Mitigation"' had been at the forefront of Australian meteorological research.[67] By 1927, the Queensland Branch of the

Royal Geographical Society of Australasia was urging the federal government to establish a series of meteorological stations 'on the outposts of the Antarctic Continent nearest to Australia'.[68] The society believed that the movements of icebergs and icefields profoundly influenced the Australian climate, particularly 'in regard to rainfall and recurring droughts', and that observations were essential to seasonal forecasting for the pastoral and agricultural industries.[69] The Australian polar explorer G H (Hubert) Wilkins had made a similar suggestion two years earlier to R G Casey, Australia's liaison officer in London, telling Casey of his vision of a ring of meteorological stations around the edge of the Antarctic connected by wireless communication for the purpose of long-range weather forecasting for the southern hemisphere.[70] But, as we shall see, the Australian prime minister of the time, Stanley Melbourne Bruce, was preoccupied in the late 1920s with Antarctic territorial acquisition rather than with the prediction of southern weather.

In the interwar period, commercial whaling intensified along the edges of the ice and the North American explorer Richard Byrd established his 'Little America' colony on the Ross Ice Shelf in 1928. A more pragmatic geopolitics began to quicken. There was, as the *Adelaide Advertiser* declared, 'A Scramble for Antarctica' that might echo the famous 'Scramble for Africa' among European powers in the late nineteenth century.[71]

Although the question of Antarctica had not been placed on the agenda of the 1919 Peace Conference, Mawson's political activism did help to persuade the Acting Secretary for the Colonies, Leopold S Amery, to give some attention to it. After discussions with the British Admiralty in early 1919, Amery proposed that 'we ought quietly to assert our claim to the whole continent'.[72] In February 1920, he sent a formal despatch to the Dominion prime ministers in which he argued that it was 'desirable that the whole of the Antarctic should ultimately be included within the Empire'.[73] He indicated that a gradual approach should be followed in order to secure the agreement of other powers. On the other hand, Amery did believe in proceeding immediately with the annexation of the Ross Sea coast to secure its lucrative whaling grounds, and he suggested that this area should be placed under New Zealand administration.[74] Whale oil from the Falkland Islands Dependencies had proven to be economically important for domestic use within the Empire, and it also had its strategic uses during the war 'owing to the need for glycerine [for explosives], in which whale oil is rich'.[75] Therefore, Amery's foremost reason for wishing to subsume Antarctica within the Empire was that a single power was better equipped to introduce effective measures to control the exploitation of 'valuable animals'.[76] In 1923, the Ross Sea Dependency was established, to be administered by New Zealand.

In his 1920 despatch, Amery did not allocate Antarctic territory for Australian administration, being constrained by the contested status of the French claim and the uncertain boundaries of Adélie Land, which lay in the middle of the Australian Quadrant. The British Admiralty advised the Colonial Office that it ranked all of Mawson's claims in the region facing Australia as 'Disputable'. According to the Admiralty, prior discovery took precedence, thus making any French claim to Adélie Land 'Indisputable'.[77] Amery had formed the view that 'France is the only Power' that could challenge any British scheme in that region.[78]

The Australian Government was disappointed at being overlooked in Amery's despatch, and was not aware at the time that the Admiralty had cast serious doubts on the status of Mawson's discoveries. Nonetheless, perceiving the despatch as only a discussion paper, Australia pressed for control of the area to its south. With the Admiralty's opinion influencing his view, Amery's initial reaction to Australian requests was lukewarm. But when Stanley Melbourne Bruce became Australian Prime Minister as well as External Affairs Minister in 1923, he actively sought to change Amery's mind. Together with strong lobbying from the Australian National Research Council, which included Mawson, Bruce began to exert significant pressure on the British Government to thwart attempts by any foreign power to establish an enclave beneath Australia's southern borders. Antarctic veterans weighed in with their opinions. Captain John King Davis, Commonwealth Director of Navigation, who had been to Antarctica as captain on Shackleton's *Nimrod* expedition and on Mawson's *Aurora,* supported Mawson's argument that Australia should be the controlling power in the sector.[79] Edgeworth David agreed, and argued that Antarctica had a most exploitable resource, a vast seam of coal.[80]

On 29 March 1924, the French Government published a presidential decree in its *Journal Officiel,* declaring hunting and fishing rights over a group of sub-Antarctic islands and Adélie (or Wilkes) Land.[81] Immediately upon learning of this action, the Australian National Research Council began a public campaign through the press, appealing to the Australian Government to challenge the French claim and to seek international sanction to administer the Australian Quadrant between 90° and 160° East, which included Adélie Land.[82] Mawson argued that this sector of Antarctica was not only Australia's closest southern neighbour but also that 'it was explored and charted by Australians with Australian money; Australians first landed there; and Australians lie buried there'.[83] Here he was referring to his lost companions, Ninnis and Mertz, neither of whom was Australian except by virtue of their sacrifice for the expedition.

Prime Minister Bruce asked Amery to advise him of what action was being taken to establish British sovereignty over the area and to place it under Australian control.[84] He stressed that the Australian

Government now felt that 'indefinite postponement of the matter will cause future difficulties'.[85] In the United States, however, Secretary of State Charles E Hughes greeted British and French imperial expansion into the Antarctic by noting that, in US eyes, only 'actual settlement' of discovered land constituted sovereignty.[86]

Since Bruce had demonstrated that Australia was unlikely to abandon its position, the question of Antarctic policy was placed on the agenda of the Imperial Conference scheduled for 1926. At the conference, an Antarctic Committee chaired by Amery proposed to assert British dominion over all of Antarctica – to paint the whole continent red, as one official confidentially put it in 1928.[87] Although that grand scheme was for some time in the future, the conference did recommend that British title over what became the Australian Antarctic Territory should be implemented by a three-step process.[88]

The first step would be to inform the international community of the special British interest in the region from approximately 160° to 45° East by publishing the 'Summary of Proceedings' of the Imperial Conference. The second involved taking possession of the territory through an authorised officer. The third step would be to issue an appropriate instrument for the government of the claimed territory.[89] The time had come to send an authorised officer south again. But the Anglo-Australian relationship continued to come under strain as Downing Street and Canberra quibbled over the responsibilities and costs of such an expedition.

Three early Australian explorers

Alessandro Antonello

Australia's status and influence in the Antarctic Treaty System is founded on its early record in science and exploration. In the period before the Treaty, three Australian explorers were particularly notable – Douglas Mawson, John King Davis and George Hubert Wilkins. In December 1928, Davis praised Wilkins (who had just completed the first flight in Antarctica) by quoting the poet John Milton: 'Whom shall we send in search of this new world, whom shall we find sufficient?'[1] Mawson, Davis and Wilkins each presented themselves as men 'sufficient' to search the new world of the Antarctic, and committed significant parts of their lives to doing so. Their physical and intellectual relationship with the Antarctic became the defining aspect of their lives.

Douglas Mawson, who overshadows all other Australian Antarctic explorers, went to Antarctica with three expeditions.[2] The first was Ernest Shackleton's British Antarctic Expedition of 1907–09, where he was a member of T W Edgeworth David's party that reached the area of the South Magnetic Pole. Mawson's second visit was with the 1911–14

Australasian Antarctic Expedition, under his own leadership. An expedition of tragedy and triumph, it saw the deaths of Mawson's sledging companions Belgrave Ninnis and Xavier Mertz, and almost Mawson's own death. The expedition eventually produced 22 published volumes of scientific results. Between 1929 and 1931 Mawson led two summer voyages to Antarctica for the British, Australian and New Zealand Antarctic Research Expedition (BANZARE), his third and final expedition to Antarctica. The chief purpose of these voyages was to claim Antarctic territory for Australia, a mission urged upon the Australian Government by Mawson himself (see chapter 1). His success as explorer and scientist in Antarctica gave Mawson a public fame and prestige that few other Australians achieve.

Mawson's vision of the Antarctic was scientific and economic. As a scientist, his interest in natural structures and processes was overwhelming – each one of his expeditions was a triumph of science as much as a political exercise. He was also deeply conscious of the potential of the Antarctic as an economic resource, advocating the exploitation of its fisheries and minerals. Throughout his life, Mawson often pursued business opportunities with natural resources, including forestry and timber, and this entrepreneurial spirit extended to Antarctica. Antarctica was not his only field of endeavour, however. He spent nearly his entire academic career as a geologist at the University of Adelaide, concentrating his work in South Australia, particularly the Flinders Ranges. He was a prominent member of Australia's scientific professions, and in 1954 was a foundation fellow of the newly chartered Australian Academy of Science.

John King Davis spent much of his life and career in Mawson's shadow.[3] For those who knew of Davis, however, Ernest Shackleton's claim that he was 'the best navigator and sailor that ever went into the Antarctic' was undeniable.[4] Davis' first visit to Antarctica was as chief officer of the *Nimrod* on Shackleton's British Antarctic Expedition of 1907–09. His second expedition to Antarctica was as second in command of Mawson's 1911–14 AAE and captain of the *Aurora.* During this expedition Davis had to make the difficult decision to leave Mawson behind at Commonwealth Bay for another year after his tragic sledge journey.[5] Davis rejoined Shackleton in 1916 to captain the *Aurora* and command the relief expedition for the Ross Sea party of the ill-fated Imperial Trans-Antarctic Expedition. His final visit to the Antarctic was with the first voyage of BANZARE in 1929–30. His relationship with Mawson on this expedition was troubled, so much so that Davis did not captain the ship for the second summer cruise. Both were strong-willed men, and their different responsibilities and priorities led to tensions.[6] In spite of their differences, they remained friends for life. Davis' contribution to BANZARE was crucial, as he guided the *Discovery* through stormy, foggy, ice-choked seas, making soundings, discovering and charting coasts and islands, and enabling flights and landings from the ship. Hand-written notes on Davis' personal collection of maps are reminders of just how uncertain the charting of Antarctic coasts and waters was at the time and just how much filling-in and checking was required.[7]

A meeting of Antarctic explorers: (from left) Phillip Law, Douglas Mawson, Norway's Hjalmar Riiser-Larsen and John King Davis at the Oriental Hotel, Melbourne in 1954. Australian Antarctic Division, © Commonwealth of Australia

At the same time as Mawson and Davis had committed their Antarctic efforts to Australia and Empire, another Australian had been charting his own path through the polar regions. **George Hubert**

Wilkins was born in rural South Australia in 1888, but after leaving Australia in 1908 travelled incessantly throughout the world, taking part in great moments of exploration and technological breakthrough.[8] He first travelled to the Arctic as second in command and cinematographer with Vilhjalmur Stefansson's disastrous and controversial Canadian Arctic Expedition (1913–6). In spite of the disappointment of Stefansson's expedition, Wilkins returned to the Arctic many times. In April 1928 he made a record-breaking 4000 kilometre flight from Alaska to Spitsbergen, mostly over unknown territory – a feat for which he received a knighthood from George V and major awards from the Royal Geographical Society and the American Geographical Society. In 1931 he attempted, but failed, to reach the North Pole in the submarine *Nautilus* – a feat only achieved nearly 30 years later, by another *Nautilus.*

Wilkins' first expedition to Antarctica was with J L Cope's largely unsuccessful expedition to Graham Land in 1920–21, and he joined Ernest Shackleton's *Quest* expedition the following summer. With the patronage of US newspaper magnate William Randolph Hearst, Wilkins' greatest Antarctic achievement was completing the first flight in Antarctica on 16 November 1928. It was his second path-breaking feat of polar aviation for that year – the first being his Arctic triumph in April – and the news electrified the world. His four final Antarctic expeditions took place between 1933 and 1939, with Lincoln Ellsworth, another American millionaire.

It was with Ellsworth's fourth Antarctic expedition in the summer of 1939 that Wilkins visited the Australian Antarctic Territory, the first and only visit he would make to the Antarctic lands claimed by his country of birth. Ellsworth's plan was to fly over the South Pole, though both men had other intentions as well. Ellsworth announced on the outward journey that he had been instructed to claim any lands he visited for the United States – a claim he qualified under questioning from Wilkins. Wilkins, for his part, had prepared some nationalistic acts too. He had made quiet inquiries with the Australian Government about the possibility of asserting or reasserting sovereignty in the Australian Antarctic Territory. Despite some wariness on the part of the Secretary of the Department of External Affairs, Wilkins was granted 'general authority to enter upon, explore and report on the Australian Antarctic Territory'. Wilkins stepped onto Australian Antarctic lands on 8, 9 and 11 January 1939, flew the Australian flag and deposited a record of his visit. It was a deeply nationalistic act, on behalf of a nation he had not lived in for decades, and with which he had an equivocal relationship.[9]

World War II intervened to stall the momentum of Antarctic affairs. After the Allied victory, Mawson renewed his efforts to have Australia fully realise its place in Antarctica. He declared in October 1945 that 'my interest is to try to establish a permanent connection between Antarctica and Australia'.[10] He and Davis were invited to be part of a government interdepartmental committee in December 1946, where Mawson dominated proceedings, demonstrating both his fluency in all fields of Antarctic enquiry and his vision for the Australian Antarctic. This committee's recommendations, covered with Mawson's fingerprints, were accepted by Chifley's Cabinet.

Mawson and Davis were both prominent members of the Executive Planning Committee established in 1947 to advise the government on its Antarctic activities, and both men were overwhelmingly supportive and complimentary of the Australian National Antarctic Research Expedition's work. Mawson, however, was sometimes frustrated with decisions made by the Antarctic Division's director, Phillip Law. Reading Mawson's correspondence from the 1950s and the minutes of the Executive Planning Committee, one certainly gets the sense that he felt that his vision for Australia's Antarctic work was not being fulfilled.[11] In championing ANARE, he was deeply conscious that it should not merely collect 'tabulated but uninspiring physical data', as he wrote to Davis in 1956, but that it should ask fundamental and important scientific questions.[12] Moreover, he was committed to the idea that ANARE must be able, in some measure, to pay for itself by opening up resources in Antarctica. On several occasions Mawson annoyed Law by offering his thoughts directly to Richard Casey, Minister for External Affairs. Davis, who held the position of Director of Navigation in the Commonwealth Government from 1920 until his retirement in 1949, was happy to give advice and assist the new generation of explorers. Wilkins also continued to support polar exploration after World War II, acting as an adviser to the United States' International Geophysical Year program.

These three men's names are now inscribed on the Antarctic map. In February 1954, Australia's first continental station was named to honour Mawson. A second station opened three years later in January 1957 was named to honour Davis, who was also, fittingly, the eponym for the Davis Sea in East Antarctica. In 2008 the Australian Antarctic Division completed a runway for its Australian–Antarctic air services near Casey Station, and named it after Wilkins for his role in pioneering aviation at both poles.

Notes

[1] *Argus* (Melbourne), 8 December 1928.

[2] Biographical details have been taken from Jacka (1986) and Ayres (1999).

[3] Biographical details have been taken from Béchervaise (1981).

[4] Ernest Shackleton, quoted in Tyler-Lewis (2006) 21.

[5] Davis (1915).

[6] See, for example, Jacka and Jacka (1988) xlv–xlvii.

[7] Davis' personal collection of maps is held by the National Archives of Australia (NAA), Hobart, Series P2819.

[8] Biographical details have been taken from Nasht (2005) and Swan (1990).

[9] See documents in NAA, Series A981, Item ANT 22, including GH Wilkins, Letter to RG Casey, 6 August 1938; WR Hodgson, Minute to Minister for External Affairs, 8 September 1938; WR Hodgson, Letter to GH Wilkins, 12 September 1938; GH Wilkins, Letter to WR Hodgson, 16 September 1938; and GH Wilkins, 'Report of the Ellsworth Antarctic Flight Expedition, 1938–39', 6 February 1939. See also documents in NAA, Series A981, Items ANT 4, ANT 23 and ANT 44.

[10] *Argus* (Melbourne), 24 October 1945.

[11] See the Executive Planning Committee files in NAA, Series A1838, Items 1495/3/4/1 Parts 1–4.

[12] D Mawson, Letter to JK Davis, 23 July 1956, MS8311, 3270/9, John King Davis Papers, La Trobe Collection, State Library of Victoria.

The BANZARE voyages, 1929–31

Douglas Mawson was chosen to command the British, Australian and New Zealand Antarctic Research Expedition (BANZARE) and immediately set about acquiring the *Discovery,* which had been built for Scott's 1901–04 expedition.[90] Bruce's 'eyes and ears' at Whitehall, R G Casey (to whom Bruce frequently referred as 'our Richard'), energetically pursued Australia's Antarctic interests with the British Government and insisted that it fulfil the recommendations of the 1926 Imperial Conference.[91] As a result of Casey's determined negotiations in London, the British Government provided the *Discovery* free of charge for two expeditions. Two summers would allow the BANZARE voyages to map the coastline for the proposed Australian sector and to raise the flag as a symbol of exercising control, as well as leaving space to undertake scientific research. British and Australian government funds were supplemented by a donation of £10,000 from Macpherson Robertson, the Melbourne 'chocolate king'; hence Mawson's naming of Mac. Robertson Land in eastern Antarctica.[92] Mawson's secret instructions from the Australian prime minister were to 'plant the British flag wherever you find it practicable to do so'.[93]

Like Scott, Mawson was haunted by Norwegians. In 1929, he wrote that 'apparently they are out to race and are working in secret, as Amundsen did when he beat Scott to the South Pole'.[94] Forestalling Norwegian activities was one of the goals of the BANZARE voyages. There was a feeling that Australia had neglected its backyard, and the Norwegians had seized the opportunity to extend whaling into these waters and to seek their own slice of the Antarctic continent. 'It had come about that this very important industry had been allowed to fall into the hands of others', Mawson lamented to the press.[95] He believed that any commercial development was 'Australia's birthright'.[96]

By the end of the 1920s the Antarctic coastline was thick with the traffic of Norwegian whalers. On a single day in the vicinity of Enderby Land in the summer of 1929–30, the *Discovery* encountered three chasers and two factory ships in the morning, met Commander Hjalmar Riiser-Larsen's ship *Norvegia* in the middle of the day, and after tea-time was passed by four more chasers going east. It became quite difficult to assert their status as intrepid explorers. 'If that is a factory ship we cannot let her be further south than we are', wrote expeditioner Stuart Campbell in his diary.[97] When the *Discovery* was running low on coal, Commander Riiser-Larsen offered supplies from a nearby whaling ship, but Mawson declined.

Douglas Mawson with the Discovery in the background during the British, Australian and New Zealand Antarctic Expedition (BANZARE) of 1929–31. National Archives of Australia: B941, HISTORIC/ANTARCTIC/1

Mawson was unhappy about competing with the Norwegians.[98] He had hoped that British diplomats stationed in Oslo would negotiate an agreement with Norway that would lead to the *Norvegia* exploring beyond 40° East longitude and ensure there was no overlap with the area he was proposing to claim for the Empire.[99]

When the two men met in Antarctic waters, Mawson explained that he had no intention of sailing westward beyond Enderby Land and urged Riiser-Larsen to explore further west and take possession of the unclaimed territory between Enderby Land and Coats Land. When they set sail again after their meeting, Mawson believed that they had reached an understanding.

In London and Oslo, however, British diplomats continued to prevaricate. And the Norwegians were 'incensed' at the extension of British jurisdiction over new territories and whaling grounds – first the Falkland Islands Dependencies, later the Ross Dependency.[100] The Norwegians held the view that Britain was unfair in including Norwegian discoveries in its territories. An added insult was the payment of heavy fees for whaling licences to Britain and New Zealand.[101] If discovery and taking possession remained essential prerequisites for an Antarctic claim, then the Norwegians, by sailing beyond Enderby Land, could put forward a claim that at least the British Empire would recognise.

Claiming something as slippery as ice was fraught with frustration and laced with comedy. It was not an easy task to see the land, let alone get onto it. Heavy ice and considerable wind forced the *Discovery* to travel slowly. It was not until 13 January 1930, when a party of men landed on a small rocky island off eastern Antarctica (Proclamation Island), that Mawson was able to claim 'full sovereignty of the territory of Enderby Land, Kemp Land, Mac-Robertson Land, together with off-lying islands as located on our charts constituting a Sector of the Antarctic Continent etc'.[102] They attached a tablet to a pole facing south, gave three cheers for the King and sang 'God Save the King'.[103] While the *Discovery* was steaming back to Australia, the *Norvegia* was working beyond Enderby Land mapping new territory and sending reports to Oslo of its discoveries.[104]

The doom and gloom of the Great Depression was the backdrop for the second BANZARE cruise. As the Depression deepened and the excitement of Antarctic exploration died down, the Australian press began to speculate about whether the Scullin Labor government would support another expedition in the present economic climate.[105] Would Macpherson Robertson's generosity again be needed? He did not disappoint, volunteering an additional sum of £6000 if the government would match it, which it did.[106]

The scientific lobby in Australia had taken the initiative in Antarctic exploration, and now sought to promote the possibilities of commercial gain in order to attract private donations. As well as marine and mineral resources, Mawson added water to the list, and others on the second BANZARE expedition contributed their own ideas. Photographer Frank Hurley (a veteran of Mawson's AAE, Shackleton's *Endurance* expedition and the first BANZARE voyage) described Antarctica as 'Nature's fairyland [and a] glorious playground for venturesome youth; a haven of rest for the sick [as well as a] land with wonderful commercial possibilities'.[107] Dr W Ingram, physician on the first BANZARE cruise, said that the Antarctic could become a summer health resort due to its 'microbe-free atmosphere' and would be 'excellent for lung cases'.[108] Privately, even Mawson must have reflected that Antarctica had expertly protected its treasures from human exploitation for millennia and was likely to continue doing so. The principal aims of the second BANZARE were to map and investigate the area between Adélie Land and Queen Mary Land and to undertake scientific observations, including an investigation of the fauna, notably whales and seals.[109]

That the aims of the two summer BANZARE voyages were accomplished successfully, and without any loss of life, owed much to the Antarctic expertise that existed in Australia at the time. Mawson had reminded Bruce that there was 'nobody else available in British circles with the experience we have of Antarctic conditions and exploration, or with such a successful record in those matters'.[110] The British Government was now looking to Australian polar explorers to help it consolidate its territorial claims in Antarctica. Fearful of the threat that the American polar explorer Richard Byrd could pose to British sovereignty claims, Britain recruited Australia's Hubert Wilkins (who was sponsored by the American newspaper magnate William Randolph Hearst) to fly from Graham Land to the Ross Dependency and claim the uncharted sector between these two claims. On 16 November 1928, Wilkins made the first flight in Antarctica – and thus it was that an aircraft was used for the first time to reinforce sovereignty over Antarctic territory.[111]

Wilkins believed that Graham Land was actually separated from the mainland by a deep strait, but that proposition was later proven incorrect by another Australian explorer, John Riddoch Rymill.[112] Like Wilkins, Rymill was recruited by the British Government to confirm its claim to the Falkland Islands Dependencies.[113] Rymill's British Graham Land Expedition (1934–37) in the *Penola* (named after his hometown in South Australia) succeeded in making valuable geographical discoveries in the region as well as conducting scientific research. In 1939 Rymill was awarded the David Livingstone Centenary gold medal of the American Geographical Society of New York. The medal's citation described the survey work of the expedition as 'probably the largest contribution of accurate detailed surveys of the Antarctic Continent made by an expedition'.[114]

After the Scullin Labor government was defeated in December 1931, the United Australia Party under the leadership of Joseph Lyons formed government. Fortunately for the smooth continuation of Australian Antarctic involvement, J G Latham, the former Attorney-General in the Bruce government, who had a significant record in Antarctic matters, was appointed both Attorney-General and Minister for External Affairs. One of Latham's first tasks was to formalise under Australian control the territory that had been recently discovered and proclaimed as British by Mawson. Latham sailed to London to discuss the appropriate legal instruments to bring what was now being called the 'Commonwealth Sector' under Australian control.[115]

Consolidating the claim

The passing of the *Australian Antarctic Territory Acceptance Act 1933* by the Commonwealth Parliament formalised the constitutional arrangements that allowed the Australian Government to be the controlling authority over the Australian Antarctic Territory, a sovereignty claim for more than 42 per cent of Antarctica (see chapter 2). In his speech to the House of Representatives, Latham observed that the territory was of strategic significance to Australia because of its proximity and that it was also of 'considerable, actual and potential economic importance'.[116] This was due not only to the existence of a whaling industry, but also to the potential commercialisation of furbearing animals and of bird life. Latham drew parallels with Alaska, which had once been thought valueless but which contained great goldfields and was now 'one of the later Eldorados of the world'.[117] Australian control in Antarctica was justified partly on conservation grounds. Australian governance, the minister declared, 'was rendered urgent by the fact that a boom in whaling was commencing', making it essential to take measures to protect the whales and other Antarctic fauna and birds from extermination.

The passage of the Act began the era of Australian consolidation and control over its territory. Since the economic situation prevented another expedition from sailing immediately to Antarctica, the government turned its attention to demonstrating its Antarctic credentials to the world in other ways. It did so by clarifying French and Norwegian claims on its borders, publishing the scientific data collected by Mawson in 1911–1914 and in 1929–31, encouraging Wilkins' visit to Antarctica with the American Lincoln Ellsworth in 1938–39, beginning the planning of another expedition, and compiling a comprehensive map of Antarctica.

The *Australian Antarctic Territory Acceptance Act* had not resolved the problem of Adélie Land, and the era of aviation had now raised the question of the legal status of Australians flying over French territory. The British Government had tried unsuccessfully before the Great War to negotiate the Adélie Land boundaries with France, but the problem remained unresolved (due mainly to a comical succession of clerical errors). At the urging of the Australian Government, negotiations between French and British diplomats were finally concluded in 1938 when France agreed to limit Adélie Land to a sector that met at the South Pole and covered 136° to 142° East longitude.[118] In addition, the governments agreed to reciprocal rights of air passage over Adélie Land and any British territories in the Antarctic.[119]

From the British perspective, Norway presented another problem. Private Norwegian expeditions had targeted the Enderby Land coastline, and the British Government knew that Norway could not be easily dismissed, particularly after the *Norvegia–Discovery* encounter.[120] The passage of the *Australian Antarctic Territory Acceptance Act* coincided with a crucial international legal decision on sovereignty in the Arctic. In July 1931, Norway had declared its intention to occupy territory in eastern Greenland, causing Denmark to institute proceedings against Norway in the Permanent Court of International Justice in The Hague. Denmark had already claimed sovereignty over Greenland.[121] Norway challenged the status of old territorial claims that had remained without 'effective occupation' and where no administrative control had been instituted.[122] The court, however, held that in polar regions effective occupation required little actual exercise of rights. In April 1933 Norway lost the *Eastern Greenland* case and the British Government therefore felt confident to negotiate the reciprocal recognition of the AAT at the other end of the earth and any unclaimed territory that Norway wished to claim. Britain indicated its willingness to recognise a Norwegian claim to 'territories between Enderby Land and Coats Land in return for Norwegian recognition of British sovereignty over the Commonwealth Sector and the Falkland Islands Sector'.[123] On 14 January 1939 Norway issued a decree placing under its sovereignty an area on the Antarctic continent extending from Coats Land to the western border of the AAT.[124] On the same day Norway recognised the boundaries of the Australian territory.[125]

In 1938, when Australia's Hubert Wilkins was to accompany the American Lincoln Ellsworth on an Antarctic flight, the Australian Government took the opportunity to show the flag in the western part of the AAT.[126] Although the Department of External Affairs was conscious that the Australian claim should be visited frequently in order to consolidate control, it was concerned that if Wilkins made a proclamation and hoisted the flag 'it might give offence to Mawson and make him think we doubted the validity of his work'.[127] But Cabinet decided that the act of consolidation was worth that risk. Consequently, on 8, 9 and 11 January 1939, Wilkins flew the 'Commonwealth of Australia' flag at several locations in the AAT and deposited one with a record of his visit at the northernmost island of the Rauer Group, and others at the western and eastern ends of the Vestfold Hills. Ellsworth had not secured Australian approval to fly into the AAT, but the government believed he would honour an earlier commitment not to make any claims for the United States. However, Ellsworth revealed to Wilkins on the journey that he intended to make claims on behalf of his country, and did so. In his report to the Department of External Affairs, Wilkins explained Ellsworth's act as patriotic rather than deceptive.[128]

The most significant consolidation of the AAT would be the establishment of a permanent presence on the continent itself. Acting on Mawson's advice, Cabinet decided to purchase Ellsworth's purpose-built motorised sailing vessel, the *Wyatt Earp.*[129] On 8 February 1939 the Melbourne *Argus* carried a statement from the prime minister that the *Wyatt Earp* had been purchased for approximately £4400. The purchase included two aeroplanes, stores and all equipment.[130] In the late 1930s the Australian Government had been considering the idea of another Antarctic expedition with its BANZARE partners. However, as war loomed again, the idea was abandoned because the 'present defence policy and campaign [called for] onerous financial commitments and national effort'.[131]

The government believed that compiling a comprehensive map of Antarctica would also demonstrate to the world Australia's significant investment in the region. In 1939 a map of Antarctica was completed through the collaborative work of John Cumpston, an official of the Department of External Affairs, and E P Bayliss of the Department of the Interior, the chief draughtsman (see front endpaper). Cumpston and Bayliss undertook extensive research using the records of the major expeditions, the charts of the British Admiralty and those issued by Norwegian whalers.[132] Mawson and Davis provided all of their original material and Wilkins, Ellsworth and Rymill supplied sketches and maps. The American Geographical Society and the Royal Geographical Society also contributed their latest information. Cumpston noted that 'every effort' had been made to obtain the 'most authentic material relating to the Antarctic'.[133]

When it was published in 1939, the Australian map of Antarctica (see front endpaper), together with an explanatory booklet, was recognised as the most accurate and complete map of its day. In 1941 the Intelligence Branch advised that, for security reasons, the sale of all maps of the Commonwealth and Territories, except that of Antarctica, would cease during the course of the war.[134] This exception was probably to ensure that Australian sovereignty claims in the south remained prominent at such a tense time. The *Canberra Times* aptly observed that, while Europe's leading powers were 'engaged in a death struggle to determine a new map of Europe', Australia 'applied the arts of peace to give the world the most reliable map possible of a new continent'.[135]

Throughout the 1930s, Australia worked to consolidate its status as the major claimant state in Antarctica, but it would not be until 1954 that it was able to establish a continental station, appropriately named Mawson. By then, the international political climate had changed significantly. The British Empire no longer held sway, and Australia found itself still seeking to secure its slice of Antarctic territory, this time in a new international order. Now its efforts would be reliant less on the expertise of its explorers than on that of its diplomats.

Notes

[1]   'Our great frozen neighbour', *Adelaide Advertiser,* 26 February 1929, NAA: Series A 461/8, Item H413/2.

[2]   For a detailed study of the complex interaction between Australian science, exploration, politics and diplomacy in the foundation of the Australian Antarctic Territory between 1901 and 1945, see Kawaja (2010) (co-author Kawaja conducted primary research for her doctoral thesis, on which this chapter is based, at the National Archives of Australia).

[3]   Beaglehole (1974) 431–36.

[4]   Lovering and Prescott (1979) 26–27.

[5]   Price (1962) 5.

[6]   Mawer (2006). The area became the Ross Dependency, now under New Zealand control.

[7]   Maury to Robert FitzRoy, 25 February 1859, quoted in Gibbs (1975) 9.

[8]   These words were spoken by Baron F von Mueller in his address at the inaugural meeting of the Victorian Branch of the Royal Geographical Society of Australasia, quoted in Swan (1961) 40.

[9]   See 'Du Faur, Frederick Eccleston (1832–1915)', *Australian Dictionary of Biography,* online edition (2006) Australian National University <www.adb.online.anu.edu.au>.

[10] Sprent (1887) 154. See also Swan (1961) 57–58.

[11] Sprent (1887) 154.

[12] Letter Royal Society of Victoria, 8 April 1887, in *Royal Society of Tasmania, Papers and Proceedings for 1887* (1888), Office of *The Mercury,* Hobart, vii.

[13] Recommendations from the Antarctic Committee, appointed by the Royal Society of Victoria and the Royal Geographical Society of Australia (Victorian Branch) to the Hon The Premier, in *Royal Society of Tasmania, Papers and Proceedings for 1887* (1888) April, Office of *The Mercury,* Hobart, ix.

[14] *Royal Society of Tasmania, Papers and Proceedings for 1887* (1888) ix.

[15] Griffiths, GS (1990) 'Antarctic exploration – the duty of Australia' (1888), quoted in Cole (1990) 27.

[16] *Progress Report of the Antarctic Exploration Committee of the Royal Society of Victoria and of the Royal Geographical Society of Australasia (Victorian Branch)* (1887), Papers of the Royal Society of Tasmania, Royal Society of Tasmania Library (Morris Miller Library), University of Tasmania, 1. All papers relating to the Royal Society and Royal Geographical Society quoted in this chapter are located at the Morris Miller Library.

[17]   *Progress Report of the Antarctic Exploration Committee* (1887) 23.

[18]   *Progress Report of the Antarctic Exploration Committee* (1887) 3.

[19]   Letter AC Macdonald, Hon Secretary, Royal Geographical Society of Australasia, Melbourne, 30 July 1890, *Papers and Proceedings for 1890* (1891) May, Office of *The Mercury,* Hobart, xxi. Baron Adolf Erik Nordenskiöld was the uncle of Dr Otto Nordenskjöld, who led a Swedish Antarctic expedition in 1901. Note the difference in the spelling of the names.

[20]   Quoted in *Copy of Progress Report of the Joint-Committee of the Royal Geographical Society of Australasia (Victorian Branch) and the Royal Society of Victoria* read on 22 August 1890, 12.

[21]   *Royal Society of Tasmania, Papers and Proceedings for 1890,* Proceedings, August, xxiii.

[22]   Funds placed on the estimates of the colonial governments' budgets were New South Wales £2000, Queensland £1000 and Tasmania £300. Quoted in Royal Society of *Tasmania, Papers and Proceedings for 1890* (1891), Proceedings, May and June, Printed at the Office of *The Mercury,* Hobart, v–viii.

[23]   *Report of deputation which waited upon the Minister for External Affairs in Melbourne on*

23 March 1911, with a 'Request for Financial Assistance in Connection with the proposed Mawson Antarctic Expedition', NAA: Series A 1/15, Item 1915/5159, 5–6.

[24] On Borchgrevink's career, see Evans and Jones (1975) and Baughman (1990). Headland (1994a) assesses the various claims to be first.

[25] Bernacchi (1901).

[26] For a comprehensive study of the *Southern Cross* Expedition see Crawford (1998). The author is the grand-daughter of Louis Charles Bernacchi.

[27] *Mercury,* 6 December 1898, 2.

[28] Letter Henry Copeland to Edmund Barton, 1 February 1901, NAA: Series A 1/15, Item 191/14438.

[29] 'Extract from note by Admiral RN Custance, Director of Naval Intelligence', 30 January 1901, attached to Letter Henry Copeland to Edmund Barton, 1 February 1901.

[30] *The Age,* 12 November 1901, EA, Correspondence Files 1901, 'Discovery Expedition' 1901–1902, NAA: CRS A 6, Item 01/1585. See also Swan (1961) 104–05.

[31] Shackleton (1909) vol1, 3.

[32] Ayres (1999) 97 and Swan (1961) 11–12.

[33] Shackleton (1909) vol1, 2.

[34] Commonwealth Parliamentary Debates (henceforth cited CPD) (1907) volXLII,

7491–92, in Greenwood and Grimshaw (1977) 551.

[35]   Shackleton (1909) vol2, 20.

[36]   Branagan (2005) 193.

[37]   The Dependencies comprised South Georgia and the South Sandwich Islands, the South Orkneys, the South Shetlands and the Antarctic continent between 20° and 80° West longitude. Bush (1988) volIII, Doc UK 21071908, 251–52.

[38]   Bush (1988) volIII, Doc UK 21071908, 253.

[39]   Norwegian enquiries of the British Government about the sovereignty of territories between 35° and 80° West and 40° and 65° South prompted the British Government to annex what became the Falkland Islands Dependencies. The purpose of the annexation was to secure British control over the lucrative whaling industry in the seas around the Dependencies. See Bush (1988) volIII, 239–65.

[40]   For example see Bush (1988) volIII, Doc UK27121881, 226. For a more complete record of the various documents that constituted British Government actions in laying claim to various sub-Antarctic islands refer to the United Kingdom Section in Bush (1988), volIII, 215–51.

[41]   Bush (1988) volIII, 246–47.

[42]   Shackleton (1919); Spufford (1996) 45–46; Huntford (1986) 597–99, 602.

[43]   Hayes (1928).

[44]   'Proposed Antarctic Expedition', a report of a meeting between Senator GF Pearce, Minister for Defence, Professor Orme Masson and Douglas Mawson, 18 January 1911, NAA: Series A 1/15, Item 1915/5159. Mawson linked the Antarctic quadrants by name to an adjacent continent or ocean: the American Quadrant, below South America, between $0°$ and $90°$ West, the African Quadrant between $0°$ and $90°$ East, and the Australian Quadrant, sometimes referred to by Mawson as the Australasian Quadrant, which also extended to below New Zealand and lay between $90°$ and $180°$ East. Mawson titled the fourth section the Pacific Quadrant, since ocean alone lies to the north of it. Mawson (1915) 3.

[45]   Mawson (1915) xiv; Ayres (1999) 33.

[46]   Mawson (1915) volII, xiv; Ayres (1999) 33.

[47]   For an excellent recent biography of Taylor, see Strange and Bashford (2008).

[48]   Ayres (1999) 34–42, Mawer (2006) 188.

[49]   *Argus,* 6 January 1911.

[50]   'Proposed Antarctic Expedition', report of a meeting between Senator GF Pearce, Minister for Defence, Professor Orme Masson and Douglas Mawson, 18 January 1911, NAA: Series A 1/15, Item 1915/5159.

[51]   'Proposed Antarctic Expedition'.

[52]   'Proposed Antarctic Expedition'. The Klondike gold diggings in Alaska were discovered in 1896.

[53]   'Proposed Antarctic Expedition'.

[54]   'Proposed Antarctic Expedition'.

[55]   *Argus,* 14 September 1911. NAA: Series A 1/15, Item 1915/5159.

[56]   *The Proposed Australian Antarctic Expedition,* paper by Orme Masson dated 21 March 1911. Orme Masson's paper outlined the background to and goals of the expedition, NAA: Series A 1/15, Item 1915/5159, 2–3.

[57]   Mawson (1915) vol1, xvii.

[58]   The Government of New South Wales donated £7000; the Victorian Government £6000; the South Australian Government £5000 and the Tasmanian grant was £500, Mawson (1915) vol1, Appendix VI, 311.

[59]   Undated letter Mawson to Colonial Office, probably sent on 26 June 1911, NAA: Series A1/15, Item 1915/5159. A copy of the response from the Colonial Office to Mawson dated 8 July 1911 indicates that it was a reply to Mawson's request, written on 26 June, to raise the flag. See copy of response in Bush (1982) volII, Doc AU08071911, 92.

[60]   Bush (1982) volII, Doc AU08071911, 92.

[61]   Undated letter Mawson to the Colonial Office, NAA: Series A1/15, Item 1915/5159.

[62] For a perceptive study of the AAE see Hains (2002b).

[63] Mawson (1915), Jacka (1986).

[64] Correspondence from Sir Douglas Mawson re Macquarie Island, Claim to Antarctic Lands, The New Hebrides Question, New Guinea, 25 May 1916–7 June 1917, Personal Papers of Australian Prime Minister, WM Hughes, NAA: Series CP 359/2, Item 9.

[65] Correspondence from Sir Douglas Mawson to WM Hughes, 25 May 1916 – 7 June 1917.

[66] Correspondence from Sir Douglas Mawson to WM Hughes, 25 May 1916 – 7 June 1917.

[67] Letter Royal Geographical Society of Australasia, Queensland to Rt Honourable the Prime Minister, 25 January 1927, NAA: Series A 461, Item G 372/1/2.

[68] Letter Royal Geographical Society of Australasia, 25 January 1927.

[69] Letter Royal Geographical Society of Australasia, 25 January 1927.

[70] Letter Casey to Bruce, Personal and Confidential, 21 February 1929, in Hudson and North (1980) 78–79. See also Nasht (2005).

[71] Headline in the *Adelaide Advertiser,* 8 April 1929, quoted in Collis (2004) 45.

[72] For an elaboration of the British Government's Antarctic goals, see Beck (1983a, b). These two papers, published in separate scholarly journals, explore the same thesis,

although the second article is more expansive. See also his major study (Beck 1986a).

[73] Despatch LS Amery, for Secretary of State, to Governor-General R Munro Ferguson, 6 February, 1920, NAA: Series CP 46, Item 41, NAA: Series A 981, Item ANT 4, pt 1, and NAA: Series A 2910, Item 404/16/1, pt 1.

[74] LS Amery to Governor-General R Munro Ferguson, 6 February 1920.

[75] LS Amery to Governor-General R Munro Ferguson, 6 February 1920.

[76] LS Amery to Governor-General R Munro Ferguson, 6 February 1920.

[77] Dominions No.99, 'Territorial Claims in the Antarctic Regions', Compiled in the Hydrographic Department of the Admiralty, 1919, Dominions Office, August 1925, 3–12, NAA: Series A 2910, Item 404/16/1, pt 1.

[78] LS Amery to Governor-General R Munro Ferguson, 6 February 1920.

[79] Letter John Davis to PL Piesse, Department of External Affairs, 5 July 1920, NAA: Series A 2910, Item 404/16/1, pt 1 and Series A 981, Item ANT 4, pt 1.

[80] Letter TW Edgeworth David to ML Shepherd, Prime Minister's Department, 29 November 1920, NAA: Series MP 1185/9/0, Item 453/204/938.

[81]   Adélie Land was frequently interposed with Wilkes Land and *vice versa* as the early name of today's Australian Antarctic Territory.

[82]   Brisbane *Daily Mail,* 13 July 1924, NAA: Series A 981, Item ANT 4, pt 1.

[83]   Melbourne *Herald,* 5 March 1925, NAA: Series CP103, Item Bundle 10. On 5 March 1925, the Melbourne *Herald* carried two separate articles on Antarctica.

[84]   Cablegram Governor-General to Secretary of State for the Colonies, 4 December 1924, NAA: Series A 981, Item ANT 4, pt 1. The channel of communication between the Australian Government and the British Government was through the Governor-General in Australia.

[85]   Cablegram Governor-General Secretary of State for the Colonies, 4 December 1924, NAA: Series A.981, Item ANT 4, pt 1.

[86]   Bush (1988) volIII, Doc US13051924, 430–32.

[87]   Minute by RH Campbell, First Secretary, Foreign Office, 23 August 1928, cited in Beck (1983b) 461.

[88]   Secret E 130 (Revise), Imperial Conference, 1926, Committee on British Policy in the Antarctic, Copy No 167, Printed for the Imperial Conference, November 1926, NAA: Series A 981/4, Item ANT 4, pt 3. '(Revise)' refers to a paper that has been revised. On revision the original may have been withdrawn from circulation.

[89]   Secret E 130 (Revise).

[90]   Record of conversation between Dr Walter Henderson and Sir Douglas Mawson held on 12 October 1928, NAA: Series A 981, Item ANT 4, pt 5.

[91]   Hudson and North (1980) introduction, viii and Edwards (1983) chapter 3, 73.

[92]   *Sydney Morning Herald,* 3 May 1929, NAA: Series A 461/8, Item H413/2.

[93]   Bush (1982) volII, Doc. AU12091929, 117–18. See also Ayres (1999) 173.

[94]   Reported in the *Cape Times* and quoted in Swan (1961) 191.

[95]   *Argus,* 12 April 1930.

[96]   'Sir Douglas Mawson explains polar voyage', Melbourne *Herald,* 5 August 1929.

[97]   Diary of Stuart Campbell, Microfilm CY 4317, Mitchell Library, Sydney, 6 and 9 February 1931.

[98]   Letter Mawson to Casey, 9 October 1929, NAA: Series A 981, Item ANT 4, pt 9 and Cable Mawson to Casey, 11 October 1929, NAA: Series A 981/4, Item ANT 51, pt 2.

[99]   Secret sailing orders to Sir Douglas Mawson, Commander of the British, Australian and New Zealand Antarctic Expedition *[sic]* His Majesty's Research Ship 'Discovery', 12 September 1929, signed SM Bruce, Prime Minister, NAA: Series A 461/8, Item N413/1.

[100]   Price (1962) 15.

[101]   Price (1962) 15.
[102]   Jacka and Jacka (1988) 310.
[103]   Jacka and Jacka (1988) 314. For a cultural analysis of this ritual, see Collis (2004).
[104]   Copy of Despatch Charles Wingfield to Arthur Henderson, Foreign Office, 25 February 1930, NAA: Series A 981, Item ANT 51, pt 2.
[105]   *Herald,* 28 April 1930, NAA: Series A 461/8, Item A413/2.
[106]   Extract from Minutes of Meeting of the Antarctic Committee held in Melbourne, 13 April 1930, NAA: Series A 981, Item ANT 4, pt 8.
[107]   *Sydney Morning Herald,* 5 April 1930, NAA: Series A 461/8, Item A413/2.
[108]   *Herald,* 3 April 1930, NAA: Series A 461/8, Item A413/2.
[109]   Secret sailing orders addressed to Sir Douglas Mawson, Commander of the British Australian and New Zealand Antarctic Expedition, His Majesty's Research Ship 'Discovery', sgd John J Daly, for Acting Prime Minister, 30 October 1930, NAA: Series A 461/8, Item N413/1.
[110]   Letter Douglas Mawson to Bruce, 7 February 1928, NAA: Series A 981, Item ANT 4, pt 5.
[111]   Nasht (2005) 176–85.
[112]   Béchervaise (1988) 501–02. See also Nasht (2005) 183 and Swan (1961) 178–79.

[113] Beck (1986a) 28–29.

[114] Béchervaise (1988).

[115] Memorandum Attorney-General's Department to Secretary, Department of External Affairs, 2 March 1932, NAA: Series A 981, Item ANT 2, pt 1.

[116] CPD vol139, Senate and House of Representatives, period 27 April to 31 May 1933, Government Printer, Canberra, Australian Antarctic Territory Acceptance Bill, Second Reading, 26 May 1933, 1952.

[117] CPD, vol139, 1953.

[118] Cable Stirling to Department of External Affairs, 20 April 1938 NAA: Series A 981/4, Item ANT 48, pt 3. See also Bush (1982) volII, Doc FR05031938, 504–05 and Doc FR01041938, 505–06.

[119] Letter CW Dixon, Dominions Office, to Alfred Stirling 19 April 1938, NAA: Series A 981/4, Item ANT 48, pt 3.

[120] For other work on this subject see Barrett (2009).

[121] Hyde (1933) 732.

[122] For full text see Hyde (1933). The judgment found in favour of Denmark by 12 votes to 2.

[123] Copy of Letter RA Wiseman, Dominions Office to FG Shedden, Australian High Commission, 24 June 1933, NAA: Series A 981, Item ANT 2, pt 2.

[124] Memorandum Alfred Stirling to the Secretary, Department of External Affairs, 27 January 1939, NAA: Series A 981 Item ANT 48, pt 3.

[125] Letter Erik Colban to Viscount Halifax, 14 January 1939, NAA: Series A 2910 Item 404/16/1 and Series A981, Item ANT 48, pt 3.

[126] Department of External Affairs copy of Cabinet Submission 4 July 1938, NAA: Series A1838 Item No.1495/3/2/1/1 Part 1 and NAA: Series A461/10 Item T.413/6.

[127] Memorandum Department of External Affairs to the Minister 8 September 1938, NAA: Series A981/4 Item ANT 15.

[128] Hubert Wilkins to Minister of External Affairs, 'Report of the Ellsworth Antarctic Flight Expedition, 1938–39', 6 February 1939 Series A1838/1 Item 1495/1, and Bush (1988) volI-II, Doc. US22101938, 439.

[129] Department of External Affairs For Cabinet Agenda No 537, 'Offer by Ellsworth to sell his vessel "Wyatt Earp" to the Commonwealth Government', 7 February 1939, NAA: Series A 1838/283, Item 1495/3/2/1/1.

[130] *Argus* 8 February 1939, NAA: Series A 461/10, Item T413/6. According to the *Argus,* the *Wyatt Earp* was purchased by Lincoln Ellsworth about three or four years earlier. It was built in Norway for sealing.

[131]   Draft Cable to External Affairs Officer, London, NAA: Series A 461/10, Item T413/6. Although the copy on file is marked 'Draft' the indications are that the cable was sent on 24 November as Alfred Stirling responded to it on 2 December 1938 in a letter to External Affairs. See Letter Alfred Stirling to Secretary, Department of External Affairs, 2 December 1938, NAA: Series A 461/10, Item T413/6.

[132]   Report (undated) by JS Cumpston regarding the preparation of the 1939 map of Antarctica, NAA: Series A 981, Item ANT 9, pt 2.

[133]   Cumpston report regarding the 1939 map of Antarctica.

[134]   Note for file from Intelligence Branch, 21 November 1941, NAA: Series A 2910, Item 404/16/1, pt 1.

[135]   *Canberra Times,* 1 March 1940, NAA: Series A 876, Item GL191, pt 1.

2

Sovereignty

Donald R Rothwell and Andrew Jackson

Australia's claim to some 42 per cent of Antarctica has underpinned national policy on Antarctica for over 75 years. Sovereign interest spurred Australia's approach to the negotiation of the Antarctic Treaty in 1959, which neatly accommodated differences of view over territorial claims and protected the Australian interest. While Australia has taken a leading role in post-World War II Antarctic affairs, there have also been challenges. An ongoing debate has taken place as to the relative weighting of the scientific value of Antarctica as against its economic value. Long-term projections of Antarctica's potential mineral wealth have resulted in speculation that some claimant states may be keeping their Antarctic claims in reserve for the future.[1] In this respect, Australia has increasingly sought to take a more assertive stand on certain Antarctic matters which go to the heart of Australian sovereignty over the Australian Antarctic Territory (AAT), particularly with respect to offshore sovereignty around the Antarctic coastline. This chapter looks at how Australia's Antarctic sovereign interests evolved, and have been maintained, so that Australia's claim remains as strong as ever.

The legal basis of the Australian claim

Any consideration of the basis upon which Australian sovereignty in Antarctica is founded requires an appreciation of international law governing the assertion of title to territory and of the actions of an individual state in seeking to assert that title. For unoccupied lands subject to discovery, of which Antarctica is one of the classic examples, international law recognises that acts of discovery which are accompanied by assertions of title, such as proclamations and/or legislative acts, provide a sound basis for a claim. However, any such act on its own results only in an inchoate title and requires further action by the claimant state in order for title to territory to be perfected.[2] Nevertheless, the 1933 *Eastern Greenland* decision of the Permanent Court of International Justice acknowledged that a lesser standard may be applied in polar than in more temperate lands, which are subject to easier access and sovereign control.[3] Title to lands could also be acquired by way of cession, by which the title acquired by one state could be transferred to another. There was certainly a polar precedent for this, with the 1867 'Alaska Purchase' seeing the United States acquire title to the territory of Alaska by way of transfer of title from Russia. This then was the legal context within which initial consideration was given to an Australian claim to Antarctica in the early decades of the twentieth century.

As to Australian activities in Antarctica forming the basis for a territorial claim to the continent, the first Australian Antarctic expedition took place in 1911 under the command of Douglas Mawson. This expedition had both a scientific and political significance and resulted in the discovery of new Antarctic lands – accompanied by the inevitable 'planting of the flag' in King George V Land and Queen Mary Land, which were claimed for the British Crown in March 1912 and December 1912 respectively.[4] Mawson was well aware of the significance attached to the Australasian Antarctic Expedition with respect to potential territorial claims to the continent, noting in 1911 that:

> If ever in the history of Australia an expedition is to set out under favourable circumstances, it must be immediate. No time is to be lost. So surely as it lapses a moment foreign nations will step in and secure this most valuable portion of the Antarctic continent for themselves, and for ever from the control of Australia.[5]

The proclamation of King George V Land on 5 January 1931 at Cape Denison, which had been occupied by the Australasian Antarctic Expedition (AAE) in 1912–13. James Francis (Frank) Hurley, Australian Antarctic Division

Proclamation

In the name of His Majesty, King George the Fifth, King of Great Britain, Ireland and the British Dominions across the Seas, Emperor of India.

By Sir Douglas Mawson

Whereas I have it in command from His Majesty, King George the Fifth, to assert the Sovereign rights of His Majesty over British land discoveries met with in Antarctica. Now, therefore, I, Sir Douglas Mawson, do hereby proclaim and declare to all men that, from and after the date of these presents, the full sovereignty of the Territory which we have discovered and explored extending continuously from Adelie Land, westwards to MacRobertson Land being that part of the Antarctic Mainland and offlying Islands (Including amongst others, Drygalski Island, Hordern Island, David Island, Masson Island, Henderson Island, Haswell Islds and an Island in Longitude 103° 15′ East shown on our charts) situate between meridia 133° and 60° East of Greenwich and south of Latitude 64° as far as the South Pole, vest in His Majesty King George the Fifth, His Heirs and Successors forever.

Given under my hand at this spot in MacRobertson Land on the eighteenth day of February 1931.

Douglas Mawson
B.A.N.Z.A.R.E.

One of the proclamations signed by Mawson in 1931, asserting the sovereignty of King George V over Antarctic lands. National Archives of Australia: B1759, 1931/2

Australia continued to sponsor and support voyages and expeditions to Antarctica, and became increasingly aware of the importance of ensuring that proclamations of sovereignty were made, even by private companies such as the Kerguelen Sealing and Whaling Company Ltd, which was urged in 1928 to 'assert British sovereignty in this area at as many points as possible ... so that we will be in a position to meet any challenge to our right of sovereignty with which we may be faced in the future'.[6]

Formal proclamations of what would become the AAT were made in 1930–31, although these claims were accompanied by the hoisting of the British flag and assertion of British sovereignty.[7] Nevertheless, by late 1931 the law officers of the British Government, following Mawson's activities and reports, prepared a legal opinion which outlined the steps for placing certain Antarctic territories under Australian control.[8] The formal transfer of sovereignty from Britain to Australia took place in 1933: first with a British order-in-council asserting British rights over the AAT and placing it under the administration of the Commonwealth of Australia, followed by the enactment of the *Australian Antarctic Territory Acceptance Act 1933* (Cwth). The Territory was defined as:

> all the islands and territories other than Adelie Land south of the 60th degree of South Latitude lying between the 160th degree of East Longitude and the 45th degree of East Longitude.[9]

Australia thereby gained sovereignty in Antarctica through a mixture of British claims, 'Empire' claims and Australian claims, made by Mawson and others. Proclamation of the AAT was at the time contested only by Norway; however, this objection was withdrawn in 1939 following a compromise that Norwegian whalers would not be faced with onerous licensing requirements in waters adjacent to other territorial claims.[10]

Legal recognition of the Australian claim

In the period from 1933 until the negotiation of the Antarctic Treaty, Australia took various steps to support its claim to sovereignty over the AAT, mindful of the decision by the International Court in the *Eastern Greenland* case, also delivered in 1933.[11] The only direct challenge to the Australian claim occurred during the private expedition of Lincoln Ellsworth, who, with Australian aviator Hubert Wilkins, undertook an aerial reconnaissance over the interior of Princess Elizabeth Land in 1939 and claimed 77,000 square miles on behalf of the United States on 11 January.[12] However, the United States refrained from adopting or ratifying Ellsworth's actions and as a result never attained an inchoate title to the territory.[13]

In order to perfect its claim to the AAT, Australia set about engaging in traditional sovereign acts, consistent with the limitations that applied to polar lands and which had been recognised in the *Eastern Greenland* decision. Various laws were adopted, including the *Whaling Act 1935* (Cwth), which purported to apply to the waters adjacent to Australian territories, including the AAT. In 1954, in order to provide for a more complete legal regime for the AAT, the *Australian Antarctic Territory Act 1954* (Cwth) was adopted, which applied the laws of the Australian Capital Territory (other than criminal laws) and the criminal laws of the Jervis Bay Territory to the AAT (see chapter 4).[14] This period was also one in which Australia's Antarctic research programs were further developed through the Australian National Antarctic Research Expeditions (ANARE), established in 1947. These operations were consolidated and expanded in preparation for the International Geophysical Year, which also resulted in the building of Australian bases on the continent at Mawson in 1954 and Davis in 1957, in addition to the earlier ANARE bases established at Macquarie Island from 1948 and Heard Island (1947–55).

Australia's Antarctic claim is specifically recognised by four other states – the United Kingdom (from whom the AAT was transferred), France, New Zealand and Norway – and Australia reciprocates by recognising their claims. The Antarctic territories of the last three states share borders with the AAT and (unlike the situation in the Antarctic Peninsula; see below) are not the subjects of dispute or counterclaim.

Argentina and Chile, the other two claimants, maintain their own claims but do not recognise the AAT, while most other states are silent on the issue of recognition of Antarctic claims. The validity of the territorial claims, including the AAT, has never been put to the test and Australia continues to avoid such a situation.

Sovereignty and the Antarctic Treaty

The 1959 Antarctic Treaty negotiations in Washington were pivotal to the future of the continent and the sovereignty claims which had been made. Notwithstanding the assertion by that time of all seven territorial claims, their legal status in international law remained dubious, even without allowing for the fact the Argentinean, Chilean and UK claims to the Antarctic Peninsula overlapped. The contentious nature of the claims had been highlighted by the 1955 *Antarctica* cases brought before the International Court of Justice by the United Kingdom against both Argentina and Chile.[15] While these cases were discontinued in March 1956, they did serve to highlight the fragile nature of sovereignty in Antarctica and the potential for legal challenge.

Accordingly, when Argentina, Australia, Belgium, Chile, France, Japan, New Zealand, Norway, South Africa, the Soviet Union, the United Kingdom and the United States, the 12 states with Antarctic interests, convened in Washington in late 1959, the ongoing status of the existing sovereignty claims was a key issue for resolution, especially if there were to be any prospect of continuing the spirit of scientific collaboration which had developed during the International Geophysical Year. The resolution of this question via Article IV of the Antarctic Treaty proved to be a masterstroke, which won ready acceptance from the claimants, including Australia, and also from the United States and the USSR. Article IV contains two parts, one addressing the status of current and potential claims and the other addressing future activities. Article IV (1) provides as follows:

Nothing contained in the present Treaty shall be interpreted as:

(a)　a renunciation by any Contracting Party of previously asserted rights of or claims to territorial sovereignty in Antarctica;

(b)　a renunciation or diminution by any Contracting Party of any basis of claim to territorial sovereignty in Antarctica which it may have whether as a result of its activities or those of its nationals in Antarctica, or otherwise;

(c)　prejudicing the position of any Contracting Party as regards its recognition or non-recognition of any other State's right of or claim or basis of claim to territorial sovereignty in Antarctica.

The position of Australia, as a state which had already asserted its territorial claim to the continent, was therefore clearly accommodated in paragraph 1(a), but Australia's interests were also reflected in the wording of paragraph 1(c) with respect to any competing claims or activities by other states incompatible with Australia's sovereign rights. In essence, Australia did not have to do anything to protect its sovereign interest other than maintain the Antarctic Treaty. While ever the Treaty is in force, nothing would change with respect to the pre-existing claims.

Nevertheless, the strategic positioning of the stations of other nations in the AAT did not go unnoticed. This was particularly so for the United States' Scott-Amundsen base at the South Pole (initially located at the apex of all the claims made by other countries, but now, by the movement of the glacial ice on which it is built, wholly within Australia's claim) and Wilkes on the AAT coast. Russian bases were also built in Australian territory for the International Geophysical Year – Vostok, in the inland heart, and the coastal stations Mirny and Oasis. Subsequently the United States transferred Wilkes to Australia, while the USSR built Leningradskaya and Molodezhnaya at the eastern and western extremes respectively of the AAT.

Where Article IV(1) sought to deal with pre-existing sovereignty issues, Article IV(2) sought to deal with future issues. It provided as follows:

> No rights or activities taking place while the present Treaty is in force shall constitute a basis for asserting, supporting or denying a claim to territorial sovereignty in Antarctica or create any rights of sovereignty in Antarctica. No new claim, or enlargement of an existing claim, to territorial sovereignty in Antarctica shall be asserted while the present Treaty is in force.

The effect of this provision for Australia (as for all other claimants) is that it potentially rendered irrelevant and ineffective any direct efforts to reinforce its claim for the duration of the Treaty. But neither of Article IV's provisions prevents the claimants from taking actions that would otherwise be consistent with claims. Indeed, the claimants continue to act as they might be expected to act, lest a change of behaviour be interpreted as a change of attitude. Most do not take actions that might be seen as unnecessarily provocative, but there are many examples of routine symbolic acts that serve to remind others of the existence of sovereignty – Australia, for example, continues to issue stamps for the AAT. More significant is the limitation this article places on a claimant's capacity to expand its territorial sovereignty through the assertion of new territorial claims.[16] However, Article IV(2) also provided Australia with significant reassurances regarding the ongoing activities within the AAT of other states, such as the United States and the USSR (and more recently China, India and Romania) – that their presence through their research stations did not provide a basis for a potential competing claim while the Treaty was in force. The crucial test for Australia would come if a state that is not party to the Treaty sought to establish a base in the AAT.

Some reference should also be made in this context to the import of Article VIII, which effectively complements Article IV by placing limitations on the exercise of traditional state sovereignty in Antarctica.

One of the characteristics of a sovereign state in international law is its capacity to exercise jurisdiction and control over all events which occur within its defined boundaries. Importantly, this includes the application and enforcement of its laws. However, any such overt expression of such a sovereign right in Antarctica had the potential to highlight sovereignty disputes. Article VIII leaves the question of jurisdiction over individuals unresolved, other than providing that observers and scientific exchange personnel are subject only to the jurisdiction of the party of which they are nationals. The practical effect of this is that Treaty parties, including Australia, have in general limited the application of law in Antarctica to their nationals, whether they be engaged in scientific expeditions or other activities such as tourism or fishing (see also chapter 4).

Sovereignty and other Treaty instruments

Notwithstanding the scope of the Antarctic Treaty, there was always the potential that as a result of the Consultative Meetings additional legal instruments would be added which would raise the spectre of sovereignty. The first occasion where this arose was in 1964 with the adoption of the Agreed Measures for the Protection of Antarctic Fauna and Flora. However, as this instrument fell directly within the ambit of the Antarctic Treaty, the limitations created by Articles

IV and VIII remained. The negotiation in 1972 of the Convention on the Conservation of Antarctic Seals did have the potential to raise sovereignty issues, but it was made explicit in Article I to the Convention that the provisions of Article IV of the Treaty were reaffirmed. Likewise, as the Convention relied upon flag state implementation via nationals and flagged vessels, it avoided issues that may have arisen from the direct application of law based on territorial claims.

When it came to the negotiation of the 1980 Convention on the Conservation of Antarctic Marine Living Resources (CCAMLR), however, the Treaty parties were confronted with challenges in addressing issues related to sovereignty that had not arisen in 1959. The first was that the area of operation of CCAMLR extended beyond the Treaty limits of 60° South into parts of the Southern Ocean properly characterised as sub-Antarctic, and for Australia this immediately raised issues as to the status of the Heard and McDonald islands. The second was that for any effective legal regime to be developed that sought to apply and enforce laws and regulations dealing with fisheries there would be a need for the recognition of traditional coastal state sovereign rights and also flag state rights. The way that this was resolved was via Article IV of CCAMLR, which sought to distinguish between the application of the convention within the Antarctic Treaty area, in which the contracting parties remained bound by Article IV of the Antarctic Treaty, and areas to the north of 60° South and within the

CCAMLR boundary limits, where sovereignty over territory is uncontested. CCAMLR does this by restating the Antarctic Treaty's Article IV formula but without seeking to extend the operation of that article into the sub-Antarctic. This was not only a significant concession to the interests of the sub-Antarctic claimants, but also recognition that Australian sovereignty over the Heard and McDonald islands was uncontested and would be unaffected.

The 1991 Madrid Protocol to the Antarctic Treaty also raised issues of sovereignty, though in ways which were distinct from earlier Antarctic Treaty System (ATS) instruments. The most significant was that by its Article 7 the Protocol placed a prohibition on mineral resource activities in Antarctica. This was a significant issue for Australia and proved to be contentious in some of the debates within government as to whether Australia should have supported the Convention on the Regulation of Antarctic Mineral Resource Activities (CRAMRA) or, alternatively, the Protocol. However, the Protocol did not seek to extend the reach of the basic limitations of Article IV of the Antarctic Treaty, but provided a 'supplement' to the Treaty.[17]

Australian sovereignty during the Treaty era

The Antarctic Treaty has now been in force for 50 years. This means that, in more than half of the time in which Australia has asserted a claim to Antarctica, the claim has been subject to the limitations agreed to in the Treaty. Nevertheless, successive Australian governments during this time have never sought to downplay Australia's Antarctic claim, notwithstanding the potential impact of the Treaty upon the status of that claim while the Treaty remained in force. For example, in 1978 a Joint Parliamentary Committee on Foreign Affairs and Defence was of the view that a 'challenge to Australia's sovereignty to the Territory by an individual nation is probably unlikely – no country has a better claim if based on early exploration activities'.[18] This confidence in the Australian claim was restated a year later by the Minister for Foreign Affairs, Andrew Peacock, who asserted in Parliament:

> Australia's title in international law rests on acts of discovery and formal claims of title by British and Australian explorers, the formal transfer of the territory from Britain to Australia and Australian acceptance by legislation, and subsequent acts showing an intention by Australia to exercise sovereignty over the Territory. This intention is demonstrated, *inter alia,* by the application by Australia of legislation to the Territory, the negotiation and conclusion of Treaties affecting the Territory and by engagement in a degree of administrative activity there.[19]

Consistent with this approach throughout the duration of the Treaty, and far from abandoning its

Antarctic claim or even taking a less assertive approach, Australia has been from time to time forthright in asserting its sovereign interests. This can be highlighted in two ways. The first relates to the assertion of new maritime claims to the Southern Ocean within Antarctic Treaty limits, and the second to the enactment and enforcement of new laws which apply to Antarctica and the Southern Ocean.

Australian maritime claims

In accordance with developments in the international law of the sea, and in particular the 1982 UN Convention on the Law of the Sea, Australia has claimed a range of maritime zones offshore Antarctica, including:

- a 12 nautical mile territorial sea
- a 200 nautical mile exclusive economic zone
- a 200 nautical mile continental shelf.

Australia has also claimed a 200 nautical mile 'Australian Whale Sanctuary' offshore the AAT, which is coterminous with the exclusive economic zone.[20] All of these claims have raised issues as to whether Australia's actions are consistent with Article IV(2) of the Antarctic Treaty and the limitations placed therein on the assertion of a 'new claim, or enlargement of an existing claim' while the Treaty is in force. The most contentious, and the one which has generated the most significant diplomatic response to a potential Australian assertion of sovereignty while the

Treaty has been in force, is that dealing with an outer continental shelf (see chapter 12).

In November 2004 Australia submitted its claim for an outer continental shelf to the Commission on the Limits of the Continental Shelf (CLCS).[21] The Australian claim, made under Article 76 of the Law of the Sea Convention, will, when formally proclaimed, give Australia a total continental shelf of approximately 3.4 million square kilometres. This, when combined with its land territories, will create one of the largest areas of jurisdiction in the world. A particular feature of the claim is the assertion of an outer continental shelf offshore the sub-Antarctic Heard and McDonald islands in the Southern Ocean.[22] It is important to note, however, that the successful assertion of an outer continental shelf does not generate sovereign territory – it is, rather, the delineation of an area where a coastal state might exercise exclusive rights as a consequence of the existence of an existing territorial claim. The difficulty for Antarctic claimant states seeking to exercise this right is that to achieve it implies recognition by the CLCS of a valid territorial claim. To pursue this would invite judgment on an Antarctic sovereign claim by a body external to the Antarctic Treaty, and one not constrained by the accommodating norms of Article IV. Seeking such external legitimisation of an Antarctic claim would be problematic.

Accordingly, recognising the sensitivity for the international community and under the Antarctic Treaty of the assertion of an outer continental shelf claim in Antarctica, Australia worked with other interested states to find ways around the dilemma. As a result, Australia chose the option of requesting the CLCS 'not to take any action for the time being' with respect to that part of the claim offshore the AAT. This defused the potential for conflict within the Treaty and had the effect that the prospect of an outer continental shelf off the AAT is effectively set aside for an indefinite time.[23] This neatly allowed Australia to meet its obligations and preserve its rights under the Law of the Sea while also protecting its interest in maintaining stability within the Treaty system. As anticipated, the Australian claim generated responses from seven other Antarctic Treaty parties – France, Germany, India, Japan, the Netherlands, the Russian Federation and the United States. With the exception of France, each of these states made direct reference to the provisions of the Antarctic Treaty, particularly Article IV, and restated their well-known positions with respect to their non-recognition of Antarctic claims and rights over the seabed or adjacent offshore waters surrounding Antarctica.[24] These responses supported the diplomatic approach Australia had taken in working with its Antarctic partners during the CLCS submission and were done in a way that ensured the positions of claimant and non-claimant states were protected. The status quo and Treaty harmony were thus pre-served.

As anticipated, when the CLCS made its 2008 recommendations with respect to Australia, no reference was made to the outer continental shelf offshore Antarctica. However, the Australian submission with respect to the area offshore the Heard and McDonald islands was endorsed, and it is now anticipated that Australia will take action under the *Seas and Submerged Lands Act 1973* (Cwth) to proclaim the outer limits of the continental shelf in the near future. If Australia does assert new outer continental shelf claims under Australian law within the Antarctic Treaty area, then it is possible that Australia will be asserting that the area over which it could exercise exclusive rights extends over the seabed south of 60° South. Whether the assertion of such a continental shelf claim provokes a response from other Antarctic Treaty parties remains to be seen.

Australian law in Antarctica and the Southern Ocean

An essential aspect of any sovereign claim is the capacity of a state to apply its laws to the territory under its control. Like other claimant states, Australia has established a legal regime for the AAT to achieve this. However, the impact of the Treaty was to alter that dynamic with the effect that Australia's sovereignty was not perfected. This is not to say that Australian law does not extend to foreign nationals in the AAT, and it can be argued that it is a sovereign act to decide whether or not to apply the law to any individual, foreign or otherwise. Indeed, as noted earlier, the Treaty itself does not prevent the application of Australian law against foreign nationals (other than observers and scientific exchange personnel, as provided for in Article VIII). Australian practice, however, is to exercise jurisdiction only over its own nationals, except in the few cases where foreign nationals have voluntarily subjected themselves to Australian legislation (such as nationals from parties that recognise the AAT). This is done both in the pursuit of goodwill and cooperation and for the reason that any attempt to enforce its laws could be contested on the grounds that Australia's sovereignty claim was not recognised. Nevertheless, Australian law in Antarctica has become increasingly complex, especially following the adoption of the Madrid Protocol, which resulted in significant adjustments to the *Antarctic Treaty (Environment Protection) Act 1980* (Cwth).[25]

The application of Australian law and its implications for Australian sovereignty in Antarctica has been highlighted in recent years with respect to those areas offshore Antarctica and Australia's sub-Antarctic possessions. This has especially been the case with the enforcement of Australian fisheries laws in the waters adjacent to the Heard and McDonald islands, over which Australian sovereignty is uncontested and which under the terms of CCAMLR can be subject to Australian law without question. Several high-profile arrests of illegal fishers have occurred within these waters as a result of the take of Patagonian toothfish.

In addition to the range of maritime zones contemplated by the Law of the Sea which Australia has asserted offshore its Antarctic territories, an Australian Whale Sanctuary which is conterminous with the exclusive economic zone has been proclaimed under the *Environment Protection and Biological Diversity (EPBC) Act 1999* (Cwth). The EPBC Act prohibits the taking, killing, injuring, treating or possession of whales within the Australian Whale Sanctuary and makes no exceptions for foreign nationals or vessels.[26] Yet while a good deal of Australian law applies within these various maritime areas offshore the AAT, there has been no instance to date of such law being enforced against non-Australian nationals or foreign vessels. This approach is therefore one which has sought to maintain the integrity of Australia's Antarctic claim and the accompanying maritime sovereignty and jurisdiction which any coastal state enjoys over its offshore areas, while also respecting the limitations on the active assertion of sovereignty and jurisdiction imposed by the Antarctic Treaty.[27] A prominent exception to this position is whaling (see chapter 4).[28]

The value of Australian sovereignty

Successive Australian governments have identified six national Antarctic policy interests and (although not necessarily listed in priority order) without exception have placed at the top of the list the wish 'to preserve our sovereignty over the Australian Antarctic Territory, including our sovereign rights over the adjacent offshore areas'. This reflects the strategic value of Antarctica to Australia, and the consequential national and regional security concerns that would arise if sovereignty over the AAT was compromised or lost.[29]

There are several reasons why the AAT is important to Australia. The traditional reason, and the one that inspired Australia's Antarctic pioneers such as Douglas Mawson, is the potential economic value to the nation. Mawson and his successors predicted that Antarctica's inevitable mineral wealth would, at some future time, bring dividends to Australia. That may well be true, even if there is no foreseeable prospect of this occurring, given the constraints imposed by the Madrid Protocol. It can be argued, however, that Australia should hold onto its sovereign claim against the day, perhaps many generations hence, when circumstances may change. In addition, there may be other kinds of non-mineral resources not yet identified and which may be extracted from Antarctica or the near-shore region and for which a regulatory regime provides a special privilege to states asserting a territorial claim. Such optimism takes us into the realm of wild and long-term speculation.

Accordingly, one should look to more realistic, albeit less tangible benefits. Heading these is national pride. Australians are generally well aware of their country's long heritage of involvement in the Antarctic region, starting in the heroic era, and many would also be aware of the size of the Australian claim. National pride is a potent force and the AAT has its part to play in that.

Australians are also generally conscious of the proximity of the AAT to Australia's south and the additional potential authority this gives the nation as a player to be taken seriously in southern hemisphere, if not global, affairs. This status can be used to great effect by a nation relatively small in terms of population, while, of course, the primary forum for this influence is the Antarctic Treaty System. As a claimant Australia was able to be an architect of the Treaty and an original signatory, and over the subsequent years has been influential in strengthening the system. It has done this in ambitious ways, including, notably, in the negotiation of the Madrid Protocol – a strategy that carried risks for Australia and for the Treaty but which eventually significantly enhanced the Treaty and global environment protection. As noted earlier, more recently Australia has used its position as a claimant to influence the way the Treaty interfaces with the Law of the Sea. It has also been actively engaged in management of the Southern Ocean, particularly through CCAMLR, and has used its influence to drive responses to illegal fishing in the Southern Ocean and in turn to achieve global impact by setting an example to other fisheries. Being a claimant has required Australia to remain engaged in the AAT, even in times of economic constraint when others have reduced their presence. This has brought the advantage of long-term involvement in science at a level which might not otherwise have been sustained, and that, in turn, has had unforeseen national and global benefits, at present especially in the context of climate research.

The converse to giving a value to Antarctic sovereignty is to consider what value would be gained by relinquishing the AAT. It is hard to imagine any gain to be made, especially in the absence of any compelling alternative governance structure for the continent. Australian policy makers were aware of 'Seward's Folly', the uncharitable description given at the time to the United States' 1867 purchase of Alaska from Russia for a little less than six cents per hectare. It serves as a lesson in taking a long-term view. US Secretary of State William Seward would not have been aware that generations later his gamble would pay off handsomely in terms of resources and strategic advantage. One can only speculate on what Russia would do now if given the opportunity to revisit the decision to sell. What current minister would like to be remembered in the future as the one who gave away the AAT because he or she could not foresee its future strategic or economic value?

Status of Australian sovereignty

There have been two phases of Australian sovereignty in Antarctica: pre-and post-Treaty. Before the adoption of the Treaty, Australia, alongside Britain, sought to affirm its sovereignty over the AAT and its sub-Antarctic possessions. Since the entry into force of the Treaty in 1961 Australia has worked within the Treaty system not only to ensure its success but also to ensure where appropriate an acceptance of its rights as a territorial sovereign, as can be seen in the CCAMLR and CRAMRA negotiations. The current status of Australian sovereignty in Antarctica is, therefore, that under the provisions of the Treaty, Australia's position has not been diminished – and it has probably taken as proactive a position as it could to reaffirm its claim within the Treaty context. Any counter-claims to Australian sovereignty could only feasibly be made by the United States or Russia building upon their long-standing scientific presence within the AAT (China being a relative latecomer). Notwithstanding the size and extent of those scientific operations and the consequent 'foothold' for both of those states, as Triggs argues, 'these activities were not undertaken *à titre de souverain* and were at the invitation and with the consent of the State claiming to be sovereign'.[30] Events over the past few years highlight Australia's awareness of the sensitivity of its actions, as is demonstrated by its request to the CLCS to not consider the outer continental shelf claim offshore the AAT, and the refusal of the Rudd Labor government in 2008 to seek to enforce the orders of the Federal Court of Australia in the *Humane Society International* case. In conclusion it can be observed that Australian sovereignty over the AAT is probably as strong as it has ever been, given the constraints of the Treaty and of the very particular issues that exist in effectively asserting sovereignty over polar lands. It can also be argued that no other state has a superior claim to the AAT.

Notes

[1]   Bergin (1991).

[2]   These principles are outlined in decisions of international courts and tribunals, especially the *Island of Palmas* arbitration (The Netherlands v. United States of America) (4 April 1928) 2 RIAA 829; and *Clipperton Island* arbitration (France v Mexico) (28 January 1931) 2 RIAA 1105.

[3]   *Legal Status of Eastern Greenland* (Norway v Denmark) (1933) PCIJ Reports, Series A/B No.53.

[4]   Triggs (1986) 105.

[5]   Triggs (1986) 105.

[6]   Bush (1982) AU03101928.

[7]   Triggs (1986) 107.

[8]   Anon (1971) 316–28.

[9]   Australia, *Commonwealth of Australia Gazette,* 1933, no 15, 365 (16 March 1933).

[10]   Triggs (1986) 110.

[11]   Triggs (1986) 115.

[12]   Triggs (1986) 111.

[13]   Auburn (1982) 62.

[14] *Australian Antarctic Territory Act 1954* (Cwth) s. 6.

[15] *Antarctica Cases* (United Kingdom v Argentina; United Kingdom v Chile) Application Instituting Proceedings (May 1955).

[16] By virtue of Article VI some flexibility remained with respect to maritime rights, which were beginning to emerge in the late 1950s as matters of some significance, given the developments that had been taking place in the international law of the sea.

[17] 1991 Protocol on Environmental Protection to the Antarctic Treaty, Article 4.

[18] Australia (1978) 74.

[19] Peacock, Andrew (1979) House of Representative Debates 116: 3502.

[20] EPBC Act 1999 (Cwth) s 225.

[21] Downer, Ruddock and McFarlane (2004).

[22] Downer, Ruddock and McFarlane (2004), Serdy (2005) 208–09.

[23] Jabour (2006) 198.

[24] Rothwell and Scott (2007) 16.

[25] Bush (2000).

[26] EPBC Act 1999 (Cwth) ss 229–30.

[27] Rothwell and Scott (2007).

[28] For full discussion of these issues see Mossop (2005), Rothwell and Nasu (2008), and Donald R Rothwell 'Australia v Japan: JARPA II Whaling Case before International Court of Justice' The Hague Justice Portal (2 July 2010) at <www.h

aguejusticeportal.net/eCache/DEF/11/840.htm
l>.
[29]   Rothwell and Nasu (2008).
[30]   Triggs (1986) 122.

3

Australia and the negotiation of the Antarctic Treaty

Rob Hall and Marie Kawaja

On 1 December 1959 Australia, together with eleven other states, signed the Antarctic Treaty at a formal ceremony in Washington. The treaty entered into force on 23 June 1961, and several weeks later the first Antarctic Treaty Consultative Meeting established under Article IX convened in Canberra. The foundation was thus laid for what has become known as the Antarctic Treaty System (ATS). This chapter traces Australia's involvement in the international efforts to create the treaty.

The impetus for an international agreement on Antarctica stemmed from what became known in the 1940s and early 1950s as the 'Antarctic problem'. Australia's initial responses to several internationally based solutions to this problem were negative because it feared internationalisation would lead to Australia giving up sovereignty of the Australian Antarctic Territory (AAT). That fear was tempered, however, with a desire to participate in any international discussions on the matter. Between 1955 and early 1958, this reluctant, sceptical Australian position remained essentially the same. However, during formal international negotiations that were conducted between June 1958 and December 1959, Australia played a constructive role – a role that came to embrace the values of the emerging treaty.

The 'Antarctic problem'

By 1939, the seeds of the problem were rapidly germinating. In January of that year, Norway claimed Queen Maud Land in Antarctica. This brought to five the number of states that had claimed Antarctic territory: Britain's claim of 1908 (amended in 1917) was the first, followed by those of New Zealand (made initially by Britain in 1923 over the Ross Sea sector, as a New Zealand Dependency), France (1924) and Australia (1933).

In response to the Norwegian claim, the Soviet Union immediately cautioned Norway in a diplomatic note that reserved Soviet opinion about the status of territories discovered by Russian citizens.[1] An added dimension to the problem was that none of these claims had been recognised by the United States, which had in 1924 enunciated and subsequently adhered to a doctrine that denied their legitimacy and, moreover, had reserved US rights in the region.[2]

A further development occurred in 1940, when Chile claimed a broad sector of Antarctica that overlapped part of Britain's claim to what was then known as the Falkland Islands Dependencies – the region below South America. Japan, which had had an expedition in the Ross Sea area between 1910–12 and had been engaged in whaling in the Southern Ocean since 1934, responded by sending a diplomatic note to Chile stating that it regarded itself 'as one of the countries holding interests and rights' in Antarctica.[3] All these events stirred Argentina into considering its Antarctic interests, and in February 1943 Argentina claimed sovereignty over Antarctic territory that also overlapped parts of Britain's and Chile's claims.[4]

After the conclusion of World War II, increasing tension between Argentina, Chile and Britain over these conflicting claims posed a problem for the United States, which wished to avoid favouring any of the rival claimants and at the same time to secure its own interests in the region. US military strategists perceived Antarctica as a desirable venue to train its military forces in polar warfare, and a US Navy exercise (Operation Highjump) was relocated from the Arctic to the Antarctic in 1947 to lessen any possible provocation of the Soviet Union at a time of growing Cold War animosity.

The search for a solution begins and falters

Between late 1947 and mid-1948, the United States reassessed its Antarctic policy and, after consulting with Britain, developed a proposal for the establishment of an Antarctic regime in the form of a condominium, the terms of which were to be agreed upon by the United States and the seven claimants.[5]

It then conveyed this internationalisation proposal to Chile and Argentina. The initial Chilean reaction was negative but, in discussions between the US envoy and the principal Chilean representative, the latter presented a counter-proposal that called for interested countries to establish a 'standstill' arrangement for Antarctica for a period of five or ten years, during which time all claims and rights would be frozen and scientific cooperation encouraged.[6] Several days later, the US envoy in Buenos Aires received a strongly unfavourable reaction from Argentina to its proposal.[7]

After gaining British approval of the condominium idea in late July, the United States approached the four remaining claimant countries for their views. A variety of responses was forthcoming: New Zealand joined Britain in expressing favourable interest in the internationalisation proposal; France requested more information; Norway viewed internationalisation as unnecessary; and Australia was sceptical about the necessity for internationalisation but indicated a desire to cooperate in working out a solution. Indeed, the Australian Minister for External Affairs, H V Evatt, in a note informing Prime Minister Ben Chifley about Australia's opposition to the US proposal, indicated that this stance was based on Australia's desire not to forgo the right to control minerals and other resources in the AAT, which would otherwise be surrendered.[8] He informed the United States that Australia supported the view that instead of pooling sovereignty what was required was a reasoned agreement retaining sovereignty, including Australia's sovereignty over its Antarctic territory, but with the interested states also agreeing to assist each other in the development of Antarctica.[9] Thus, by the end of 1948, the United States had been unable to secure an agreement to negotiate a solution to the Antarctic problem.

An attempt to revive the US initiative to form an international Antarctic regime came from an unlikely source. In early 1949 the All-Union Geographical Society of the Soviet Union adopted a resolution demanding Soviet participation in all international decisions concerning Antarctica.[10] Despite the organisation's non-official status, both France and Britain sought US reaction, eliciting the response that the United States was now using the Chilean standstill proposal as a basis for study.[11]

By September, events began to gather pace. The United States handed to Britain for comment copies of a draft declaration on Antarctica embodying a modified version of the Chilean proposal that sought to address some major sticking points. These were: the freezing of all claims and rights in territory south of latitude 60° South for the period of the declaration (five or ten years); the exchange of scientific information; the freedom of scientific research in the region; and the establishment of a consultative committee consisting of one member from each party.[12] Britain responded positively the following month, and in early 1950 the United States began informal discussions with Chile about the proposal, and informed Australia and New Zealand of developments.[13] New Zealand expressed support. Australia, on the other hand, was opposed on the grounds that: the consultative committee might give the Soviet Union an easy entry to Antarctic control; occupation or activity by the Soviet Union or any other non-signatory during the standstill period might be recognised at international law as constituting a title to territory; and Australia's own claim needed consolidation through the despatch of expeditions and other activities.[14]

The Soviet position on Antarctica became official in June 1950. In a memorandum simultaneously addressed to the United States and six of the claimant countries (Argentina, Australia, the United Kingdom, France, New Zealand and Norway), the Soviet government warned that it could 'not recognize as legal any decision regarding the regime of the Antarctic taken without its participation'.[15] However, the outbreak of the Korean War in June 1950 meant that the United States had more pressing matters to contend with, and during the remainder of 1950 and throughout 1951 little further effort was expended on achieving a solution.[16] The proposal thus became moribund. However, events were in train in the international scientific community that were to influence the approach of the interested governments. These events were associated with the 1957–58 International Geophysical Year (IGY), one of the components of which was an Antarctic scientific program.

Antarctica, the IGY and Australia

Although originally proposed to be a Third Polar Year, the International Council of Scientific Unions (ICSU) subsequently expanded the scope of research to encompass worldwide studies of the Earth and its cosmic environs. Accordingly, it sent out invitations to member states to participate in the International Geophysical Year to be held from July 1957 to December 1958.

At a planning and coordinating meeting held in Rome in 1954, two significant developments occurred. The Soviet Union indicated it would participate in the IGY, and it was decided that the study of Antarctica and outer space would receive special attention. The decision to focus on Antarctica resulted in the establishment of a special Antarctic conference to coordinate the activities of the twelve countries planning to undertake research there. These were Argentina, Australia, Belgium, the United Kingdom, Chile, France, Japan, New Zealand, Norway, South Africa, the Soviet Union and the United States – all of which had declared claims, rights or interests in Antarctica.

At the first Antarctic IGY conference, held in Paris in early July 1955, the locations of the projected scientific stations were discussed. Numerous stations were proposed for the Antarctic Peninsula region, primarily by Argentina, Chile and the United Kingdom, for what appeared to be political rather than purely scientific reasons. The Soviet Union, on the other hand, planned to establish three stations in the AAT, much to the immediate consternation of the Australian government. The US Department of State was also concerned at the imminent Soviet penetration of Antarctica.[17]

These proposals triggered two reactions. First, Richard Casey, Australian Minister for External Affairs, had been anticipating a test to Australia's Antarctic credentials during the course of the IGY. He was aware that both the United States and the Soviet Union were scheduled to participate in the program and also aware that neither would seek Australian permission to establish scientific bases in the Australian sector, as that would be an admission of Australia's sovereignty. Sensing the problem, Casey made a significant diplomatic move in the form of a public statement in which he welcomed the interest of other countries in the IGY and offered Australia's help to those wishing to undertake scientific research in the AAT.[18] Casey's initiative was at the same time a face-saving device and an assertion of Australian sovereignty. On 30 July 1955, he noted in his diary that Cabinet had agreed 'I should make a public statement welcoming the Americans and the Russians to make observations. As we can't stop them, we'd better take it with good grace.'[19]

Second, the two South American states were wary not only of the projected level of increased British activity in the Peninsula region, but also of the imminent Soviet presence on the continent. In an attempt to protect their claimant positions, the Argentine and Chilean delegations presented a joint resolution at the final plenary session of the meeting in which participants would acknowledge that the establishment of the various national bases was temporary and that activities undertaken during the IGY did not modify the existing status in the Antarctic of relations between the participating countries.[20]

All of the delegations present approved the resolution. Although not binding their respective governments, the resolution came to be viewed as a mutual understanding to place a moratorium on the claims issues, thereby allowing non-claimant participating countries to establish stations anywhere in Antarctica as part of the IGY program without political repercussions. At the same time, the resolution provided a measure of protection for claimant participating states against the erosion of their positions. It was, in short, an informal variant of the Chilean standstill idea. This understanding resulted in the diminution of overt friction in Antarctic affairs during the period leading up to and including the IGY. Australia, however, continued to be particularly perturbed about the location of Soviet stations on the AAT and there was much speculation in the press about their possible military and strategic value.[21]

Richard Casey

Richard Casey, as British Minister of State in the Middle East, with Winston Churchill in Cairo, January 1943. National Library of Australia: nla.pic-vn4319600

Carl Murray

Born in Brisbane in 1890 and schooled in Melbourne, Richard Gardiner Casey had a career that would be impossible today. In the words of his biographer, he was 'the last of a kind. Australia's evolution towards full independence ... meant that no Australian could ever again enjoy the range of appointments which fell to him'.[1] In Australia he held a succession of ministries, including Commonwealth Treasurer, External Affairs and first Australian Minister to the United States. In the United Kingdom, Winston Churchill appointed him British Minister of State in the Middle East (Prime Minister Curtin was reportedly annoyed at 'having his No 1 diplomat taken from him by Winnie'), member of the UK War Cabinet and Governor of Bengal.[2] At one time or another Casey was also Federal President of the Australian Liberal Party, Governor-General of Australia, Australian of the Year, life peer, Privy Counsellor and Knight of the Garter, the highest British honour. This glittering gold chain of positions is all the more remarkable because Casey was a shy and reserved man and a mediocre public speaker. On the other hand, he was born into a prosperous and well-connected family, was hard-working and, above all, possessed an exceptional talent for diplomacy.

After a year at the University of Melbourne, Casey moved on to Cambridge, graduating as an engineer in 1913. He would later tell a conference of engineers that they were 'the salt of the earth' and should be more involved in policy making.[3] Before the start of his own political career he served as a major in World War I (winning the Military

Cross and the Distinguished Service Order) and worked in the United States and New Guinea for Australian gold and copper mining interests. He believed enthusiastically in the economic and social benefits offered by science and technology, and his own efforts in this regard, including vigorous advocacy of the CSIRO and of the establishment of the radio-telescope at Parkes, would lead to his election as a Fellow of the Australian Academy of Science in 1966.

Casey's enduring interest in Antarctica dated from the 1920s when, as Australian Political Liaison Officer in London, he had lent invaluable support to Mawson in the preparations for and during BANZARE, among other things arranging the loan of the *Discovery* from the British Government. In 1933 he strongly supported Australia's taking over responsibility for Antarctic territory previously claimed in the name of the Crown, stating that this was 'the culminating point of twenty years of continuous and concerted effort on the part of Australians to consolidate their interests in the Antarctic'.[4] And following Australia's request that British policy for Antarctica be included on the agenda of the 1937 Imperial Conference in London, Casey chaired the Polar Committee.[5] From 1951–60, as Minister for External Affairs, he took charge of all Australia's Antarctic activities. He made himself uncommonly available to Antarctic Division director, Phillip Law, and involved himself personally in the planning of research expeditions and the establishment of Australia's continental Antarctic stations. He emphasised the vital national importance of these endeavours on strategic and scientific – in particular meteorological – grounds and also because of Antarctica's potential food and mineral resources. When in 1953 he announced the expedition to found Mawson Station (Antarctica's first) in a region 'of vital importance to Australia ... [and] so close to Australia's back-door', Minister Casey had a statesman-like eye on his country's past and future:

The present generation is the trustee for Australian posterity. For us to neglect the Antarctic could be as serious as if our forefathers had confined themselves to a small strip of coastal settlement in Australia and left it to others to develop the resources of the rest of the continent. Today the Antarctic is a challenge – which cannot be ignored – to Australian courage and imagination, and the proposed expedition shows that we will grasp our opportunity.[6]

When Prime Minister Robert Menzies welcomed delegates to the first Antarctic Treaty Consultative Meeting in Canberra on 10 July 1961, he expressed his 'one personal regret' that Casey, who had recently become a member of the House of Lords, was not present, as 'my former colleague ... played a most active role in the negotiation of this

[Antarctic] Treaty'.[7] Indeed, it was Australia's contribution, led by Casey, to the successful signing of the Treaty which had resulted in the unanimous selection of Canberra as the venue for the first ATCM.[8] The 1959 Conference on Antarctica in Washington had been preceded by considerable preliminary negotiation, and it was in both phases that Casey was most significantly involved. He helped to smooth out major difficulties with the Latin American and French delegations and, most importantly, in private conversations in Australia with the Soviet Deputy Foreign Minister some months previously had overcome the USSR's rejection of the crucial Article IV.[9] A statement Casey made saluting the Antarctic Treaty when it was finally signed exemplifies his dual patriotic and global aspirations for the region. The entry into force of the agreement, he declared, would represent:

both a practical settlement of potentially difficult issues in an area of close and immediate concern to Australia, and a hopeful example of cooperation between East and West which might help to restore the confidence so sadly lacking in the post-war international scene.[10]

In recognition of Lord Casey's long service to Australian Antarctic expeditions and research, the nation's third continental station was named Casey in 1969. An Antarctic range, a glacier, a cape, a bay and an inlet also bear his name.[11]

Notes

1 Hudson (1993) 385.

2 *Argus* (Melbourne) 2 June 1945.

3 *Argus* (Melbourne) 17 March 1953.

4 *Records of the Australian Academy of Science,* vol3, no 3/4, Canberra, 1977, 60.

5 Cablegram 115 to the Secretary of State for Dominion Affairs, 28 November 1936, NAA: Series A461, Item C 326/1/4, i; Kerr (2009) 233.

6 Swan (1961) 264–65.

7 Australian Government (1984) vol2, appendix 23, 240.

8 Bowden (1997) 186; Swan (1961) 325.

9 Hudson (1986) 279; Bowden (1997)185–86 and 181–85.

10 Casey (1959) 667.

11 Australian Antarctic Data Centre, Composite Gazetteer of Antarctica, http://data.aad.gov.au/aadc/gaz/scar/.

Getting to the negotiating table

While the international scientific community was organising its onslaught on Antarctica, so were the politicians. The Soviet announcement of its intention to establish three IGY stations in Antarctica had prompted an immediate reassessment of US Antarctic policy. On 8 September 1955, the Australian Minister for External Affairs, Richard Casey, visited the State

Department to seek information about the US position. He was informed that the United States favoured negotiation among the seven claimant countries so that conflicting claims could be reconciled, but was not disposed to include the Soviet Union, believing that it would be less problematic to reconcile conflicting claims without a Soviet presence.[22] Casey responded that he strongly opposed the idea of the internationalisation of Antarctica, that Australia wanted the status quo maintained and that he saw no reason for international action, given that Antarctica remained free of serious international friction.[23] By 24 September 1955, at an Australia, New Zealand and United States (ANZUS) Council meeting in Washington, Casey did express the hope, though, that the United States, New Zealand, Britain and Australia 'could get together to concert their positions with regard to Antarctica'.[24]

Further consultation along such lines was not to occur for another two years, however, as US Antarctic policy was under continuous reassessment. During this time, the State Department was generally favouring the position that the United States should claim Antarctic territory – a position supported by Casey, who believed that an American presence would counter any Soviet ambitions in the region.[25] It is likely that Casey also considered that, if the United States made an Antarctic claim, it would then seek reciprocal recognition with Australia.

On 12 August 1957, the Department of External Affairs informed the Australian High Commissioners in London and Wellington and the Australian Ambassador in Washington that Cabinet still felt that international control as a solution to the Antarctic problem was premature and that Australia 'must work to sustain' its claim to sovereignty. External Affairs also informed its representatives that forthcoming discussions on Antarctica in London, to be held in August and September between Australia, the United Kingdom, New Zealand, South Africa and Canada (the 'Old Commonwealth'), would explore the issues without commitment to the participating governments.[26] These discussions were to be initially at 'officials level' to clear the way for the more formal examination of the subject in September, when Casey planned to meet in London with other senior policy makers from Britain and New Zealand.

The outcome of the senior-level 'Old Commonwealth' discussions was a working paper that was to be used by Australia, Britain and New Zealand in preparation for four-power discussions with the United States scheduled for early October in Washington. The paper set out the arguments for and against a continuation of the status quo, analysed the principal problems that would arise in establishing an international regime and compared the rival merits of the plans so far canvassed. Notably, too, at Australian insistence the idea of a demilitarisation program for Antarctica was included in the paper, to be explored at future meetings. The British government had also shifted its preference from the establishment of an Antarctic condominium to a version of the standstill proposal. It now favoured establishing an international authority which included the Soviet Union: the legal status quo in Antarctica would be frozen and would not be affected by the subsequent activities of any member nation.[27]

The four-power discussions began in Washington in early October 1957. Representing the State Department, Ambassador Paul Daniels indicated that the United States was not convinced about the desirability of Soviet participation in an international Antarctic regime, although he could foresee eventual Soviet inclusion, provided that the Soviets accepted the conditions and purposes of a regime. From the outset, Britain argued strongly for Soviet inclusion on the grounds that otherwise the four powers could not hope to achieve their basic objectives for the area.[28] On the matter of Australia's suggestion regarding the demilitarisation of Antarctica, Daniels stated that the basic objective of US policy was the removal of the Soviet military threat rather than demilitarisation per se, for which he assumed a regime would provide. In response to Daniels, Arthur Tange, Secretary of the Australian Department of External Affairs, emphasised that there was considerable scepticism in Australia about solving the Antarctic problem with an international regime. Australia wanted Antarctica demilitarised and preferred a solution of the conflict on claims.

Tange added that any international regime should include the Soviet Union and that if an arrangement for the whole of the region could not be concluded Australia thought it worth studying whether a more limited arrangement might be attempted. However, if demilitarisation could not be achieved, and if the issue of conflicting claims could not be solved except by unacceptable Australian concessions, Tange indicated that Australia might prefer to live with the status quo.[29] Although positions at that stage remained fluid, there was general agreement by the four that their discussions should continue, in secret and on an informal basis, exploring three major objectives: preventing Antarctica from being used as a base for military threat, encouraging scientific research in the Antarctic, and providing for the equitable exploration and exploitation of the natural resources of the region.[30]

Daniels soon became impressed with the logic of the British arguments in favour of an international regime based on the standstill principle ('freezing' the issue of claims and rights) and of the inclusion of the Soviet Union. He suggested, in addition, that a convenient nondiscriminatory criterion for membership of the international regime would be engagement in scientific activities in Antarctica. This would, in effect, limit participation to the present claimants and the United States, the Soviet Union, South Africa, Belgium and Japan.[31]

Objections to this suggestion were immediately raised by the representatives of Australia and New

Zealand, who emphasised their countries' opposition to Japanese membership.[32] In early February 1958, Malcolm Booker of the Australian Embassy called on Daniels and advised him that Australia was firmly against an early attempt to achieve any general internationalisation of Antarctica. He asked if the United States would be willing to discuss what he called a 'functional approach' to the Antarctic problem, whereby sovereignty would not be renounced but agreement would be sought solely on demilitarisation and scientific cooperation. Booker added that Australia hoped to include the Soviet Union in such an arrangement.[33] Daniels replied that it would be possible to discuss this as a possible fall-back plan at the next round of meetings and asked Booker to summarise the proposal in writing to facilitate analysis.

At this point the secrecy of the four-power talks was exposed by a front-page article in the London *Daily Telegraph,* reporting that Britain had proposed to the United States a tentative plan for the internationalisation and demilitarisation of Antarctica. The report went on to say that the plan was currently being prepared by Britain in consultation with Australia and New Zealand.[34] This sparked immediate action by Daniels, and all countries with Antarctic claims or interests were quickly informed of the US position and their views sought as to the broad objectives that might inform a common Antarctic policy.[35] Despite some initial misgivings about the US position on the part of Argentina and Chile, by the end of February they were in general agreement. Norway's preliminary reaction was also favourable, and France, the other remaining claimant, replied that it would provide a view in due course.[36]

But while these early reactions would have been encouraging to the State Department, the Australian position still represented an area of potential disagreement. The essence of Australia's functional approach was set out in a statement which asserted that scientific cooperation could only proceed on the basis that all activity in the Antarctic should be exclusively peaceful in character and intent, and that the parties agreed that Antarctica would not be militarised and on the right of all countries to have free access to each other's bases in the Antarctic.[37]

This approach reflected Australian scepticism about the possibilities of obtaining Soviet agreement to any elaborate provisions on inspection and control in Antarctica. Casey expressed his belief that any insistence on such provisions would jeopardise the chances of securing general acceptance of the principles of international scientific cooperation and of demilitarisation.[38] In the light of this assessment, Booker provided Daniels with the draft declaration setting out the functional approach and told him on 28 February 1958 that, while Australia had not gone so far as to abandon the concept of internationalising Antarctica, it wanted to confine its efforts at the onset to the realm of the possible: 'Australia would agree only to minimum concessions and would be reluctant to "give anything away".'[39] He added that the Australian government felt that negotiations for an agreement might also break down on the point of control over economic exploitation.

In early March 1958, US President Dwight D Eisenhower approved a directive that authorised the United States to seek a peaceful solution to the Antarctic problem through an international regime that included the Soviet Union.[40] Over several days, Daniels consulted with representatives of Australia, Britain and New Zealand. Through Booker, Australia indicated that it preferred that an agreed position be established among the claimant powers and the United States before any approach was made to the Soviet Union. In addition, Booker reiterated Australia's preference for a limited agreement, questioned the need for administrative machinery in any Antarctic arrangement, and expressed Australia's concerns about inspection and control to guarantee the demilitarisation of the region and about the inclusion of any provision related to economic exploitation.[41] Taking up these concerns, Daniels asked whether the deletion of a paragraph on resources 'might soften the blow for the Australian Government'. Booker responded that this suggestion would help, although Daniels added that such a deletion would not mean that the United States had abandoned the idea.[42]

Several weeks later, the United States sought further confirmation of the views about a treaty from the eleven other countries that had participated in the Antarctic program of the IGY.[43] Britain immediately gave a favourable reply, adding that Australia had come up with the idea of a pre-conference working group to meet in Washington, a suggestion that the Foreign Office also approved.[44] Having gauged the general view about possible directions and goals for an international regime on Antarctica, the US Government began the formal process that would lead to the signing of the Antarctic Treaty. On 2 May 1959, President Eisenhower invited the eleven other nations that had participated in the Antarctic program of the IGY, which included the Soviet Union, to participate in a conference on Antarctica. By early June, all eleven countries had accepted this invitation and the table was set for the negotiation process to follow.

At the negotiating table

The formal negotiation of the Antarctic Treaty lasted for 18 months. It took two forms. From June 1958 to mid-October 1959, a total of 60 preparatory meetings was held in Washington, attended by two representatives from each of the eleven invited nations and three or four from the United States. These were followed by the full-scale conference, which began on 15 October 1959 and concluded on 1 December 1959 with the signing of the Antarctic Treaty. The conference was attended by delegations of all twelve states and included two representatives of each.

The fact that so many preparatory meetings were required before the conference suggests that problems and obstacles arose that delayed efforts to reach agreement. Between June and October 1958, progress was slow due to the repeated insistence of Andrei Ledovski, head of the Soviet delegation, that discussion should be confined to procedural matters only. Both the Australian and British representatives frequently expressed their governments' strong opposition to this Soviet view and their belief that matters of substance should be discussed.[45] In early November, Daniels, the head of the US delegation, initiated a more accommodating approach toward the Soviet Union which soon led to more substantive matters being negotiated. Draft texts of what might become the Antarctic Treaty were now the main preoccupation of the meetings.[46] If broad agreement could be reached at the preparatory meetings, the negotiations at the main treaty conference could be conducted in a more positive and consensus-driven environment.

Slowly, by mid-March 1959, unanimous agreement was reached on the objectives of the first three draft articles. These referred to the use of Antarctica for peaceful purposes only, to freedom of scientific investigation and to international cooperation. But there were still disagreements, reservations and misgivings in regard to the nine others. By far the most significant problem at this stage was the draft Article IV, which concerned the 'freezing' of the legal status quo. Nine parties agreed to the text. France, which had earlier resisted the draft, had subsequently shifted ground and wanted a minor change in language. Argentina also had reserved its position on one portion of the article. But the Soviet Union had adopted a more radical position, suggesting that the best way of setting aside the question of territorial claims and consequent political rivalry was not to mention them in the treaty at all.[47] Soviet rejection of this article was clearly a major unresolved issue.

When talks resumed in mid-July after a brief intermission, Yuri Filippov, the new head of the Soviet delegation, announced that although Article IV was the most controversial, his government 'was now prepared to agree to inclusion of an article on rights and claims in view of its policy of seeking to conclude a treaty'.[48] The removal of Soviet opposition here meant that discussions could now continue on the remaining unresolved matters.

Away from the table

The change in the Soviet position concerning the draft of the crucial Article IV – at the core of the proposed treaty – was a turning point in the negotiations. It resulted from a diplomatic meeting 16,000 kilometres away from Washington. On 12 March 1959, during an Economic Commission for Asia and the Far East conference in Queensland, Australia, Casey had a private conversation with the leader of the Soviet delegation, Deputy Foreign Minister Nicolai Firubin, about the mutual reinstatement of their embassies in Moscow and Canberra following their suspension five years earlier over the Petrov affair.[49] During the course of this conversation, Casey also raised the issue of Antarctica, and 'explained Australian objectives and interests in orthodox but forceful terms'.[50] Firubin responded by outlining what he believed to be his government's views on Antarctica, indicating that the Soviet Union believed that the matter of territorial rights and claims in the region should not be part of the current deliberations on Antarctica but should be dealt with separately, perhaps at a separate conference to be held in due course.[51]

The following day, Casey gave Firubin a letter expressing Australia's view regarding the freezing of territorial claims in the region and inviting Firubin to comment. The letter indicated that Australia felt strongly on the matter and would have substantial doubts about participating in a treaty that did not in substance contain the provisions that it had in mind. Casey explained that he believed that there was a 'fundamental misapprehension in the Russian position'. In contrast, Australia supported a provision that was designed to hold in abeyance all unresolved questions of territorial sovereignty and to create a legal situation in which no activity in the Antarctic by any country, claimant or not, after the Treaty came into effect would improve its legal claim to sovereignty or its existing state of rights, whatever that might be.[52] The Australian Government, Casey continued, believed that the draft Article IV being discussed at the Washington meetings could achieve this objective and that it could 'do so without in any way damaging the legitimate interests and aspirations of the two great non-claimant powers interested in the Antarctic, namely the United States of America and the USSR'.[53] Accordingly, he explained that Australia saw no advantage in concluding a treaty which failed to achieve this objective and if the Soviet Union felt any doubt that the text proposed for the article did fail in this regard, then his government would examine any alternative draft.[54]

On 28 April 1959, Filippov advised Daniels at the State Department that his government was now considering at least two alternative versions of Article IV. He also advised Daniels for the first time that the hitherto rigid Soviet attitude on this point was being reassessed.[55] Within a fortnight Daniels was invited to lunch at the Soviet Embassy in Washington with Ambassador Mikhail Menshikov. Points of difference relating to Antarctica were discussed, and after several follow-up meetings with Soviet representatives Daniels came to the conclusion that the United States and the Soviet Union disagreed only on the questions of accession to the treaty and the settlement of disputes.[56] In other words, the impasse regarding Article IV's freezing of the legal status quo appeared to have been overcome.

This was confirmed in early June when Firubin responded to Casey's letter.[57] Firubin said that he was pleased to be able to tell Casey that the 'representative of the Soviet Union at the talks in Washington has been given instructions to agree to Article IV of the draft Treaty'.[58] Booker passed on the contents of Firubin's letter to the representatives of Argentina, Britain, Chile, New Zealand and the United States at a meeting held in Washington on 13 June, where it was agreed that the impasse could be assumed to have been solved. Booker reported to Canberra that the representatives felt considerable gratification and had expressed their appreciation of the part Casey had played in securing this result.[59] Clearly, Casey's initiative was a significant act of diplomatic leadership. By persuading the Soviet Union to reconsider its stance on the issue and change its position, his intervention had cleared away a major obstacle to convening the conference on Antarctica.

The Conference on Antarctica

As delegations were gathering in Washington before the conference, an unexpected development was in store for the American hosts. On 12 October the French representative, Ambassador Pierre Charpentier, called on Ambassadors Daniels and Herman Phleger of the US delegation at the State Department. He told them that he had been instructed that 'under no circumstances was France to agree to an article such as Article [IV] which provides that nothing in the treaty shall be interpreted as a recognition by any party of any other country's right to territory or claim or basis of claim to territorial sovereignty in Antarctica'.[60]

Daniels expressed his surprise at this reversal of the French position. After being informed that Britain had already been notified of the decision, Daniels suggested that Charpentier should discuss the matter with other claimant countries, particularly Australia.[61] Charpentier took up the suggestion and called at the Australian Embassy in Washington on the following day. He informed Casey, who had arrived to lead the Australian delegation, about the French decision. Casey recorded in his diary that the two had 'an active hour discussing the devastating French decision' and that he had told Charpentier that if it were an unalterable one, it would destroy the conference and the treaty.[62] Incensed at this turn of events, Casey sent an impassioned, personal message to the French Foreign Minister, Maurice Couve de Murville, on 13 October expressing his grave concern that the conference would fail and 'the high hopes that have recently been entertained for the successful conclusion of a unique and progressive Treaty would be destroyed'.[63] He added that other countries were approaching the conference in a flexible frame of mind with regard to outstanding issues and so, if the conference failed, 'the responsibility might well seem to rest solely upon France'. He concluded by saying how deeply he personally would regret such an eventuality and with the earnest hope that Couve de Murville might reconsider the French position before the start of the conference in two days' time.[64] But it would take longer for Casey's hope to be fulfilled.

The opening Plenary Session of the Conference on Antarctica began in Washington two days later, attended by delegations from the twelve participating countries. On the following morning, rules of procedure were adopted, including a rule that the text of the treaty would be submitted for signature only if approved unanimously.[65] Although the Conference did finally result in a consensus document, the various committees that had been established worked tirelessly to hammer out contentious issues. For example, discussion to resolve the French opposition to the crucial draft Article IV began on 20 October. But it was not until early November – following numerous private discussions, drafting subcommittee work and texts suggested by both France and Britain – that the critical impasse on claims and rights was overcome and France announced that it accepted a British draft of the article.[66] Casey's diplomacy had again been constructive. Also in early November, the Soviet Union accepted in essence the draft article on inspection, thus removing the reason for Australia's earlier hesitation about the possibility of concluding a satisfactory treaty.[67]

Howard Beale, Australia's ambassador to the United States and Head of Delegation for the second half of the Conference on Antarctica, signing the Antarctic Treaty for Australia in Washington on 1 December 1959. National Archives of Australia: M4619, 216

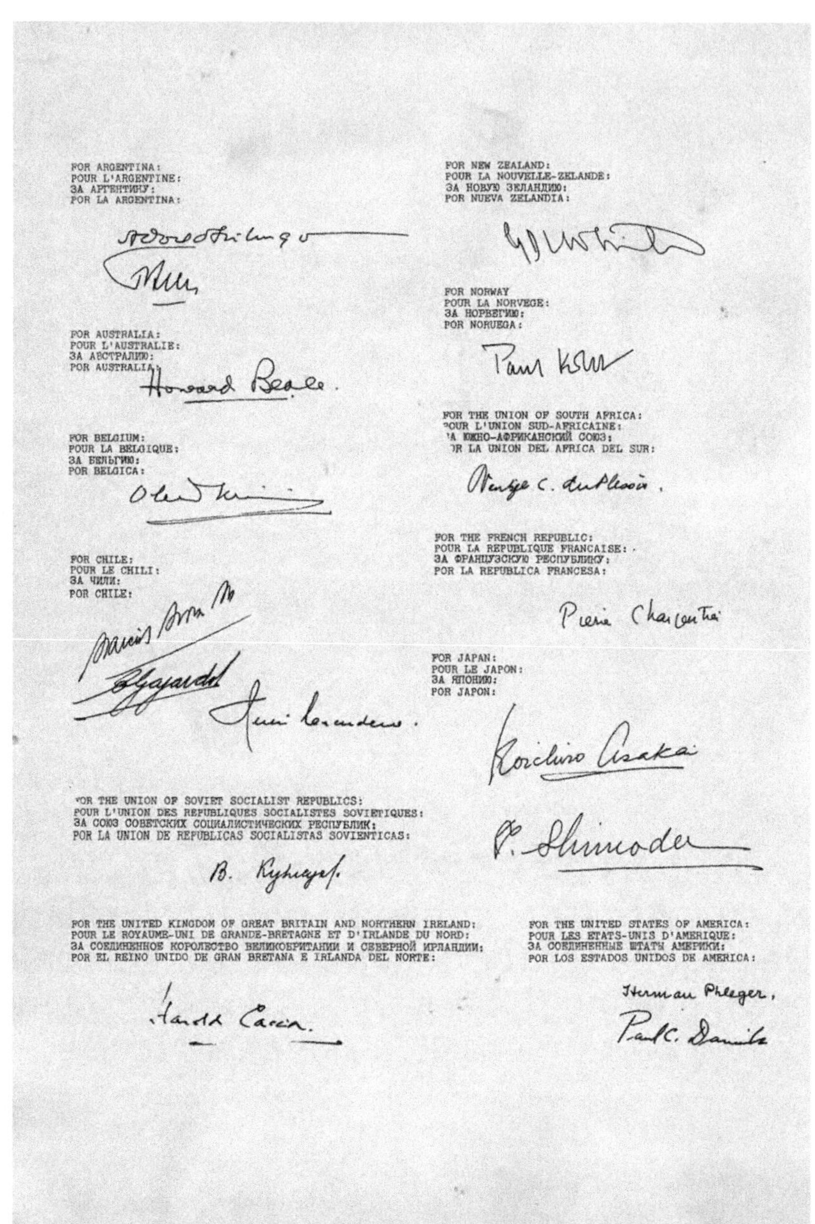

The 12 original signatories to the Antarctic Treaty. Courtesy
Australian Department of Foreign Affairs and Trade

Courtesy Australian Department of Foreign Affairs and Trade

By 24 November 1959, the last unresolved issue related to nuclear testing and explosions in Antarctica. It turned out to be the most significant sticking point of all. This topic had been introduced on 20 October, when, in discussion on draft Article I (peaceful purposes), Argentina proposed that such activity be prohibited in Antarctica, regardless of its character and purposes.[68] Although the proposal was withdrawn after it had been pointed out that all weapons testing was already banned by Article I, the topic struck a responsive chord with delegations from the southern hemisphere, particularly Australia.

On 28 October, a new article was suggested in a joint Australian– Argentine proposal. This provided that 'no nuclear or thermo-nuclear experiments or explosions of a non-military nature, and no disposal of fissionable waste material, shall take place in Antarctica except after notice and consultation among the High Contracting parties'.[69] The Soviet representative objected to the exception on the grounds that it would undermine Article I (peaceful purposes) and complicate inspection.[70] Numerous redrafts of the article were formulated and rejected until, four weeks later at the final Heads of Delegation meeting on 28 November, all other delegations agreed to the final text insisted upon by the Soviet Union.[71]

The path was thus cleared for the final Plenary Session of the Conference on 1 December 1959, at which the Antarctic Treaty was signed by the representatives of the twelve states meeting in Washington.[72] The Australian Cabinet endorsed the terms of the treaty on 7 March 1960. The *Antarctic Treaty Act 1960* then passed through both Houses of Parliament and received assent on 2 November 1960.[73] Six months later, on 23 June 1961, the treaty came into force when Australia, Argentina and Chile – the final three signatory states to do so – deposited their instruments of ratification with the United States. In this way the foundation stone of the Antarctic Treaty System was laid and the representatives of the parties obliged under Article IX to meet in Canberra within two months.

***

Specifying a city as the venue for the inaugural meeting is an honour almost unknown in treaty negotiations. But Australia had been a committed partner in all the long consultations and its diplomats had played a significant role in overcoming opposition to the critical Article IV and, through their advocacy of demilitarisation and support for the prohibition on nuclear testing and explosions in particular, in shaping a treaty that Australia came to embrace. There were major benefits, which the Australian delegation report summarised. The Treaty was a document that, except in times of a global war, safeguarded 'our back door' by prohibiting nuclear activity which might be a risk to Australia and ensuring that Antarctica would not become an arena of great power rivalry, either in terms of militarisation or the Cold War. It also protected Australia's position with respect to claims by maintaining the status quo and consolidated the basis for international scientific cooperation. All in all, the report concluded, the Antarctic Treaty was a sound and valuable one for Australia. Subsequently hailed as the first arms control treaty of the nuclear age, the Australian government foresaw it would set a precedent for any future international negotiations in such areas as outer space.[74]

Notes

[1]   *Izvestia* (Moscow), 28 January 1939, cited in Hanessian (1965) 29.

[2]   Hall (1989).

[3]   Hanessian (1965) 44.

[4]   Christie (1951) 269. In 1946, Argentina amended the boundary of its Antarctic claim by extending its western limit.

[5]   Draft Agreement Prepared by the Department of State, Washington, undated, *Foreign Relations of the United States, 1948,* 997–1000.

[6]   The Ambassador in Chile (Bowers) to the Secretary of State, Santiago, 19 July 1948, *Foreign Relations of the United States, 1948,* 995. The US envoy was Caspar Green and the principal Chilean representative was Professor Julio Escud-

126

ero, former Legal Adviser to the Chilean Foreign Ministry and unofficial consultant to the Ministry.

[7] The Chargé in Argentina (Ray) to the Secretary of State, Buenos Aires, 21 July 1948, *Foreign Relations of the United States, 1948*, 995–96.

[8] Letter from HV Evatt to JB Chifley, 8 February 1949, National Archives of Australia (hereafter, NAA): Series A1838/2, Item 1945/18/2.

[9] Memorandum no 188 dated 5 March 1948 from the Secretary DEA to EA Officer, London, NAA: Series 1838/2, Item 1495/3/2/3, Part 1.

[10] Russian Antarctic claims, *The Times*, 12 February 1949. This organisation based its demand on the Soviet rights in Antarctica as a result of the prior discoveries of the Antarctic continent by Russian explorers in 1819–20.

[11] Memorandum of Conversation, by the Chief of the Division of Northern European Affairs (Hulley), Washington, 23 March, *Foreign Relations of the United States, 1949*, 795–96.

[12] For the text, see Draft Declaration on Antarctica, Prepared by the Department of State, Washington, undated, *Foreign Relations of the United States, 1949*, 807–09.

[13] Footnote no 3, *Foreign Relations of the United States, 1949*, 807; Memorandum by the Officer in Charge of British Commonwealth and Northern European Affairs (Hulley) to the Director of the Office of North and West Coast

Affairs (Mills), Washington, 4 January 1950, *Foreign Relations of the United States, 1950,* I, United States Government Printing Office, Washington, 907–08; Memorandum of Conversation, by Mr Caspar D Green of the Office of British Commonwealth and Northern European Affairs, Washington, 17 February 1950, *Foreign Relations of the United States, 1950,* 908–09.

[14] Australian claims in the Antarctic, Volume II, Agenda Papers, Paper no 8, Antarctica, Commonwealth Prime Ministers' Conference, 1956, NAA: Series A1838/2, Item 1495/1/9/1 Part 1.

[15] The Embassy of the Soviet Union to the Department of State, Washington, 8 June 1950, *Foreign Relations of the United States, 1950,* 911–13. The memorandum was not sent to Chile, the remaining claimant, because the Soviet Union had not established formal relations with the South American country at this time.

[16] Hanessian (1960).

[17] On Australian reaction, see Cabinet Submission by RG Casey, Minister for External Affairs, 19 January 1956, NAA: A1838/2, 1495/1/9/4 Part 2. US Department of State's concern is reported in Cablegram 817, 25 July 1955, NAA: Series 1838/2, Item 1495/13/1 Part 2. Eventually, the Soviet Union established six stations in Antarctica during the IGY.

[18]   Secret and Guard, Commonwealth Prime Ministers' Conference 1956, Volume II, Agenda Paper no 8 – Antarctica. NAA: Series 1838/283, Item 1495/1/9/1 (Part 1).

[19]   Lord Casey's diaries originals, Box 28, Entry Saturday, 30 July 1955, National Library of Australia MS 6150.

[20]   First CSAGI Antarctic Conference (Paris, 6–10 July 1955) *Annals of the International Geophysical Year* IIB (1959) 409.

[21]   Swan (1961) 374.

[22]   Memorandum of a Conversation, Department of State, Washington, 14 September 1955, *Foreign Relations of the United States, 1955–1957,* XI, United States Government Printing Office, Washington, 624–25.

[23]   Ibid.

[24]   Editorial note, *Foreign Relations of the United States, 1955–1957,* 627–28.

[25]   Casey from Spender, Washington, 5 June 1957, NAA: Series A1838/2, Item 1495/19/1 Part 2.

[26]   Cablegram to Australian High Commission, London; Australian Embassy, Washington; Australian High Commission, Wellington; August 12, 1957, NAA: A1838/2, 1495/19/1 Part 2.

[27]   The text of this working paper is enclosed with Memorandum no 1150/57, 23 October 1957, NAA: Series A1838/2, Item 1495/17/1 Part 1.

[28]   Tange, Washington, 9 October 1957, NAA: Series A1838/2, Item 1495/19/1 Part 2. Britain's

position was based on the premise that the Soviet Union would remain in Antarctica after the end of the IGY and that it would be impracticable to eject it by force. This premise was confirmed when the Soviet Union announced in September 1957 that it intended to remain in Antarctica to continue research – an announcement which led to a decision by ICSU to establish a Special Committee on Antarctic Research (SCAR) to plan for scientific exploration after the IGY.

[29]   Ibid.

[30]   Ibid. See also Memorandum from Kevin to The Minister, 29 November 1957, NAA: Series A1838/2, Item 1495/1/9/1 Part 3.

[31]   Draft Memorandum of Conversation, Washington, 17 January 1958, Department of State, Central Files, 702.022/1-1758.

[32]   In Australia's case this probably reflected its long concern about the presence of what it perceived as an unfriendly power in Antarctica. After WW II, Australia had sought to prevent Japanese whaling activities in Antarctica. Although unsuccessful in this endeavour, it did secure a clause in the 1951 Japanese Peace Treaty that required Japan to renounce all rights and interests in Antarctica.

[33]   Memorandum of Conversation between Daniels (G), Wilson (ARA) and Booker (Australian Embassy), Border (Australian Embassy), 5 Febru-

130

ary 1958, Department of State, Central Files, 702.022/2-558.

[34] Memorandum of Conversation between Daniels (G) and Lord Hood (British Embassy), Washington, 12 February 1958, Department of State, Central Files, 702.022/2-1258, plus attached text of the United Press report. See, also, footnote no 2, *Foreign Relations of the United States, 1958–1960*, 471.

[35] Circular Telegram from the Department of State to Certain Diplomatic Posts, Washington, 15 February 1958, *Foreign Relations of the United States, 1958–1960*, 471–72.

[36] Memorandum of Conversation between Daniels, Owen (ARA), Luboeansky (ARA), Guyer (Argentine Embassy) and Goni (Argentine Embassy), Washington, 20 February 1958, Department of State, Central Files, 702.022/2-2058; Memorandum of Conversation between Daniels, Luboeansky (ARA) and Bianchi (Chilean Embassy), Washington, 28 February 1958, Department of State, Central Files, 702.022/2-2858; US Embassy, Oslo, to Secretary of State, Department of State, Central Files, 702.022/2-1958; American Embassy, Paris, to Department of State, Washington, 27 February 1958, Department of State, Central Files, 702.022/2-2758.

[37]   Cabinet Submission no 1040, from Casey, Minister for External Affairs, 22 February 1958, NAA: Series A4926./XM1, Vol 42.

[38]   Ibid. Casey had come to this conclusion because of the impasse at this time over inspection at the Geneva test ban negotiations: the US had insisted upon inspection and control, which the USSR had rejected. Casey could not envisage either changing its position in Antarctica and accordingly believed that regular visits between national expeditions and stations would be the closest to inspection and control that could be achieved.

[39]   Memorandum of Conversation between Daniels, Luboeansky (ARA) and Booker (Australian Embassy), Border (Australian Embassy), Washington, 28 February 1958, Department of State, Central Files, 702.022/2-2858.

[40]   National Security Council Report, Washington, 8 March 1958, *Foreign Relations of the United States, 1958–1960,* 479–87.

[41]   Memorandum of Conversation, Embassy of New Zealand, Washington, 10 March 1958, *Foreign Relations of the United States, 1958–1960,* 494-7; Memorandum of Conversation between Daniels, Luboeansky (ARA), Neidle (L), White (New Zealand Embassy), Audland (British Embassy), Booker (Aus-

tralian Embassy) and Border (Australian Embassy), Washington, 13 March 1958, Department of State, Central Files, 702.022/3-1358. The Australian government believed that any approach to the Soviet Union before an agreed position among the claimant powers and the United States was established would have serious political implications for it at home. This position was probably related to the 1954 defection by a Soviet diplomat, who provided evidence of Soviet espionage in Australia, creating a political furore. For a succinct account of the 'Petrov Affair' and its repercussions, see Millar (1978) 346–49.

[42] Draft Memorandum of Conversation between Daniels, Luboeansky (ARA), Neidle (L), White (New Zealand), Audland (British Embassy), Booker (Australian Embassy) and Border (Australian Embassy), Washington, 13 March 1958, Department of State, Central Files, 702.022/3-1358. The tenor of Australian views expressed at these meetings was reiterated to US Secretary of State Dulles when he discussed Antarctica briefly with the Australian Minister for External Affairs on 11 March during the SEATO Council Meeting in Manila. See footnote no 3, *Foreign Relations of the United States, 1958–1960,* 497.

[43] Aide mémoire from the Department of State to Certain Embassies, Washington, 24 March

1958, *Foreign Relations of the United States, 1958–1960,* 497–99.

[44]   Telegram to the United States Embassy, London, 1 April 1958, Department of State, Central Files, 702.022/4-1958.

[45]   Memorandum of Meeting, 24 June 1958, Department of State, Central Files, 702.022/6-2458.

[46]   These related to the use of Antarctica for peaceful purposes; freedom of scientific research; international cooperation in scientific research; 'freezing' the legal status quo; criminal and civil jurisdiction; inspection rights; administrative measures; the relationship of the treaty to non-parties; zone of application; settlement of disputes; and ratification and depository requirements. See Memorandum of Meeting, 18 November 1958, Department of State, Central Files 702/022/11-1858.

[47]   Memorandum from the Director of the Antarctica Staff (Owen) to the Deputy Assistant Secretary of State for International Organization (Walmsley), Washington, 13 March 1959, *Foreign Relations of the United States, 1958–1960,* 539–47.

[48]   Memorandum of Meeting, 23 July 1959, Department of State, Central Files, 702.022/7-2359.

[49]   Millar (1972) 316. See also note 41 above.

[50]   Savingram to Australian Embassy, Washington, 18 March 1959, NAA: Series A1838/2, Item 1495/13/1 Part 2.

[51]   Ibid.

[52]   Ibid.

[53]   Ibid.

[54]   Ibid.

[55]   Memorandum of Conversation between Daniels, Gleysteen (EUR/EE), Fisher (G) and Filippov (Embassy of the USSR), Washington, 28 April 1959, Department of State, Central Files, 702.022/4-2859.

[56]   Memorandum of a Conversation, Soviet Embassy, Washington, 11 May 1959, *Foreign Relations of the United States, 1958–1960*, 563–66.

[57]   The British Embassy received the letter on 1 June and although the fully translated text was not received by Casey until 12 June, its contents were communicated through the British Foreign Office to Australia on 9 June. See, Cablegram from Australian High Commission, London, NAA: Series A1838/2, Item 1495/3/2/1/4.

[58]   Ibid.

[59]   Cablegram from Australian Embassy, Washington, 13 June 1959; NAA: Series A1838/2, Item 1495/3/2/1/4.

[60]   Memorandum from Phleger, 12 October 1959, Department of State, Central Files, 702.022/10-1259.

[61]   Ibid. See also Cablegram from Tange to Casey, Washington, 15 October 1959, NAA: Series A1838/2, Item 1495/3/2/1/4.

[62]   Millar (1972) 330.

[63]   Ibid.

[64]   Ibid.

[65]   Memorandum from the Head of the US Delegation to the Conference on Antarctica (Phleger) to the Secretary of State, Washington, 16 October 1959, *Foreign Relations of the United States, 1958–1960,* 581–82.

[66]   Millar (1972) 333.

[67]   Memorandum of a Conversation, Department of State, Washington, 7 November 1959, *Foreign Relations of the United States, 1958–1960,* 608.

[68]   Memorandum from the Head of the Delegation to the Conference on Antarctica (Phleger) to the Secretary of State, Washington, 20 October 1959, *Foreign Relations of the United States, 1958–1960,* 583–55.

[69]   Memorandum from the Head of the Delegation to the Conference on Antarctica (Phleger) to the Secretary of State, Washington, 28 October 1959, *Foreign Relations of the United States, 1958–1960,* 594–96.

[70] Memorandum from the Head of the Delegation to the Conference on Antarctica (Phleger) to the Secretary of State, Washington, 3 November 1959, *Foreign Relations of the United States, 1958–1960,* 601–02.

[71] Memorandum from the Head of the Delegation to the Conference on Antarctica (Phleger) to the Deputy Under Secretary of State for Political Affairs (Merchant), Washington, 28 November 1959, *Foreign Relations of the United States, 1958–1960,* 631–32.

[72] Casey did not sign the Antarctic Treaty on behalf of Australia as he had left the Australian Delegation on 6 November. He was replaced as Head of Delegation by Howard Beale, Ambassador to the United States.

[73] See, For Cabinet Submission No 575, 7 March 1960, NAA: A1838/283, 1495/3/2/1/1; Memorandum for the Minister: Antarctic Treaty Ratification, 22 September 1960, NAA: Series A432/5, Item 1953/3228.

[74] Australian Delegation Report, NAA: Series A1838/269, Item 1495/1/2/Part 1.

4

Law

Stuart Kaye, Michael Johnson and Rachel Baird

The governance of the Australian Antarctic Territory (AAT) and Australia's broader interests in Antarctica are affected by international and domestic law. Since 1961 the Antarctic Treaty has provided the basis for a remarkable legal regime which maintains, in a unique way, equilibrium between the interests of Antarctic claimants and others. The formation of a system of international legal instruments around this treaty has transformed a continent essentially empty of regulation into a model of international cooperation and stewardship. It is within this context that Australia, as both a claimant and an active supporter of the system, negotiates and balances its interests and frames its laws. This chapter outlines the matrix provided by the Treaty itself, in areas that are vital to Australia's policy objectives, before considering the implications for Australian sovereignty in Antarctica and the domestic legal structures that Australia has in place for the AAT.

The Antarctic Treaty System

At its core, the Antarctic Treaty System (ATS) encompasses four international treaties (the Antarctic Treaty,[1] the Convention for the Conservation of Antarctic Seals,[2] the Convention on the Conservation of Antarctic Marine Living Resources[3] and the Protocol on Environmental Protection to the Antarctic Treaty[4]) as well as the decisions and measures adopted by parties under those treaties.[5] Across these legal instruments exists a raft of legally binding provisions regulating the actions of States Parties in Antarctica. This chapter focuses principally upon the system's central and constituting instrument, the Antarctic Treaty itself, rather than its other elements, which are the subjects of several other chapters within this work.

The legal instruments create an important foundation for the functioning of the system by entrenching key, indispensable principles and setting out basic obligations on matters such as environmental protection. But while the system is underpinned by legal provisions, its whole is more than the sum of its treaty obligations. The real 'life' of the ATS exists in the actions of its parties. The parties run the system and, jointly and collaboratively, steer it on its path to address new challenges as they arise. As Richards states, the Treaty with its 14 Articles is 'a short and elegant document', creating a flexible regime 'capable of evolving to address new challenges in Antarctica, consistent with the policy priorities of Treaty parties'.[6]

What really characterises the ATS in a very practical and real sense is consensus and collaboration among the Treaty parties. These two elements colour everything that happens within the system, and how every party, including Australia, engages with Antarctic issues. As Powell and Jackson state, 'Australia cannot achieve anything for the future of Antarctica until there is international consensus'.[7] The primary forum within which the consensus and collaboration occur is the annual Antarctic Treaty Consultative Meeting (ATCM), a critically important part of the system that is fundamental to understanding how it operates on a practical level.

The Antarctic Treaty Consultative Meeting

The ATCM is established by Article IX of the Treaty. That provision specifies that representatives of the original Contracting Parties to the Treaty, as well as those of any acceding state that demonstrates an interest in Antarctica 'by conducting substantial research activity', shall meet:

at suitable intervals ... for the purpose of exchanging information, consulting together on matters of common interest pertaining to Antarctica, and formulating and considering, and recommending to their Governments, measures in furtherance of the principles and objectives of the Treaty.

The parties which are entitled to attend these ATCMs have come to be known as Consultative Parties,[8] and they also allow so-called non-Consultative Parties to attend, albeit formally by invitation and without the right to participate in the taking of decisions.

Members of the Australian delegation (central group) at the 26th Antarctic Treaty Consultative Meeting, Madrid 2003. Andrew Jackson, Australian Antarctic Division, © Commonwealth of Australia

The work of the meeting is facilitated by the submission of papers – Working Papers, Information Papers and Secretariat Papers. Both parties and observers can submit papers[9] on a variety of topics under the various items on the agenda, which itself is settled by consensus among the parties. Although consensus acts as a filter to keep out any topics which some parties do not wish to discuss, the operation of the ATCM allows the parties acting together to raise and discuss any issue relevant to Antarctica. Through the ATCM, the Antarctic Treaty System is therefore a living and evolving regime, able to be steered by the parties in a variety of directions.

Ongoing treaty-making

As mentioned above, Article IX of the Treaty empowers representatives to formulate 'measures in furtherance of the principles and objectives of the Treaty' and to recommend them to their governments. Paragraph 4 of Article IX provides that these measures become effective when subsequently approved by all Consultative Parties. Although admittedly not perfectly clear on its face, this provision results in measures becoming legally binding. This mechanism for what is essentially delegated legislation under the auspices of the Treaty, together with the open-ended empowering clause about the subject matter of such measures, gives real teeth to the work of the ATCM. As a result, not only can the ATCM discuss any matter that arises in the Antarctic context, it can also adopt binding obligations with respect to it.

Until 1995, these 'measures' were referred to as Recommendations. At ATCM XIX in 1995, the parties decided to clarify the various purposes of its Recommendations by adopting Decision 1 (1995), which divided the nomenclature of Recommendations into Measures, Decisions and Resolutions.[10] Measures are the legally binding motions requiring subsequent approval by all Consultative Parties before becoming effective, whereas Decisions cover administrative or 'internal organisational' matters within the Treaty system, and Resolutions are hortatory, non-binding declarations.

The importance of consensus

The consensus requirement in Article IX(4) for Measures to become effective has infiltrated the rest of the ATCM's proceedings – consensus is also required for the adoption by the ATCM of Decisions and Resolutions,[11] and indeed in practice applies to all aspects of the conduct of the ATCM.[12]

Consensus is sometimes portrayed as a weakness of the ATS, although arguably it is what makes the system so strong. In international law generally, there is little merit in negotiating the strongest possible text if, as a result, few states ultimately ratify it. This is even more poignant in the Antarctic context, where a range of factors makes a collaborative approach the only realistic means of achieving a stable and sustainable political climate for the continent. The risk inherent in proceeding on any issue without the concurrence of all is that ill-affected parties may begin acting unilaterally. Although consensus sometimes results in the 'lowest common denominator' being adopted, it means that all parties are taken on board when decisions are made. Antarctic Treaty parties move together as one.

It is the consensus approach that allows states with differing interests and views on a range of matters to come together to manage the continent cooperatively, safe in the knowledge that their interests are protected from a bloc of states acting in an unfavourable way. To choose just one issue as an example: while consensus limits Australia's ability to incorporate the protection of its sovereign interests over the Australian Antarctic Territory (AAT) into ATS decision making to any great degree, it also protects those very same interests from being significantly compromised at the hands of other parties. Consensus creates a power of veto for every party, allowing it to avoid discussion of any topic prejudicial to its interests. It therefore provides a very strong protection for claimants' interests within the ATS.

Of course, this approach sometimes stifles action too, and can result in progress on specific issues moving slowly. One prominent example is the almost 13 years it took to negotiate the Liability Annex to the Environmental Protocol, from the beginning of negotiations in 1993 to its final adoption by the ATCM in 2005.[13] However, as progress could not be made on any issue without the stable framework provided by the ATS, the maintenance of that system is always the most important priority. Generally, seeking to advance an isolated issue at the expense of the health of the ATS as a whole would be a very short-sighted strategy, with significant consequences for broader interests in Antarctica. This is not to say that where a party considers that a specific issue is sufficiently important, it is not willing to 'push the envelope' – Australia itself has been willing to take this approach on carefully selected issues, such as with the CRAMRA minerals regime. Even in these rare circumstances, however, the integrity of the ATS is still the ultimate goal. Australia believes in the importance of the system: it 'remains the best way to achieve Australia's policy interests in the region'[14] and its maintenance is often cited as the first goal of the Australian Antarctic Program.[15]

Australia's influence

It is often said that science is the currency of the ATS. While that is certainly true, influence is also achieved by the approach taken by a party within the diplomatic and political realms of the system, the centre of which is the ATCM.[16] Australia has built an enviable reputation through its strong participation in these realms over many decades and, buttressed by its valuable scientific program, is now definitely a major player in the ATS.[17] Australia always contributes strongly to the work of the ATCM by way of submitting papers and leading debates. Proposals it raises are paid significant attention, its views are well respected and its support for the proposals of other parties is highly valued. Add to this the substantial role Australia has played over many decades on a range of issues of particular significance to Antarctica – including 'the Question of Antarctica' (see chapter 9), the establishment of the Antarctic Treaty Secretariat[18] and pioneering an approach suitable to all sides for the delineation of the continental shelf[19] – and the sum of influence is considerable.

Peace and security

The Antarctic Treaty's very first Article sets the parameters for all activity within, and adjacent to, the continent. It declares that Antarctica is to be used for peaceful purposes only.[20] Military activity, including the establishment of military bases, fortifications, military manoeuvres and the testing of weapons, is prohibited.[21] Nuclear explosions are specifically prohibited in Article V. The result of these two Articles is that Antarctica has been free of military activity and 'nuclear free'[22] since 1959, save for the permitted 'use of military personnel or equipment for scientific research or for any other peaceful purpose'.[23]

Given that there are 60 bases established south of 60° South, involving 23 nation-states, the Antarctic Treaty framework has been well tested.[24] Additional states with expressed interests in the continent, as evidenced by their ratification of the Treaty, bring the total number of Treaty parties to 48, including the 12 original signatories and the seven claimant states.[25] With the arrival of various national scientific research expeditions, the local population surges during summer to well over 4000. By all accounts the model is working. Australia maintains a permanent presence in the AAT through its three bases. However, in accordance with the Treaty, it also has to accept a number of foreign bases, and Russia, China and France have established stations in the AAT.

The Treaty contains provision for oversight 'to promote the objectives and ensure the observance of the provisions of the present Treaty'. Under Article VII, 'each Contracting Party whose representatives are entitled to participate in the meetings referred to in Article IX of the Treaty shall have the right to designate observers to carry out any inspection provided for by the present Article'. These inspections can be unannounced and the Article provides for 'complete freedom of access at any time to any or all areas of Antarctica'. This includes all stations, installations and equipment within those areas, and all ships and aircraft at points of discharging or embarking cargoes or personnel in Antarctica. Further, aerial observation may be carried out at any time over any or all areas of Antarctica by any of the contracting parties having the right to designate observers.

Now in its 50th year of existence, the framework is not only functioning well but also has the benefit of incumbency should there be suggestions in the future that a replacement framework be explored to facilitate interests in natural resources.

Science within the Antarctic Treaty

Reflecting its origins in the International Geophysical Year (IGY), the Antarctic Treaty has a strong emphasis on science. This is most unusual in an international agreement of any type – and where the agreement also deals with disarmament issues and sovereignty over territory, it is without precedent. The Treaty accords scientific cooperation between the Antarctic Treaty States great prominence, and given that much of the diplomatic activity between states concerning Antarctica has been in the interest of national scientific programs, this highlighting of science has proved far more than lip service to an ideal.[26] Without downplaying the importance of other political factors, it is clear that the inherently collaborative nature of scientific research and the fact that it has been a perennial motivator for human presence on the continent have combined to reinforce the need noted above for states to engage cooperatively in Antarctica.

From the preamble of the Treaty on, there is explicit encouragement to scientific cooperation. After acknowledging the importance of this cooperation, the preamble stresses that the freedom of scientific investigation established during the IGY provides a basis for ongoing scientific cooperation and progress for all people.[27] Several provisions reflect this view. Article II explicitly restates the principle of scientific cooperation adopted informally during the IGY.[28] In essence, cooperation hinges on freedom of movement and access throughout the continent, without regard to competing national claims, and on exchange of scientific data between the parties. The institution of these highly successful arrangements with no fixed term gave the Treaty a stable starting point based on successful state practice, which is also unusual for an international agreement.[29]

However, the IGY mode of cooperation needed to be further defined. Ad hoc arrangements intended to operate for 18 months could leave some matters to be airbrushed over, as whatever problems might be encountered could be resolved at the end of the IGY. A Treaty intended to operate indefinitely could not leave matters unconsidered, so Articles III, VII and VIII clarified the status of scientific personnel within areas of national claim, and ensured the open sharing of data would continue.[30]

In addition to a framework for the sharing of data, Article III provides for broader cooperation. Personnel may be exchanged between expeditions and stations, and plans for operations should be made available to others to permit 'maximum econo-my and efficiency of operations'.[31] This encourages individual states to combine resources in their Antarctic operations. Such cooperation, while never universal between all Antarctic Treaty Consultative Parties, has been a feature of a number of programs, on both an ongoing and an ad hoc basis.[32]

Interestingly, Article III(2) also encourages the 'establishment of cooperative working relations' with relevant specialised agencies of the United Nations with an interest in Antarctica. Such cooperation as has occurred over the past half century has been restricted to agencies such as the International Maritime Organization and the Food and Agriculture Organization.[33]

The other provision dealing with science in Antarctica, albeit less directly, is Article VIII. This article enshrines a crucial compromise that permits the operation of expeditions and stations in a manner consistent with Article II. The Treaty leaves unresolved the issues of the exercise of jurisdiction, but Article VIII provides that observers, scientific exchange personnel and their support staff are subject only to the jurisdiction of the Party of which they are nationals.[34] This means that scientific personnel and support staff operate under the jurisdiction of their home state and its national Antarctic program, rather than under the jurisdiction of a claimant state. This ensures that there is freedom of movement for scientific expeditions throughout the continent, and that problems that might have been engendered by the lack of recognition for claims under Article IV do not arise.[35] From an Australian perspective the arrangement works, and Australian staff stationed at the three Australian bases are governed by domestic law via the *Australian Antarctic Territory Act 1954* (Cwth).

Application of domestic laws and the issue of sovereignty

Australian domestic law in Antarctica had its beginning with the assertion of Australian sovereignty. On 7 February 1933, King George V issued an order-in-council placing what was to become the Australian Antarctic Territory under the authority of the Commonwealth of Australia, and defining it as comprising all the land on the continent between 45° and 160° East, with the exception of the as yet undefined French claim over Adélie Land.[36] The Commonwealth Parliament then passed the *Australian Antarctic Territory Acceptance Act 1933* (Cwth), which came into effect some three years later.

However, the creation of an Australian territory was not mirrored by legislative enthusiasm to provide it with a legal system. Surprisingly, in spite of the official support only a few years earlier for the British, Australian and New Zealand Antarctic Research Expedition, which provided the basis for the assertion of sovereignty, the *Australian Antarctic Territory Acceptance Act* did nothing to support the administration of law in the AAT, but was merely an acknowledgment by the Australian Parliament of the transfer of sovereignty by the King. Further, the legislation provided almost nothing with respect to how the Territory would be governed or what laws might apply there. It provided only for ordinances, and did nothing to establish any legal structure.

No further development of Australian law occurred for almost 20 years, reflecting Australia's absence from Antarctica before and immediately following World War II. However, with Australia's planned return to Antarctica through the Australian National Antarctic Research Expeditions (ANARE), the domestic legislative regime needed to be updated. With the likely influx of foreign scientists and related personnel during the International Geophysical Year, this updating became all the more urgent. Parliament therefore passed the *Australian Antarctic Territory Act 1954* (Cwth) to provide for the extension of Australian law to the AAT. Although the Act has since been altered, it still forms the basic structure for Australian law operating in the AAT today.

Domestic law in the AAT

There are significant difficulties in operating a legal system in a remote and largely uninhabited place. Where the volume of human activity is very low, the implementation of a complete legal system is effectively impossible. A functioning justice system typically needs law enforcement officers, judges and court officials, gaols and mechanisms for sanction for offences. A fully functioning legal system also needs courts and laws to deal with the multitude of civil disputes that may arise across the range of human activity. This could encompass tort, contract, company law, environmental law and administrative law. Any legal system must have laws in place in order to deal with disputes or breaches of the law across any of these areas. The establishment of permanent bases and even expeditions to Antarctica requires consideration of the law applicable to the AAT.

In the absence of a permanent population of any great size, the organic development of a legal system is effectively impossible. The amount of government support required to administer and renew a legal system is not insignificant, and in Antarctica would likely be disproportionate to the human presence. In addition, the small size of the population in the AAT makes it less likely that breaches of the law or civil disputes would take place. This can be demonstrated by comparison with another Australian external territory, Norfolk Island. Norfolk Island has a population of approximately 2500, which includes the number of tourist visitors.[37] Even with this population, which is considerably more than the number of people in the AAT at any given time, Norfolk Island has no gaol, sees only a handful of cases through its courts each year, and has had only two murders committed in 150 years.

Consequently, for a largely empty territory like the AAT, there is a need to incorporate a fully functioning legal system from another jurisdiction. This is accomplished through the wholesale adoption of that system, subject to two provisos: first, that the laws are applied insofar as they can be given conditions in the territory; and, second, that there is a mechanism to provide for local modification of the adopted legal system where necessary. Such a system was used in the original incorporation of English law into the Australian colonies in the eighteenth and nineteenth centuries, and has been used in a number of Australian external territories since World War II. The AAT follows this pattern for remote and sparsely inhabited territory by applying the laws of another Australian jurisdiction, supplemented by specific ordinances designed for the AAT itself. The structure and operation of this system are discussed below.

The laws of the AAT operate in a clear hierarchy.[38] First, the Governor-General is empowered to make laws for the peace, order and good government of the AAT. Although delegated legislation, these ordinances are superior to other received law in the AAT, with the exception of the Commonwealth statutes. In theory, the ordinances could be used to provide all the AAT's laws; in practice, they are rarely used. In the past two decades, only three ordinances have been passed, including the *Criminal Procedure Ordinance 1993* (AAT) and the *Weapons Ordinance 2001* (AAT).

Second, the basic structure of the AAT's law is provided by the adoption, subject to their application to the conditions of the AAT, of the laws of the Australian Capital Territory (ACT) for all purposes save criminal law, which is derived from the criminal laws of the Jervis Bay Territory.[39] The selection of the criminal law of the Jervis Bay Territory is not an isolated case. In addition to being used for a number of other sparsely settled external territories, the criminal law of the Jervis Bay Territory is used to provide for a wide range of general criminal offences (as opposed to offences directed towards the maintenance of service discipline) for the Australian Defence Force. By virtue of the *Crimes at Sea Act 2000* (Cwth), it also applies aboard Australian-registered vessels which are geographically remote from Australia, including in the waters around the AAT, or similarly remote ships of any nationality whose next port of call is an Australian port.

The rationale for the selection of the Jervis Bay Territory for criminal law and the ACT for civil law appears to be based on a number of factors. The laws used are derived from a Commonwealth territory rather than a state within Australia. And, by virtue of section 122 of the Constitution, there is no restriction on the Commonwealth's ability to legislate for a territory – unlike the constitutional limitations on its ability to affect state law. This gives the Commonwealth overarching control as to the content of the law, not merely through the mechanism of ordinances, but also of the territory legislation. While the Commonwealth has not intervened very often to amend a self-governing territory's laws, it can intervene to amend the criminal laws of the Jervis Bay Territory with relatively little difficulty or public complaint.

The most likely application of law in a remote location is criminal law. Disputes over contractual arrangements or in tort can often find alternative forums where they can be dealt with in a more convenient fashion. The lack of people in a territory also means a lack of legal practitioners familiar with its law, and a lack of publishing services indicating the content of that law. Civil actions are more likely to be brought in other jurisdictions more convenient to the parties where the law in question is more accessible to all concerned. This is borne out by the fact that to date all civil actions brought before Australian courts and tribunals concerning activities in Antarctica have avoided the Supreme Court of the Australian Capital Territory, which functions as the superior court of record for the AAT.[40] Using the criminal law of the Jervis Bay Territory gives the Commonwealth complete and absolute control over the content of the law, with the ability to change this content quickly and simply through delegated legislation in the form of ordinances. Since the Jervis Bay Territory has no elected government, changes are unlikely to antagonise an elected legislature.

The third element of the AAT's legal system is that Commonwealth statutes will continue to apply, with the exception of criminal laws under Chapter 2 of the *Criminal Code Act 1995* (Cwth), to the extent they are already dealt with under the laws of the Jervis Bay Territory. This provides a wide-ranging substructure to the laws of the AAT, covering an ever-widening range of matters.

Relationship of domestic law with the Antarctic Treaty

The application of Australian domestic law was modified in 1960 to reflect Australia's obligations under the Antarctic Treaty, which was intended to make Antarctica a zone of peace and international cooperation where scientific exploration and research could be undertaken by participating states without regard to the territorial claims of the various parties. In order to ensure this could take place with assertions of sovereignty by states like Australia with territorial claims, the Treaty contains Article VIII:

1. In order to facilitate the exercise of their functions under the present Treaty, and without prejudice to the respective positions of the Contracting Parties relating to jurisdiction over all other persons in Antarctica, observers designated under paragraph 1 of Article VII and scientific personnel exchanged under subparagraph 1(b) of Article III of the Treaty, and members of the staffs accompanying any such persons, shall be subject only to the jurisdiction of the Contracting Party of which they are nationals in respect of all acts or omissions occurring while they are in Antarctica for the purpose of exercising their functions.

As a party to the Antarctic Treaty, Australia was obliged to amend the operation of its law in the AAT to accommodate the presence of foreign nationals to whom Australian law did not apply. This was accomplished by the passage of the *Antarctic Treaty Act 1960* (Cwth). In practice, the lack of application of Australian law to visiting scientists and their support staff seems to have been extended to any foreign presence outside Australia's bases. This is explored further below.

The law affecting the AAT has also been augmented as the Treaty system has grown. The *Antarctic Treaty (Environment Protection) Act 1980* (Cwth) has incorporated into Australian law mechanisms for species protection, collection permits and site protection derived from the Recommendations adopted at Antarctic Treaty Consultative Party Meetings. In addition it was extensively amended in 1992 to provide for the environmental impact assessment regime required under the Madrid Protocol.

Enforcement of laws and the practice of states

Although Australia has embraced applying its domestic laws to the Australian Antarctic Territory, at least in a prescriptive sense, it has taken a more circumspect approach to enforcing those laws against foreign nationals. Several authors have noted that the legal provisions of the ATS do not prevent Australia from enforcing its domestic laws against foreign nationals in the AAT.[41] Indeed, a 1992 report of the House of Representatives Standing Committee on Legal and Constitutional Affairs noted: 'It is both in

Australia's sovereign interests and consistent with Australia's obligations under the Antarctic Treaty to extend and apply Australian law to foreign nationals in the Australian Antarctic Territory.'[42]

It is true that the legal instruments do not prevent Australia from enforcing its laws against foreign nationals in the AAT (with the exception of the narrow scope of Article VIII, discussed above). However, the mere absence of a prohibition is not sufficient reason to engage in an action, especially in the Antarctic context, where action is rightly influenced by more than just legal obligations. Although a number of authors validly raise the maintenance of Australia's sovereignty as cause for enforcing domestic law, it is appropriate for Australia to refrain from such enforcement for several reasons.

The 'freezing' of territorial claims by Article IV of the Treaty was a key element in garnering support from states on both sides of the sovereignty issue.[43] The importance of all interested states being able to participate in the ATS notwithstanding differences of views on some issues has been discussed above, and sovereignty is a prime example of such an issue. Although not reduced to a legally binding obligation, there is a clear understanding among Treaty Parties that they enforce their domestic law in Antarctica only against their own nationals.[44] The practice of not enforcing domestic laws against nonnationals is consistent with the compromise embodied in Article IV.

This approach also helps to subdue the sovereignty issue within Antarctica. As Richards notes, the practice of non-enforcement 'removes the need others may feel to buttress their own positions by protesting, for example, application of Australian laws in the Australian Antarctic Territory to non-Australian nationals'.[45] More formally, the practice also serves to avoid active challenge to Australia's claim, such as through dispute resolution mechanisms.[46] Although Australia's sovereignty over the AAT is explicitly recognised by only four other parties, its claim is also not actively contested. Australia wishes 'to maintain this status quo: it would not be in [Australia's] interests to incite others actively to contest [its] claim by ignoring this practice'.[47]

Sovereignty is a significant underlying issue in the ATS. However, on a practical level, all parties see that it is very rarely the subject of contentious discussion at ATCMs. Non-claimants accept that sovereign interests will be protected to a certain point, whereas claimants accept that they will not go past that point. This creates a balanced status quo, allowing collaboration to flourish and not be eroded by straying into the contentious territory of sovereignty.

Domestic law offshore

Most human activity in the Antarctic Treaty Area arguably takes place in the marine environment. Antarctic tourism has been increasing at a steady rate over the past decade and has been concentrated in cruise ship tourism, particularly around the Antarctic Peninsula. In addition, fishing and the exploitation of other marine living resources have also increased dramatically since the 1980s, and there has been more scientific whaling by Japan in the waters adjacent to the AAT. All this activity raises the issue of Australian enforcement of law in the waters around the AAT.

The application of Australian law is potentially not limited to its Antarctic land territory. Like the rest of Australia, the AAT is surrounded by a 12 nautical mile territorial sea. However, most of the AAT's coastline is ice shelves, extending in places many miles out to sea, interspersed with rocky shores. The status of ice-covered coasts at international law is unsettled, and therefore the precise position of the territorial sea has not been promulgated. Although the establishment of the baselines is implied by the submission of Antarctic data to the Commission on the Limits of the Continental Shelf, the Australian Government has not publicly indicated its position on this issue and no straight baselines have been proclaimed in the AAT.[48]

Australia has proclaimed areas of extended jurisdiction out into the ocean that have affected the AAT. In 1978, it proclaimed the Australian Fishing Zone (AFZ), which still provides the basis for jurisdiction for Australia's principal piece of fisheries legislation, the *Fisheries Management Act 1991* (Cwth). Six weeks after the AFZ was declared another proclamation was made exempting the waters around the AAT from its operation. As such, the waters around the AAT are no longer part of the AFZ and the *Fisheries Management Act* does not apply to them.[49] Interestingly, there was some change in 1994, when Australia proclaimed an Exclusive Economic Zone (EEZ). The proclamation of the EEZ applied to all Australian external territories, including the AAT, and in this case no equivalent exemption was made, so the Australian EEZ operates off the AAT. However, since the bulk of Australian offshore fisheries law is contained in the *Fisheries Management Act,* the effect is to limit the operation of law off the AAT to those matters which are regulated using the EEZ rather than the AFZ. This essentially restricts those matters which are subject to domestic regulation to environmental measures and the protection of whales under the *Environment Protection and Biodiversity Conservation Act 1999* (Cwth) (EPBC Act).

Given that one of the activities taking place around the AAT is the scientific whaling program operated by Japan, the application of Australian domestic law to protect whales is a matter of some political significance. That Australian domestic law does extend to these activities was confirmed by the Federal Court of Australia in *Humane Society International Incorporated v Kyodo Senpaku Kaisha Ltd,*[50] where it held that Japanese whaling activity in the exclusive economic zone off the AAT was contrary to the EPBC Act. Of course, since the Federal Court orders were obtained from legal proceedings not involving the Australian Government as a party, it is not the government's place to directly enforce them. If it were to take action, it would be by way of enforcing the laws themselves. However, consistent with its general approach to enforcement, and in spite of public pressure from environmental non-government organisations, the Australian Government has refrained from imposing its domestic laws on Japanese whalers, preferring to pursue a diplomatic solution. Even in the face of a failure of a negotiated end to Japanese whaling, the Commonwealth has indicated it will seek to have the matter resolved by the International Court of Justice rather than through the application of Australian domestic law.[51]

Domestic law of the Australian sub-Antarctic islands

Australia has sovereignty over two groups of sub-Antarctic islands, and domestic legal matters for these islands are distinct from those applicable on the Antarctic continent. Macquarie Island is legally part of the state of Tasmania, and therefore Tasmanian law operates there in the same form as it operates within the rest of Tasmania. Macquarie Island lacks a permanent population, but has been the site of a scientific and meteorological station periodically since 1911 and permanently since 1948. Any disputes or prosecutions would fall within the jurisdiction of the

Supreme Court of Tasmania or the Tasmanian Court of Petty Sessions.

The second group of islands comprises the Territory of Heard Island and McDonald Islands. The territory has no permanent base, unlike the AAT; instead, the largest island, Heard, is occupied by scientific expeditions every few years.[52] As an external territory, however, its laws are organised in the same fashion as those of the AAT, being derived essentially from the civil law of the Australian Capital Territory and the criminal law of the Jervis Bay Territory. The *Heard and McDonald Islands Act 1953* (Cwth) provides for a similar system of ordinances to replace or augment the operation of the derived law: once again, very few of these have been passed.

The need for a domestic legal system has been less pressing for the Territory of Heard Island and McDonald Islands. On the other hand, because its surrounding waters are part of the Australian Fishing Zone – unlike the waters off the AAT – since the 1990s there have been several high-profile attempts to enforce Australian law on vessels fishing illegally around the territory. However, these enforcement actions have been pursuant to alleged breaches of the *Fisheries Management Act* and not the laws of the territory. Consequently, it has been Commonwealth law rather than the laws of the Heard and McDonald Islands Territory under which action has taken place.

***

The enforcement of domestic law in the AAT will probably present increasing challenges for Australia. With greater numbers of visitors to the territory comes a greater need to ensure compliance with the law, especially in the context of protecting natural and cultural heritage. And given that the visitors will not necessarily be Australian nationals, the compromise at the heart of the Antarctic Treaty in Article IV could itself come under some pressure, especially if the visitors are not nationals of another party to the Treaty.

Notes

[1]   [1961] ATS 12.
[2]   [1987] ATS 11.
[3]   [1982] ATS 9.
[4]   [1998] ATS 6.
[5]   Various definitions of the Antarctic Treaty System can be found in Article 1(e) of the Environmental Protocol; on the Antarctic Treaty Secretariat website www.ats.aq/e/ats.htm; and in the third recital to the *Washington Ministerial Declaration on the Fiftieth Anniversary of the Antarctic Treaty,* <www.state.gov /g/oes/rls/other/2009/121339.htm>.
[6]   Richards (2010). Penny Richards served as Senior Legal Adviser in the Australian Department of Foreign Affairs and Trade from August 2006 until May 2010, and led the Australian

delegation to the Antarctic Treaty Consultative Meetings from 2007 until 2010.

[7]   Powell and Jackson (2007) 38.

[8]   See Rule 1 of the *ATCM Revised Rules of Procedure* (2008), www.ats.aq, and Article 1 of the Environmental Protocol, on the Antarctic Treaty Secretariat website, www.ats.aq/e/ats .htm.

[9]   Observers and non-Consultative Parties can generally only submit Information Papers; see Rules 30 (non-Consultative Parties), 35 (Observers) and 45 (Experts) of the *ATCM Revised Rules of Procedure* (2008), <www.ats.aq>.

[10]   Available on the Antarctic Treaty database, on the Antarctic Treaty Secretariat website, <www.ats.aq>.

[11]   Rule 24, *ATCM Revised Rules of Procedure* (2008), <www.ats.aq>.

[12]   Although the Rules of Procedure permit majority vote on some decisions, most notably those of a procedural nature, in practice consensus is sought in the first, and indeed almost every, instance.

[13]   Annex VI: Liability Arising from Environmental Emergencies (not yet in force); the status of Measure 1 (2005), which adopted the Annex, is available on the Antarctic Treaty database on the Antarctic Treaty Secretariat website, <www.ats.aq> (viewed 20 June 2010).

[14]   Powell and Jackson (2007) 53.
[15]   <www.aad.gov.au/default.asp?casid=18> (viewed 20 June 2010).
[16]   Also see Haward, Hall and Kellow (2007) 26.
[17]   See Powell and Jackson (2007) 53, Haward, Hall and Kellow (2007) 24.
[18]   Haward, Hall and Kellow (2007) 25, Powell and Jackson (2007) 43.
[19]   Powell and Jackson (2007) 45–46.
[20]   Article I (1), Antarctic Treaty.
[21]   Article I (1), Antarctic Treaty.
[22]   It is noted that from 10 July 1962 to 1972 a nuclear reactor (the PM-3A) was used at the US McMurdo Station to generate electricity and steam for fresh water. It was decommissioned in 1972. See 'Proposed Addition of the Plaque Commemorating the PM-3A Nuclear Power Plant at McMurdo Station to the List of Historical Sites and Monuments', Agenda item CEP7B(Doc number WP005), presented by the USQ. ATCM XXXIII, 3–14 May 2010, Uruguay.
[23]   Antarctic Treaty, Article 1 (2).
[24]   <www.ecophotoexplorers.com/antarcticastations.asp> (viewed 1 September 2010).
[25]   <www.antarctica.gov.au/antarctic-law-and-treaty/treaty-partners?casid=80> (viewed 1 September 2010).
[26]   Budd (1986) 103.
[27]   Preamble, Antarctic Treaty; see also Roots (1986) 172–73.

[28]   Article II, Antarctic Treaty.
[29]   See Bush (1982) vol1, 53–54.
[30]   Bush (1982) vol1, 53–56.
[31]   Article III, Antarctic Treaty.
[32]   For example, the American and New Zealand Antarctic programs have a long history of co-operation in air transport.
[33]   Hamzah (2010, 189) notes the increasing engagement with UN specialised agencies in recent years, such as the FAO and IMO, was in part responsible for the moderating of Malaysian diplomatic concern over the Antarctic Treaty.
[34]   Article VIII, Antarctic Treaty.
[35]   Bush (1982) vol1, 75–82.
[36]   Bush (1982) vol2, 142.
[37]   2006 *Norfolk Island Census,* p 6, <www.info.gov.nf/>.
[38]   Kaye, Rothwell and Dando (1999) 10.
[39]   *Australian Antarctic Territory Act 1954* (Cwth), s 6.
[40]   *Australian Antarctic Territory Act 1954* (Cwth), s 10; see *Kay and Comcare*[2006] AATA 50; *Saldanha and Comcare*[1995] AATA 580; *Spurr and Comcare*[1999] AATA 43; *Wayne Ross Richards and Commission of the Safety Rehabilitation and Compensation of Commonwealth Employees Compensation*[1993] AATA 164.
[41]   For example, see Stephens and Boer (2007) 55–59.

[42]   Australia. House of Representatives Standing Committee on Legal and Constitutional Affairs (1992) 15 (¶2.32).

[43]   Commonwealth Attorney-General (2005) Outline of Submissions of the Attorney-General of the Commonwealth as *Amicus Curiae* (filed on 25 January 2005, in the Federal Court case of *Humane Society International v Kyodo Senpaku Kaisha),* available at <www.hsi.org.au/editor/assets/legal/AG_submissions_25_January_2005.pdf, 2 (¶7)>.

[44]   Richards (2010); Commonwealth Attorney-General (2005), 2 (¶10).

[45]   Richards (2010).

[46]   Rothwell and Scott (2007) 11.

[47]   Richards (2010); see also Commonwealth Attorney-General (2005) 3 (¶17).

[48]   Kaye (2004).

[49]   Proclamation made on 31 October 1979: reprinted in Bush (1982), vol2, 208–09. It should be noted that Australian fisheries legislation applies to Australian fishing vessels in the waters off the AAT: Bush (1982), vol2, 209; Orrego Vicuña (1988) 108. The reason given for making an exception of the waters of the AAT was that it was thought it might prejudice the negotiations for CCAMLR: Gardam (1985) 286–87.

[50]   *Humane Society International Incorporated v Kyodo Senpaku Kaisha Ltd*[2008] FCA 36.

[51]   Media release, Australian Minister for Foreign Affairs and Minister for the Environment, 28 May 2010, www.foreignminister.gov.au/releases/2010/fa-s100528.html.

[52]   Australian Antarctic Division, <www.heardisland.aq/about/human_activities.html>.

5

Already a special case? Australian Antarctic policy in the first decade of the Antarctic Treaty

Alan D Hemmings and Julia Jabour[1]

All decades, with hindsight, seem to carry some particular flavour, to bear some common characteristics. But the 1960s were recognised even at the time as a decade of profound change, a period within which the transformation from the post-war world to something more recognisably similar to our present times occurred, a change clearly evident in Australian society of this period.

To scan the issues of Australia's premier weekly, *The Bulletin,* through the decade is to see this transformation unfold. During the 1960s, the patriarchal framing, unembarrassedly sexist cartoons, overt racism, and concern with communist penetration of the waterfront set in the context of a Cold War standoff with the Soviet Union, gave way to coverage of the emancipation of women, the recognition of Aboriginal rights, and the redirection of concerns about communism towards China and neighbouring South-East Asian states, especially Vietnam (with which Australia would become directly engaged).[2] Internationally, the reportage ranged from UK Prime Minister Macmillan's 1960 'Winds of Change' speech in Cape Town to American landings on the Moon in 1969. However, *The Bulletin* showed not the slightest interest in the Antarctic throughout the 1960s, not even reporting on the First Antarctic Treaty Consultative Meeting (ATCM), which was held in Canberra on 10–24 July 1961, following the entry into force of the Antarctic Treaty on 23 June 1961. The media in general were remarkably uninterested in Antarctica as a political issue throughout the decade. From the start, Antarctic politics was a niche concern.

Four Australian prime ministers held office through the 1960s: the Liberal Party's Robert Menzies until January 1966, Harold Holt (Liberal) until his drowning in December 1967, the former deputy prime minister (and Country Party leader) John McEwen until January 1968, when Liberal John Gorton took over (and remained until March 1971). In other words, the government of the entire period was in the hands of one side of politics, and notwithstanding significant changes post-Menzies, reflected throughout consistent assessments of international relations and Australia's interests and role in the world.

We start by giving the general flavour of the ATCMs from 1961 to 1970 and summarising the main concerns of the six meetings. Thereafter, our consideration of specifically Australian policy through the decade is assembled under four thematic headings. These are:

- *institutional* – concerning Australia's engagement with shaping and building the Antarctic system and influencing its *modus operandi*
- *conservation* – an early major focus, and one with which Australia engaged quite strongly
- *resource management* – not always entirely distinct from conservation, but often so, and most obviously focused on the question of how to manage any future resumption of commercial sealing; and what we have termed
- *strategic interests* – while in a sense all the foregoing are also strategic interests, what we attend to here are essentially the deep interests around Australia's sense of rights and entitlement as a territorial claimant.

We conclude the chapter with an assessment of Australian policy over the decade.

Overview of the decade's Antarctic Treaty Consultative Meetings

The 1960s were characterised by a soft and sure approach to decision making by the Antarctic Treaty Consultative Parties, who desired to make headway and earn each other's respect, along with that of the international community, by avoiding contentious issues. This approach gave them a solid start and, 50 years on, still partly explains the longevity of the regime. The first six ATCMs reveal the exclusivity of their membership and a clear recognition that some issues already had been resolved to the extent possible in the Treaty negotiation and should not be revisited. Others had been only partially resolved or not at all, and would require a sensitive approach if there were to be any likelihood of progress. There was thus a certain expediency to the decision making, which was consistent with the parties' general aversion to risk.

Only the original 12 signatories attended either the preparatory or Treaty meetings throughout the decade, and their deliberations were recorded in no more than a cursory fashion, which later earned criticism for being secretive and exclusive.[3] It was to remain that way until 1970, when the process became marginally more transparent.[4] At each of the intersessional preparatory meetings the parties took the opportunity to discourage each other from raising particularly sensitive issues. These private meetings, convened primarily so that the parties could agree on the agenda for the next meeting, provided opportunities to test reactions to controversial items and to exclude the possibility of unwelcome surprises. The parties' overriding concern during the decade was to concentrate on specific items about which 'rapid progress [can] be achieved [because] the future is bound to depend on the initial impetus given'.[5]

Prime Minister Robert Menzies (standing at rear left) welcoming delegates to the first Antarctic Treaty Consultative Meeting, Canberra, 10 July 1961. National Archives of Australia: AT19

The first ATCM, in Canberra, was opened by Prime Minister Robert Menzies, who was also the Minister for External Affairs, and chaired by John Gorton, the Minister for the Navy and Minister assisting the Minister for External Affairs. Thereafter, Australian politicians, like those of other Antarctic Treaty Consultative Parties (ATCPs), were not directly engaged with the Antarctic diplomatic forums. These were left in the care of officials – a quite different situation to that obtaining across many other areas of Australian international interest. The Canberra meeting was attended by 12 Australian officials in addition to Gorton.[6] Other ATCM delegations in the decade were generally much smaller, and often included a local ambassador, sometimes as head, and other embassy staff.[7] (Australia routinely has delegations the size of its Canberra complement again today.)

As might be expected, the first ATCM was substantially occupied in realising commitments made in the Treaty and establishing the administrative norms for this and further meetings, including the question of Secretariat support for the Treaty. Australia took a lead role in this last matter, including offering to host the institution in Canberra. Rules of procedure were adopted, and discussions were held on the central role assigned to science, and on the Special Committee on Antarctic Research (SCAR) as a source of advice. There were discussions (and further technical meetings agreed) on operational matters such as radio communications and cooperation around mail delivery. Two obviously big-ticket issues stand out. Consideration of the 'preservation and conservation of living resources' resulted in Recommendation I-VIII, which first used the terms 'conserve' and 'living resources' and agreed on 'general rules of conduct for preservation and conservation of living resources in Antarctica', the first step on the road to the Agreed Measures (see below). Discussion of the sensitive 'exchange of information and advice relating to the application of nuclear energy in the Treaty Area' resulted in the guarded Recommendation I-XIII:

> Taking into consideration the provisions established in Article V of the Antarctic Treaty, the Representatives recommend to their Governments

that they exchange *by all means deemed advisable* information on the application of nuclear equipment and techniques in the Treaty Area (emphasis added).[8]

The second ATCM was held a year after the Canberra meeting, in Buenos Aires, from 18–28 July 1962. Thereafter meetings were biennial: ATCM III, 2–13 June 1964 in Brussels; ATCM IV, 3–18 November 1966 in Santiago; ATCM V, 18–29 November 1968 in Paris; and ATCM VI, 19–31 October 1970 in Tokyo. With two-year gaps between main sessions, a practice developed until the late 1970s of holding multiple short preparatory meetings in advance (a practice which persisted until ATCMs became annual events, following the adoption of the Protocol on Environmental Protection to the Antarctic Treaty in 1991). Including ATCMs, preparatory meetings and various technical meetings outside the ATCM, the period saw some 60 meetings – a surprisingly large number and comparable to the overall level of the wider Antarctic system today. The first six ATCMs were characterised by the exclusivity of the membership (just the 12 original signatories to the Antarctic Treaty, the ATCPs), the establishment of the administrative norms and modus operandi that inform the Antarctic system to the present, and the identification and first work on some of the key resource management and environmental issues that, in time, led to the addition of new legal instruments, and what became the Antarctic Treaty System.

The second ATCM had an even more administratively focused agenda than the first, again considering science and the availability of scientific data, communications and logistics cooperation, and how to approve recommendations from ATCMs domestically. Recommendation II-VI established that diplomatic channels would be used to advise any changes to Antarctic activities previously reported under Article VII(5) of the Treaty. The second ATCM added nothing to the discussion of nuclear issues, but Recommendation II-II referred back to conservation issues addressed in Recommendation I-VIII, required the collection and exchange of information, and indicated an intention to develop measures on the protection of living resources at the third ATCM.[9] That meeting did indeed adopt the first new substantive obligations since the Treaty: Recommendation III-VIII on Agreed Measures for the Conservation of Antarctic Fauna and Flora. Aside from this, ATCM III was again concerned with telecommunications and logistics (on this occasion aircraft landing facilities).[10]

Further development of the Agreed Measures dominated proceedings at the fourth ATCM, with designation of 15 Specially Protected Areas, of fur seals and the Ross seal as Specially Protected Species, and two recommendations on cooperation in implementing the article on permits and information exchange on native animals and birds. With the Agreed Measures in a sense underway, ATCM VI also saw the first substantive work on seals, which resulted in the adoption of Recommendation IV-21: Interim Guidelines for the Voluntary Regulation of Antarctic Pelagic Sealing. Perhaps more unexpected was the fact that the first official discussion of tourism took place, with Recommendation IV-27: Effects of Antarctic Tourism, as the outcome. The concern was that tourism might 'prejudice the conduct of scientific research, conservation of fauna and flora and the operation of Antarctic stations', issues that would, with the addition only of search and res-cue, characterise the ATCM debate around tourism in the 2000s (see chapter 10). Logistics and com-munications were again touched on.[11]

The fifth ATCM saw the now regular addition of Specially Protected Areas, and agreement to draw up a list for a new category of Historic Mon-uments. The continuation of previous discussions finally resulted in the substantive Recommendation V-2: Measures for Improving Antarctic Telecommu-nications. Tourism was again on the agenda, without any apparent outcome. But it was the marine environment that dominated the meeting and led to Recommendation V-3 on the Southern Ocean, which welcomed the proposed study by the International Oceanographic Commission and en-couraged SCAR to engage with it. There were also major developments in relation to seals. A seven-page Draft Convention for the Regulation of Antarctic Pelagic Sealing was discussed, and at-tached as Annex 2 to the ATCM's Final Report.

Annex 1 to the report was a four-page SCAR analysis of the sealing issue: Modified Version of the Report of 1968 to National Antarctic Committees by the Scientific Committee on Antarctic Research (SCAR).[12]

With the sixth ATCM in 1970, documentation in final reports became much more comprehensive, including a list of documents presented and delegations attending.[13] An important precedent for ATS development was established, with the decision that further consideration of the draft sealing convention would occur 'outside the framework of the Antarctic Treaty, since the conservation of seals in the sea does not fall within the scope of the latter and is of interest to countries that are not Parties to the Antarctic Treaty'.[14] In this connection, informal meetings were held, separate from the Consultative Meeting. The convention text was redrafted, and renamed a Draft Convention for the Conservation of Antarctic Seals, the name under which it was subsequently adopted in 1972. Tourism was discussed, and Recommendation VI-7 required tourists to act consistently with the Treaty and Recommendations, to arrange visits to stations beforehand and to comply with any conditions imposed. Also, any expedition not organised by an ATCP but proceeding from its territory must now be reported by it as part of the advance notice information expected under the Antarctic Treaty. A number of recommendations were adopted relating to Specially Protected Areas and to conservation of flora and fauna under the Agreed Measures.

The really new development at the sixth ATCM was the appearance for the first time of obligations in relation to environment and ecosystems and of the term 'wise use'. This was reflected in Recommendation VI-4: Man's Impact on the Antarctic Environment, which recognised that 'in the Antarctic Treaty area the ecosystem is particularly vulnerable to human interference', that much of the Antarctic's importance '[derives] from its uncontaminated and undisturbed condition', that there '[is] an increasingly urgent need to protect the environment from human interference' and that ATCPs should assume responsibility for this and for 'the wise use of the Treaty area'. In a sense, the modern concern with environmental protection arrived in Antarctica with this recommendation. Its realisation was the dominant project of the decades ahead.

Australian policy in the ATCMs

Institutional

For the Antarctic Treaty to succeed and last, Australia saw that it had to develop robust administrative and institutional practices. From the start, Australia was thinking about the Treaty's architecture, and it went into the first ATCM with the idea of establishing a headquarters (offering to host it in Canberra – links with its wider strategic interests were obvious) with a secretariat, albeit with initially quite limited functions.[15] This turned out to be the most contentious issue of all at ATCM I and the proposal failed. (An Antarctic Treaty Secretariat was not in fact agreed to until 2001, and formally commenced operation in Buenos Aires on 1 September 2004.[16]) Before the attainment of consensus on that location, the Tasmanian State Government led a major effort to see the secretariat located in Hobart. However, within these 1961 discussions Australia took the lead to broker a deal which has stood the test of time: namely, that the ATCP hosting the ATCM would perform the essential administrative services, and that the next host would consult to set a date for that meeting and, through diplomatic channels, resolve its agenda. Australia saw this as a useful brake on what it feared would otherwise be an unhelpful strengthening of influence of the Treaty's depositary government, the United States.[17]

However, Australia sided with the United States at ATCM IV in 1966, regarding the relationship between meetings (ATCMs and ad hoc sessions) and expenditure. The United States argued that neither ATCMs nor Antarctic Treaty meetings of experts had any authority to commit governments to expenditure. As a result the parties adopted Recommendation IV-24, which outlined how meetings of experts could be established 'to discuss practical problems related to Antarctic activities' and subsequent reports submitted to the consultative parties for their consideration, unless otherwise agreed. Recommendation IV-25, on the other hand, made it plain that the special meeting on logistics to be held in Japan in 1968 was different to a meeting of experts. It outlined how in this case the host government would circulate reports to all other governments to take whatever action they might wish as a result of deliberations among them.

Four states acceded to the Treaty in its first ten years: Poland in 1961, Czechoslovakia in 1962, Denmark in 1965 and the Netherlands in 1967. None of the newcomers were admitted to consultative meetings, however. They were deemed not to be Article IX(2) parties because they did not conduct substantial research activity, such as the organisation of an expedition or the building of a research base in Antarctica. According to Australian delegation briefs, there was even discussion about whether or not the four new signatories should be included in circulation lists for the exchange of information in accordance with Article III(1)(a). Information exchange was considered to be a test of the good faith of the consultative parties to act cooperatively. The question of whether or not to exchange information with *all* signatories related to persistent suspicions about the activities of the Soviet Union. What complicated matters further was the fact that scientists from the Eastern bloc countries (Poland and Czechoslovakia) routinely travelled to Antarctica with the Soviet Union's Antarctic program and were included in exchanges of information by the Soviets. Australia did not appear to have the same objections to either Denmark or the Netherlands receiving exchanged information. Politics was never far below the surface, even in relation to supposed administrative decisions.

Conservation

Influence in any diplomatic context often follows a winding path, and necessarily involves blending with other inputs. But the general rules of conduct for preservation and conservation of living resources in Antarctica found in Recommendation I-VIII have an early Australian connection. The rules were based on a paper from SCAR, and the SCAR internal process that led to that paper goes back at least to 1959 and the third meeting of SCAR in Canberra, where the working group on biology chaired by Robert Carrick (the head of ANARE's biology program) raised the need to protect Antarctic fauna and flora. In 1960 Carrick developed this theme in a paper entitled 'Conservation of nature in the Antarctic', and this in turn was subsequently developed through SCAR.[18] As Riddle and Goldsworthy note, 'the direct lineage from his 1960 paper ... to the Agreed Measures is very obvious [and] Robert Carrick should be recognised as being the first to set eyes on the goal of a comprehensively protected Antarctic continent'.[19] Interestingly, in 1961 Australia was cautious both about SCAR acquiring the direct scientific advisory role with the ATCM that in fact eventuated, and about the risk that SCAR's recommendations on the conservation of living resources would stray into the problematical area of jurisdiction. Australia was supportive of SCAR as the international coordinating body, but preferred its advice to feed in via the separate national science bodies – in its case, the Australian Academy of Science. There were several reasons for this stance: a sense that SCAR itself might not welcome entanglement in the political arena; a concern that its scientific independence should be preserved; a general disinclination to building too much institutional apparatus around the Treaty too soon; financial parsimony; and an evident concern that too great a role for an international science body risked undercutting the standing of states, and particularly claimant states such as Australia. The fear was that greater SCAR autonomy might pose a challenge to Australia's sovereignty interests. The safest option, in Australia's view, was in the first instance a voluntary code.

Technical debates such as those around the Agreed Measures raised Australian awareness of the need for technical advice to be available to delegations. Although approving the Agreed Measures in principle and giving practical effect to them at Australian stations, there was ongoing concern about the jurisdictional implications of interpretations and developments favoured by some states, including arrangements for permits.[20] Indeed, Australia deferred approving the Agreed

Measures pending clarity about these issues, particularly the differences between the United Kingdom and Chile in relation to amending Article II (Australia inclined towards Chile's position).[21] Australia favoured allowing protection for ocean areas adjacent to Specially Protected Areas, but recognised that, as with the concurrent discussion around seals, there were legal issues to be resolved, and wanted SCAR meanwhile to report to the ATCM on the practical scientific benefits.[22]

What is revealed here is a three-level Australian engagement with the unfolding Antarctic conservation debate. Australian scientists, most obviously Robert Carrick, were seemingly in the vanguard of awareness of Antarctic vulnerabilities and, with international colleagues through SCAR, provided the ATCM with the advice and even drafting guidance that led, through a series of recommendations, to the Agreed Measures. This was a major step in Antarctic, and indeed global, attention to conservation. Australian officials were supportive of the general thrust of these developments, but keen to assess the implications of any new obligations and their potential consequences for the complicated juridical situation. Australia was also, particularly earlier in the decade, always alert to the supposed possibilities of the Soviet Union making mischief. So even conservation was never decoupled from Australian strategic interests.

Resource management

The substantive resource management issue arising in the first decade of the Treaty was around the question of sealing, which had been a major motive for early interest in the Antarctic and sub-Antarctic regions. By 1964 there were indications of a possible revival of commercial sealing within the Antarctic Treaty Area, and sealing appeared on the agenda of the third ATCM, with an interim recommendation, III-XI: Pelagic Sealing and the Taking of Fauna on Pack Ice, being adopted. Some regulatory structure for pelagic sealing was considered necessary. The central question was whether the Treaty had the competence to elaborate whatever structure was required, in view of its reservation of high seas freedoms. In relation to seals, and to the broader question of the competence to impose special protection on ocean areas around Antarctica, some states, including the claimants Argentina and Chile, did not believe the Treaty provided a basis. Australia took a different position: that the Southern Ocean was covered by the Treaty without this prejudicing high seas rights. Indeed, Australia argued that unless the Treaty was seen as applying across the entire area south of 60° South, its non-militarisation provisions would not be effective.[23]

This topic was part of the broader discussion about the area of application of the Agreed Measures and about the form of regulation for pelagic sealing.

Australia was cognisant of the importance of the pack ice, and pushed for the sealing regulations to apply to the taking of seals off the pack ice as well as in open water. Finally, in relation to seals, there were potential sealing nations, such as Canada, which were not parties to the Antarctic Treaty.

Australia thought that there were three options for addressing the sealing question: by Measures adopted through a Recommendation, along the lines of the recent Agreed Measures; by a convention 'formally divorced from the Antarctic Treaty context'; or by a 'voluntary system of control'.[24] It was decided that after preliminary development in, and on the fringes of, the ATCMs, the final stages of the negotiation of what became the Convention for the Conservation of Antarctic Seals should be conducted through a stand-alone diplomatic process. Australia came around to this position somewhat reluctantly. Accepting the need for regulation of pelagic sealing in the Southern Ocean, it noted that 'such sealing has not yet taken place'. It thought three papers prepared by SCAR's Working Group in Biology formed an acceptable basis for developing a regulatory system, although it was surprised that the six zones identified in these proposals did not seem to cover the entire 360° circumference of the continent. Because of the non-Treaty states with a potential interest in sealing, Australia finally decided that a separate convention was the best option. The question then became the manner in which this convention would be drawn up, since this could hardly be done at an ATCM, where such non-parties would have no standing. The remaining substantive problem was the area of application of a putative seals convention, which Australia thought should be decided by a separate international conference, since it might not be appropriate for the ATCM to propose a region that extended beyond its own area of responsibility.[25]   The final development, and shape, of the Convention for the Conservation of Antarctic Seals was not resolved until the second decade of the Antarctic Treaty (see chapter 7).

Strategic interests

Australia's strategic interests in the Antarctic, and therefore in the Treaty, centred on its territorial claim to the Australian Antarctic Territory (AAT). On that front, even the United States, which Menzies called Australia's 'great and powerful friend', needed to be watched. Running alongside this at the start of the decade was a practical concern about the implications for Australia's safety of any military use of Antarctica and, as part of the wider Cold War context, anxiety about the containment of the Soviet Union. By the end of the decade, satellites and ballistic missiles had rendered much of this concern moot. Even attitudes towards the Soviet Union changed throughout the 1960s, so that by the fifth ATCM, while still 'unpredictable', it was also characterised as responsible and moderate.[26]

Australia saw the Treaty as the best compromise it could get, and one that it could argue met its main political objectives, namely the non-militarisation of the area and its opening up to peaceful international and, in particular, scientific cooperation, without weakening Australia's position on sovereignty, and 'freedom of action to explore and exploit resources'.[27]

One sees a perfect encapsulation of almost all these interests (although nothing on resources) in Menzies' opening speech at the first ATCM. He drew attention to Lady Mawson's presence, thereby invoking Australia's greatest explorer, upon whose work much was based. He carefully noted that 'we have agreed to set aside *the argument* about territorial claims' (emphasis added) and, lest this was not clear enough, added 'Nobody abandons his own'. And noting that four nuclear powers were present, he wittily applauded the demilitarisation provisions: 'It would not, perhaps, be grammatically accurate to say that it is demilitarized, because it has never been militarized; but it is to be non-militarized, and this is of tremendous importance.'[28]

Leading the Australian delegation (with John Gorton as chair of the meeting), R L Harry used his opening statement to catalogue Australia's engagement in Antarctica, from 'Australian sealers and whalers' in the nineteenth century to the present day, and mentioned all the Australian Antarctic worthies: Mawson (of course), but also Hubert Wilkins and John

Rymill.[29] Other ATCPs did likewise, but nobody would have been unaware that Australia's enduring interest was sovereignty over the AAT.

Australia gave careful attention to the stances of other original signatories to the Treaty, including other claimants, in relation to jurisdiction. It classified fellow ATCPs into categories: claimants who would not relinquish their claims (Argentina, Australia, Chile); claimants who would allow internationalisation (United Kingdom, New Zealand); those who had not claimed but might if the Treaty broke down (United States, USSR); and those who could not claim and favoured internationalisation (Japan, South Africa, Belgium).[30]

Throughout the decade, any agenda item or proposal for discussion was viewed through the sovereignty prism. What implications were there for Australian sovereignty and the careful *modus vivendi* of the Treaty, whether the issue was postage stamps, inspection, nuclear energy, administrative arrangements under the Treaty, the role of SCAR or conservation – let alone manifestly problematical matters such as jurisdiction? Jurisdiction was probably the most sensitive issue among Treaty parties, and the one most likely to lead to Treaty breakdown.[31] This ensured that alongside a generally sympathetic approach to proposals to promote science, logistic cooperation, the conservation of natural resources, and institutional support of the Treaty, there was a more anxious imperative to avoid, at nearly any cost, 'contentious' issues.[32] Remarkably, Australian delegates were briefed that the first ATCM should be 'non political', its role being instead to establish procedures and machinery as the foundation for future progress.[33] Of course the ATCMs were never anything other than political and a number of contentious issues had to be addressed, albeit hesitantly, over the decade. As a result, in the later 1960s a more expansive view obtained. Australia now saw its main diplomatic objective *vis-à-vis* Antarctica as preserving the Antarctic Treaty (and soon the Antarctic Treaty System) in an international climate whereby the Treaty's principles and objectives were delivered through gradually developing international cooperation across a number of fields.[34] Disputes, of course, still had to be avoided.

Australia in the first decade of the Antarctic Treaty: an assessment

While administrative arrangements rarely appear exciting, the norms and capacities developed in this first decade had significant consequences for the sort of institution the ATS would become and, thereby, a critical bearing on the issues it could tackle, and on its longevity. We now know that the Antarctic Treaty has lasted for more than half a century. This was not a certainty in the early 1960s. Australia cannot claim a pre-eminent role in ensuring this success, but it was one of the Treaty's most committed state parties through the first decade and thus a significant contributor to its bedding-in and to the establishment of the norms and *modus operandi* of the period, which were subsequently extended across the emerging ATS.

Whether it was simply a product of the huge area of the Australian Antarctic Territory (AAT) and of a domestic experience of operating across continental distances, or was also from deliberate political choice, Australia established a capacity for autonomous Antarctic facilities and logistics exceeded only by that of the United States and the Soviet Union. No doubt influenced also by its membership of the then relatively dominant Anglophone bloc, Australia seems a particularly confident participant in the ATCMs, more assured than its position in the international community at that time might otherwise lead one to imagine. Antarctica had become an arena in which Australia could exercise disproportionate influence.

Of course Australia aimed to exercise such influence, because it hoped to have influence proportionate to the 42 per cent of the continent that it claimed as the Australian Antarctic Territory. This was its key strategic interest. Having contained (as it saw it) the worst challenges to its position through the 1959 Treaty, Australia, like others, then sought to guide the Treaty's implementation in directions congenial to its interests. In this it was perhaps aided by its wider historical international connections. Australia was firmly located within the Western bloc throughout the Cold War. It had historical ties to the United

Kingdom which included, like New Zealand, common imperial roots for its Antarctic claim. Australia was coupled to the United States (again with New Zealand) in the tripartite ANZUS Treaty. (These connections were reflected, *inter alia,* in its active engagement in *Konfrontasi* and Vietnam.) Alongside the natural advantage of relative proximity to Antarctica, at least in comparison with northern hemisphere claimants, Australia also had strong domestic science traditions and capacities, which were a material advantage in the new science-mediated Antarctic polity.

In addition to institutional development, Australia built upon its already well-established Antarctic operating and scientific experience, its high-level engagement during negotiation of the Antarctic Treaty, and the unusual identification of its national capital in the text of that treaty as the venue for the first meeting following its entry into force, to establish an important role in brokering negotiations (if not agreements) and putting forward ideas on how to deal with the practical day-to-day idiosyncrasies of operating in the Antarctic.

The two major policy outcomes of the ATCMs of the 1960s relate to conservation and resource management: the general moves that led to the 1964 Agreed Measures, and the particular focus on how best to conserve and manage seals should commercial sealing again become a major activity. The latter was institutionally addressed in the following decade through the 1972 Convention for the Conservation of

Antarctic Seals. In both cases it is important not to anachronistically confuse the later concern with the general protection of the Antarctic environment with the narrower conservation imperative of the time. In both of these developments, but particularly in relation to the Agreed Measures, Australia played an important role. The Agreed Measures established species and area protection, and general conservation principles that were subsequently developed in the new instruments of the ATS, and in that sense it might be termed a proto-environmental agreement. Its main elements remain to this day (updated through the Madrid Protocol) at the core of the ATS's commitment to environmental protection, the development of which in the late 1980s and early 1990s again saw Australia play a major role (see chapters 11–14). The Convention for the Conservation of Antarctic Seals was the first instrument in a sequence addressing emergent resource management issues. While historicism can be a risky business, one can argue that to the extent that it played a role in the debates around conservation and resource management in the 1960s, Australia helped to set in train, and to shape, the future cast of the collective Antarctic project. Given the size of the Antarctic Treaty Area, and the persistence of the ATS, this is no mean achievement.

The hybrid nature of the political reality presented by Antarctica, and specifically by the AAT, was (and remains) crucial to the sorts of stances Australia took and to the significant resources it put into its Antarctic engagement. Inescapably, there were major foreign affairs components to Australian Antarctic policy. These included the containment of any challenges to Australia's asserted territorial sovereignty over the AAT, and ensuring that Antarctic norms and relationships were appropriately situated within the prevailing Cold War framework. The latter nonetheless required careful management of some of its allies' differing perspectives on territorial issues. Russia may have been, especially in the early years, the greatest worry, but it was not the only state that Australia kept an eye on. Thus one sees Australia taking care around the significant fact that its prime ally (the United States) does not recognise any territorial claims, and periodically in relation to the United Kingdom and New Zealand who, while themselves claimants, sometimes frame the claimant position differently to Australia.

But Antarctica also had *domestic* significance in the context of Australia's evolving post-war sense of nationhood and place in the international community. The facts of being a claimant, of being geographically relatively proximate to Antarctica and thus to some degree finding it easier to operate there than some other states, and of emerging from the status of a British Dominion (indeed formally acquiring its Antarctic territory partly as a consequence of past imperial connections with Great Britain) also gave Antarctica a standing in Australian domestic affairs. The AAT and Australia's consequent sense of itself as a significant player in the new Antarctic system can therefore be seen in part as manifestations of Australian nation-building, even if this sense was largely confined to elite levels in the bureaucracy. As previously noted, this did not mean that there was necessarily widespread popular or media interest in Antarctica. Antarctica was, for Australia, a special case precisely because it did not fit neatly into either an international or domestic pigeonhole.

It is a commonplace that in the contemporary world the boundaries between what is domestic and what is international have substantially eroded. Modern information and other technologies have shrunk the world, but this was less obviously the case in the 1960s. The hybrid nature of Australia's Antarctic engagement, as both an international and domestic issue, probably cast that part of the world in a different light from any other place in the Australian imagination. The legacy of this framing is still with us.

Notes

[1]   We thank the staff at the Australian Antarctic Division; Newspapers and Microforms Reading Room at the National Library of Australia, Canberra; and National Archives of Australia, Canberra, for assistance with their collections.

[2]   See Rolf (1979); Wiley KG (1961) Where a vote could mean disaster: NT Aborigines unfit for citizenship, *The Bulletin* 82 (4250), 29 July 1961, 20–21; three pieces by Alan Reid in consecutive numbers (4248, 4249, 4250) of *The*

Bulletin 82 in July 1961; Hoad B (1969) Equal pay: money ... or status? *The Bulletin* 91 (4339), 8 February 1969, 29–32; Anon (1968) What happened to the Gurindji and their land? *The Bulletin* 90 (4610), 13 July 1968, 17; and Anon (1970) We shall overcome (by 1972). *The Bulletin* 92 (4696), 21 March 1970, 27–29 [on law reform and aborigine rights]; Horne D (1968) If America leaves. *The Bulletin* 90 (4601), 25 May 1968, 32–37; and Anon (1970) Close-up of a domino's domino. Special Report. *The Bulletin* 92 (4693), 28 February 1970, 33–35.

[3]   The final Treaty meeting reports generally contained an opening and closing paragraph and the text of recommendations from the meeting to the governments of those countries represented, but little else. There were no working or information documents available publicly from these intersessional, expert or consultative meetings during the 1960s.

[4]   In that year the final report from ATCM VI also included opening speeches (included in ATCM I as well), a list of participants and a list of documents.

[5]   Australia (1961b) 27.

[6]   Four from External Affairs, three from the Antarctic Division (then within External Affairs), two from CSIRO and one each from the Attorney-General's and Postmaster-Generals' depart-

ments and the Bureau of Meteorology. Source: Australia (1961b).

[7]   The delegation to ATCM V in Paris in 1968 comprised five officials: the Ambassador to The Hague, a Third Secretary from the Paris Embassy, and one each from External Affairs, the Antarctic Division, and the Department of Supply (at that stage the Antarctic Division's parent department). Source: Australia (1968) 12–13.

[8]   Australia (1968) 12–13.

[9]   Argentina (1962).

[10]   Belgium (1964).

[11]   Final Report of the Fourth Antarctic Treaty Consultative Meeting, in Argentina (1969).

[12]   France (1968).

[13]   Delegations were listed in the printed report of the first ATCM, but do not appear in the typescript reports available for ATCMs I–IV inclusive, available at the Antarctic Treaty Secretariat<website www.ats.aq> or in the hard copies in the authors' possession.

[14]   Paragraph 10 in Japan (1970).

[15]   Australia (1961a).

[16]   Antarctic Treaty, Decision 1 (2001), Measure 1 (2003).

[17]   Australia (1961c).

[18]   Riddle and Goldsworthy (2002) 564–66.

[19]   Riddle and Goldsworthy (2002) 564–66.

[20]   Australia (1966).

[21]   Australia (1968).

[22]   Australia (1968).
[23]   Australia (1964).
[24]   Australia (1964).
[25]   Australia (1968).
[26]   Australia (1968).
[27]   Australia (1968).
[28]   Australia (1961b).
[29]   Australia (1961b).
[30]   Australia (1968).
[31]   Australia (1968).
[32]   Australia (1961b).
[33]   Australia (1961b).
[34]   Australia (1968).

6

Science

Michael Stoddart and Marcus Haward[1]

Few people taking the ferry from Louisville on Tasmania's east coast to Maria Island know of the link between their point of departure and Antarctica. The place is named after Louis Bernacchi, born in Belgium in 1876 to Italian parents. Bernacchi spent much of his childhood on Maria Island, where his father tried to make a success of a number of business ventures; he attended school in Hobart and went on to study astronomy at Melbourne University. At the age of 23 he accompanied Carsten Borchgrevink's 1899 Antarctic expedition aboard the *Southern Cross* as an astronomer, overwintering at Cape Adare. When Bernacchi joined Captain Robert Scott two years later aboard the *Discovery,* he was the only member of the expedition who had been to Antarctica before. Perhaps fortunately, family commitments prevented him from accepting a later invitation to accompany Scott on the fateful *Terra Nova* expedition, which was to cost Scott and four companions their lives. Australia's long association with Antarctic science began with Bernacchi's southern sojourns.

A few years later T W Edgeworth David, Professor of Geology and Palaeontology at the University of

Sydney, sailed south as chief scientific officer on Ernest Shackleton's *Nimrod* expedition (1907–09), accompanied by his former student, Douglas Mawson. Edgeworth David led the first ascent of Mount Erebus and, with Mawson and the Scot Alistair Mackay, was the first to reach the vicinity of the South Magnetic Pole. Also on the expedition was Raymond Priestley, an English geology student, later the co-founder with Australian geologist Frank Debenham of the Scott Polar Research Institute in Cambridge and Vice-Chancellor of the University of Melbourne. Priestley and Australia's Thomas Griffith Taylor were scientific members of Scott's 1910–13 *Terra Nova* expedition. Taylor, too, would go on to a distinguished international career, as head of geography at Sydney University and professor at Chicago and Toronto universities. The publications of all these men set the scene for the geological work of many decades to come.

In 1911–14, Mawson led his own Australasian Antarctic Expedition (AAE) and, in 1929–31, he led the two official cruises of the British, Australian and New Zealand Antarctic Research Expedition (BANZARE). The 22-volume scientific reports of the AAE took until 1947 to complete. BANZARE also collected scientific data on land and at sea, from Enderby Land to Oates Land, in fields including geology, meteorology, zoology and botany. Publication of its reports ran to 13 volumes and was finally completed in 1975. As the 1930s ended and war encompassed the world, scientific study of Antarctica was forced to take a back seat.

When peace returned, Douglas Mawson resumed his quest to stimulate Australian government interest in the Antarctic, and a scientific expedition was assembled and a team of scientists recruited. Among them was Phillip Law, a physics lecturer at the University of Melbourne, whose task was to coordinate the science program and to make observations on cosmic rays from the expedition's ship, the *Wyatt Earp*. As Bowden notes, meteorology and geology were the main scientific focus, as they were the priorities of a government which already sensed that Australia's climate was profoundly influenced by its proximity to Antarctica.[2] And so it was that, in 1947, Australia's National Antarctic Research Expeditions (ANARE) were born.

Phillip Garth Law: the architect of ANARE

Tim Bowden

If ever a man found himself in the right place at the right time – and seized the opportunity – it was Phillip Garth Law. He later became known in Australia as 'Mr Antarctica', an appellation that was richly deserved.

Law was lecturing in physics at the University of Melbourne in July 1947 when he arranged a secondment to the fledgling organisation ANARE (Australian

National Antarctic Research Expedition) as its senior scientific officer. Later that year he sailed on the quaintly named HMAS *Wyatt Earp,* a former Norwegian sealing boat, in an attempt to reach the coastline of the Australian Antarctic Territory and select a site for a scientific station. It was the last time a wooden ship with sails would attempt such a Herculean task, and the *Wyatt Earp* was hopelessly inadequate. Although it failed to penetrate the pack ice, Phillip Law, with his customary drive and dedication, did manage to record valuable readings of cosmic ray activity down south with his instruments, despite the boat's ferocious capacity for rolling (through 35 degrees in five seconds!). This work formed the basis for further pioneering cosmic ray work in Antarctica in later years.

When it became clear that a station could not be built on the Antarctic continent immediately due to the lack of suitable shipping, the leader of ANARE, Group Captain Stuart Campbell (who had been the pilot of a Gypsy Moth float plane during Sir Douglas Mawson's BANZARE voyage of 1929–31), lost interest and Phillip Law was appointed acting officer in charge on 1 January 1949, and eventually ANARE's director for the next 17 years. A man small in stature, a boxer, keen skier and bushwalker, Law combined rare qualities of incisive management skills, great personal courage and a clear vision for the development of scientific programs which would

Phillip Law (left) and surveyor Syd Kirkby (see text box pages 186–7) at Law's 90th birthday celebration, Melbourne 2002. Jonothan Davis, Australian Antarctic Division, © Commonwealth of Australia

sustain Australia's Antarctic program as a permanent activity.

Despite being chronically seasick on every one of the 28 voyages of exploration and re-supply he led until his retirement from ANARE in 1966, Law personally directed the exploration and accurate charting of some 5000 kilometres of unknown coastline of the Australian Antarctic Territory.

Until ice-strengthened ships became available in 1954, Law used the sub-Antarctic Macquarie and

Heard islands as training grounds for the eventual assault on the continent, and for scientific observations, particularly in meteorology and physics. He encouraged over-wintering doctors to become amateur biologists, doing albatross, penguin and seal counts. With Australia rather short on glaciers, he persuaded physicists to take on the science of glaciology, and Heard Island, a 3000-metre volcano rising sheer out of the Southern Ocean, had both glaciers and enough ice and snow to train sledge dog teams.

In the immediate post-war period, ANARE had to make do with what military or naval equipment could be scrounged. Huts for Heard Island, originally designed for the tropics, had to be modified to rid them of the high louvred windows designed to let in cooling breezes. Heard Island had an abundance of those. Clothing had to be similarly adapted. The first trained geologists, Graham Chittleborough and Tim Ealey, went to Heard in 1949, with Law (a physicist) acting as their supervisor. Chittleborough recalls they had no waterproof clothing, and attempted to rubberise their parkas by boiling them in an improvised solution, which lent them a 'somewhat distinctive odour'.

Law was keen to make sure that the all-male stations did not become bastions of ockerdom, although the word was not in vogue then. He insisted that each station had a library of the polar classics and a good encyclopaedia, as well as novels. Gramophones were provided, with classical and popular 78 rpm records, and 35 mm feature films were reduced to 16 mm format for evening screenings. Then, as now, a film could take over the culture of a station. In 1949, *Pride and Prejudice* was played at least 100 times. The sound was often turned down while the expeditioners supplied their own, sometimes bawdy, dialogue. When Law relieved the station he thought the whole team of winterers had gone potty, as they were talking among themselves in the genteel language of Jane Austin's nineteenth-century England. A request to pass the butter was likely to elicit the response: 'Such affability, such graciousness, you overwhelm me.'

OICs (officers in charge) were allocated a quantity of bottled wine for formal mess dinners on Sunday nights, when best clothes were donned and formal toasts drunk – in an era when wine was regarded by some as plonk drunk by derelicts out of bottles hidden in brown paper bags.

On 11 February 1954, the chartered Danish ice-strengthened ship *Kista Dan* broke through the fast ice into what is now Mawson Harbour – the only sheltered anchorage on the entire coast of Greater Antarctica. The expedition's first task was to build the prefabricated huts to house the ten men to winter there. No one knew what lay behind their small patch of exposed rock but before the year was out, some of them, using dog teams and primitive over-snow vehicles called 'weasels', became the first to see the great northern ranges of the Prince Charles Mountains, which held back the Lambert Glacier, the largest in the world.

Greater Antarctica was the last great geographical unknown on earth. Law quickly organised the building of Antarctica's first permanent hangar at Mawson, and extended the range of exploration by using Auster and Beaver light aircraft. At the same time he developed what he called the technique of 'hit and run exploration' – each year he would choose a section of unexplored coastline, and on his way to and from resupplying the stations take advantage of any brief windows of good weather to land, either by launch, fixed-wing aircraft or helicopters when they became available, and work around the clock to maximise the time ashore. Law was rather scornful of the 'heroic era' explorers who, when they did manage to get ashore, often wasted time by playing football matches, photographing penguins and not really taking advantage of the situation before the weather inevitably closed in and they had to return to their ships.

One of the first priorities of 'hit and run' operations was to team up a geologist and a surveyor. While the geologist chipped the rocks in search of mineral discoveries, the surveyor took an astrofix (which could be done in daylight) to pinpoint their actual position, and biologists assessed the wildlife before the weather broke, as it always did. All the coastal maps of the day were approximations. In later years Law would say jokingly that these groups explored more virgin Antarctic Territory than Mawson, Scott and Shackleton combined. Law also personally chose the sites for the other continental stations, Casey and Davis. These ice-free areas, including Mawson Station, were prime pieces of Antarctic real estate, and Australia got to them first.

This pleased ANARE's parent department, External Affairs, which was keen for Australia to demonstrate its claim to 42 per cent of the entire Antarctic continent. External Affairs was less comfortable with overseeing the logistics of running and building the stations and, after grumbling about the money, left Law and his team to organise everything. Phillip Law's aggressive promotion of the Antarctic Division ruffled the feathers of the diplomats of External Affairs, who could be both petty and mean-minded – in 1960 refusing to allow Law to travel to Britain to receive personally the prestigious Royal Geographical Society's Founders' Medal.

Phillip Law realised that only a vigorous and innovative science program could justify the continuing expense of maintaining an Australian presence in Antarctica. Most of the programs he set up – upper atmosphere physics, biology, glaciology, meteorology and marine science – are running to this day, when

Antarctica's influence on global warming is now known to be pivotal and Australia is well positioned to be a world leader in this discipline.

The International Geophysical Year of 1957–58 was of crucial importance. The Antarctic Treaty was still to be negotiated and the Cold War was at its height. The prospect of the Soviet Union building stations on Australian-claimed territory (and never leaving) caused great anxiety in Canberra. On 30 January 1956, while the Russians were building their Mirny Station halfway between Wilkes (later Casey) Station and Mawson Station, Law and his relief party for Mawson called in. He did not know how they would be received, but the Russian leader, Mikhail Somov, received them warmly, and was keen to take advice from the more experienced Australians. Much vodka was drunk, and Law's uncanny resemblance to Vladimir Ilyich Lenin had the delighted Russians snapping photographs of him standing beside a bust of the Russian revolutionary hero outside the main hut. Remarkably, the Cold War never came to Antarctica.

Law was very much an expedition man and scientist, but he also played his part in diplomacy, including at the 1959 Washington conference negotiating the Treaty and in Canberra at the first Antarctic Treaty Consultative Meeting. His pragmatism showed in the first debate on establishing a secretariat – he wanted it to help meet the Treaty

Parties' obligations for information exchange, as he thought it unnecessarily cumbersome to have to notify every other Party individually of his annual expedition plans.

In 1966 Law's frustrations with the Department of External Affairs (DEA) mandarins came to a head when they would not approve his proposals for properly funded and adequately salaried positions for his scientific staff, and he resigned as Director of the Antarctic Division. He was then 55, and went on to a second career as executive vice-president of the Victoria Institute of Colleges. Although he endured bureaucratic frustrations in that role as well, he was successful in his campaign to have diplomas replaced by degrees. His interest (and influence) in Antarctic matters continued unabated for the rest of his long life.

His wife, Nel Law, who died in 1990, was the first Australian woman to set foot on the Antarctic continent when her husband took her south in 1961 as a guest of the Lauritzen Line. Although normally a stickler for the rules, Law was not averse to bending them if it suited him. Nel's voyage was nearly scuppered by the DEA just as the *Magga Dan* was to leave from Fremantle, but was saved by Senator John Gorton, representing the Minister for External Affairs, who gave his dockside imprimatur. Nel's superb oil paintings of that Antarctic visit are an enduring legacy.

The DEA never endorsed the knighthood that many felt Phillip Law should have received when he retired from ANARE, but a long life eventually showered many honours upon him. In 1993, then aged 80, Law was interviewed by Andrea Stretton for Film Australia's *Australian Biography* TV series and he told her that most people were not recognised for what they did until 50 years later. By the time Phillip Law died on 20 February 2010 at the age of 97, his list of honours and awards was impressive – including Australia's highest, an AC, the equivalent of the knighthood denied him all those years ago. Law took some pleasure in having all his honours listed. It seems appropriate to do so again here: PHILLIP GARTH LAW, AC, CBE, MSc, DAppSc (Hon. Melb), DEd (Hon. Vic), DSc (Hon. La Trobe), Hon. FRMIT, FANZAAS, FAIP, FRSV, FTSE, FAA.

In 2011 Law's ashes were taken to Mawson to be interred, along with those of Nel, beneath a stone cairn on the west arm of Horseshoe Harbour.

I once cheekily said to Phillip Law, 'One of the advantages of a long life is that you can dance on the graves of your enemies.' He made no comment in response, but a quiet smile played about his lips.

The International Geophysical Year (IGY, 1957–58) made Antarctica a focus for concerted and collaborative research. Twelve countries committed scientists and technicians to the Antarctic program of the IGY and research was conducted at some 50 stations. These included the UK's Halley Station, Japan's Syowa Station and several stations opened by the Soviet Union. Australia's Mawson Station, the oldest continually operating station south of the Antarctic Circle, had already been in existence for three years when in December 1956 the *Kista Dan* sailed for the Vestfold Hills in East Antarctica to establish Davis Station. By this time Australia had been involved in scientific research in Antarctica for almost eight decades, albeit on an opportunistic and uncoordinated basis. During the IGY, however, in Phillip Law's view, Australia produced more valuable scientific data than almost any other nation because 'we were the only ones, apart from the British, who'd had enough experience beforehand to set up a decent scientific program'.[3] Australian work centred on geophysics and Antarctica's structure, the ice sheet and upper atmospheric physics, and it was at this time that glaciology entered the program.

Government support for IGY science was a turning point for Australia, despite the prevailing view that during the pre-IGY period Australian involvement in the Antarctic served the interests of sovereignty and not science. The cause of science was nevertheless much advanced by both Mawson and Law being scientists of high standing. Law fought hard for funds to enable scientific research to be undertaken, but not always with the success enjoyed by later Australian

Antarctic Division (AAD) directors. Both men in their own way ensured that Australian science would become an increasingly valuable currency within the Antarctic Treaty System.[4]

It is hard to assess the influence that early Australian scientific research had on the Antarctic Treaty. As noted above, before the IGY science was not the currency in Antarctica, though it was a useful pastime. Australian contributions to upper atmospheric physics, geology and glaciology, as well as support of the Commonwealth Trans-Antarctic Expedition of 1955–58, meant that Australia came to be regarded as a significant force in newly emerging research fields in Antarctica. The IGY changed the world's perspective about Antarctica by introducing a central theme of the Antarctic Treaty – that Antarctica is to be used for the peaceful pursuit of science. The Treaty enshrines the principle of scientific cooperation and collaboration in Articles II and III, which remain defining characteristics of Antarctic science.[5] Nevertheless, through the work of Bernacchi, Taylor, Priestley, Mawson, Edgeworth David and Law, at the time of the IGY Australian science was widely known throughout the then small world of Antarctic science, and held in high regard. More importantly, it was the solid foundation upon which Australia's influence within the Treaty was to be built.

In the decades following the IGY – and particularly since 1991, when the ATCM declared 1991–2000 the Decade of International Scientific Cooperation – col-

214

laborative research has increased 13-fold and the number of scientific papers published worldwide has doubled. If science has become the currency of Antarctica, Australia has played an important role in maintaining its value. An analysis of published papers with the word fragment 'Antarc' in their titles suggested that Australian scientists published almost 10 per cent of the world's total of scientific papers about Antarctica in the quarter century to 2004, the third largest contribution after the United States and the United Kingdom.[6]

Australia's Antarctic science program, post-IGY

Australia's current Antarctic research program has certain characteristics that set it apart from those of other long-established Antarctic nations. Although it is one of the oldest national programs, the intellectual environment in which the program has evolved has not been stable. For the first 20 years of its existence (1948–68) the Australian Antarctic Division was a part of the Department of External Affairs, which had only a peripheral interest in science. After 1968 the division's home changed several times and sometimes quite rapidly, via the Department of Supply (1968–72), Department of Science (1972–74), Department of Science and Consumer Affairs (1974–75), Department of Science (1975–78), Department of Science and the Environment (1978–80), Department of Science and Technology (1980–84) and Department of Science yet again (1984–87). In these 20 years, while under the umbrella of the Department of Science in its various manifestations, the focus on science was maintained; with the advent of the Antarctic Science Advisory Committee in the early 1980s, financial support was provided to enable participation of university scientists in the program. This committee, established by and reporting to the minister, is charged with overseeing Australia's Antarctic research program. From July 1987 to the present day the Antarctic Division has been in an environment portfolio rather than a science portfolio, but the focus on science continues. Today it is part of the Department of Sustainability, Environment, Water, Population and Communities.

This administrative history helps establish the milieu in which the Australian Antarctic research program has evolved. Unlike the programs of most parties to the Antarctic Treaty, in which the Antarctic program is independent of government, Australia's program is part of government, with advantages for the continuity of long-term monitoring work, but concomitant disadvantages through the exclusion of AAD scientists from most national competitive research grant schemes.

As we have shown above, Australia's program of scientific research in Antarctica was initially driven largely by the enthusiasm of those in charge, although it is fair to say that the world's fascination with physics provided a powerful driver until the 1970s. First the Australian Academy of Sciences and later the Antarctic Science Advisory Committee provided advice on the strategic directions for the science program, and in 1995 the latter prepared the first formal science strategic plan. Before 1995 much fundamental work was conducted on the ice sheet and the cryosphere generally, setting the foundations for the present focus on high-latitude climate science.[7] Early work on penguins – mainly conducted after 1970, when the then director, Bryan Rofe, appointed a biologist to the Australian Antarctic Division – and in marine biology, introduced 15 years later, laid important foundations for Australia's commitment to the Convention on the Conservation of Antarctic Marine Living Resources (CCAMLR).

Successive strategic plans have focused on areas of science directly relevant to government positions on environmental protection, including climate science, Southern Ocean fisheries science and, more recently, cetacean biology and conservation. Most countries support the best Antarctic science which is offered and supportable within the constraints of logistics. Australia requires in addition that the science funded by the national Antarctic program also supports the policy objectives of government. Thus only research about the Antarctic which addresses major strategic questions is supported. Strong research themes are high-latitude climate science (in collaboration with CSIRO, the Bureau of Meteorology and several universities), marine ecosystem conservation in support of CCAMLR and environmental protection in support of the agenda of the Committee for Environmental Protection, which was established by the Madrid Protocol to advise the ATCM. Climate research in support of the government's climate science agenda and contributing to the work of the Intergovernmental Panel on Climate Change is delivered through a strongly collaborative research initiative, the Antarctic Climate and Ecosystems Cooperative Research Centre (CRC), established in 2003 and succeeding previous Antarctic CRCs (see appendix). Despite the fact that the instruments of the Antarctic Treaty System deliberately exclude whaling from their consideration, the Australian Antarctic science program has recently contributed substantially to knowledge of Antarctica's whale stocks and cetacean biology and conservation.

Structure of the current science program

Australia's program of scientific research has, since its absorption into the environment portfolio, been pursued jointly by research scientists employed by the department and by researchers in Australian and overseas universities and research agencies. Australia's Antarctic science program is coming under the direction of a new strategic plan scheduled to start in the 2011–12 season. Three themes – Climate Processes and Change; Terrestrial and Near-shore Ecosystems: Environmental Change and Conservation; and Southern Ocean Ecosystems: Environmental Change and Conservation – will continue to support Australia's policy and resource management needs, while a fourth theme – Frontier Science – will provide an opportunity for research that addresses Australia's national science priorities without the requirement for policy relevance. The program's broad strategic directions are set by the Antarctic Science Advisory Committee (ASAC), which is also charged with the conduct of periodic reviews of the quality of the program. The most recent of these, conducted in 2003, concluded that Australia is 'well served by its Antarctic science program', which represents 'a remarkable contribution by Australia to world science'. The international steering committee charged with undertaking the review very strongly endorsed the quality of the overall program. About 200 scientists travel south each year to conduct research in more than 100 projects, each of which has been approved by ASAC following evaluation by national and international referees.

International standing of Australia's Antarctic science program

Mention has already been made of Australia's high productivity in Antarctic research, relative to other nations with large Antarctic programs. In terms of its ranking in international collaborations, Australia is in fifth position, after the United States, the United

Kingdom, France and Germany (although the funding requirements for European Union science emphasise collaboration and therefore favour European nations in the analysis). In recent analyses, the Australian Antarctic Division and the University of Tasmania rank third and fourth respectively in a listing of the world's most productive.[8] Australia also has five of the 47 most productive authors (three from the Australian Antarctic Division and two from the University of Tasmania). Of course, bibliometric analyses impose their own constraints on reality and must be interpreted with caution.

International standing is also evidenced in the roles taken by Australian scientists in the organisation of international science programs, and there are few significant international research programs in Antarctica or the Southern Ocean which do not include Australians in leadership positions. Over the years Australia has had a high profile in the Scientific Committee on Antarctic Research and its many programs, standing committees and other bodies. It has provided a number of vice-presidents for these bodies (but as yet no president). Australian scientists have played influential roles on the steering committees of international oceanography programs (such as the World Ocean Circulation Experiment, the Climate Variability and Predictability Program, the Climate and Cryosphere Program, and the International Program for Antarctic Buoys), the International Geosphere-Biosphere Program (such as the Joint Global Flux

Experiment, and the Global Ocean Ecosystem Dynamics Program) and on the Intergovernmental Panel on Climate Change.

In the recent International Polar Year (IPY 2007–08) an Australian scientist held the position of co-chair of the IPY; Australian scientists played leadership roles in five IPY programs and were the lead coordinators of others. The programs spanned Antarctica's climate, its sea ice, solar influences on atmospheric processes, introduced organisms and marine biodiversity. Some contributed to existing, ongoing international research activities: 'Aliens in Antarctica' and 'Census of Antarctic Marine Life' were designed *de novo* for the IPY. All have produced scientific reports, special volumes of journals and many papers, and have created valuable baseline data for further research. They have done much to maintain Australia's reputation for leadership in Antarctic research.[9]

Australian contributions to Antarctic science

High-latitude climate science

As already noted, the IGY saw the first steps taken by Australia to study Antarctica's ice sheet. Data have been collected on the rate of ice flow, changes in ice thickness and other parameters on oversnow traverses, and an array of automatic weather stations has been established in East Antarctica. Many of the stations have continued to operate unattended and have provided weather data for over 20 years. In addition, some 5000 kilometres of coastal perimeter have been surveyed. Fifty years of data are showing that the East Antarctic ice sheet is in slight imbalance, with less flowing away from the continent than is being added as snow. The total imbalance of the East Antarctic ice sheet is about 38 cubic kilometres annually, equal to an annual drop in sea level of 0.1 mm. Data such as these on ice sheets and on the mechanics of ice deformation, which were introduced into the program in the 1970s, are important for models of future climates. The 4th Assessment Report of the Intergovernmental Panel on Climate Change noted that the role of the great ice sheets is the largest unknown element in the estimation of future sea-level rise. In the early days data were obtained by scientists in the field, but today the emphasis is shifting towards remote sensing, using satellites with a far wider coverage than can be achieved by people on the ground. There are many examples in the scientific literature of pioneering work conducted four decades ago linking to contemporary satellite observations of Antarctic change – and nowhere is this more topical than in the area of sea-level rise. Governments around the world are struggling to understand and quantify the risk to their coastal developments and port infrastructure.

Drilling an ice core at Law Dome, a small ice cap near Casey Station, in December 2008. Ice cores from this expedition are currently being analysed to obtain detailed information about past climates in the region and links between Antarctic and Australian climates. Courtesy Joel Pedro, Australian Antarctic Division

Exterior view of the Australian ice-core drilling camp at Law Dome, following a week-long blizzard in December 2008. A group of seven spent a month at the site collecting detailed environmental records of changes in atmospheric chemistry during the past several hundred years. Courtesy Joel Pedro, Australian Antarctic Division

Along with this long-term research into ice sheets, the last 15 years or so have seen Australia develop a strong program in understanding the role of sea ice in the climate story, as well as in the biology of the Southern Ocean's food chain. Australia's work is central to the validation of international satellite-based instruments measuring parameters such as the extent of sea-ice cover, the ice thickness, the depth of snow cover, and the ice's temperature, albedo (ability to reflect heat back into space) and drift rate.

Australia started its ice-core research in the late 1960s, although it was almost two decades before this research found its place in studies leading to a reconstruction of ancient climates. Ice cores taken from Law Dome are of international significance because they come from a location where precipitation rates are very high, providing a detailed and fine-scale overview of the past 80,000 years. Cores from elsewhere in Antarctica provide low-resolution overviews of almost 800,000 years. Australia's cores fill a crucial place in the analysis of Earth's climate in the recent past.

Research into the Southern Ocean's central role in Earth's climate system has provided observational support for a new conceptual model of the ocean's dynamics, in which three-dimensional ocean circulation, eddy fluxes, water-mass conversion, wind forcing and topographic interactions are intimately linked. The rate at which water is transferred from the surface to the deep ocean determines how much heat and carbon dioxide the ocean can store, and thus influences the rate and magnitude of climate change. This process links ice research with oceanography. As temperatures drop, sea ice forms on the surface of the ocean and releases a dense brine that sinks to the ocean floor, followed by more as the sea ice thickens. As this dense, saltier water spills over the edge of the continental shelf it moves away from Antarctica, transporting oxygen and nutrients far into the northern hemisphere and driving the so-called conveyor belt of water movement around the Earth. Australian research conducted along standard transects at repeated intervals is showing that these deep-water masses are becoming warmer and less salty more rapidly in Antarctica than elsewhere, which is consistent with the pattern of global warming predicted by climate models.

Because of its early start in scientific research in Antarctica, Australia has collected one of the longest continuous weather records of any nation there, a record which is today accessed by scientists around the world through the World Meteorological Organization. These data are used in global and regional numerical weather prediction systems and are of immediate and practical value to operators of aircraft and ships, particularly in East Antarctica, the region where Australia has focused its forecasting efforts. Early international collaborative work on the measurement of atmospheric ozone concentrations, initiated by Phillip Law and others during the IGY of 1957–58, led to the subsequent discovery by British scientists at Faraday Station (now run by Ukraine and renamed Vernadsky) of the thinning of the ozone layer. This observation eventually enabled the introduction of the Montreal Protocol banning the use of chemicals that destroy atmospheric ozone.

Convention on the Conservation of Antarctic Marine Living Resources (CCAMLR)

Australia has had a major involvement in science underpinning the work of CCAMLR, including key roles in its scientific committee and scientific working groups. This research work has evolved as Australia's interests have broadened with the development of active Australian fisheries within the CCAMLR area in the mid-1990s. In addition, Australia's scientific contributions have been influential in the implementation of CCAMLR's ecosystem approach to management and of the precautionary approach.[10] Australia was at the forefront of ensuring that CCAMLR maintained its commitment to these principles, noting concern at CCAMLR IV that 'the directions being taken within the Commission are diverging from the fundamental principles upon which the Convention ... is based'.[11] As Constable has noted, the development of a precautionary approach to the krill fishery was a major achievement and borrowed a number of principles from approaches developed in the IWC in the early 1980s.[12]

Australian scientists have been active in developing models to guide decisions within CCAMLR. An early contribution by W K de la Mare provided a base for a 'krill model', later adapted and extended to model fish stock.[13] This modelling provides support to CCAMLR's decision making in Patagonian toothfish and mackerel icefish fisheries.[14]

These scientific commitments have been supported by institutional developments. The Antarctic Marine Living Resources Program, established in the Australian Antarctic Division in 1999 and now known as the Southern Ocean Ecosystems Program, has a specific aim to support research relevant to CCAMLR.

Committee for Environmental Protection

Australia has been an active member of the Committee for Environmental Protection (CEP) since its formation under Article 11 of the Environmental Protocol. The Committee first met in 1998 and has developed into a key institution. Australia held the chair between 2003 and 2006 and currently holds the vice-chair. The Committee's role is to provide advice to the ATCM on matters concerning the implementation of the Protocol's six annexes. It does so by addressing the state of the Antarctic environment and considering 'the need for scientific research, including environmental monitoring, related to the implementation of this Protocol'.[15] The Committee is also responsible for assessing measures developed under the Protocol and evaluating environmental impact assessment procedures. While science is involved in the implementation of at least five of the annexes, science also contributes to debates about how environmental issues should be approached. The Committee is now increasingly working with the Scientific Committee on Antarctic Research and CCAMLR to provide the best possible advice.

In the mid-1990s Australia was the first country to establish a research program on the scientific aspects of human impact in Antarctica. Early work focused on human interactions with penguins and seals, establishing guidelines for safe approach distances, and on the biological consequences of rubbish-dump run-off into coastal marine habitats. Recently the CEP has identified a list of issues which it wants to address. One of the first is the role of introduced species – a field in which Australia offers leadership. The 'Aliens in Antarctica' program of the 2007–08 International Polar Year focused on compiling an inventory of introduced species accidentally carried into Antarctica in the clothing and belongings of tourists and government researchers, and assessing the dimensions of the threat to native species. The study was based on the pioneering work of Frenot and others, which identified a range of biological threats from a number of groups of organisms.[16] The onset and progress of climate change makes the less climatically extreme areas of Antarctica increasingly vulnerable to invasive species. The CEP is developing a non-native species manual, to be completed in 2015, in which Australia's research will figure.

A second priority is climate change, in which Australia has a high international reputation, and a further priority is marine spatial protection and management in collaboration with CCAMLR. An area of lower priority for the Committee, in which Australian science is developing high international visibility, is how to clean up hydrocarbon and other contaminants left behind in sites of past activity. Australia argued that this issue be given the highest priority but was unable to achieve consensus on the ranking because the issue is not faced by all parties, and the Council of Managers of National Antarctic Programs already has processes underway to address the issue. When Annex VI (Liability) comes into force, and national Antarctic programs are forced to evaluate the costs of cleaning up abandoned work sites, Australia's timely investment in this area of science will reveal its true importance.

International Whaling Commission

Australia has made a longstanding contribution to the work of the International Whaling Commission's scientific committee. In the 1980s work by W K de la Mare was instrumental in reforming the Commission's management procedure, providing a scientifically rigorous critique of current practice and ensuring that increased work was undertaken on ecosystem interactions. This work was critical to the development of the Commission's revised management procedure, which formed the basis of the revised management scheme.[17] Work on ecosystem interaction and modelling presented within the International Whaling Commission made an important contribution to CCAMLR's early work (see chapter 7).

The Australian Government's long-standing and bipartisan commitment to banning commercial whaling has resulted in a research program that addresses whale population dynamics and ecosystem interactions. The Australian Marine Mammal Centre, based at the AAD's Science Branch, coordinates this non-lethal research.

Agreement on the Conservation of Albatrosses and Petrels

Australian science includes work on seabird taxonomy and population studies. This has an emphasis on five albatross species (wandering, black-browed, shy, light-mantled sooty and grey-headed) that have breeding colonies on Macquarie and Heard islands, as well as on rocks and islands within mainland Australia's Exclusive Economic Zone. Australian scientists were instrumental, along with colleagues in the United Kingdom, South Africa and New Zealand, in initiating action to address the incidental catch of seabirds in long-line fishing operations. Initial research, working from observations recorded in catch records from Japanese pelagic long-line tuna fishing within Australian waters, provided an estimate of the incidental or by-catch of albatrosses in fishing operations. Australia presented a paper to the Scientific Committee of CCAMLR in 1990 on albatross mortality associated with long-line tuna fisheries. Although the data were obtained from outside the convention area, it was estimated that 44,000 albatrosses were killed annually.[18]

Australian research with Japanese long-line pelagic tuna fishing vessels also provided data on effects of mitigation methods, including the use of 'bird poles' and streamers to inhibit interactions between seabirds and the setting of baited hooks. The significant 85 per cent decline in the seabird catch rate when these devices were used was presented to the scientific committee of CCAMLR along with evidence of the economic benefits.[19] This contributed to the development of conservation measures mandating use of mitigation methods within the CCAMLR area.

AAD research has also been directed at practical measures to address seabird by-catch. This has included pioneering programs (in collaboration with the fishing industry) on the sink rates of different types of lines, experiments with weighted fishing lines, and the use of line-setting tubes and 'brickle curtains' (a form of bird-exclusion device used when hauling in the catch) on line hauling. This research, funded by the Pew Conservation Trust and internationally recognised, is providing workable solutions to the seabird problem. Australian scientists have also continued to provide support to the technical advisory committee of the Agreement on the Conservation of Albatrosses and Petrels.

Future development of Australia's Antarctic science program

Australia's Antarctic science program is directed by an evolving series of strategic plans, each identifying those aspects of high-latitude science needed to support Australia's positions in the Antarctic Treaty and its associated instruments and the broader environmental agenda set by the Australian Government. *How* our science is done will surely change, and perhaps quite rapidly, with the advance of technology.

In his reflection on the 50th anniversary of ANARE in 1997, scientist John Heap (formerly of the UK Foreign and Commonwealth Office) addressed the question bedevilling all nations running Antarctic research programs – do logistics drive science, or does science drive logistics?[20] Heap noted the nub of the riddle – that governments have already invested great sums of money in fixed sites in Antarctica and, as a consequence, logistics drive science. Recent trends, however, indicate that this stranglehold might be weakening and thus opening opportunities for new science in locations previously unattainable. Although ships are relatively free to work wherever needed in the Southern Ocean, provided they are not too close to uncharted coasts, continental-based science has considerable logistical challenges. The investment by Australia in fixed-wing aircraft for Antarctic use is likely to greatly extend the research possibilities. Complex and important physical processes are occurring high on the plateau about which we have only the slimmest of knowledge. But even with light and manoeuvrable aircraft the costs of supporting deep-field research are comparable to the expense of maintaining a research vessel in the Southern Ocean. Until and unless very considerable recurrent expenses can be saved through the reduction of fixed infrastructure, Australia's ability to operate where the scientific questions can be best studied will remain fettered.

We can expect to see the development of remote-sensing technology replacing and supporting field observations. Satellites, which began to be used to monitor Antarctica only a little over 30 years ago, will increasingly replace people on the ice. Already it is abundantly clear that satellite technology is allowing observations to be made across vast swathes of Antarctica with sensors that can accurately measure surface elevation, temperature and roughness, sea-ice extent and concentration, and the movement of icebergs. Instruments such as Landsat and the Ice, Cloud and Land Elevation Satellite have revolutionised our understanding of how Antarctica is responding to climate change, but they depend upon the presence of light to illuminate the surface. Satellites carrying instruments that emit radar beams, such as the new synthetic-aperture radars, are able to penetrate through clouds and provide high-resolution images of the land below. The world's interest in climate change is encouraging the deployment of an expanding array of satellite-borne sensors to monitor the height, temperature and condition of the ice sheet, ice shelves and sea ice. For example, the European Space Agency's Earth Observation satellites provide coordinated observations of both the Arctic and the Antarctic. The Global Interagency IPY Polar Snapshot Year project during the recent International Polar Year pulled together the huge amount of data coming from a range of satellites. The European Space Agency's CryoSat-2 satellite enables mapping of the change in thickness of Arctic, Greenland and Antarctic ice – essential information in the climate change debate.

Improved microelectronic devices which can be affixed to seals and penguins are even now enabling significant advances in understanding ocean currents and water properties. Devices known as 'crittercams' – small video cameras mounted on the heads of seals – allow detailed examination of seal diet and hunting behaviour, with only minimal interference when the apparatus is fitted and retrieved. New sensors will enable additional variables to be observed, such as the pattern of patchiness of biological productivity in relation to seal feeding locations. The recent history of the electronics industry leads to the view that such devices will become ever tinier, perhaps eventually being fitted to small fish and even invertebrate species.

The next few decades will see the emergence of scientific programs requiring increased collaboration and the sharing of logistics among research teams and national programs. While issues of sovereignty and the politics of Antarctica are never far away, the world has woken up to the fact that Antarctica is no longer a remote, far-away place visited only by adventurers and explorers, but is very much the canary in the global coal-mine and also the powerhouse behind much of the world's weather and ocean quality. Australia's long and impressive record of scientific research in Antarctica has helped to establish the basis for future work.

Notes

[1]   We are grateful to Drs Gwen Fenton and Andie Smithies of the Australian Antarctic Division for assistance with this chapter.
[2]   Bowden (1997) 14.
[3]   Bowden (1997) 177.
[4]   Herr and Hall (1989).
[5]   Green (2002).
[6]   Dastidar and Ramachandran (2008).
[7]   Stoddart (2008).
[8]   Dastidar and Persson (2005), Dastidar and Ramachandran (2008). Other Australian institutions included in the listing are the CSIRO (rank 13), the University of Melbourne (rank 18), the Antarctic Cooperative Research Centre (rank 23), the Australian National University (rank 33) and Macquarie University (rank 48).
[9]   Australian Antarctic Division (2009).
[10]   Constable et al. (2000), Constable (2001).
[11]   Orrego Vincuña (1991) 25.

[12]   Constable (2001) 76.
[13]   Beddington and de la Mare (1985), de la Mare (1987), Constable and de la Mare (1996).
[14]   Constable (2001).
[15]   Madrid Protocol Article 12(k).
[16]   Frenot et al. (2005).
[17]   Haward and Vince (2008).
[18]   Hall (2007) 121.
[19]   Hall and Haward (2001).
[20]   Marchant et al. (2002).

7

Managing marine living resources, the 1970s–1990s

Stuart Kaye, Marcus Haward and Rob Hall

The Southern Ocean ecosystem has distinctive characteristics that influence choices about its conservation. Much of it depends on krill, and its waters are affected by some of the most difficult weather conditions anywhere and are influenced by the Antarctic Convergence – producing a region unlike any other on the planet.[1] All of this presents significant challenges to resource management, challenges that are matched only by the difficulties of ensuring compliance with agreed regimes in such remote and forbidding locations. Analysis of the development of Antarctic marine living resources regimes from the 1970s through to the present, and Australia's contribution to them, reveals a concerted focus on conservation, and a commitment to redressing the legacies of past overexploitation.

Early efforts

The history of overexploitation in the Southern Ocean is well known (see chapter 10). Various species of fur seals were hunted intensively in the first half of the nineteenth century. Beginning in the early twentieth century, exploitation of whales in Antarctic waters increased until it reached a highpoint in the two decades immediately before World War II. The increasing targeting of finfish and krill from the 1960s was viewed with concern, given the failure to constrain catches of whales.[2] It was realised that a failure to regulate the harvesting of krill, in particular – the cornerstone of the entire Antarctic marine ecosystem – could have major consequences. The vulnerability of the marine life of the Southern Ocean had already been attested by the destruction of whales and seals in the sub-Antarctic.[3]

There was very little in the Antarctic Treaty itself that dealt with living resource management, with the exception of Article IX(1)(f), which provided for measures on the 'preservation and conservation of living resources in Antarctica'.[4] This absence was in part covered by Article VI of the Treaty, which provided that high seas rights within the waters of the Treaty Area would not be prejudiced. Given that the Treaty was concluded before the advent of the concept of the exclusive economic zone in international law, high seas rights essentially meant fishing rights, as whaling was by then regulated under the International Convention for the Regulation of Whaling (ICRW) and the continental shelf was provided for under the 1958 Convention on the Continental Shelf.[5] In such a situation, the states that negotiated the Treaty did not need to address issues of living resource management. It was also recognised at the Antarctic Conference in Washington in 1959 that consensus on this topic would be hard to achieve (see chapter 3).

Despite this initial reluctance, a complex set of instruments, built upon the original political compromise reached in the Antarctic Treaty and including conventions and recommendations arising from Antarctic Treaty Consultative Meetings (ATCMs), has grown up with the aim of protecting the marine environment, regulating human activities in Antarctica and conserving marine living resources.

This process began in Brussels with the adoption at ATCM III in 1964 of the Agreed Measures.[6] The Measures were intended to provide the most basic environmental protection of plants and animals within the Treaty Area (that is, south of 60° S). They were to be monitored and enforced by each state party for its own nationals, and were never intended to function as a regulatory regime for marine living resources.

To this point Australia's interest in the Southern Ocean's living resources was dealt with adequately by the ICRW – Australians were not interested in fishing or sealing, but were actively whaling. Nevertheless, Australia had taken the view that fishing was a high seas right protected by Article VI of the Treaty. As a claimant, it optimistically hoped for a special recognition by others fishing in the waters off the AAT. In Australia's mind, freedom to exploit resources was not a corollary of the freedom to conduct science.

In 1972, the Antarctic Treaty Consultative Parties (ATCPs) concluded the Convention for the Conservation of Antarctic Seals (CCAS) in London.[7] This was a specialised convention that dealt solely with certain species of seal found in the Treaty area and explicitly preserved the vital compromise contained in Article IV.[8] The convention provides for a regulatory regime, administered on a national basis by state parties, to restrict seal harvesting to specified limits set out in its Annex. CCAS was an important step towards increasing marine living resource protection within the Antarctic Treaty System (ATS). It applied to the ocean and thus extended resource management and conservation beyond the terrestrial focus of the Agreed Measures. It is important to note that there has been virtually no interest on the part of the ATCPs, or any other state for that matter, in harvesting Antarctic seals on a commercial basis. Given the lack of any strong international demand for fur, such exploitation is unlikely to recommence in the foreseeable future.[9]

Conserving marine living resources in Antarctica

By the time the Agreed Measures entered into force (on 1 November 1982), the Convention on the Conservation of Antarctic Marine Living Resources (CCAMLR) had also entered into force (on 7 April 1982), and efforts were advancing towards more substantial progress in marine living resource management.[10]

The development and operation of what was to become the marine living resources regime has been discussed by a number of commentators.[11] Concerns over the impact on the Antarctic ecosystem of an unregulated krill fishery by heavily subsidised Eastern bloc fleets were first raised in the mid-1970s. Krill, small shrimp-like crustaceans, are critical elements in the food chain within the Southern Ocean. Krill fishing began in the early 1970s and grew steadily, with a catch of 448 266 tonnes recorded in 1980–81.[12] These concerns over the potential unregulated harvesting of krill were the impetus for the negotiations over Antarctic marine living resources. The Scientific Committee on Antarctic Research (SCAR) held a conference on the living resources of the Southern Ocean at Woods Hole Oceanographic Institution, Massachusetts, in 1976, which led to the creation of BIO-MASS, the Biological Investigation of Marine Antarctic Systems and Stocks. The Scientific Committee on Oceanography (SCOR) established a group of specialists on the living resources of the Southern Ocean that became the planning group for BIOMASS.

BIOMASS was a particularly important initiative. It was the first large-scale multinational research program focusing on the marine ecosystems and resources of the Southern Ocean, and at the time the largest study of its type ever carried out. BIOMASS had direct and significant effects on Australian research efforts in the Southern Ocean and the direction of discussions over these issues by ATCPs and within Antarctic Treaty forums. Many of the scientists who took part in BIOMASS became integrally involved in the deliberations within the ATCM over management of marine living resources within the Treaty Area. The involvement of scientists resulted in the development of the innovative multi-species ecosystem approach to management, pioneered in what became the Convention on the Conservation of Antarctic Marine Living Resources (CCAMLR), which also established a core principle of rational use that balanced resource conservation with exploitation.

As discussed in more detail in chapter 12, Australian politicians, scientists and diplomats had a major role in ensuring that the convention was satisfactorily concluded and that CCAMLR became an integral part of the ATS. In particular, Australia hosted the first and final sessions of the Special Antarctic Treaty Consultative Meeting (SATCM) and also its diplomatic conference, which were tasked with establishing a definitive conservation regime. As noted above, the ATCPs had become increasingly drawn to the question of the conservation and management of marine living resources. In the negotiations Australia was firmly in the 'conservation' group (along with the United States and the United Kingdom) – as opposed to the 'fishing' group led by the USSR and Japan. Two decades later, in the late 1990s, Australia developed a fishery around its sub-Antarctic islands (see following). It is important to emphasise that this fishery has been highly controlled and conducted within the framework of CCAMLR Conservation Measures: the management tools established by the convention's Commission.

In addition to its strong commitment to the ecosystem approach embodied in Article II of CCAMLR, and working with other likeminded states to ensure that this provision remained a central plank of the instrument, Australia also worked hard to resolve the challenging sovereignty issues that emerged. Fishing rights were an important issue for claimant states, but there was no prospect of the claimants achieving any exclusive rights to living resources in the waters off their territories. While it was agreed that the convention would include a reference to Article IV of the Antarctic Treaty so as to avoid prejudice to the claimants' interests, the matter of sovereignty was to become even more complicated. Early in the negotiations it was recognised that to provide an effective ecosystem-based approach to management, the boundaries of the regime would need to extend northwards from the Treaty area. This would mean that the CCAMLR area would include sub-Antarctic islands over which the existence of state sovereignty was recognised.

While a number of states, including Australia, had territory within the area proposed for the new convention, France in particular was concerned about the implications of extending the boundary of the convention outside the Antarctic Treaty Area. As a result, the matter of sub-Antarctic islands became a major item in the negotiations. The matter was resolved through the inclusion of the chairman's statement in the Final Act of the diplomatic conference, and thus of CCAMLR, which addressed France's specific concerns – and provided the same opportunities to other states with sub-Antarctic territories. Interestingly,

Australia has never enacted the chairman's statement in relation to the Territory of Heard Island and McDonald Islands, instead implementing domestic law and regulations that may be stronger that the CCAMLR measures. Australian efforts in marine biological research also increased following the establishment of BIOMASS, and continued as such research was needed to support its commitments to CCAMLR's principles of the rational use of resources and the effective management of the Southern Ocean ecosystem. The Australian-chartered supply vessel *Nella Dan* was refitted to support such research, and marine scientific research capability has been a major element of Australia's research program and research budgets from this time (see chapter 6).

CCAMLR was opened for signature on 20 May 1980, and entered into force following ratification by all of the then ATCPs within two years.[13] Its negotiation has been recognised as a major achievement that established path-breaking concepts in the regional management of marine living resources.[14] The most significant ensuing challenge was to implement the ecosystem management concept and to establish the Commission and the Scientific Committee.[15] The slow pace of formulating rules of procedure was an early point of criticism.[16] Significant difficulties were experienced from 1982 to 1987 in the relationship between the Commission and Scientific Committee, and over the role of the latter.[17]

The first meeting of the committee ended in deadlock, with no agreement on its role: Australia, the United States and the United Kingdom argued that it was a consultative body to provide scientific conclusions to the commission, while the USSR saw the members as national representatives.[18] The committee's adoption of procedural rules reinforced consensus as the model of decision making, and by 1987 institutional relationships had been rebuilt, with the commission requesting advice from the committee and the committee requesting guidance from the commission.[19]

The functioning of CCAMLR

CCAMLR has a number of elements that are common to most regional living resource management agreements. It has a headquarters with a secretariat, and Article XIII provides that the headquarters be in Hobart. This location reflects the central role played by Australia in the convention's negotiation. Whereas the venue for Antarctic Treaty meetings is rotated among parties and is not linked to the location of the new secretariat in Buenos Aires, CCAMLR states that unless parties decide otherwise, the meetings of its commission are to be held at the secretariat, and to date this has always been the case. The secretariat in Hobart provides logistical and translation support for these annual commission meetings, as well as acting as a conduit for data exchange and management and assisting in the coordination of research programs. It also provides a contact point for many other international organisations, including bodies engaged in marine living resource management.[20]

The CCAMLR Commission is the principal decision-making body under the convention. As with other Antarctic instruments, full membership rights are vested in the original States Parties, or to acceding parties which have research or fishing interests in the Southern Ocean.[21] Similarly, decision making is by consensus, effectively giving any party a veto.[22] The commission has a broad range of powers, which include formulating and revising conservation measures – the principal means by which it manages the Southern Ocean ecosystem. As with other marine living resource agreements, the measures that can be implemented are quite varied and wide-ranging, as provided in Article IX(2), and include those which relate to the impact upon the ecosystem as a whole.[23]

In establishing a scientific committee, the parties intended to create a permanent scientific consultancy for the commission to assist it in the complex task of implementing an ecosystem management approach.

The committee provides the technical expertise and data required to analyse and monitor the state of the ecosystem which CCAMLR is obliged to protect from harm. Its central importance can be seen in the fact that the commission must publish and 'take full account' of its advice and recommendations.[24] The convention also encourages participation of non-governmental organisations and intergovernmental organisations – an unusual feature at the time it was negotiated; the resulting network of relationships has already been referred to. There is provision for observers and specialists from these other organisations to be present at CCAMLR meetings, and their involvement reflects the work of parties such as Australia and the United States in addressing criticisms about a lack of engagement of ATS forums with such 'specialised agencies'.[25] This criticism was to continue through the 1990s (see chapter 9).

The approach to the management of living resources adopted within CCAMLR reinforces the principal desire of the ATCPs to ensure that any exploitation of Antarctic marine living resources would only take place in a sustainable fashion, following what would be later termed the 'precautionary approach' to ensure the protection of the Antarctic environment. This saw the ATCPs adopt a management strategy based on the ecosystem, rather than using the recently adopted maximum sustainable yield approach used in the Law of the Sea Convention or single species regulation.[26] This policy was evident even before formal negotiations for CCAMLR commenced, being reflected in interim guidelines for Antarctic marine living resource conservation.[27] Subsequent negotiation did not remove this emphasis upon a broad ecosystem-based approach, and it is embedded in the provisions of the Convention.[28] Even the CCAMLR Area, 'the largest targeted conservation area on Earth', reflects this strategy.[29]

Similarly, rather than focus on certain species of possible commercial or regulatory interest, CCAMLR explicitly defines the subject of its regulation, the Antarctic marine ecosystem, in an expansive fashion: 'The Antarctic marine ecosystem means the complex of relationships of Antarctic marine living resources with each other and with their physical environment'.[30] However, although the intention is to deal with the ecosystem as a whole, the convention also provides that nothing in it is to derogate from either the Convention for the Conservation of Antarctic Seals or the International Convention for the Regulation of Whaling.[31] Although whales and seals are important parts of the Antarctic ecosystem, CCAMLR has had no direct role in their management.

Australia, CCAMLR and illegal, unreported and unregulated fishing

In the mid to late 1990s CCAMLR members noted with increasing concern the amount of fishing activity undertaken by vessels of nonmember states. What was initially termed 'illegal' or 'irregular' fishing within the CCAMLR area was recognised as posing significant management challenges for the Commission, particularly in relation to the catch of high value Patagonian and Antarctic toothfish *(Dissostichus* species).[32] Toothfish species have been subject to increasing fishing effort from the 1990s, as the market value of the fishery and fishing techniques improved.[33] It is recognised that vessels linked to CCAMLR member states undertake much of this illegal fishing. These vessels may also use a flag of convenience or complex ownership structures that mask the beneficial owner.[34]

Edeson notes that 'the terminology "Illegal, Unreported and Unregulated [IUU] Fishing" is generally accepted as having been initiated in the context of CCAMLR ... and in particular at its sixteenth session' in 1997, where this was one of the major topics discussed.[35] A number of parties urged action, with Australia noting the need for states to ratify the UN Fish Stocks Agreement.[36] Norway commented that the report of the scientific committee gave 'an alarming picture, in particular with regard to the drastic decimation of the stocks of the Patagonian toothfish and the threatening of the collapse of seabird populations killed off as by-catch'.[37] Australia, the Meeting Report recorded:

> seeks urgent, integrated and coordinated action by all CCAMLR nations to address the issue of illegal fishing, which is driven by the high eco-

nomic value of the fish and is doing so much damage to the Southern Ocean ecosystem and to the legitimate interests of legal fishers working in accordance with CCAMLR requirements.[38]

The following decade saw concerted effort by the Commission, on many occasions responding to Australian initiatives, to introduce measures designed to limit the effects of IUU fishing. Australia's involvement was in equal part influenced by the determination to defend the integrity of CCAMLR and by the direct challenge to Australian interests as the illegal fishing fleet moved eastwards across the Indian Ocean to embrace Australia's Heard Island. Within CCAMLR Australia vigorously advanced measures such as the *Dissostichus* Catch Documentation Scheme, the centralised vessel monitoring system and enhanced use of inspection procedures. Domestically, Australia responded with on-the-water patrols, concentrated on the waters around Heard Island, using Defence vessels and chartered Customs vessels to apprehend illegal fishers with spectacular success. Bilaterally, Australia negotiated with France the 2003 Agreement with the Government of the French Republic on Cooperation in the Maritime Areas adjacent to the French Southern and Antarctic Territories (TAAF), Heard Island and the McDonald Islands.

In addition to the decisions made in the CCAMLR Commission, Australia (with support from Norway) raised the problem of IUU fishing at the UN Food and Agriculture Organization's Committee on Fisheries meeting in February 1999.[39] Following a series of negotiations, the Committee on Fisheries approved by consensus the International Plan of Action on 2 March 2001, and urged all members to implement it effectively. The Australian Government, instrumental in fostering this initiative, welcomed the development of the plan of action, noting that it complemented other international plans of action in helping to 'promote more responsible and accountable world fisheries practices'.[40]

Australia's commitment to addressing problems of IUU fishing for toothfish did, however, lead to tensions within CCAMLR. Australia proposed the listing of toothfish on Appendix II of the Convention on International Trade in Endangered Species of Wild Flora and Fauna (CITES) at the 12th Conference of Parties to CITES held in Santiago, Chile in November 2002. Such listing was seen by Australia as strengthening CCAMLR's catch documentation and trade monitoring arrangements and helping to close loopholes related to claims of 'out of area' catches and illegal, unreported and unregulated fishing.[41] Non-governmental organisations and the Australian and Chilean fishing industries supported this initiative.[42] But Australia's proposal attracted broad opposition at CCAMLR XXI – recorded in 75 paragraphs – and only New Zealand supported it.[43] The strength of this criticism surprised Australian delegates. The proposal also attracted strong opposition at the CITES 12th Conference of Parties from Norway and Japan, states which, while critical of Australian actions in seeking CITES listing, had supported CCAMLR's program against illegal, unreported and unregulated fishing.

More recently Australia has worked with other CCAMLR parties in improving measures on port state control, implementing electronic catch documentation and introducing a Measure on control of nationals involved in IUU fishing. Australia continues to take a leading role in efforts to deter and eliminate IUU fishing in the CCAMLR Convention Area.

Conservation of seabirds

As noted above, CCAMLR member states readily recognised the link between fishing and the incidental catches of seabirds, with concomitant impacts on seabird populations. Most southern hemisphere albatross and petrel species range through the CCAMLR area. The issue of incidental mortality associated with fishing operations was first raised at the third meeting of the commission in 1984.[44] The need to collect data on incidental catch was also discussed at both the fourth and fifth meetings of 1985 and 1986. In 1985, the commission agreed that steps should be taken to record and report non-target species caught during fishing operations, and that the Executive Secretary should distribute material on measures developed by members to assess, avoid and mitigate accidental and incidental mortality of Antarctic marine living resources.[45] It was not until 1989, however, that the issue of incidental catch re-emerged on the agenda of the scientific committee. The development of a separate agenda item indicated the increasing attention paid to the issue as a result of the emerging problem and a growing concern with the introduction of long-line fishing in the convention area.

At its eighth meeting the commission asked the scientific committee to evaluate and provide advice on the ways to assess and minimise this mortality.[46] In adopting Resolution 5/VIII, 'the Commission reiterated its concern at the commencement of an unregulated fishery of a type known elsewhere to cause substantial incidental mortality of seabirds'.[47] Incidental catches of albatrosses received considerable attention at the ninth meeting, in 1990. Australia presented a paper to the scientific committee that described albatross mortality associated with long-line tuna fisheries outside the convention area. A conservative estimate of the number killed annually was 44,000.[48] Australian delegates also presented information on Australian–Japanese efforts to reduce the incidental catch of albatrosses through use of 'bird poles' and streamers. The significant decline in catch rate of 88 per cent using these devices was presented to the committee along with the economic benefits of such devices.[49]

The commission agreed that modifications of long-line fishing techniques within the convention area should be implemented. As well as the deployment of bird poles and streamers, these techniques included the use of baits which sink immediately they are immersed in the water, the setting of long-lines at night and the dumping of trash and offal only after long-line operations have ceased. Recommendations were prepared as a draft Conservation Measure, although this was not approved at this meeting of the commission. Some delegations wanted more time to consider technical detail, while others wanted additional measures to be implemented as soon as possible.[50] The delegates did agree, however, that formal adoption of a Conservation Measure would be discussed again at the next meeting.[51]

At the 1991 meeting, the scientific committee noted that, despite requests for detailed information from members on the incidental catch of seabirds from long-lining, this data had not been provided. The committee recorded that incidental mortality had been underreported by a minimum of 33 per cent in 1990–91, and that recommendations agreed in the previous year had not been followed by those under-taking fishing activities in the convention area. As a result, Conservation Measure 29/X required specific action in the conduct of long-line fisheries aimed at minimising such incidental mortality, a measure which remains in modified form today.[52]

Further conservation measures have been developed in more recent years, including the delaying of the opening of fishing seasons until most albatrosses and petrels have finished breeding. Seabird mortality in regulated long-line fisheries in the CCAMLR area has subsequently reduced, and where over 6589 birds were reported killed in 1997, this number had reduced by more than 99 per cent to only 15 birds in 2003. Later CCAMLR reports indicate further reductions, and no albatrosses were reported taken in regulated long-line fisheries in 2006.[53] Of course, despite the effectiveness of these measures, IUU fishing remains a substantial problem in the CCAMLR area.

Work by CCAMLR member states led directly to the development of the Agreement on the Conservation of Albatrosses and Petrels. Australia's offer to initiate meetings was accepted, and 12 'range states' and five international organisations attended a meeting in Hobart in 2000 that agreed on fundamental principles.[54] The Agreement on the Conservation of Albatrosses and Petrels (ACAP) was adopted by consensus in Cape Town in 2001 and the convention entered into force on 1 February 2004. Its secretariat is in Hobart.

The agreement's conservation measures apply the precautionary approach, and it recognises that many other international instruments contain measures that are or can be directed to the conservation of albatross and petrel species.[55] Although ACAP has achieved much, improving the conservation status of albatrosses and petrels has been impeded by the absence of data on the by-catch of these species. To address this issue, the parties have recently signed a number of memorandums of understanding with relevant high seas fisheries management organisations, including

CCAMLR, to facilitate access to such data and collaboration in areas that are relevant to both their conservation efforts.

***

The development of instruments and regimes to manage marine living resources saw a significant broadening of the Antarctic Treaty arrangements. CCAMLR's emphasis on an ecosystem-based approach was very different from those underlying other fisheries or marine resource conventions of the time, and is still distinctive.[56] The strength of such an approach is that harvesting of commercial stocks cannot be allowed to endanger the ecological relationships between all fauna in the CCAMLR Area. The protection of non-commercial species was the intention from the outset of negotiations.[57] The vulnerability of the Antarctic food chain, particularly with its reliance upon krill as a staple, was a real concern during the negotiations, and the ecosystem approach was used specifically as a counter to this vulnerability.[58]

Australia contributed in important ways to the initiation of CCAMLR and to maintaining the integrity of the fundamental provisions of the ecosystem approach as embodied in Article II. As host nation of the secretariat and depositary state, it has continued to support other states acceding to the instrument and becoming members of the Commission. Australia's well-resourced Antarctic marine science program has allowed it to meet its own policy objectives and CCAMLR's needs for a sound basis for its decisions and to help drive initiatives in tackling IUU fishing and conserving seabirds. Australia's engagement in CCAMLR has been positive and sustained, although at times it has proposed initiatives such as the listing of toothfish by CITES that have not gained the support of other parties. In seeking to advance issues in CCAMLR, Australia has retained its commitment to effective management of the resources of the Southern Ocean.

Notes

[1]   The Antarctic Convergence (now called the Antarctic Polar Front) is that zone where cold Antarctic waters are subducted beneath warmer more northerly waters. This convergence is up to 80 kilometres wide, and forms a physical and biological oceanographic boundary that separates Antarctic and sub-Antarctic from more temperate waters.
[2]   Chittleborough (1984) 144.
[3]   Fogg (1992) 38–40. For 1970s Russian and Japanese fishing practices, see Kock (1992) 183–89.
[4]   402 United Nations Treaty Series 71.
[5]   161 United Nations Treaty Series 72.

258

[6]   Agreed Measures for the Conservation of
       Antarctic Fauna and Flora: reprinted in Bush
       (1982) vol1, 146–69.
[7]   1080 United Nations Treaty Series 175.
[8]   The species protected are the southern elephant
       seal *Mirounga leonina,* leopard seal *Hydrurga
       leptonyx,* Weddell seal *Leptonychotes weddellii,*
       crabeater seal *Lobodon carcinophagus,* Ross
       seal *Ommatophoca rossii,* and the southern fur
       seals, *Arctocephalus* species. The content and
       operation of the CCAS have been examined
       separately by Rothwell and Joyner: Rothwell
       (1996) 121–23; Joyner (1998) 120–22.
[9]   Note, however, reports in 1988 that the USSR
       had engaged in commercial sealing operations.
       At the review of the operation of the Convention
       for the Conservation of Antarctic Seals in
       September 1988, it was found there was insuf-
       ficient evidence to substantiate the claims: see
       Marchal (1989) 142; Rothwell (1995).
[10]   Negotiation of a marine living resource conven-
       tion began in 1977, after having been explored
       at the 1975 ATCM-VIII in Oslo: see Bush
       (1982) vol1, 348–51; see also Resolution VIII-
       10: Bush (1982) vol1, 323–24.
[11]   For example see Barnes (1982); Howard
       (1989); Powell (1990); Orrego Vicuña (1991);
       Stokke (1996); Kaye, Rothwell and Haward
       (2001); Herr (2001).
[12]   Chittleborough (1984) 147.

[13]   [1982] Australian Treaty Series No 9; CCAMLR entered into force on 7 April 1982.

[14]   Powell (1990); Orrego Vicuña (1991).

[15]   Powell (1990).

[16]   Howard (1989); Orrego Vicuña (1991).

[17]   Howard (1989).

[18]   Orrego Vicuña (1991) 30–31.

[19]   Orrego Vicuña (1991 32–33.

[20]   Relationships exist with the Food and Agriculture Organization, the Commission for the Conservation of Southern Bluefin Tuna, the Indian Ocean Tuna Commission, the Scientific Committee on Antarctic Research, the Scientific Committee on Oceanic Research, the Western and Central Pacific Fisheries Commission, the Advisory Committee on Albatrosses and Petrels and the International Whaling Commission. The Scientific Committee also has a close relationship with the Committee for Environmental Protection established under the Madrid Protocol; [1994] ATS No.16; [1996] ATS No.20

[21]   CCAMLR, Article VII. Article VII(2)(c) also permits membership of regional economic integration organisations – with what became the European Union firmly in mind. To date the EU is the only member of this type.

[22]   Joyner (1985).

[23]   CCAMLR, Article IX(2)(i).

[24]   CCAMLR, Article IX(4).

[25]   CCAMLR, Article XXIII(4). The provision was utilised when ASOC, an umbrella environmental NGO, was granted observer status in 1988.

[26]   Fogg (1992) 239.

[27]   Recommendation IX-2(2), 19 September 1977. Reprinted in Bush (1982) vol1, 349

[28]   Barnes (1982) 242–60.

[29]   Joyner (1998) 123. Unlike the arbitrary political boundary of the Treaty Area (Article VI), the CCAMLR Area is defined in relation to the Antarctic Convergence, a boundary which reflects the ecological realities of the range and habitats of creatures in the Southern Ocean, since almost no creatures cross it except migratory whales.

[30]   CCAMLR, Article I(3); 'Antarctic marine living resources' are defined in CCAMLR, Article I(2).

[31]   CCAMLR, Article VI; see Edwards and Heap (1981).

[32]   CCAMLR (1996) Annex 6: 163–64.

[33]   Haward (2004).

[34]   Haward (2004).

[35]   Edeson (1999) 94. Edeson comments that 'this initiative almost certainly has the ugliest acronym in the area of fisheries and probably beyond it'. Molenaar (2000, 502) comments that 'the term IUU fishing has obviously been preferred above something like "FOC Fishing"'.

[36]   CCAMLR (1997) 12.

[37]   CCAMLR (1997) 8.

[38]   CCAMLR (1997) 12.

[39]   Australia's position on illegal, unreported and unregulated fishing and its actions in supporting the development of the International Plan of Action to Deter, Prevent and Eliminate Illegal, Unreported and Unregulated Fishing (IPOA-IUU) can be seen as part of a continuum in its work on high seas fisheries. Australia's commitment to 'achieving practical outcomes and in securing a widely accepted agreement from ... negotiations' at the UN Conference on Straddling Fish Stocks and Highly Migratory Fish Stocks continued through Australia's work on illegal, unreported and unregulated fishing. See Bergin and Haward (1995).

[40]   *Australian Maritime Digest,* no 90, 1 April 2001.

[41]   Antarctic and Southern Ocean Coalition (ASOC) (2002). One argument in favour of CITES from the viewpoint of its supporters was the initiative's broad reach – with 160 States Parties, as opposed to CCAMLR's then 24 members.

[42]   ASOC argued that as CITES can designate CCAMLR as the management and/or scientific authority, CCAMLR would remain 'the appropriate body for management of toothfish'.

[43]   CCAMLR (2002); see also *Mercury* (Hobart) 30 October 2002, 18.

[44]   United States of America (1984) 4.

[45]   CCAMLR (1985) 7.

[46]   CCAMLR (1989) 5.

[47]   CCAMLR (1989) 28.

[48]   Hall (2007).

[49]   CCAMLR (1990) 16.

[50]   CCAMLR (1990) 16–17.

[51]   Hall (2007) 121.

[52]   Hall (2007) 121 – 22.

[53]   CCAMLR (2006) 22.

[54]   ACAP defines a range state as 'any State that exercises jurisdiction over any part of the range of albatrosses or petrels, or a State, flagged vessels of which are engaged outside its national jurisdictional limits in taking, or which have the potential to take, albatrosses and petrels.' Art I(2)(p).

[55]   ACAP Article II(1) and Article II(3).

[56]   Burke noted in 1994 that CCAMLR remained the only marine living resource convention based on an ecosystem management approach: Burke (1994) 114; see also Belsky (1985) at 761–62; note that such an approach is used in UNESCO's *Man and the Biosphere Programme:* Howard (1989), 113.

[57]   Bush (1982) 350.

[58]   Edwards and Heap (1981) 355–56.

8

Mapping

Shirley V Scott[1]

Mapping and geodesy have been integral to international scientific and political cooperation during the life of the Antarctic Treaty System (ATS). The contributions of Australian officials at Antarctic Treaty Consultative Meetings have been paralleled by those of Australian cartographers and geographers in the succession of Scientific Committee on Antarctic Research (SCAR) bodies devoted to mapping and geodesy. While mapping is neither pure science nor pure politics it has important implications for both. This chapter situates Australian leadership in Antarctic mapping and geodesy at the intersection of Antarctic politics, history, science and law. It begins before the signing of the Antarctic Treaty because Australia's participation in the ATS was grounded in its pre-existing territorial claim, for which maps provided essential support. But its chief focus is on the 1950s and 1960s, a period in which Australians actively promoted international cooperation on Antarctic mapping while at the same time ensuring that such work would not be detrimental to territorial claims.

Science has been the core activity in Antarctica and, despite the fact that mapping was not a specific scientific activity of the 1957–58 International Geophysical Year (IGY), mapping and associated fields have provided an essential geographical framework for Antarctic science since the signing of the Antarctic Treaty.[2] Surveying and geodesy have been important fields of enquiry, although they are sometimes regarded less as sciences in their own right than as service providers.[3] Scientists have depended on detailed and accurate maps for planning and conducting scientific fieldwork, for navigation and as a basis for scientific reporting.[4]

In one sense, mapping could be said to have reduced in political and legal significance with the establishment of the Antarctic Treaty System, since Article IV 'froze' all territorial claims. Yet, while commentators from non-claimant states tend to paraphrase Article IV in such a way as to suggest that it rendered the whole territorial problem a non-issue, for claimant states it was vital precisely because it permitted them to participate in the Antarctic Treaty System while retaining their pre-existing views as to the legal status of the continent. The Treaty does not constitute a renunciation of territorial claims nor require any state to renounce its claim. This meant that mapping continued to be an important Australian Antarctic activity in the decades following the establishment of the ATS.

Mapping and the proclamation of Australia's claim to the AAT

The Australian Antarctic Territory (AAT) was delimited by a British order-in-council of 7 February 1933. The Australian Parliament passed the necessary legislation to accept the AAT as a territory under the authority of the Commonwealth of Australia on 13 June 1933 and the order-in-council came into operation on 24 August 1936. An official Australian map of Antarctica had been produced in 1929, primarily for use in the BANZARE voyages of 1929–31, but it was now considered necessary to prepare a new and more detailed map because of the formalisation of the claim. E P Bayliss of the Department of the Interior began revising the map, and in 1936 was joined by Dr J S Cumpston of the Department of External Affairs. The map and accompanying handbook were published in 1939 (see chapter 1 and front endpaper), becoming the first in a continuing series of 1:10,000,000 maps.[5]

Maps do not 'prove' sovereignty, but they can support the establishment of territorial title. In the *Eastern Greenland* case, the Permanent Court of International Justice identified two essential elements of territorial sovereignty: the intent and will to act as a sovereign and the actual exercise of authority by the state in question.[6] A state making a case for its intent and will to act as a sovereign could reasonably be expected to draw on cartographic evidence.[7]

Recognition of one's title by another state, whether express or implied, may assist in confirming title. Associated with the concept of recognition is that of acquiescence. International tribunals have placed considerable weight on the failure of a state to protest acts of sovereignty by a state with a competing claim. It is therefore vital that a state claiming territorial rights act as a sovereign – exercising authority and protesting any state-like acts within that territory on the part of another state. Such acts and responses are logically premised on a belief that the territory in question is one's own. Maps play a vital, albeit often indirect, role in establishing and reinforcing that belief, and may speak to both a domestic and international audience. Maps, and in particular the placenames inscribed on maps, thus reflect as well as help create the political imagination. Placenames impart historical and cultural information and serve as a record – or denial – of discovery and effective occupation.

Post-war mapping and the consolidation of Australia's Antarctic claim

Efforts to consolidate Australia's claim after World War II were largely prompted by a massive US expedition in 1946–47 to explore, photograph and map the continent. Operation Highjump, led by Admiral R

E Byrd, succeeded in photographing virtually the whole coastline as well as several hundred thousand square kilometres of the interior.[8] The work was supplemented the following year by astronomical fixes and ground mapping visits to the Windmill Islands and the Bunger Hills.[9] The work undertaken by Operation Highjump was so extensive that not only were these photographs used to choose the site of Mawson base in 1954, but they were still being used (in conjunction with Australian-produced data) to make Australian Antarctic maps in the late 1950s.[10]

Australia was disconcerted by such energetic American activity because the United States did not recognise Australia's Antarctic claim and had made no formal approach to the Australian Government to enter the AAT.[11] The Soviet Union also developed potential claims in Antarctica, and Australian apprehension regarding Soviet intentions continued to drive Antarctic exploration and mapping endeavours throughout the 1950s and 1960s. Australian officials were well aware that it would be difficult to compete in exploration and mapping with the United States or Russia, but over the following decades the smaller scale on which Australia conducted its operations did give it the advantage of nimbleness.[12]

Norway had also been active in mapping the area claimed by Australia. Up to the end of World War II, the most comprehensive exploration and geographic information about the AAT was that generated by the Lars Christensen Expeditions of 1929–30 and

1936–37.[13] Lars Christensen had in 1937 explored from Amundsen Bay to the West Ice Shelf,[14] resulting in the so-called Hansen Atlas, a series of maps covering most of the coast and 'tens of kilometres inland' from 0° eastward to 90° East longitude, published in 1946.[15] Australians used these maps in 1954 when approaching Horseshoe Harbour to establish the first permanent mainland Antarctic station at Mawson, and again at Davis in 1957.[16] Up until 1960 the Hansen maps remained the best available of many parts of the AAT.[17]

The Australian National Antarctic Research Expedition (ANARE) was created in 1947 and the Antarctic Division was established within the Department of External Affairs in May 1948.[18] A Cabinet decision of 4 May 1948 set up the ANARE Executive Planning Committee as 'an advisory body to the Department of External Affairs and Antarctic Section on matters connected with the exploration, scientific research, development etc of the Territory'. Other than the routes mapped by Douglas Mawson in 1908–09 and the Australasian Antarctic Expedition in 1912, the inland of the AAT was completely unknown at the time ANARE was established.[19]

Phillip Law, later Director of the Antarctic Division from 1949 to 1966, was in 1947 appointed senior scientific officer of ANARE. His first task was to draw up a scientific program for submission to the ANARE Executive Planning Committee.[20] Law was aware that the main priority was Australia's territorial claim:

There's no doubt that everyone interested in Antarctica in those days was in it because of the territorial acquisitions, the value of possible minerals, the whaling industry, the fishing rights – all the commercial interests of colonialism. And that was accentuated, of course, by the fact that seven nations had claims in the Antarctic [hence] all this fuss about whether other people would recognise them or not. The scientific work was literally put in as a bit of softening of that hard approach.[21]

It is difficult to demonstrate effective control of territory that remains unknown; thus surveying and map-making were important to consolidate the Australian claim. Indeed, the very process of exploring and surveying contributed towards the 'effective occupation' of the AAT. Originally the Antarctic Division had responsibility for Antarctic mapping but in 1958 responsibility was transferred to the Division of National Mapping, which established an Antarctic Mapping Branch led by Thomas Gale, who was to make a formidable contribution to the mapping program.[22] The next two decades were busy ones with the Branch creating and disseminating many maps.

Under Law's direction a program of basic exploration of more than 5000 kilometres of coastline and of inland mountain ranges and peaks was set in place. The Prince Charles Mountains were sighted for the first time in 1954. From 1954 to 1960, but particularly in 1956–57, more of the AAT was sighted and explored than at any other time.[23] From 1956 to 1960 aircraft were kept at Mawson throughout the year, which meant that survey and geology parties could be dropped hundreds of kilometres away. Syd Kirkby, who was surveyor and/or leader of the wintering parties at Mawson for 1956–57, 1960–61, 1980–81 and a member of ANARE summer operations in 1961–2, 1962–3, 1964–5 and 1979–80, was said by Law to have explored more of Antarctica than Scott, Shackleton, Amundsen and Mawson combined.[24] This included considerable exploration of the Prince Charles Mountains in 1956 and 1960. ANARE had completed basic reconnaissance exploration of the AAT by the end of the 1960s, but the task of comprehensive mapping was still ahead when the Antarctic Treaty was signed.

Syd Kirkby

Lynette Finch
Sydney L Kirkby, Australian Antarctic surveyor, was born in Perth in 1933 and, by the time he was five years old, had survived three infant killers: whooping cough, diphtheria (twice) and polio. In 1954, while still a cadet surveyor, he scored the plum role of navigator and astronomer on an expedition into the Great Sandy Desert of Western Australia, an area that was home to Aboriginal people but would soon become part of the Woomera Rocket

Range and a site of intensive oil exploration. His challenge was to map a desert the size of Spain. Before any cohesive mapping system could be established over such a vast area, Syd had to create a large-scale primary network of control points, each separated by tens of kilometres. Only then could mapping surveyors add secondary and tertiary points within the grid. Before satellite positioning and electronic surveying, points (astrofixes) were mostly determined with respect to the stars, and they were typically taken from the highest landscape feature. Scrambling over low desert sandhills was rather different to scaling the mountain ranges of blizzard-blown Antarctica, but Syd's survey of the Great Sandy Desert did lead directly to his life as a 'Polyarnik' (polar man).

In 1956 the number of astrofixes that had been taken all over Antarctica could be counted on the fingers of both hands. Aided by ANARE planes, RAAF pilots, dog teams and World War II tracked sand vehicles ('weasels'), Syd established mapping control with astrofixes taken as close as possible to each degree of latitude and the equivalent distance apart in longitude. He worked along the coasts and wherever rock broke the monotony of the ice plateaus of the 5,896,500 square kilometres of the Australian Antarctic Territory – probably the biggest ground control that a single surveyor has ever created anywhere in the world.

Syd spent three winters and four summers at Mawson Station. In the summer of 1961–62 he worked in Oates and Victoria Lands to establish mapping control from Cape Bage to 350 kilometres beyond the eastern border of the Australian Antarctic Territory. In 1962–63 he went to King George and Wilkes Lands and mapped 480 kilometres of coastline and 52,000 square kilometres of previously unknown territory. In 1964–65 he explored and mapped Enderby and Kemp Lands on the western extremity of the Australian Antarctic Territory. His Antarctic swan song was as leader of the 1979–80 regional scientific study of Enderby, Kemp and eastern Queen Maud Lands.

One D4 Caterpillar in a crevasse near Mount Cresswell in the Prince Charles Mountains while going to the aid of another. The driver of the vehicle pictured escaped with minor injuries. With virtually no tools, a team which included Syd Kirkby took four days to winch out the still functioning Caterpillar. Henrick

(Hank) Geysen, Australian Antarctic Division, © Commonwealth of Australia

Syd's most eastern astrofix is beyond the eastern boundary of the Australian Antarctic Territory; his most western is more than 5000 kilometres away. You can stand anywhere in East Antarctica and be certain that within 400 nautical miles (or about 750 kilometres) of your position there is a first landing or a first astrofix made by Syd Kirkby.

Antarctic placenames

Before 1952 there was no procedure in Australia for approving Antarctic names, but Australia and New Zealand had representatives on the Antarctic Place-Names Committee in the United Kingdom.[25] In considering the placename questions arising from the work of Antarctic expeditions after 1928, the Committee had agreed in 1934 on a statement of principles. The statement stipulated that, while it was customary and natural for an explorer to suggest names for discoveries, ultimate responsibility for the adoption of names rested with the administrative authority of the territory in which the places were situated. Names should be selected with regard to euphony, brevity and appropriateness, and new or altered names should not as a general rule take the place of names already in common use. Where explorers had suggested more than one name for the same place or geographical feature, regard should be paid to 'authoritative priority of discovery'. The statement was sent to the Australian and New Zealand governments with a note expressing the hope that it would also commend itself to these governments.[26]

The UK committee was reconstituted in 1948 under the chairmanship of Sir Gerald Fitzmaurice, Second Legal Adviser to the Foreign Office.[27] Although this was a subcommittee of the Polar Committee, the fact that the Polar Committee itself was secret meant that the subcommittee was known publicly as the Antarctic Place-Names Committee.[28] Australian officials were invited to circulate lists of Australian decisions on placenames to ensure that they were incorporated into official British publications.[29]

On the suggestion of Phillip Law, an Antarctic Names Committee of Australia was established in 1952 to advise the Minister for External Affairs. The committee reviewed all existing names in the Australian Antarctic and sub-Antarctic territories, providing the Antarctic Division with details of names for publication in a gazetteer, and assisting with the revision of maps. The committee examined names given by explorers of all countries in the AAT and names proposed by members of ANARE. Names agreed on by the committee were submitted to the Minister for External Affairs. If approved, they became official and were used on official Australian maps of Antarctica.[30] Save for an 18-month period, Law chaired the committee from 1952 to 1981.[31]

It was accepted that the explorer who discovered a feature had a right to name it, but it was not always clear who had seen it first, particularly if the country in question did not distribute the information before another country's nationals visited. The British Antarctic Place-Names Committee, the Antarctic Names Committee of Australia and the New Zealand Geographic Board came to accept each other's decisions in relation to the British Antarctic Territory, the Australian Antarctic Territory and the Ross Dependency. Each also recognised the names given by Norway and France in their respective territories, and maintained close informal relations with the Advisory Committee on Antarctic Names of the US Board on Geographic Names.[32]

The Advisory Committee followed official US policy of ignoring all questions of national sovereignty in the Antarctic, which meant in practice that its members regarded Argentinean and Chilean name proposals as on the same footing as British proposals. Where conflicts arose, the Committee most often used priority of naming as its chief criterion for acceptance. Following the extensive aerial photography provided by Operation Highjump, the Advisory Committee had undertaken 'saturation mapping', giving names to all features on the photographs even where little or no ground control had been used. The US policy of according priority to early naming contrasted with the British approach of prioritising discovery and postponing naming until either a practical need had arisen or a reliable map became available. The Antarctic Names Committee of Australia approved some US placenames, deferred decision on some, and rejected others.[33]

Australian influence in the SCAR working group on cartography

The principal work of the Scientific Committee on Antarctic Research (SCAR) has been undertaken in a series of permanent working groups, whose titles and subject matter have evolved in line with developments in Antarctic science. As in broader Antarctic politics, the diplomatic situation was complicated by the fact that, although the United States was a principal ally of Australia, the United States and the USSR were both non-claimants. This meant that they had common interests that differed from those of claimants such as Australia. Australian influence (especially through the work of Phillip Law) ensured that international cooperation on mapping within the ATS took shape in a manner compatible with Australia's interests. Reflecting on Australia's achievements during the early post-IGY years, Law acknowledged the political clout of Bruce Lambert and other members of the ANARE executive planning committee.[34] And, as will be seen, Professor K E Bullen, the first vice-president of SCAR, was also influential in shaping the role of the working group on cartography.

At the second meeting of SCAR, held in Moscow in August 1958, the Soviet Union proposed creating a map of the whole Antarctic continent. According to the proposal, Russia would map one-third of the continent within the next three to five years, leaving it to SCAR to organise how other countries would map the remainder. Russia proposed that SCAR set up a cartographic commission composed of representatives of countries participating in the production of the map. Professor Bullen, the Australian representative at the meeting, acknowledged the importance of mapping but noted that the scheme was highly ambitious and that he had no powers to commit Australia to a course of action in the matter, suggesting that consideration be deferred 'until governmental issues were clearer'.[35] When a vote was imminent, Bullen expressed the view that SCAR was exceeding its constitutional powers in setting up a cartographic commission with powers to divide the Antarctic into sectors where particular nations would work. In response to concerns that this would render SCAR ineffective, Bullen argued that the proposal could lead to problems and that scientists had a duty to promote concord, not discord, between nations.[36] The matter was left open until the final plenary session, at which it was decided that a working group be established to meet at the next SCAR meeting, and that it be convened by Georges

Laclavère, French cartographer and SCAR president from 1958 to 1963.

Aware of proposals under which the UN Mapping Office or the Scott Polar Research Institute would assume a coordinating role in Antarctic mapping, Australia offered at the third meeting of SCAR, held in Canberra on 2–6 March 1959, to establish an Antarctic mapping centre. The centre would produce international maps of the Antarctic, act as a repository for cartographic and hydrographic information concerning the Antarctic and the surrounding seas, and help coordinate international mapping efforts. Although the proposal was not accepted in its original form, the meeting decided that a permanent secretary of the working group on cartography be appointed who would, *inter alia,* maintain and distribute a catalogue of cartographic material, receive and distribute recommendations for standardised conventional signs for maps, and collect and circulate information about current proposals. Bruce P Lambert, Australian Director of National Mapping, was appointed permanent secretary of the working group on cartography.[37] Richard Casey, Minister for External Affairs, regarded Lambert's appointment as recognition of Australia's status in Antarctic science.[38] From an undercurrent of the United States and the USSR jostling each other for position, Lambert had secured an outcome favourable to Australia.[39]

The Antarctic mapping centre was established in Melbourne within the Antarctic branch of the Division of National Mapping, Department of National Development, and it both looked after Australian interests in Antarctic cartography and functioned as a SCAR secretariat. Lambert went on to forestall any immediate action on Russia's mapping proposals at the 1959 conference by undertaking to seek the views of participating nations on the proposals. Australian officials were thus active in determining the form that international cooperation in Antarctic mapping took in the early years of SCAR, emphasising national mapping programs and bilateral collaboration rather than collective programs on the basis not only that mapping by committee would be inefficient but that it could also serve to dilute any advantage Australia might gain from its mapping activities in respect of its sovereignty claim.[40]

Lambert continued to chair the SCAR working group for some two decades and under his leadership the group undertook much useful work. At its fourth meeting at Cambridge in 1960, for example, SCAR approved a set of symbols and recommended that members use them in their topographic maps of Antarctica.[41] Although by then there was already considerable universality of conventional representation on topographic maps, this was not true of maps of Antarctica. In 1961 the Australian Division of National Mapping, on behalf of SCAR, published *Stan-*

dard symbols for use on topographic maps of Antarctica. [42]

The issue of placenames also came before the working group on cartography at its third and fourth meetings. At its third meeting SCAR adopted the recommendation that SCAR members exchange their gazetteers, and at the fourth meeting that they distribute amendments. It was also resolved that any member nations finding themselves in conflict over placenames should endeavour to resolve their differences bilaterally.[43] The issue was raised again in 1964, when the Russians suggested that the SCAR working group on geodesy and cartography address the question of placenames.[44] Australia preferred to have SCAR's role confined to consideration of generic terms as opposed to the actual naming of features, officials deeming the naming of features a political, as opposed to a scientific, exercise.[45]

The Russian proposal was not accepted.[46] By the mid-1960s France, the United Kingdom, New Zealand, the United States and the USSR had all published their own gazetteers.[47] Australia published a provisional gazetteer in June 1961, and the 'first comprehensive attempt to rationalise the names of new and formerly named features' in 1965.[48] The number of placenames was at this stage increasing at a rapid rate; between 1956 and 1980 the number of generally recognised placenames in Antarctica rose from 3400 to about 12,000.[49]

Australian leadership in SCAR bodies on mapping and geodesy

Australians have assumed leadership roles in the succession of SCAR working groups in cartography and related spatial sciences. Key figures have included A G (Tony) Bomford, C Veenstra, G Lindsay, Drew Clarke, John Manning, Phil O'Brien and Henk Brolsma. The name of the group has changed several times. In 1961 the title became the Working Group on Geodesy and Cartography. By 1988 it was felt that, with the increasing demand for a geographic information system for Antarctica and the resulting need for a common geodetic reference system, the primary responsibility of this working group should be to provide a homogeneous ground-related spatial framework for specialised information systems developed by other SCAR working groups, and its name was accordingly changed to the Working Group on Geodesy and Geographic Information.[50] Drew Clarke, who chaired the Group from 1992, restructured its work into projects with individual leadership responsibilities. The Group now saw one of its core tasks as gathering and maintaining Antarctic geographic data in a coordinated digital and graphic form. Its activities were subsequently amalgamated with geology and solid earth geophysics, and an expert group on geospatial information was established within the standing group for the geosciences. By 2006 the expert group had largely broken down, and at the 19th SCAR meeting in Hobart in 2006 it became the separate Standing Committee on Antarctic Geographic Information, chaired by Brolsma.[51]

Establishing a survey control network for mapping in 1971 in the Prince Charles Mountains, 500 kilometres south of Mawson Base. Here radio operator Patrick Moonie is aligning the signalling lamp to allow the surveyor at the next station to read a precise angle. The electronic distance measurer stands on a tripod in the observation tent. John Manning, Australian Antarctic Division, © Commonwealth of Australia

Australia has led and/or been actively involved in a number of initiatives of the succession of SCAR bodies on mapping and geodesy, including the production of information products. The *SCAR catalogue of*

Antarctic maps and charts was first published by the Division of National Mapping in 1960, with subsequent editions in 1961, 1969, 1974 (revised 1976) and 1988. The Australian Antarctic Division now maintains this as an online catalogue, with member countries able to edit and add maps.[52] Australia, with input from the United Kingdom, Germany and Canada, also developed the *SCAR feature catalogue,* which contains detailed descriptions of standard geographic features as agreed by the SCAR Antarctic community.[53] Australia continues to host the catalogue.[54]

Satellite geodesy was introduced into Antarctica in 1969, with the setting up of four geodetic satellite observation stations on the continent to link it with the worldwide network of stations.[55] This technology was in the early 1970s superseded by microwave geodesy using the TRANET Doppler system, making it possible for the first time to accurately measure the geodynamic relationship between Antarctica and other southern landmasses.[56] The following decade saw the advent of the global positioning system (GPS). At the 20th meeting of SCAR in Hobart in 1988 it was decided to undertake a cooperative GPS survey to determine the rates of relative motion within the Antarctic tectonic plate and between this plate and adjoining tectonic plates. Australia, on behalf of SCAR, arranged an international GPS geodetic pilot survey in 1989–90 with dual-frequency equipment. An interim report was presented to the meeting of the SCAR Geodesy and Geographic Information Working Group in Frankfurt in June 1990, and the work produced the first substantial GPS baselines between Australia and Antarctica.[57] The Geodetic Infrastructure of Antarctica project was begun in 1992 to provide a common compatible network of control for spatial information. Australia led this project for ten years, developing a network of permanent GPS observatories that transmitted data to control centres in Europe, the United States and Australia, and thereby permitting enhanced real-time positioning accuracy on a worldwide basis. Germany then led the project until 2009, when Australia once again assumed leadership.[58]

The SCAR composite gazetteer of Antarctica was first produced in 1998. The German national representative on the working group had in 1992 advocated the 'one feature one name' concept, leading after initial hesitation to a decision to attempt to avoid future duplication of names. The composite gazetteer was compiled, maintained, printed and hosted by Italy for over ten years and in 2007 the Australian Antarctic Division became host. The composite gazetteer, now available at the Division's website, includes some 36,000 names corresponding to some 17,000 features and is thus the product of a sizeable undertaking. Names are submitted by the national names committees from 22 countries and linked to those committees, to map publishers, map retailers and small-scale maps showing the distribution of flora and fauna. The composite gazetteer has experienced several problems, including that not all new names are forwarded for inclusion and that requests for the information are either ignored or take a very long time to be answered.[59]

After a decade with less Australian Antarctic mapping activity (from the late 1970s to late 1980s), responsibility for Antarctic mapping was in 1988 returned to the Australian Antarctic Division (AAD), with geodesy being assigned to the Australian Surveying and Land Information Group. The AAD data information centre is arguably the leading Antarctic data centre. Among other functions, it manages a metadata catalogue of all Antarctic spatial databases and services and continues to make its spatial data freely available.

Mapping the extended continental shelf

Australia's largest mapping exercise in the Antarctic in recent years was its comprehensive survey of the continental shelf off the AAT in preparation for lodging its submission to the Commission on the Limits of the Continental Shelf (CLCS). The continental shelf is the area of the seabed and subsoil that extends beyond the territorial sea to a distance of 200 nautical miles from the territorial sea baseline and beyond that distance to the outer edge of the continental margin. In order to define the outer limits of its continental shelf beyond 200 nautical miles from the baseline (the 'extended continental shelf'), a state is required to submit data to the Commission within ten years of the entry into force of the convention for that state.[60] Over the two Austral summer seasons 2000–01 and 2001–02, the ice-strengthened research vessels *Polar Duke* and *Geo Arctic* completed around 24,000 kilometres of bathymetric and seismic survey along 5500 kilometres of the Antarctic coast. The survey was designed to profile the continental shelf along transect lines perpendicular to the coast, spaced approximately 90 to 95 kilometres apart and running from the continental slope to the deep ocean (4500 metres depth).[61] The *Polar Duke* conducted 58 days of survey in the first season, and *Geo Arctic* spent 102 days at sea in the first and 93 days in the second, providing data which allowed Geoscience Australia to produce the most comprehensive mapping of the Antarctic seabed ever undertaken, at a cost of over $40 million.[62] As part of the mapping of the extended continental shelf off the AAT, Geoscience Australia also defined and mapped the coastline of the AAT (see back endpaper).[63]

Australia had the earliest deadline for submission to the CLCS of any Antarctic coastal state, and therefore faced a particular challenge in fulfilling its obligations under the UN Law of the Sea Convention while not breaching – in letter or in spirit – its obligations under Article IV of the Antarctic Treaty.[64] Australia had hitherto strongly defended the ATS, rather than the United Nations, as the appropriate forum in which to address Antarctic matters, and Australian officials engaged in five years of sustained high-level discussions in an unsuccessful attempt to amend Law of the Sea Convention practices on the application of Article 76 to Antarctica.[65] Australia's submission included Antarctic data and was accompanied by a diplomatic note requesting that the Commission not take any action for the time being in relation to the information in the submission relating to Antarctica. The CLCS accepted Australia's request when adopting its recommendations in relation to Australia's extended continental shelf areas in April 2008.

***

Antarctic mapping and geodesy have constituted an important although generally under-recognised dimension of Australia's national engagement with Antarctica and participation in the Antarctic Treaty System. Maps and mapping-related activities were constitutive of Australia's original territorial claim, contributed to its consolidation as a demonstration of Australia's administration of the AAT, and continue to be a way of demonstrating to the world at large the existence of the AAT as a political and legal entity. Australia shaped the nature of the activities initially undertaken by the SCAR Working Group on Cartography so that it functioned to coordinate national mapping programs by assisting in the exchange of information and the standardisation of scales, symbols and projection used in Antarctic mapping rather than developing joint mapping programs. This was deemed in the best interests of effective and efficient mapping of the continent while at the same time being compatible with staunch support of Australia's territorial claim. Australia went on to take a significant role in large-scale projects in geodesy and topographical information in SCAR cooperative projects. The approach towards inclusion of data on the extended continental shelf off the AAT adopted in the Australian submission to the Commission on the Limits of the Continental Shelf can be understood as a recent manifestation of Australian leadership in the politics of Antarctic mapping and spatial sciences.

Notes

[1]   The author would like to thank John Manning and Syd Kirkby for their helpful comments on an earlier draft. I remain responsible for any errors or omissions.

[2]   Thompson (1997) 371.

[3]   Thompson(1997) 371.

[4]   Antarctic Science Advisory Committee (1991) 62.

[5]   Bayliss and Cumpston (1939). In 2008 the Australian Antarctic Division issued a special edition facsimile copy of the 1939 map. Manning (2010) 26.

[6]   Prescott and Triggs (2008) 155.

[7]   The weight that an international tribunal could be expected to attach to any particular map will depend on a range of factors including its provenance, clarity, scale, technical and professional skill and accuracy, official status, institutional affiliation of the map-maker, circumstances under which it was prepared and the subsequent use made by it. *Eritrea-Ethiopia Boundary Commission*, 2002, cited in Prescott and Triggs (2008) 193.

[8]   Bowden (1997) 9.

[9]   Manning (2002) 55.

[10] The site for the station had been selected from aerial photographs taken during Operation Highjump. Bowden (1997) 104; Division of National Mapping, 'Notes on Compilation of the Provisional Map of Coast of Oates Land and King George V Land'. NAA: Series A3092, Item 221/16/1/1.

[11] Bowden (1997) 10.

[12] Minutes of the meeting of the ANARE Executive Planning Committee, 6 June 1957, at 4; NAA: Series A1838 (A1838/1), Item 1495/3/4/1 Pt 3.

[13] Kirkby (1993) 12.

[14] Manning (2002) 54.

[15] Kirkby (1993) 12.

[16] Bowden (1997) 123; email communication with John Manning, 24 November 2010.

[17]	Email communication with John Manning, 24 November 2010.

[18]	It has since 1968 been located within the departments responsible for science or the environment.

[19]	Manning (2002) 54.

[20]	Law (2002) 15.

[21]	Cited in Bowden (1997) 52.

[22]	Personal correspondence with Syd Kirkby, 24 November 2010.

[23]	Kirkby (1993) 12.

[24]	Address entitled 'Some Antarctic Leaders' given to the Royal Society for the Arts in April 1996. Draft of 15 February, p 8. Personal correspondence with Syd Kirkby, 9 January 2011.

[25]	Bowden (1997) 256–57.

[26]	Antarctic Place-Names Committee, 'Antarctic Place-Names: Notes for the Guidance of Explorers and Cartographers' APC(48)1. NAA: Series A3318 I, Item L1948/3/7/4.

[27]	'Polar Committee. Establishment of Sub-Committee on Place Names in the Antarctic' 5 March 1946. NAA: Series A1066, Item IC45/39/2.

[28]	Antarctic Place-Names Committee, 'Draft Minutes of Meeting at the Commonwealth Relations Office on Monday, 27th September, 1948 at 4pm'. NAA: Series A3318, Item L1949/3/7/4.

[29]   Brian Roberts, Foreign Office to J Rowland, External Affairs, 24 June 1949. NAA: Series A3318, Item L1949/3/7/4.

[30]   Kenneth Anderson to the Rt Hon William McMahon, Minister for External Affairs, 16 October 1970. NAA: Series M425P, Item I22 Part 4.

[31]   Bowden (1997) 256–57.

[32]   GW McKinnon, Geographical Officer, Antarctic Division, 19 July 1960. NAA: Series A1838, Item I1495/1/8 Pt 6; Brian Roberts (1964).

[33]   GW McKinnon, Secretary, Antarctic Names Committee of Australia to Mr Gervais Coles, External Affairs, 9 October 1968. NAA: Series A1838, Item I1495/1/8/2.

[34]   Law (2002) 15.

[35]   Australian National Antarctic Research Expeditions, Minutes of the Executive Planning Committee Meeting, 7 November 1958. NAA: Series A1838, Item I1495/3/4/1 Part 4.

[36]   'Extracts, Relating to Mapping, from Professor KE Bullen's Report of Second Meeting of SCAR at Moscow, August 1958', Appendix B, to Australian National Antarctic Research Expeditions, Minutes of the Executive Planning Committee Meeting, 7 November 1958. NAA: Series A1838, Item I1495/3/4/1 Part 4.

[37]   Savingram from External Affairs to Australian Embassy, Washington, 23 June 1959. NAA: Series A3092, Item 221/16/1/1.

[38] RG Casey, Minister of External Affairs to Senator the Honourable WH Spooner, MM, Minister for National Development, 11 August 1959. NAA: Series A1838, Item I1495/3/4/1 Part 4.

[39] Australian National Antarctic Research Expeditions, Minutes of the Executive Planning Committee Meeting, 27 April 1959. NAA: Series A1838, Item I1495/3/4/1 Part 4.

[40] Telegram from Australian Embassy, Washington to External Affairs, Canberra, 16 December 1958. NAA: Series A3092, Item 221/16/1/4.

[41] Lambert and Laclavère (1961) 1.

[42] Division of National Mapping (1961).

[43] APC(60)46 'Antarctic Place-Names Committee, 'Recommendations relating to place-names made by the Special Committee on Antarctic Research', 23 September 1960. NAA: Series A1838, Item I1495/1/8 Part 6.

[44] Notes on the provisional agenda of ANARE Executive Planning Committee Meeting, 28 July 1965. NAA: Series A1838 (A1838/2), Item 1495/3/4/1 Part 7.

[45] Secretary, External Affairs to the Director, Division of National Mapping, 13 March 1964. NAA: Series A1838, Item 1495/1/9/15/2.

[46] See report in SCAR Bulletin 37 (January 1971) in *Polar Record* 15: 97 (1971), 619–49.

[47] For details, see Roberts (1964).

[48] Manning (2002) 66; Bowden (1997) 256.

[49] Hattersley-Smith (1989) 299.

[50] 'Meeting of SCAR Working Group on Geodesy and Cartography: Summary Report', *SCAR Bulletin* 92 (January 1989), 11–12 at 11.

[51] 'Report to SCAR Excom – June 2007. SCAR Standing Committee on Antarctic Geographic Information SC-AGI', <www.antsdi.scar.org/eggi> (accessed 9 November 2009).

[52] <http://data.aad.gov.au/aadc/mapcat/search_mapcat.cfm>.

[53] 'Report to SCAR Excom – June 2007. SCAR Standing Committee on Antarctic Geographic Information SC-AGI', <www.antsdi.scar.org/eggi> (accessed 9 November 2009).

[54] <http://data.aad.gov.au/aadc/ftc/>.

[55] Lambert (1971).

[56] Manning (2002) 58.

[57] Manning (2002) 64.

[58] Email communication with John Manning, 24 November 2010.

[59] 'Report to SCAR Excom – June 2007' <http://portal.uni-freiburg.de/AntSDI/sc-agi-report-to-scar-excom-washington-june-2007/view> (accessed 9 November 2009).

[60] In May 2001 a Meeting of States Parties to the Convention resolved that for those states for whom the Convention entered into force before 13 May 1999, the 10-year period should be taken to have commenced on that date. UN Doc SPLOS/72 (29 May 2001) para (a). By SPLOS/83 (20 June 2008) a Meeting of States

Parties decided that it be understood that the deadline could be satisfied by submitting preliminary information indicative of the outer limits of the continental shelf beyond 200 nautical miles and a description of the status of preparation and intended date of making a submission.

[61] *Ausgeo News* (2002) vol66, 18–19.

[62] <www.un.org/Depts/los/clcs_new/submissions _files/submission_aus.htm> (accessed 4 February 2011).

[63] Ibid.

[64] Powell and Jackson (2007) 45.

[65] Powell and Jackson (2007) 46.

9

Australia, the United Nations and the Question of Antarctica

Marcus Haward and David Mason

The most significant external challenge to the Antarctic Treaty in the early 1980s was Malaysia's initiation of debate within the United Nations on what was termed the Question of Antarctica.[1] The focus of this debate evolved over the two decades that it remained on the United Nations General Assembly (UNGA) agenda, but its key elements centred on a critique of the privileged position accorded the Antarctic Treaty Consultative Parties (ATCPs). There was concern about the way in which Antarctica was to be administered and a plea for greater involvement by the United Nations to ensure that future exploitation of Antarctica's resources could benefit all nations, not just those with economic and technological capability. This debate was seen by both ATCPs and the claimant states, including Australia, as a serious challenge, 'perhaps the strongest external attack on the legitimacy of the ATS to date'.[2] The Question was introduced in 1983 and ran as an annual item at the UNGA, although in 1994 it shifted to a biennial item and in 1996 to being considered each third year, until it was finally removed from the UNGA agenda in 2005.[3]

Examining this period provides important insights into how Australia was able to provide leadership and exert influence while working to ensure that the values of the Antarctic Treaty System (ATS) – collaboration, consensus and minimising discord – were maintained. While this was not the first time the United Nations had been linked to management of Antarctica,[4] the response to the Question had a significant impact on both the internal operation and the external presentation of the ATS in relation to its governance of Antarctica.[5] Australia recognised the significance of the Malaysian challenge but also judged that it was best addressed by ensuring a united response from the ATCPs, an end to which considerable effort was devoted. In particular this involved coordinating the work of Treaty parties through the Antarctic Treaty Group in New York, a group chaired by Richard Woolcott, Australian Permanent Representative to the United Nations from 1982 to 1988. The Treaty Group provided a forum to discuss strategies and tactics over the Question, including preparations for the UNGA debates. Australia's support for this forum, along with Woolcott's role, was pivotal in the response to Malaysia.

Richard Woolcott addressing the United Nations in 1985.
Courtesy Richard Woolcott

Malaysia's focus on the Question of Antarctica was undoubtedly driven by Prime Minister Mahathir bin Mohamad, shaped by his leadership of the Non-Aligned Movement (NAM).[6] During the long period of debate over the Question, Mahathir antagonised two Australian prime ministers – Bob Hawke and later Paul Keating – although on issues unrelated to Antarctica. As Richard Woolcott, a major protagonist in the management of the Question, has noted, one result of these external factors and of Australian leadership of the Treaty parties at the United Nations was that the Question entangled Malaysia and Australia as much as it was a debate between the ATCPs and their critics.[7] Despite this tension Woolcott, who had spent time in

Malaysia as an Australian diplomat, was able to work closely with his Malaysian counterparts. It is equally evident that this bilateral relationship built on Australia's extensive engagement with Malaysia since its independence in 1957.

Australia, Malaysia and the United Nations debate on the Question of Antarctica

Mahathir bin Mohamad became Prime Minister of Malaysia on 16 July 1981 and in this position committed Malaysia to a lead role in the Group of 77 (G77) of developing non-aligned states.[8] This commitment became clear in Mahathir's first address to the UNGA in September 1982, where he introduced a theme that he would continue to link to Antarctica: the problem of the dissonance between developed and developing states and what he saw as the neo-colonial behaviour of developed states.[9] Mahathir considered that 'the world continues to remain in the grip of crises of various kinds stemming from unresolved political and military conflicts, economic stagnation and recession, widespread poverty and privations, and various inequities all of which seem to defy solution'.[10] He argued that the concept of the 'common heritage of mankind' – given effect in the UN Law of the Sea Convention – provided a model for the future in protecting the interests of the developing world, and declared that Antarctica did not belong to the claimant states, in the same manner that colonial territories did not belong to colonial powers.[11] While Mahathir concurred with the Antarctic Treaty's core commitments to peace and scientific research, he called for uninhabited lands (and Antarctica in particular) to be administered by the United Nations so that future exploitation of their resources could benefit all nations, reviving an argument first made in the 1950s. Mahathir returned to the neo-colonial theme to attack the ATCPs later in the decade.[12]

In 1983, Malaysia developed and intensified its challenge to the ATS and to the ATCPs.[13] Australia, as host of the 1983 ATCM XII, and through its chairing of the Treaty Group at the United Nations, took a key role in organising a response. Australia also engaged in consultations with Malaysian officials, who requested a meeting with Australian counterparts prior to the Bonn Special Antarctic Treaty Consultative Meeting (SATCM, 11–22 July 1983) to discuss Antarctica. This meeting was held in Canberra from 5–7 July.[14]

The SATCMs devoted to negotiating the minerals regime provided important opportunities for the ATCPs to consider the implications of the Malaysian initiative. The Bonn meeting saw a united position being maintained by the ATCPS and included pivotal interventions by key non-claimants, both the United States and the USSR speaking strongly against any formal dialogue with Malaysia. At the same time parties recognised that any informal bilateral discussions aimed at heading off or moderating the terms of Malaysia's initiative would be useful. They agreed that it should not be left to Australia alone to brief the contracting parties – who at this stage were not invited to meetings, or able to participate in the SATCM process on minerals.[15]

The Bonn SATCM coincided with a meeting in New Delhi in March 1983 of the NAM, the major forum Malaysia used to promote and gain support for its position on Antarctica. The Australian government worked hard to engage with members of the NAM, undertaking extensive briefings in 1983 with a range of states through the work of Australian missions in key countries.[16] This strategy of briefing NAM members and engaging in dialogue about Antarctica continued over the peak period during which discussions over the Question were on the UNGA agenda – particularly during the development of the Secretary-General's Report (see below) that was an outcome of resolution 38/77 of the UNGA. Information for Australian posts was circulated back to the Australian mission in New York, which was given carriage of the day-to-day tactics.[17]

The 1983 meeting of the NAM saw Argentina and India, two states that bridged the ATS and the NAM, playing important roles. Argentina provided a strong response to Malaysia, while India, which itself was moving towards acceding to the Antarctic Treaty, refused to co-sponsor Malaysia's statement.[18] Malaysia sought NAM support for inscription of an item on

Antarctica on the UNGA agenda. A summit of the Caribbean Community states was also held in early July. At this meeting Antigua and Barbuda – later co-sponsor with Malaysia of the inscription of the item on Antarctica – suggested the addition of the same item on the agenda of the scheduled Commonwealth Heads of Government Meeting to be held in New Delhi in November 1983, as well as on the agenda of UNGA 38. Malaysia later proposed an 'information item' on Antarctica for the Heads of Government meeting.[19]

Australia hosted the fifth SATCM in Canberra on 12 September 1983, immediately before ATCM XII (13–27 September 1983). In this meeting India and Brazil gained acceptance as ATCPs, India's request for ATCP status in particular providing a critical counterweight to Malaysia's criticism of the lack of involvement of NAM members in the ATS. ATCM XII offered a further opportunity for the parties to address the concerns expressed by Malaysia, and to establish a range of procedures and practices that fundamentally changed the way the ATCM operated.

Before the 38th Session of the UNGA in November the same year, Malaysia sought the backing of the NAM and the Association of South-East Asian Nations for its position on Antarctica and also presented its proposal to the non-governmental organisations at the United Nations to gather further support.[20] With the assistance of the NAM, and in particular Antigua and Barbuda, the 'Question of Antarctica' was entered into the UN First Committee agenda.[21] In Malaysia's opinion, 'Its allocation to the First Committee highlights the international security dimension of the subject'.[22] While Mahathir did not attend the UNGA debate, his country's permanent representative to the United Nations, Tan Sri Zainal Abidin Sulong, detailed Malaysia's challenges to the ATS.

Ambassador Sulong began by stating that Malaysia recognised that Antarctica was a site of significant scientific interest – although he noted with concern the limited role of the Scientific Committee on Antarctic Research at ATCMs – and that its living and non-living resources held great economic potential. He then asserted his country's belief that, while the aims of the Antarctic Treaty were noble, and the ATCPs should be praised for their efforts to neutralise territorial claims and to promote peace and science, 'the treaty and its system has become mired in its obsession to maintain a status quo regime advantageous to a privileged few'.[23] He reiterated Mahathir's claim that the common heritage concept should be applied to Antarctica because the continent remained 'outside the sovereignty of nations' and was one of the final reminders of 'colonialist order'.[24] Sulong criticised ATCM decision-making processes that excluded non-consultative parties and the views of the international community.[25] Foreshadowing the issue that would consume the ATCPS in the latter part of the decade, he argued that the current system could not ensure the protection of the Antarctic environment or the equitable exploitation of natural resources. Thus, he concluded, Malaysia called for a new international regime for Antarctica within the framework of the United Nations.[26]

After considerable negotiation on Woolcott's part a consensus response to the resolution was achieved.[27] Malaysia's goal of a new regime for Antarctica was countered by an UNGA resolution passed on 15 December 1983 that called for the 'Question of Antarctica' to be discussed in 1984. The resolution requested the Secretary-General 'to prepare a comprehensive, factual and objective study of all aspects of Antarctica, taking fully into account the Antarctic Treaty System and all relevant factors', and to seek the views of member states in the preparation of the study. It also requested all interested parties, including states, the United Nations and other organisations, to provide assistance to the Secretary-General.[28]

Malaysia asserted that a comprehensive study of Antarctica and the ATS was not a threat to the objectives of the Antarctic Treaty System, but would help inform serious and constructive discussion in 1984.[29] Australia, along with other Consultative Parties, did not agree with Malaysia's presentation in the debate on resolution 38/77 or with its characterisation of the Antarctic Treaty of 1959, and the ATCPs were unanimous in their objection to Malaysia's initiative and to any attempt to revise or replace the Treaty. Hamzah has argued that Malaysia did not in fact advocate this course of action, noting the statement in Mahathir's 1982 speech that 'we do not dispute what the Antarctic Treaty System has done. But what we are seeking is a broader base and firmer foundation for international cooperation on Antarctica'.[30]

Not surprisingly, 1984 was a year of major activity in response to resolution 38/77. On 8 February the UN Secretary-General, Javier Perez de Cuellar, sent a formal letter to Permanent Representatives regarding the resolution's content and inviting material for inclusion in his Report.[31] On 23 March Australia convened a meeting of ATCPs that resulted in agreement on a form of words to be drafted as an aide mémoire to be conveyed to the Secretary-General. A 'Reactions Paper' to the resolution was also prepared and distributed to selected G77 and NAM member countries.[32]

In May Malaysia released a paper presenting its position. The ATCPs believed that the Malaysian paper went beyond the terms of reference agreed to as part of the resolution.[33] Australia, as chair of the Treaty Group, conveyed this judgment to Malaysia. In early June Ambassador Tan Sri Zain Azrai called a meeting of the core group of states supporting the Malaysian initiative: Antigua and Barbuda, Ghana, Algeria, Yugoslavia and Sierra Leone. However, Antigua and Barbuda did not attend and reports received by Australian diplomats suggested that the states had diverse and potentially conflicting agendas.[34] These differences were to become evident in the later broadening of the ambit of resolutions in the General Assembly under the Question item. The matter was the focus of a number of meetings between Consultative Parties in June and July to consider a preliminary response to the Malaysian paper. Woolcott, too, met several times with Zain Azrai, and on 22 June 1984 with the UN Secretary-General to discuss Antarctica, among a range of topics.[35] On 26 June Woolcott conveyed to Zain Azrai the firm and unanimous opposition of the ATCPs to the Malaysian position paper. In early July in Canberra, Zain Azrai met Australian officials. Christopher Beeby and Colin Keating from the New Zealand Ministry of Foreign Affairs, who were in Canberra at the time as part of regular Australia–New Zealand bilateral talks, also attended part of the meeting.

In the lead-up to the release of the Secretary-General's Report on 31 October 1984[36] and the debate in the General Assembly, the ATCPs continued to meet. Australian officials recorded that the US State Department was advocating a hard line against Malaysia and noted that meetings had been held between Malaysian officials and their US counterparts in August.[37] In late November the interaction increased in intensity, with separate meetings of ATCPs and non-ATCPs discussing approaches to the forthcoming debates. The ATCPs received redrafts of Malaysia's paper just before the First Committee session. They were not happy with the redrafted paper, and Woolcott again conveyed this view to Zain Azrai. The UNGA

Richard Woolcott and Zain Azrai at the South Pole in January 1985 at the time of the workshop on the Antarctic Treaty System. Courtesy Richard Woolcott

First Committee session on 29 November 1984 dealt with Antarctica,[38] and as a result of the lengthy negotiations between Zain Azrai and Woolcott (representing the ATCPs) a consensus resolution related to the Question of Antarctica was eventually achieved.

At this point a remarkable event took place, the fruition of an idea put forward at the ATCM in Canberra a little over a year earlier. Under the sponsorship of the US Polar Research Board, 57 diplomats and scientists from 25 countries participated in their personal capacities in a workshop on the Antarctic Treaty System from 7–13 January 1985, held at a camp in deepest Antarctica, near the head of the Beardmore Glacier (a major obstacle in Shackleton's and Scott's quests for the pole). The workshop aimed to foster discussion while also giving participants experience of the practicalities of living in Antarctica. One highlight was a *Wisden*-recorded cricket match between the Beardmore Casuals, captained by Arthur Watts from the United Kingdom, and the Gondwanaland Occasionals, captained by New Zealand's Christopher Beeby – with the match going to the latter. Both Woolcott and Zain Azrai attended the workshop.

Despite the constructive and less political exchanges enabled by this event, later in the year the consensus achieved at the 1984 UNGA broke down. The immediate cause was certain topics included when the 40th session of the UNGA debated the Question. The ATCPs' primary objections centred on references to the Law of the Sea Convention and on the linking of the concept of the 'common heritage of mankind' to Antarctica.[39] At the same time, other issues, principally concerning South Africa, were being included as a result of Malaysia's discussions within the NAM and in other forums as it attempted to build support for its initiative.[40] Australia had continued to brief members of the NAM through ongoing work by its posts in a number of countries, and before the General Assembly debate Antarctica was discussed at a meeting of South Pacific missions in New York, where Australia expressed the hope that as many countries as possible would 'not participate' in the debate in order to demonstrate a belief that the General Assembly should proceed on the Question of Antarctica by consensus.[41]

The UNGA 40 debate began on 25 November 1985 in the First Committee. Malaysia opened the proceedings, followed immediately by Australia, which initially did not speak on behalf of ATCPs as it had done at UNGAs 38 and 39.[42] Twenty-one countries spoke in support of Malaysia, but not Antigua and Barbuda – one of the original co-sponsors of the resolution in 1983. All ATCPs participated in the debate, as did most contracting, non-consultative parties, the exceptions being Peru, Papua New Guinea and Cuba. Canada, although not an Antarctic Treaty party, spoke in support of the ATS. Unlike in previous debates in the First Committee, the resolutions were put to a vote.[43] At the conclusion of the debate Ambassador Woolcott gave a statement on behalf of the ATCPs regretting the breakdown of consensus on the matter.[44]

The UNGA 40 General Debate began on 12 December 1985. Australia, the United States, New Zealand, the United Kingdom, Chile and Colombia (a non-Treaty state) all spoke in favour of the ATS. Malaysia proposed establishing a UN committee to consider Antarctica, a motion that was endorsed by Sri Lanka. Angola, Togo and Kenya expressed the wish to see Antarctica managed under the principle of the common heritage of mankind. Although the final voting in UNGA 40 represented an improved result for Malaysia compared to voting in the First Committee, the ATCPs held the line, while regretting the loss of consensus and the broadening of the debate. Woolcott, 'on behalf of the treaty parties ... told the Assembly ... that it was a matter for regret that we had been unable to achieve consensus'.[45] Woolcott coordinated a new and effective approach to the vote, with the Treaty parties agreeing to neither abstain nor vote against the proposal, but to state that they were 'not participating' in the vote.[46]

In 1986 Malaysia shifted one of its key demands, effectively abandoning the objective of establishing a UN Special Committee to ensure that Antarctica was managed in the interest of all of mankind and not just an exclusive few countries.[47] Prime Minister Mahathir did, however, ensure that Malaysia maintained its challenges to the ATS and to the ATCPs. He returned to address the UNGA and argued that Antarctica should be managed under an internationally accepted regime, with a greater degree of involvement by the United Nations. He continued to view the ATS as 'undemocratic' and to insist that South Africa should be excluded from the ATS and the ATCM as a result of its racist policies.[48]

The focus on neo-colonialism in Antarctica was highlighted by Malaysia's targeting of South Africa as a Consultative Party, a matter which became the topic of a specific resolution in the 1987 debate (41/88 C) appealing to the ATCPs to exclude South Africa due to the persistence of the apartheid regime. The linking of South Africa to the Question posed challenges for both Malaysia and Australia. Australia continued to view the debate on South Africa as peripheral to the broader implications of the Question,[49] but it was also a key factor in ensuring the continued failure of consensus. Ghana, in particular, urged action on South Africa, an action that Zain Azrai, in meetings with Woolcott, had recognised could sidetrack the debate.[50] The linking of South Africa to the Question also posed challenges for the internal unity of the ATCPs. Australian officials noted that it was likely that Soviet diplomats, while remaining strongly aligned with the position of the ATCPs regarding the Question in 1987, were managing internal policy issues within their government over attitudes to South Africa. Australian diplomats in Moscow believed it unlikely that the USSR would be able to continue to support the ATCPs' position not to participate in the UNGA debate if the South African issue remained as part of the UNGA resolution.[51]

By February 1987 Australia had held the chair of the New York Group of the ATCPs for four years. This committee met regularly and was the forum to consider strategy and tactics in relation to interaction with Malaysia, and positions during debates in the First Committee and in the General Assembly. In the first meeting of the group for that year, Ambassador Woolcott broached the question of whether the time had come to rotate the chair. The parties stated in a 'chorus' that Australia had handled the task well in the past and should continue to do so in the future.[52] Accordingly, when Woolcott's term as Australia's permanent representative concluded in August

1988, his successor, Ambassador Michael Costello, took over the chair.

Any chance of returning to a consensus position at UNGA 43 in 1988 was lost with the reaction of Malaysia and others to the ATCPs' adoption of the Convention on the Regulation of Antarctic Mineral Resource Activities (CRAMRA) on 2 June 1988. Positions in the debate now hardened considerably. Malaysia's immediate response was to register its 'utmost regret and deep concern' in a letter to the UN Secretary-General[53] and to urge the ATCPs not to sign the convention.[54] New Zealand conveyed its view to Australia that it found Malaysia's response unnecessarily strong and 'pretty provocative'.[55]

While consensus was not achieved in 1988 there were developing signs that it might be possible at UNGA 44 in 1989. Malaysia supported statements on CRAMRA by the prime ministers of Australia and France, who indicated that their governments would not sign the agreement but would work instead to develop a more comprehensive environmental protection instrument. Malaysia also noted the possibility of a review conference on the Antarctic Treaty in 1991 and expressed the hope that an ATCP would avail itself of the opportunity to call for a review, since this would 'provide an appropriate occasion for the Antarctic Treaty Consultative Parties to reflect on the growing international concern on Antarctica and the environment, the weaknesses of the Antarctic

Treaty System and to accede to the changes which the international community has been calling for'.[56]

In the event, the opportunity for a review conference was not taken up. It was overtaken early in 1991 by the processes associated with the conclusion and adoption of the Protocol on Environmental Protection, the Madrid Protocol. This milestone, together with a broadening of participation at the ATCMs – including increased opportunities for involvement by UN specialised bodies and other observers and the decision by the ATCM in 1985 to make meeting documents publicly available – helped shift Malaysia's long-term relationship with the ATS. The Madrid Protocol was a signal that the Treaty parties and the international community in general were willing to ensure the protection of Antarctica's environment, and that the ATS was continuing to evolve.[57] Prime Minister Mahathir's final personal intervention on the Question occurred at the 1993 General Assembly. The tone of his comments did, however, change, such that his address can be seen as a turning point in Malaysia's relationship with the ATCPs.[58] The address followed and echoed contributions from Malaysian diplomats that emphasised the positive outcome of the adoption of the Madrid Protocol and the increasing level of engagement between the ATCPs and the UN specialised agencies that had been attending ATCMs.

After a year of recess from the UNGA agenda the Question was raised again in 1996. Relations between the ATCPs and challenging states were increasingly amenable and, as noted earlier, this meant that the Question could be shifted from a biennial to a triennial agenda item.[59] It also signalled a 'ritualisation' of the item[60] and a consensus approach being maintained between Malaysia and the ATCPs. The debate had evolved into an avenue for reporting and information provision, with Malaysia in 1998 recording its pleasure at the continued achievement of consensus.

By 2002 Malaysia had retained its support for consensus but was still challenging the ATCPs in key areas.[61] It now demonstrated a deeper awareness of current issues facing the parties, helped by greater engagement with the Antarctic Treaty System.[62] Malaysia was invited to observe the 2002 ATCM in Warsaw, an invitation that has been continued to the present. In 2002 Mahathir did not address the General Assembly; instead, his successor Abdullah Badawi spoke on general international issues,[63] mainly related to the global 'war on terror'.[64] In the debate on the Question, Malaysia reiterated its earlier concerns that although the Madrid Protocol was a landmark, a strict environmental regime would display to the world the ATCPs' dedication to environmental protection.[65] The other major issues that Malaysia raised were matters already being addressed within the ATS: the problem of illegal, unregulated and unreported fishing, and the control of tourism in Antarctica.[66]

The dynamics underpinning Malaysia's focus on Antarctica once again shifted markedly in May 2004, with concomitant changes in its relationships with the ATCPs. Mahathir, now in retirement, issued a public statement 'urging Malaysia to sign the Antarctic Treaty'.[67] As a result, 'political support for an assertive diplomatic position at the UNGA on the Question declined'.[68] Mahathir's successors, prime ministers Abdullah Badawi (2004–09) and Najib Abdul Razak (from 2009), continued their country's engagement with the ATS, including increasing involvement in the work of the Scientific Committee on Antarctic Research (SCAR). Malaysia expanded its links with other Asian ATCPs, had scientists appointed to polar research groups and participated in research in Antarctica.[69] After more than two decades Malaysian diplomats noted developments in the ATS such as the ongoing work on the liability annex within the Madrid Protocol,[70] the establishment of the Treaty Secretariat in 2004 and the continued involvement of contracting parties and observers from UN specialised agencies and non-governmental groups.

Continuity and change in the early 1980s

The early 1980s can now be seen as a period of significant institutional development within the ATS. The conclusion of CCAMLR, and its notable replication of the Antarctic Treaty's Article IV, provided important reinforcement to the system and began to flesh out its design. At the same time debates over Antarctica's resource potential were reinvigorated after the oil shocks of 1973 and 1978, caused by rapid increases in the price of oil from the Organization of the Petroleum Exporting Countries. The oil shock encouraged developed states in particular to increase exploitation of national oil and gas resources but also to look to new areas. Antarctica attracted some interest for its mineral and hydrocarbon resource potentiality, 'however speculative and hypothetical'.[71] More importantly, the 'Antarctic minerals issue served as a stimulus for the initiation of the "Question of Antarctica" in the United Nations in 1983, which was, via the invocation of "common heritage", directly linked to the outcome of UNCLOS III [the Third United Nations Conference on the Law of the Sea]'.[72] The ATCPs' discussions over minerals (1970–88) occurred in the same period as the negotiation of the Law of the Sea Convention (1967–82).

The advent of CRAMRA and Australia's role in the negotiation and eventual rejection of that instrument are recounted in chapter 11. It is important to note here, however, that the development of the minerals regime increased the number of contracting and consultative parties, including those from developing states and associated with the non-aligned movement. These countries included Brazil, Uruguay, Peru, Papua New Guinea, China, India and North Korea. Table 9.1 shows these states, the date they acceded the Antarctic Treaty and the date they achieved Consultative Party status.

Table 9.1 Key non-aligned states and the Antarctic Treaty

State	Accession to Antarctic Treaty	Consultative Party status recognised
Brazil	May 1975	September 1983
Uruguay	January 1980	October 1983
Peru	April 1981	October 1987
Papua New Guinea	March 1981	Not sought
China	June 1983	October 1985
India	August 1983	September 1983
DPRK (North Korea)	January 1987	Not sought

India's accession to the Treaty was significant, as it had been an early critic of the treaty regime. Even more interesting was the rapid acceptance of India's Consultative Party status – determined by other ATCPs' recognition that a state fulfils the requirements of Article IX of the Antarctic Treaty – less than one month after its accession to the Treaty.[73] Vidas notes that, in contrast to India's rapid acceptance as an ATCP, Poland took 16 years to achieve Consultative Party status following its accession to the Treaty in 1961.[74] India's special case can, arguably, also be seen in the light of broader geopolitical issues such as China's accession to the Treaty and the interest of Treaty parties in increasing representation from the non-aligned movement. Uruguay's achievement of ATCP status was clearly influenced by Malaysia's success in gaining support in the UNGA to discuss Antarctica, as the ATCPs appeared reluctant to question the status and commitment of its science program.[75]

Australia and the Question of Antarctica

We have seen that the progress of the Malaysian initiative in the two decades 1983–2005 was both shaped by, and helped shape, subsequent and related developments in the ATS. This is most clearly evident in reactions to the minerals regime which was developed concurrently with the Question. The Australia–France initiative that overturned CRAMRA and led to the development of a comprehensive environmental instrument in 1991 (see chapter 11) did increase internal stresses within the system but also helped moderate the external challenge posed by the Question.

Australia worked hard to promote the successes and value of the Antarctic Treaty and the Treaty system and to counter Malaysia's claims. Extensive efforts were made to inform and understand the concerns of the countries of the NAM, and to provide briefings to these countries as part of normal activities of Australian diplomatic posts. These posts provided ongoing information to both the Department of Foreign Affairs in Canberra and the Australian Mission in New York. At the same time, Australia and the other ATCPs made good use of the strong personal links between Richard Woolcott and Zain Azrai, his Malaysian counterpart, during the key period of the Malaysian challenge. As noted, Australia provided a leadership and coordinating role as chair of the ATCPs at the

United Nations; it also used opportunities to discuss the Malaysian initiative in the margins of the meetings which were called as the minerals negotiations developed. In addition to working with other ATCPs, who provided important information on the Question, Australia worked diligently to advance non-Treaty states' understanding of the operation of the ATS. Analysis of the handling of the Question thus sheds considerable light on Australia's leadership and influence within the ATS and its use of the norms and practices of the system.

The Question concluded in 2005 with Malaysia's consent and, with the chief protagonist increasingly integrated into the ATS,[76] the challenge to the legitimacy of the Treaty may have been weathered. While the return to calm has no doubt been welcomed by the ATCPs, the possibility of future storms cannot be underestimated. Will new or emergent issues rekindle the discussion? The current debate over Antarctic biological prospecting, for example, which is in essence focused on access to benefits from marine genetic resources beyond national jurisdiction in the Antarctic Treaty Area, may reinvigorate the 'common heritage of mankind' debate. On the other hand, the flexibility and innovation shown by the parties in addressing the challenge posed by the Question of Antarctica augur well for their ability to meet such future challenges as may arise.

Notes

[1]   For overall surveys of the matter see Tepper and Haward (2005), Hamzah (2010) and Dodds (2006).

[2]   Vidas (1996a) 50.

[3]   See Tepper and Haward (2005).

[4]   India and Sweden had promoted referring Antarctica to the United Nations in 1956 and New Zealand Prime Minister Nash had promoted the internationalisation of Antarctica as a means of resolving the 'Antarctic Problem'.

[5]   See Vidas (1996a) 50.

[6]   The extent to which the Question of Antarctica had domestic political clout is interesting. Hamzah (2010) notes that it had little salience as an election issue in Malaysia.

[7]   Woolcott (2003) 212.

[8]   Mahathir had had a lengthy period in Malaysian politics. He was first elected to parliament in 1964 and had served as Deputy Prime Minister since September 1978.

[9]   Tepper and Haward (2005).

[10]   Mahathir (1982).

[11]   Khoo (1995) 374; Mahathir (1982).

[12]   In AAD file 87/6239(c)--. Mahathir reiterated this criticism in a statement to the UNGA over the development of CRAMRA on 4 October 1988. New Zealand in particular, was critical of the statement. As a result many partici-

pants viewed a return to consensus at UNGA 53 in 1988 as unlikely.

[13] Tepper and Haward (2005).
[14] In AAD file 83/383.
[15] In AAD file 83/383.
[16] In AAD file 83/383.
[17] In AAD file 83/383.
[18] In AAD file 83/383.
[19] In AAD file 83/383.
[20] Malaysia (1983).
[21] Sulong (1983a).
[22] Hussain (1990).
[23] Sulong (1983b) 446.
[24] Sulong (1983b).
[25] Sulong (1983b). Ambassador Sulong also criticised a lack of cooperation with the United Nations and its specialised agencies such as the Food and Agriculture Organization, the UN Environment Programme and the Committee on Natural Resources.
[26] Sulong (1983b).
[27] Woolcott (2003) 212.
[28] Resolution 38/77 Question of Antarctica. *Official Record of the General Assembly, Thirty-Eighth Session,* Resolutions Adopted on the Reports of the First Committee, 69–70.
[29] Sulong (1983b); see also Hamzah (2010) 1.
[30] Hamzah (2010) 190.
[31] The Australian submission to UN Secretary-General's report was coordinated by Foreign

Affairs with input from the Department of Science and Technology (chiefly the Australian Antarctic Division) and other departments. There was some concern at the short lead time for submission of material. In AAD file 83/383.

[32]   In AAD file 83/383.
[33]   In AAD file 83/383.
[34]   In AAD file 83/383.
[35]   In AAD file 83/383.
[36]   Question of Antarctica; Study Requested Under General Assembly Resolution 38/77 Report of the Secretary-General A/39/583 (Part 1), 31 October 1984, in AAD file 83/383.
[37]   In AAD file 83/383.
[38]   Item 66 of the First Committee's Agenda.
[39]   Beck (1986b).
[40]   In July 1985, for example, the Organization of African Unity saw a resolution on Antarctica sponsored by Mauritius in a meeting in Addis Ababa, Ethiopia.
[41]   In AAD file 83/383.
[42]   In AAD file 83/383.
[43]   Woolcott (2003) 212.
[44]   In AAD file 83/383.
[45]   Woolcott (2003) 212.
[46]   Woolcott (2003) 212.
[47]   Mahathir (1986).
[48]   Mahathir (1986).
[49]   Australia consistently maintained this position in public and in private discussions with

Malaysia. File 83/383 Australian Antarctic Division.

[50]   In AAD file 83/383.

[51]   In AAD files 87/566 and 87/623; see also Beck (1988).

[52]   In AAD files 87/566 and 87/623.

[53]   Beck (1989); see also AAD file 87/623.

[54]   Beck (1989).

[55]   In AAD file 87/623.

[56]   Hussain (1990) 6–7.

[57]   Ismail, 'Address by Malaysia on the 'Question of Antarctica' at the 48th Session of the United Nations General Assembly', A/C.1/48/SR.32. United Nations, New York, 2–3.

[58]   Tepper and Haward (2005).

[59]   Tepper and Haward (2005).

[60]   Beck (1988).

[61]   Tepper and Haward (2005).

[62]   New Zealand invited Malaysian scientists to visit Scott Base in 1997 and Australia followed up with support for Malaysian participation in its program; see Hamzah (2010).

[63]   Abduallah Badawai succeeded Mahathir as Prime Minister of Malaysia in 2004. Mahathir's last address to the UNGA as Prime Minister occurred in 2003. This address did not mention Antarctica.

[64]   Tepper and Haward (2005).

[65]   Malaysia was represented by Zainuddin Yahya, Malaysia's Deputy Permanent Representative to the United Nations.

[66]   Zainuddin (2002) 4. Malaysia also looked forward to the establishment of an ATS secretariat, hoping that it would enable greater transparency.

[67]   Hamzah (2010) 189.

[68]   Hamzah (2010) 189.

[69]   Hamzah (2010) 190. Malaysia was appointed an associate member of SCAR in 2004 and became a full member in 2008.

[70]   Annex VI was concluded and open for signature at the ATCM XXVIII in Stockholm June 2005. It has not yet entered into force.

[71]   Vidas (1996b).

[72]   Vidas (1996b) 74.

[73]   Vidas (1996a) 53.

[74]   Vidas (1996a) 53.

[75]   In AAD file 83/383.

[76]   Hamzah (2010).

10

Resources

Julia Jabour and Marcus Haward

The potential of the resources of the Southern Ocean, the sub-Antarctic and Antarctic continent has long attracted interest. Access to and exploitation of these resources have also been influential motives for activity. The word 'resource' can, however, be misleading, frequently bearing connotations of extraction, exploitation and economic value. Certainly, at times parts of Antarctica have excited interest for their promise of extractable resources, but in the same areas and elsewhere in the far south there are also resources of a very different nature. From the tourist's or the scientist's point of view, it is the place itself: its beauty, history, physical properties or living things that are the resources – and of greatest value when they remain undisturbed. Bearing in mind, then, that Antarctic 'resources' may coexist and are often utilised in combination, we consider them in four broad categories for the purposes of discussion: biological, scientific, mineral and aesthetic (or touristic). We describe how these resources have inspired exploration, exploitation and investigation, and how a tenacious resource politics has manifested in different ways at different times.

Antarctic resources: prospects, politics and pragmatism

The reports of early explorers who described an abundance of whales and seals in the Southern Ocean encouraged sealers and whalers to follow them into the region. Systematic exploitation took place, driven by demand for oils and fats that were highly prized in Europe. The sealers' and whalers' activities in Antarctic waters were expanded by exploration in the heroic era, such that 'knowledge of the great continent was so remarkably advanced during the short period between 1901 and 1912'.[1] Research into the oceans developed understanding of krill,[2] and geological studies associated with early exploration provided samples of minerals.[3] Australian scientists Louis Bernacchi, T W Edgeworth David, Thomas Griffith Taylor and Douglas Mawson showed that, as in later decades, information on Antarctica's resource potential was a useful by-product of exploration. Taylor noted that 'Sir Edgeworth David has endeavoured to estimate the extent and possible value of coal reserves in Antarctica', and suggested that potential coal fields stretched over 12,000 square miles 'but it is unlikely that coal measures are developed throughout'.[4] An equally important consideration in the debate over Antarctica's mineral resources was the recognition that its harsh environment would be a major limitation to exploitation.

These constraints on exploitation were reasserted in later years. During the first Antarctic Treaty Consultative Meeting (ATCM) in Canberra in 1961, private discussions among parties took place on a proposal to establish a group to investigate and advise on matters such as resource exploitation that could have political implications that might upset the Antarctic Treaty. The United Kingdom felt that the first important function of this 'Article IX group' was to downplay the resource potential of Antarctica:

> Since so much nonsense is published and widely believed about the economic potentialities of the Antarctic, one of the first needs is for the Article IX Group to concert their opinions about possibilities and probabilities. This could only result in reducing suspicion and ease the political difficulties.[5]

The group would deal immediately with any relevant Antarctic problems that flared up unexpectedly, thus postponing them as political issues – but the proposal was not presented formally to the meeting and was not raised again. The idea, however, related specifically to the Antarctic's economic potential, which the Parties acknowledged could destabilise the fragile early accord provided by the Treaty. Over the following decades the interrelationship between politics and pragmatism has helped shape the Parties' responses to the potential of other, more current, activities. These include prospecting for novel biological material or processes, 'harvesting' fresh water from Antarctic ice, and perhaps even hard rock mining or hydrocarbon extraction. Clearly the latter are economic resources of a last resort on account of the difficulties of extraction and utilisation, let alone the complexities of establishing a management regime.

Biological resources

The search for and exploitation of marine mammals (seals and whales) generally shaped the first century of modern Antarctic resources history. Australian interests were active in the initial exploitation of biological resources. Sealing was the first example of living resources exploitation in the Australian Quadrant – the broad sphere of influence encompassing what later became the Australian Antarctic Territory (see chapter 1). Animal oil was 'so essential to the trade of the colony of New South Wales' that it led ships to the bountiful waters of the Antarctic and sub-Antarctic.[6] Seal harvesting began on Macquarie Island immediately on its discovery in 1810, and fur seals had been virtually wiped out a decade later. The harvesters then turned to elephant seals and the abundant penguin species, which were exploited relentlessly for several decades until they also became too scarce to be economical. Following a 60-year hiatus, during which few vessels even visited the island, the oil industry again reached full production during the 1880s, mainly under the direction of New Zealander Joseph Hatch. The last oiling party left Macquarie Island in 1919 and by 1920 Hatch's licence had been revoked.[7] At Heard Island sealing began in the 1850s and lasted until 1880, by which time thousands of elephant seal skeletons and tusks were washed up on the coastline.[8] Although these activities were located on the sub-Antarctic islands, they were the harbingers of the potential depletion of other species, especially whales and fur seals, throughout the southern seas and in the waters around the Antarctic continent. Douglas Mawson's Australasian Antarctic Expedition (AAE) of 1911–14 established and maintained a radio station on Macquarie Island and undertook studies of botany, zoology, meteorology and geology during this time. Its expeditioners also witnessed the oil industry first hand. Mawson had promoted the economic potential of Antarctic resources to gain financial support for his expeditions, but his concerns over the ecological impact of the oil industry saw him urge the creation of a wildlife sanctuary on Macquarie Island. The Tasmanian Government was to make such a declaration under Tasmanian law in 1933.[9]

The Australian colonies developed bay whaling based on abundant stocks in coastal waters. Declining whale numbers in coastal areas encouraged whalers to venture further offshore, with the Hobart-based barque *Venus* sailing as far as latitude 72° South in 1831.[10] This voyage attracted considerable attention when the ship returned with a cargo of sperm-whale oil. While whaling was an ongoing interest, Heard Island, the McDonald Islands and Macquarie Island had neither safe harbours nor safe anchorages, which constrained the development of an Australian whaling industry in the Southern Ocean.

Norwegian whalers famously explored along the Australian Quadrant in the 1930s, with Mawson on the *Discovery* meeting Hjalmar Riiser-Larsen on the *Norvegia* during the first BANZARE voyage on 14 January 1930,[11] and Kerguelen Island, relatively close to Heard Island, supported a Norwegian whaling station from 1908 to 1929. At the first ATCM in Canberra in 1961, Australia was one of a number of delegations (the others were Japan, Norway and the United States) whose opening speeches mentioned whaling, such was the industry's profile at that time. The importance of whaling in discussions of Antarctic resource exploitation cannot be underestimated, despite Article VI of the Antarctic Treaty, and more specifically Article VI of the Convention on the Conservation of Antarctic Marine Living Resources (CCAMLR), effectively quarantining the issue to the International Whaling Commission (see chapters 2 and 7).

In 1961 the United Kingdom tabled (but later withdrew) a draft 'Convention on the Protection of Wild Life in the Antarctic' at the first ATCM.[12] At the time the delegates acknowledged that 'preservation and conservation of living resources' was one of the topics mentioned expressly in Article IX(1) of the Antarctic Treaty as being part of their mandate, but recognised its sensitivity. The preferred position of Australia, along with other parties, was to avoid the issue altogether because of the possibility that it could open controversial arguments about jurisdiction, ownership and exploitation of any resources with an economic potential. From this first meeting, the parties sought ways to reduce tensions over the exploitation of biological resources. Because of the possibility of conflict over jurisdiction, Australia and the other Consultative Parties opted for a voluntary code of conduct, instead of a freestanding convention, to protect living resources in the interim while discussions continued.[13]

The Agreed Measures for the Conservation of Antarctic Fauna and Flora, concluded in 1964 as ATCM Recommendation III-VIII, was the culmination of discussions in the two previous consultative meetings and was the compromise (with some interesting alterations to terminology) between the United Kingdom's preferred convention and the interim code of conduct. The objectives of the Agreed Measures were stated to be 'protection, scientific study and rational use of [these] fauna and flora'; Antarctica itself was considered a 'special conservation area'. Protection, scientific study and rational use were to be facilitated through the issue of permits by the governments of nationals researching and operating in Antarctica. Changes to the UK draft and the final Agreed Measures were made to delete provisions that allowed the killing of native fauna for reasons of self-defence, the taking of fauna to provide specimens for private collections, and the taking of fauna to provide specimens or products for commercial purposes. In addition, the taking of native fauna for food was now permitted only if it was 'indispensable [for] men or dogs' (Article VI).

The Convention on the Conservation of Antarctic Marine Living Resources (CCAMLR) adopted in 1980 aims to conserve and protect – through fisheries management – both the ecosystem values of all marine living resources, and the economic value of targeted species. Although Australia is the Depository State, a signatory to the convention, a member of the CCAMLR Commission and the host of the Commission's secretariat, it had little direct interest in fisheries in the Southern Ocean until the 1990s. In the 1995–96 fishing season, Australian companies opened up fisheries off Heard Island and the McDonald Islands and Macquarie Island, targeting the highly prized Patagonian toothfish. This high-value catch attracted increased activity from a number of other fishing states and led to concern within the CCAMLR Commission about the potential impact of unregulated and thus unreported fishing in the Convention area. Managing the fishery/conservation dilemma outlined in CCAMLR's precautionary ecosystem approach became, and remains, compromised by illegal, unreported and unregulated (IUU) fishing (see chapter 7).[14] Australia undertook on-water surveillance and enforcement programs in response to such activities within Australian waters, off Heard and McDonald islands in particular. This resulted in the apprehension of the first suspected IUU fishing vessel within the Heard and McDonald Islands Exclusive Economic Zone in September 1997.

The focus on protection of its sovereign interests involved considerable effort and expense by the Australian Government, which has supported extensive surveillance efforts, leading to further arrests. This surveillance has included the cross-ocean 'hot pursuit' chases and apprehension of two more vessels – the *South Tomi* in 2001 and the *Viarsa* in 2005 – for illegally fishing in Australian waters off Heard and McDonald islands. Another activity that involves biological resources is bioprospecting, although it does not involve the same level of regulation or concern.

Bioprospecting

Biological prospecting (the search for material with biologically active properties capable of useful exploitation) is being undertaken in the Antarctic on an increasing scale and for a range of potential applications.[15] Because of Antarctica's extreme climate and isolation, its fauna and flora have many unusual adaptations or curious properties of interest to scientists and to the nutraceutical and pharmaceutical industries. For example, krill oil is very high in polyunsaturated omega-3 fatty acids, and the antifreeze polypeptides or glycopeptides found in some fish species have important uses in medical technology.[16]

The regulation of biological prospecting has been on Antarctic Treaty Consultative Meeting agendas since around 2002 without a substantive decision yet being made.[17] This is due in part to difficulties in separating biological prospecting from ordinary scientific research (sample collection, for example), making Parties reluctant to categorise their projects as 'bioprospecting' per se.[18] In 2009 the ATCPs decided that bioprospecting was adequately regulated for the time being by existing Antarctic Treaty System (ATS) laws, which include the obligation to conduct an environmental evaluation of all scientific research projects.[19]

Global interest in Antarctic biological resource potential is increasing. For example, an Australian-developed database of US and European patents for krill products and processes identified an upward trend in the lodging of patents, seen as a proxy for investment in research and development into diverse uses of krill.[20] The database was initiated in 2003, updated in 2008 and passed on to CCAMLR in 2009. The CCAMLR Commission will continue to use it as a source of information, tracking global interest and trends in utilising krill for a much greater range of applications than was thought possible when the krill fishery was first developed in the 1970s.[21] Toxic levels of fluoride in the carapaces of the krill meant that traditional production methods to harvest the meat could not be used with Antarctic krill. It was a number of years before this problem was solved, and there was a general hiatus in the krill fishery during that time. Australia itself is not a krill-fishing country, but it does have a strong interest in krill research. The Australian Antarctic Division hosts an international facility in which the complete life cycle of krill was observed for the first time in 2009. Experimental results from these aquaria-raised animals answer many questions about the enigmatic Antarctic krill *Euphausia superba* that is the keystone species of the ecosystem managed by the Convention on the Conservation of Antarctic Marine Living Resources, but simultaneously raise other concerns, such as how juveniles will survive in changing sea-ice conditions (see chapter 7).

The four identifiable phases of bioprospecting – sample collection, isolation, screening for bioactivity, and product development – are generally agreed upon, though not necessarily in this order. Australia's participation in biological prospecting is limited. Of the Australian interest recorded on the Bioprospector database, the organisations involved include both universities and private businesses, with international partners. Of all the potential bioprospecting activity in the Southern Ocean, it was thought that the harvesting of marine species such as krill was the least problematic scenario because of the existence of the CCAMLR regulations about fishing. Of the four phases described above, only the first is likely to occur in the Antarctic and even if re-sampling (or harvesting) is required, it is likely to be considered 'fishing' under the CCAMLR rules and regulated accordingly. It makes no difference whether krill are removed for fish food, human food or omega-3, their removal would need to be consistent with the CCAMLR ecosystem approach.[22]

Having claims to Antarctic territory and maritime zones gives Australia no current advantage in accessing or extracting biological material because, given the accommodations of Article IV of the Treaty, the practice of claimants (including Australia) is not to seek exclusive benefit. Nevertheless, access is preserved because Article IV is non-prejudicial to any Antarctic Treaty signatory state. In future, should the Antarctic Treaty fail, Australia will be free and in a prime position to exert full sovereignty over any resources that derive from the Australian Antarctic Territory. Similarly, its jurisdiction will extend from Heard Island and Macquarie Island into the Antarctic Treaty Area by virtue of its UN-ratified extended continental shelf zone boundaries, mentioned below.[23] In the meantime, and by general agreement, science is (and has always been) used to legitimise human presence in Antarctica.

Scientific resources

The Antarctic, so remote and isolated from human activity and impact that it is relatively pristine, provides an important scientific laboratory. It is uniquely placed to provide understanding of Earth as a system, and its responses to climate variation and change. Some research can only be undertaken there; in other instances, the Antarctic has particular advantages as a location. Scientific curiosity was only part of the motivation for early exploration; nonetheless it has been a driver of Antarctic endeavours for a century. It is embedded in the Antarctic Treaty and is a central policy interest for the Australian Antarctic program.[24] As Australian governments have maintained a long-standing political commitment to Antarctica, the interests driving that commitment have also remained relatively stable, albeit developing and evolving.[25] An example of such evolution in relation to the orientation of Antarctic science occurred following the 1997 review of the Australian Antarctic program (the *Foresight Review).*[26] The development of a strategic focus to science was epitomised by the development of government goals for the Australian Antarctic Program that included, *inter alia,* the commitment 'to undertake scientific work of practical, economic and national significance'.[27]

Ongoing Australian research is attempting to understand unresolved questions related to the cryosphere – the ice-covered and frozen areas of the world – and features and creatures in the depths of the Southern Ocean that are new to science. This research is investigating the unique physiological adaptations of Antarctic plants and animals to extreme conditions, which may be useful in the hunt for novel pharmaceutical or nutraceutical applications in the future. Significantly, researchers are also investigating the links between the Antarctic and Australian climates (a relationship that fascinated Mawson a century ago) which will, among other things, help to understand possible causes of rainfall decline in areas such as south-west Western Australia.[28] The early explorers also had a keen interest in the physical structure of Antarctica and several Australians made important contributions to early geological research.

Mineral resources

Following the adoption of the Antarctic Treaty in 1959, the topic of the exploitation of minerals was on the ATCM agenda for a number of meetings, beginning with ATCM VI, held in Tokyo, 19–31 October 1970. Although the Final Report of this meeting did not record the Parties having any discussions or making any decisions on the subject, 'enquiries from geophysical prospecting companies about the possibility of prospecting in the ocean surrounding Antarctica' brought the matter to their attention.[29]

A voluntary moratorium was subsequently adopted in 1977 through Recommendation IX–1, until a regulatory regime for minerals extraction could be established. So little was known about Antarctic mineral potential at the time that the whole exercise was speculative at best. In 1983, for example, Gjelsvik listed the known mineral deposits as:

East Antarctica: Deposits of iron (large, but low grade), titanium, uranium, niobium, tantalum (unknown grades and quantities), gold (low-grade, unknown quantities). A great number of industrial minerals (graphite, micas, kyanite, fluorite, rock crystal, etc.). Coal measures.

Transantarctic Mountains: Small deposits of tin and rare earth minerals. Copper, zinc and molybdenum (unknown grades and quantities). Large coal deposits.

Antarctic Peninsula: Molybdenum and copper ('porphyry copper'), and vein deposits of copper, lead, zinc and silver. Iron, chromium, nickel, cobalt. Altogether about 30 localities known, so far none of economic interest.

Deep ocean floor: Manganese nodules with low metallic values.[30]

While conceding that little effort had been invested thus far in geological exploration of Antarctica's mineral potential, Gjelsvik stated that, 'to an economic geologist, the list is not impressive at first sight'.[31] Nevertheless, the Gondwana connection – the geological links between Antarctica and mineral-rich areas in Australia and South America – was a powerful cause for optimism that at some point in the future Antarctic mineral resources would become proven and then commercially exploitable, and perhaps quite quickly under the right circumstances.[32] As Gjelsvik expressed it, 'the Gods of the environment have put the mineral deposits in Antarctica in a deep freezer for the benefit of our grandchildren or even more distant generations'.[33] Twenty years earlier Phillip Law had predicted that by 1984 year-round deep

Antarctic mining would be possible, supported by nuclear-powered townships inhabited by families.[34] This was not to be the case; the Parties adopted the Convention on the Regulation of Antarctic Mineral Resource Activities (CRAMRA) in 1988 but it failed to enter into force. Now there is a total prohibition on mineral resource activities other than scientific research under Article 7 of the Protocol on Environmental Protection to the Antarctic Treaty (the Madrid Protocol, which replaced CRAMRA), with complex decision-making rules in place should the ATCPs seek to overturn the ban (see chapter 11).

A coal seam 3 metres thick beneath arkose (a type of sandstone containing a high proportion of feldspar) in the Bainmedart Coal Measures in the northern Prince Charles Mountains in East Antarctica. J Baune, Australian Antarctic Division, © Commonwealth of Australia

During the CRAMRA negotiations parties noted that hydrocarbon deposits could exist in sedimentary basins of the continental shelves[35] and that they were likely to be the only non-renewable resource to become commercially exploitable.[36] Subsequent twenty-first century survey work has measured sediment thickness in order to establish the outer margins of these continental shelves. This data will prove to be a rich source of information about hydrocarbon potential in the future, but commercial use of the data remains constrained by the Article 7 ban.

Nevertheless, Australia is currently in the unique position of being the only Antarctic claimant to have exclusive rights over areas appurtenant to its territory confirmed by a United Nations body. This occurred when the Commission on the Limits of the Continental Shelf confirmed Australia's extended continental shelf boundaries of the Heard and McDonald Islands and Macquarie Island.[37] These areas are a sub-Antarctic inheritance for future generations.

Another potential inheritance is fresh water from Antarctica.

Fresh water harvesting

Paradoxically, the driest continent on earth has the potential to supply life-giving fresh water to parched regions of the world, including Australia – the driest inhabited continent on earth. Ice is one of the primary defining features of the Antarctic and makes up about 60 per cent of the world's fresh water. The 'harvesting' of fresh water from Antarctic ice is not a topic many people take seriously. This is strange since the quest for new sources of fresh water will intensify as climate variations bite harder into traditionally dry areas of the planet. When these dry areas become unproductive (projected under worst-case scenarios), ice from Antarctica may prove to be one of the world's most valuable commodities.[38] Australia needs new, secure fresh water sources and the federal government has committed $12.9 billion to a 10-year project, 'Water for the Future', to secure a long-term water supply for the country.[39]

Before Antarctic ice becomes commodified, inherent conceptual and practical difficulties must be overcome. Some of these relate to intellectual discussions about sovereignty and the public nature of water,[40] while others relate to more strictly technical, economic, legal or political problems. Nevertheless, good arguments could in future be made for harvesting water from Antarctica. References to ice in its various forms can be found in the Antarctic Treaty (Article VI) and throughout the Annexes to the Madrid Protocol. There is also a reference to ice-covered waters in Article 234 of the UN Law of the Sea Convention. However, none of these references substantially clarifies the legal position of Antarctic ice in relation to its use as a source of fresh water. The Final Act of SATCM IX noted that harvesting of ice was not considered to be an Antarctic mineral resources activity. CRAMRA – the failed minerals convention – excluded ice from its functional definition of 'mineral resources' (presumably on the basis that ice is renewable).[41] In 1989 the Parties adopted a recommendation on the exploitation of icebergs, and it was subsequently dropped as an agenda item.[42] The 1970s was the peak interest period for the exploitation of Antarctic icebergs and interest has lessened ever since.

Jurisdiction over icebergs was one of the sticking points in past consideration of ice harvesting and, along with questions of technical complexity and cost-benefit, contributed to a hiatus in interest since the 1970s.[43] At the First International Conference on Iceberg Utilization in Iowa in 1977, it was acknowledged that icebergs were a potential water and energy resource, although the logistical requirements of towing icebergs out of the Antarctic, and the economic viability of such a project, were preclusive then, and probably still are today. That is not to say that fresh water cannot be harvested from ice in situ and transported around the world in bulk carriers in the same way that carriers transport liquefied natural gas. During the 1970s and 1980s, several researchers undertook studies (mostly unpublished) into iceberg transportation, but feasibility remained uncertain.[44] If one considers that ice is not a mineral (and therefore not prohibited from being extracted under Article 7 of the Madrid Protocol mining prohibition), Australia could appropriate fresh water from an iceberg within the Exclusive Economic Zone off its Antarctic Territory and transport it to Australia at some point in the future. Currently, however, this is unlikely to be anything other than hypothetical given the cost and the unknown reaction to such appropriation.

Aesthetic/touristic resources

The Antarctic has been part of Australia's social heritage since the first explorers departed and returned, and their stories of tragedies and achievements were popularly reported in the colonial newspapers from the first half of the nineteenth century (see chapter 1). The Antarctic is a fertile source of material for popular culture: there is a large volume of literature, and contributions from other arts include music, paintings, television and film. Most significant, however, is the value of its appeal as a tourist destination. The Antarctic has been commodified for popular consumption and new players continue to enter the tourism market, with more vessels making more trips to the continent for longer periods of time each year.

Tourists visit the Antarctic for diverse reasons, including the wildlife, the spectacular ice forms, the mystery of the unknown. It has been speculated that a trip to Antarctica is – for some – a visit to a sacred place and 'an attempt to establish a more harmonious relationship with nature and with God'.[45] Whatever the attraction, from the beginning of commercial tourism in the 1960s the numbers of tourists, operators, vessels and voyages have risen continuously

Tourists from the ship Orion standing near king penguins at Macquarie Island Station, Buckles Bay in 2011. Gregory Stone, Australian Antarctic Division, © Commonwealth of Australia

ever since.[46] A total of 35 262 tourists visited the Antarctic in the 2009–10 Austral summer, as reported by the International Association of Antarctica Tour Operators.[47]

Tourism operations to the Antarctic favour departure from the port of Ushuaia in Argentina because of the relatively short distance across the Drake Passage to the Peninsula. While Peninsula routes make up about 95 per cent of total tourism effort, a handful of companies operate regular expedition cruises from Hobart or ports in New Zealand to the East Antarctic regions of the Ross Sea and Commonwealth Bay. Voyages to the East Antarctic involve a significantly longer time at sea – as many as seven days – compared with as few as two days for the voyage from

Ushuaia. Australian nationals made up seven per cent of this number, ranking the country fourth, below the United States, Germany and the United Kingdom, in Antarctic tourism.[48] Australian interests are represented in nearly 15 per cent of the membership of the International Association of Antarctica Tour Operators.[49]

Tourism has been on the ATCPs' agenda since the 1966 ATCM, when the parties recognised that tourist visits to Antarctic bases might 'prejudice the conduct of scientific research', not to mention potentially damage flora and fauna and generally disrupt scientific bases.[50]

More than 30 recommendations in the 50-year history of the Antarctic Treaty meetings of parties have encouraged responsible, environmentally friendly and self-sustainable tourism.[51] In 2004 the ATCPs adopted a legally binding Measure that requires tourism operators to have emergency search and rescue and medical evacuation insurance to avoid burdening scientific programs.[52] Five years later, they adopted a number of existing industry by-laws as a means of formalising non-mandatory rules.[53] Measure 15 prohibits landing passengers from vessels carrying more than 500 persons, restricts the number of passengers ashore at any one time to 100 or less, and allows only one tourist vessel to visit a site at any one time.[54] This move aims to address safety as well as enhancing protection of both environmental and aesthetic values.

Finally, perhaps the most significant decisions with consequences for tourism to come from ATCMs in recent years relate to its developing relationship with the International Maritime Organization (IMO). Most tourism is ship-borne and in 2004 the ATCPs invited the organisation – the world shipping regulator – to design a mandatory code for polar shipping.[55] A recommendatory code adopted late in 2009 outlines, among other things, new categories for vessels travelling in polar waters.[56] A vessel will be rated as belonging to one of seven polar classes and the rating will permit it to operate only under specific conditions. For example, those in category PC1 can operate year-round in all ice-covered waters, whereas those in category PC7 can operate only in summer and autumn, and only in thin first-year ice.[57] In 2009 the IMO also adopted a ban on the use and carriage of heavy-grade oils through a resolution of its Marine Environment Protection Committee.[58] The ban will come into force on 1 August 2011. The new ice ratings and the ban on heavy fuel oil, along with tougher emissions regulations[59] and Antarctic Treaty Consultative Party scrutiny, have meant that Antarctic tourism operators will be operating to the highest environmental standards. Until now, the playing field has been a fairly even one with plenty of room in the market for new operators catering to all classes of fare-paying passengers. In the future, however, extra regulation from within the ATCMs directly, or more likely indirectly via the IMO, will strengthen the natural limitations already operating on Antarctic tourism and keep numbers low. This will in turn help to protect the aesthetic values that are so inextricably tied to the environment.

***

The resources of Antarctica and the Southern Ocean have been important in enhancing early political interest in the region. The question of the natural resource potential of the continent, no matter how elusive, has continued to shape interaction within the Antarctic Treaty System. The Protocol on Environmental Protection provides a ban on future mineral exploitation, in addition to reinforcing the importance of the Antarctic environment. Extraction of minerals and hydrocarbons is unlikely for many decades. Marine living resources will continue to be exploited within the framework of CCAMLR's concept of rational use within a precautionary ecosystem approach to resources management. New activities are already in play – biological prospecting, for example, particularly from krill and krill products, has increased its market impact in recent years. Other resource activities – hydrocarbon extraction or fresh water production from ice, for example – are much longer-term prospects, if indeed they could be called prospects at all. In addition, Antarctica will continue to be a tourist destination and an area of ongoing scientific research.

Australia's interests as a claimant state and as an active Consultative Party to the Antarctic Treaty mean that it will remain engaged with the resources agenda as it has in the major Antarctic marine living resources and minerals management issues of the past. Emerging areas, such as biological prospecting and the relatively older issue of water from Antarctica, have the potential to raise the same challenges that marine living resources posed to the delegates at the Antarctic Treaty negotiations and the first ATCM.

Notes

[1]   See Taylor (1930) 2.
[2]   Taylor (1930) 224–26.
[3]   Taylor (1930) 93–107.
[4]   Taylor (1930) 100.
[5]   Government of United Kingdom (1961) Proposal for the establishment of a special body to consider technical questions under Agenda Item 19 – Administrative arrangements, ATCM I, Canberra, 1961. Document later withdrawn.
[6]   Triggs (1984).
[7]   Parks and Wildlife Service Tasmania (2010) History of Sealing on Macquarie Island, <www.parks.tas.gov.au/index.aspx?base=1822> (accessed 25 July 2010).
[8]   In 1874 the *Challenger* expedition naturalist, Henry Moseley, reported these tide lines of skeletons: quoted in Hince (2005) 124.

[9]   Parks and Wildlife Service Tasmania (2010) History of Sealing on Macquarie Island, <www.parks.tas.gov.au/index.aspx?base=1822> (accessed 25 July 2010).

[10]   Australian Antarctic Division (2010) 'Australia's Involvement in Antarctica', <www.antarctica.gov.au/about-antarctica/history/australias-involvement-in-antarctica> (accessed 29 November 2010).

[11]   Barrett (2009) 364.

[12]   Government of United Kingdom (1961) Draft Convention for the Protection of Wild Life in the Antarctic, ATCM I, Canberra, 1961.

[13]   Recommendation VIII of Meeting I, hereinafter written as Recommendation I-VIII.

[14]   Succinctly described by Stokke (1996).

[15]   Scientific Committee on Antarctic Research, 'Biological prospecting in the Antarctic region: a conservative overview of current research' Working Paper 2, Antarctic Treaty Consultative Meeting XXXIII, 2010. In this report SCAR refers to the database 'Bioprospector', which is a joint enterprise between the United Nations University and UNEP. See <www.bioprospector.org/bioprospector/antarctica/home.action>. See also Foster, Nicol and Kawaguchi (2009): the authors constructed a database from patents registered in the European and US Patent Offices since the 1970s to detect

trends in the krill fishery of the Southern Ocean.

[16]   Jabour-Green and Nicol (2003). See also 'Bio-prospector' database, <www.bioprospector.org/bioprospector/antarctica/home.action>.

[17]   Jabour (2010).

[18]   Scientific Committee on Antarctic Research, 'Biological prospecting in the Antarctic region: a conservative overview of current research' Working Paper 2, Antarctic Treaty Consultative Meeting XXXIII, 2010, 3.

[19]   This obligation is derived from the Madrid Protocol, Art. 8 and Annex I. Other obligations from the Antarctic Treaty System include the freedom of scientific research, duty to exchange and report observations and results from Antarctica and duties to protect Antarctic fauna and flora. See ATCM XXXII Resolution 9/2009, at <www.ats.aq> for full details.

[20]   Foster, Nicol and Kawaguchi (2009).

[21]   Nicol and Endo (1997) 367.

[22]   Jabour (2010).

[23]   Jabour (2008).

[24]   Brook (1984).

[25]   Haward et al (2006).

[26]   Antarctic Science Advisory Committee (1997).

[27]   Australian Antarctic Division (2002).

[28]   van Ommen and Morgan (2010).

[29]   US Department of State (2002).

[30]   Gjelsvik (1983) 62.

[31]   Gjelsvik (1983) 62.
[32]   González-Ferrán (1983) 160.
[33]   Gjelsvik (1983) 63.
[34]   Law (1964) 9.
[35]   Bergsager (1983) 169.
[36]   González-Ferrán (1983) 160.
[37]   Jabour (2008) 429–31.
[38]   Water has already surpassed crude oil in value. A bottle of water from an Australian supermarket is about $1.50/litre. Compare this with a litre of crude oil at 52¢ (assuming a barrel of oil is ~159 litres at US$81.63/barrel and using a conversion rate of 0.9787 [as at November 2010]).
[39]   Australian Government Department of the Environment, Water, Heritage and the Arts, *Water for the Future,* 2008, <www.environment.gov.au/water/australia/index.html> (accessed 24 November 2010).
[40]   Lopes P (2008) 'Water with borders: the institutional postponement of international water trade', Draft paper presented to International Studies Association 49th Annual Convention, San Francisco, 2008, 3.
[41]   CRAMRA Art 1.6: 'all non-living natural non-renewable resources, including fossil fuels, metallic and non-metallic minerals'. The implied exclusion of ice in the definition of mineral resources was expressly confirmed in the Final Act of the Fourth Special Antarctic Treaty

Consultative Meeting on Antarctic Mineral Resources, at 434 (US Department of State 2002).

[42] Recommendation ATCM XV-21 (Paris 1989), 'Exploitation of Icebergs', entered into force 29 January 2004. The recommendation urged that governments exchange information on the feasibility of commercial exploitation, technology and environmental implications and to coordinate further research through SCAR.

[43] Trombetta-Panigadi (1996).

[44] Weeks (1980).

[45] Berger (2010).

[46] Headland (1994b).

[47] International Association of Antarctica Tour Operators (2010a) Tourism Statistics, <http://image.zenn.net/REPLACE/CLIENT/1000037/1000116/application/pdf/touristsbynationality_total4.pdf> (accessed 26 June 2010). This figure represents only paying tourists, not staff or crew who also 'visit' and land on Antarctica.

[48] International Association of Antarctica Tour Operators (2010a). The numbers of Australian tourists remain high despite the distance from Australia and the expense of cruises departing from South America.

[49] International Association of Antarctica Tour Operators (2010b) Membership Directory 2010–2011, <http://apps.iaato.org/iaato/directory/list.faces;jsessionid=E6DBFF923C52854

DB5686C45365075D8> (accessed 26 June 2010).

[50]   Recommendation IV-27, 1966.

[51]   This accords with the Australian government policy on tourism: 'The Australian Government recognises the legitimacy of tourism activities in Antarctica provided they further the principles and objectives of the Antarctic Treaty and their conduct is ecologically sustainable and socially responsible.' See Australian Antarctic Division, About Antarctica, Tourism, <www.antarctica.gov.au/about-antarctica/tourism/australian-policy>. For the full list of measures regarding tourism, see the Antarctic Treaty Secretariat website, <www.ats.aq/e/ats_other_tourism.htm>.

[52]   Measure 4/2004.

[53]   Measure 15/2009.

[54]   Formerly IAATO Bylaws Article X-A.3, Article II-F and Article X-B respectively.

[55]   The process began in 2004 with a request from the XXVII Antarctic Treaty Consultative Meeting to Parties to work with the IMO towards establishing guidelines for Antarctic shipping (ATCM Decision 4(2004)). The 26th meeting of the International Maritime Organization Assembly adopted the recommendatory 'Guidelines for ships operating in polar waters' on 2 December 2009 (IMO Resolution A.1024(26)). The development of a mandatory

code is ongoing and expected to be completed in 2014.

[56] Many tourist vessels conduct both Arctic and Antarctic cruises.

[57] IMO Resolution A.1024(26), 'Guidelines for ships operating in polar waters', Table 1.1 – Class Descriptions, 10.

[58] International Maritime Organization, 'Amendments to MARPOL Annex I to add Chapter 9 – Special requirements for the use or carriage of oils in the Antarctic area,' Resolution MEPC.189(60), 26 March 2010.

[59] International Maritime Organization, '2009 Guidelines for monitoring the worldwide average sulphur content of residual fuel oils supplied for use on board ships', Resolution MEPC.183(59), 17 July 2009.

11

Mining and 'World Park Antarctica', 1982–1991

Andrew Jackson and Peter Boyce[1]

In 1959 the potential for Antarctica to hold valuable minerals that might one day be extracted was well understood, as was the potential for arguments over who should get the benefit. But the Treaty negotiators carefully avoided the question, cleared the way for the Antarctic Treaty to be adopted – and left the minerals problem to a future generation. When the issue bubbled to the surface sooner than expected, consensus was briefly reached on regulating possible mining, but promptly broken again when Australia decided that the Treaty parties had got it wrong. The subsequent agreement to a different approach became a landmark in the Treaty system's evolution. This chapter tells some of that story from the perspective of Australian officials involved at the coalface.

El Dorado on ice?

Antarctica's mineral resource potential hovered in the backs of the minds of some of its explorers, and Douglas Mawson, an accomplished mining engineer, used this to plead support for his 1911–14 expedition.

In 1964, Antarctic Division director Phillip Law predicted that within 20 years harbours would have been established for ships to load cargoes of concentrates transported by giant hovercraft from year-round inland mines.[2] The reality was more sober. While economically exploitable minerals were not discovered and there was no enthusiasm for prospecting, the potential remained. Indeed, the 1973 oil crisis sparked interest in seeking new hydrocarbon fields – including at the poles.

Digging into the issues

Australia had argued for the 1959 Treaty negotiations to sidestep the mining issue and the Treaty made no mention of minerals. There was no hurry to solve a problem that did not exist. But a decade later, in 1970, amid concerns of exploration under the guise of scientific research, the subject was broached, and it was included on the 1972 Antarctic Treaty Consultative Meeting (ATCM) agenda in Wellington – three years ahead of the arguably more pressing marine living resources issue. Those opening discussions recognised three key themes – the potential interest in minerals, the need to protect the environment, and the need to keep the Antarctic free from discord.

A simple solution would have been to ban mining then and there – and to do precisely this, in 1975 New Zealand proposed a 'World Park', an ambitious but ill-defined concept. The move was unsuccessful and ATCMs continued to refer the matter to various experts for advice.[3] Although the management issues could be identified, neither economic resources nor any interest in mining were apparent. But that was the point – in the absence of mining it would be much easier to negotiate rules to regulate it. And so, in 1977, the parties agreed to refrain from mining while progress was made towards a regulatory regime. Four years later, they decided to negotiate a minerals convention. Debate began in Wellington in 1982, when the fourth Special Antarctic Treaty Consultative Meeting (SATCM) initiated the first of 12 negotiating sessions. Much was at stake. Australia sought an influential role in minerals activities in the Australian Antarctic Territory (AAT), a share of earnings from them, stringent environmental protection, and prevention of unfair economic practices. Other delegations had equally full agendas. Given the requirement that decisions be reached by consensus, political will and diplomatic skill were required in equal measure. Christopher Beeby, New Zealand's astute head of delegation, led debate with deft diplomacy; apart from a practical regime, he had also to find a politically acceptable one. As negotiations intensified, new states acceded to the Treaty and criticism grew in the UN (see Chapter 9). Inevitably, blocs formed: claimants collaborated to protect their interests; non-claimants worked to minimise any claimant advantage. Some sought stricter environmental standards, others weaker, and developing states pleaded for concessions.

Diversity of views was also apparent within Australia's delegation.[4] Should mining or environmental interests drive the Convention, and should responsibility for implementing it lie with the government's environment or resources departments? On the one hand, Australia had strong environmental objectives, influenced by an environmental lobby whose concerns fuelled protests over construction of France's Dumont d'Urville airstrip and led to the establishment by Greenpeace of World Park Base on Ross Island. (Environmentalists also pragmatically recognised the momentum towards the minerals Convention, and proposed ways to 'plug the gaps' rather than lobby against the Convention and risk unregulated mining.[5]) Alongside the environmental concerns were the government's forthright sovereign interests: the wish for a special role in decisions affecting the AAT and the right to tax activities there, and for a substantial claimant share of net revenue from prospective mining.[6] These positions were anathema to some others.

Consensus on Antarctic mining

The final negotiations took place in Wellington in May and June 1988. Beeby progressively tackled unresolved issues. One week from the end he implored delegations to find consensus on 'a result that is tolerable to all' even though it would not be anyone's preferred position.[7] Solidarity between claimant nations wavered; Australia was risking isolation, and the prospects for its objectives of a special share of revenue and anti-subsidy provisions faded. Instructions were sought from Canberra. Ministers consulted, some proposing to hold out. On 1 June the Acting Foreign Minister, Michael Duffy, instructed the delegation to conclude the Convention rather than thwart consensus. That meant compromise. Despite disappointment about lost claimant privileges, Australia supported the consensus arrived at after six years of negotiation, in the end having achieved improved environmental measures, membership of relevant institutions and the power to veto activities in the AAT.

On 2 June 1988 CRAMRA (Convention for the Regulation of Antarctic Mineral Resource Activities) was adopted. It did not directly allow mining, but provided mechanisms to assess its impacts and, if acceptable, to regulate them. Mining could not proceed until separate liability rules were negotiated. It seemed that the minerals issue was solved in a regime with a strong environmental emphasis.

Pride in consensus was evident. France's head of delegation said the Convention should 'very shortly enter into force' and the moratorium 'not last any longer than necessary'.[8] Entry into force would require the participation of 11 developed and five developing Treaty parties – these 16 had to include all seven claimants, and the United States and the USSR. The next step would be progress towards entry into force, starting with opening the Convention for signature for one year from 25 November 1988.

Cold feet

Although some Australian ministers talked up the achievements, others quietly expressed regrets about the concessions that had been made. Not publicly known at the time, Treasurer Paul Keating on 21 September wrote to Foreign Minister Gareth Evans and other Cabinet colleagues about CRAMRA's implications for Australia's sovereignty, revenue share, and the risk that certain governments might subsidise uneconomic mining. With such matters being canvassed, there was no mood for early signature.

Environmentalist rumblings emerged on both sides of the Tasman.[9] At an 11 November meeting with conservation organisations, Environment Minister Senator Graham Richardson acknowledged the differences of view on CRAMRA within Australia, observing that the Minister for Resources, Senator Peter Cook, was against signing: 'His position and Treasury's is more to do with subsidised mining than anything else. My inclination is that we should sign'.[10] Ten days later Keating's letter was leaked, revealing a warning: Australia risked losing sovereignty if it ratified CRAMRA and would 'concede our economic claims over Antarctica for virtually nothing'.[11] He was later reported as saying, somewhat uncharitably given the difficult negotiating climate, that Australia had been poorly represented in Wellington and 'must be prepared to stand alone if necessary on this issue'.[12] The Treasurer publicly declared his outright opposition on 21 November and the following day Evans tabled CRAMRA in Parliament 'to promote community discussion'.[13]

Questioning of the Convention increased as the 25 November 1988 opening date for signature approached. In Wellington, New Zealand Foreign Minister Russell Marshall expressed surprise at Keating's opposition, hoping that 'Australia will come to the party'. An environment group representative added that Keating's concern reflected resentment at the way Australia had been treated in June.[14] Meanwhile, as non-government organisation (NGO) opposition became louder, independent Senator Jo Valentine moved a motion urging the government to establish an Antarctic 'World Park'.[15] At CRAMRA's signature ceremony two days later, nine Treaty parties committed themselves to it.[16] Australia held back.

As 1989 began, the Australian Government maintained an open mind on signing the Convention. But the first of a series of unexpected events took place to influence Australian thinking. On 28 January the Argentinean vessel *Bahaia Paraiso* capsized near Palmer Station, spilling 675,000 litres of fuel, and just one month later Peru's *BIC Humboldt* ran aground. Suddenly, Antarctic marine pollution was a real issue. But on 24 March the Antarctic Peninsula accidents were trumped when, at the other end of the world, the *Exxon Valdez* ran aground in Alaska, spilling more than 40 million litres of crude oil into waters rich with birdlife, marine mammals and valuable fisheries. For a polar disaster its scale was unprecedented. Graphic images of stricken tankers started circulating at a time of heightened debate about Antarctic mining. However hard one might promote CRAM-RA's environmental rules, there was no escaping the spectre of a similar catastrophe in Antarctica.

Antarctic issues generally had a low profile in Australia and enjoyed an unusually bipartisan political approach. NGOs mobilised a campaign of letters to ministers, achieving the highest ever public attention on Antarctica. Media interest increased the pressure. Evans championed CRAMRA's safeguards and maintaining consensus. Cook retorted that refusing to sign would put Australia in a strong position to win concessions. Within Labor Caucus minds were being made up. On 6 April Caucus Chairman Bob Chynoweth announced his opposition to CRAMRA. Ministers supporting signature were becoming isolated. Richardson recognised Keating's and Cook's concerns but continued to put the case for consensus: 'The minerals Convention did not come out of thin air ... I, for one, would not like to be the person who started it all again'.[17]

But a week later, once again on the other side of the world, another event shifted Australian thinking. Lobbying by renowned marine explorer Jacques Cousteau had made France increasingly hesitant about signing. A strong Greens showing in French elections added pressure, and a repeat was expected in European Commission elections in June. On 20 April, French Prime Minister Michel Rocard announced that he would not support CRAMRA, albeit with an important qualification: 'France will not ratify the Treaty in its present state'. He then proposed its renegotiation.[18] Given that CRAMRA required French participation, this announcement received surprisingly muted responses – some countries assuming a clarification would be announced, or that France would reconsider if it got no support. New Zealand's Foreign Minister Marshall lambasted France's environmental credentials, citing the construction of the Dumont d'Urville airstrip and the sinking of the *Rainbow Warrior*.[19]

Rocard's decision did not go unnoticed in Australia. On 27 April Keating wrote to Prime Minister Bob Hawke about his concerns over CRAMRA. This time he raised new elements – Antarctica's ecological importance, the World Park option, and the government's environmental record.[20] On 2 May Opposition Leader John Howard announced his objection to CRAMRA, saying, 'We must not let this opportunity pass' and that 'above all, we believe that mineral activity in Antarctica poses too great a threat, especially to the terrestrial environment'.[21] An Australian Conservation Foundation demonstration in Canberra that day was addressed by Labor's Chynoweth, Liberal Senator Chris Puplick and Democrats Senator Norm Sanders – all opposed

CRAMRA. Hawke was being cornered. It was predicted Cabinet would put off a decision until France had clarified its position and heat from Howard's comments had abated.[22] But on 3 May, Puplick's Senate motion to ban Antarctic mining was passed.[23] Bob Hawke was listening carefully. In a 4 May press conference he said, 'Don't try and conjure up a position that what we're going to have is the Liberals with Democrats taking a more appropriate environmental position than this Government ... we haven't reached that peculiar state of affairs.'[24]

Decision time

As Cabinet's decision date approached Cook seized the opportunity, writing to Hawke to say that with France's decision, Coalition opposition and Keating's 'World Park' suggestion, the circumstances had changed. Across the Tasman, New Zealand Environment Minister Geoffrey Palmer urged signature, arguing that some protection from mining was better than nothing. Hawke weighed the issues – the importance of Treaty consensus; CRAMRA's environmental provisions; Australia's sovereign interests; international pressure to sign up and domestic pressure not to; and an impending election in Tasmania, where in 1983 he had first established his environmental credentials.

Coincidentally, Australian diplomats were gathering in Paris at a crucial meeting to set the agenda for October's biennial ATCM. The environment was already on the agenda, partly inspired by the *Bahaia Paraiso* incident. Chile had proposed comprehensive environmental measures – not to replace CRAMRA but to integrate existing requirements.[25] There was intense interest in France's position and speculation about Australia's. CRAMRA was at risk – just three more participants were needed: Australia and France, plus either China or India.

A hostile Senate made Antarctic mining legislation impossible and France had already cast doubt on CRAMRA's future. Was this Australia's opportunity? On 8 May Canberra sent the delegation in Paris last-minute instructions to test 'alternative scenarios to straightforward signature and ratification, and you are requested to circumspectly canvass opinion accordingly'.[26] On 11 May the domestic ground shifted again when the Labor Caucus decided to oppose mining. Hawke telephoned Rocard to gauge French thinking. The delegation in Paris circulated a paper proposing a 'catch-all convention to protect the Antarctic environment' and over time subsuming existing instruments, referring to CRAMRA with the ominous phrase 'should it enter into force'.[27] The reaction was immediate and hostile. Once-close friends of Australia were appalled. Even some NGOs thought it too ambitious and questioned the wisdom of tabling it.[28] By the meeting's end there was resigned acceptance that Australia and France had moved the issue into a political realm where diplomats could only watch developments.

On 16 May officials scrambled to meet Hawke's request for a briefing on what 'World Park' actually meant. Keating increased his attack, branding CRAMRA a 'starter's gun for mining'; Richardson prepared to retreat from his support for the convention; and the media predicted Cabinet would reject it.[29] Puplick railed against Hawke: 'This Labor Government is now desperately hoping the French, by not signing the Convention, will relieve them of their clear moral obligation to make a decision.'[30] But the sentiment was not universal – Antarctic veteran Phillip Law blustered that by not signing Australia would be utterly discredited and 'branded naïve, ignorant and obstructive ... an Antarctic World Park is doomed to failure'.[31]

On 22 May 1989 Cabinet was to make its decision. Hawke woke to front-page news that Evans' Cabinet submission had leaked – it would recommend Australia not sign CRAMRA but instead explore a World Park.[32] That same day NZ Prime Minister David Lange wrote to Hawke urging signature and reminding him that a World Park had been rejected in 1975. Lange was too late. Hawke announced Cabinet's decision that Australia would not sign, but instead promote a comprehensive environmental regime to prohibit mining in an Antarctic Wilderness Reserve.[33] Even though Hawke's announcement had included the acknowledgement that CRAMRA was better than nothing, the Convention was now at serious risk.

Whose idea was it?

According to Paul Keating, during the 1988 debate about CRAMRA's merits, only he and Peter Cook argued against signing it. He says that Hawke ridiculed his arguments for opposing CRAMRA.[34] Significantly, Keating did not at that time propose the World Park option, an idea he later claimed to have suggested to Michel Rocard in October 1988. Why Keating did not reveal that option until April 1989 is not clear.

Hawke's recollections of the circumstances of his decision to oppose CRAMRA differ from Keating's and are difficult to reconcile with media reportage of the period. A 2010 history of Hawke's prime ministership contains a strong and puzzling claim: 'Quite unknown to the electorate, but of further irritation to his Cabinet colleagues, Hawke in 1989 had undertaken another environmental initiative that would be difficult to manage and would win the government not a single vote'.[35] Hawke's wife and biographer, Blanche d'Alpuget, reports that after reading CRAMRA over the weekend he decided to take it to Cabinet and oppose it. Hawke's chief of staff at the time, Craig Emerson, is quoted as having agreed with the prime minister's verdict on CRAMRA that same weekend, while noting that the prime minister was 'confronted with strong advice from Foreign Affairs, PM and C and Treasury that we should hold our horses'.[36] This is odd because Foreign Affairs had been arguing for adoption of CRAMRA while Treasury had been consistently opposed. More seriously, d'Alpuget appears to have overlooked earlier vigorous discussion among key ministers from late 1988, ignoring Hawke's silence and implied neutrality on the matter over many months. She acknowledges that the so-called 'environmental initiative' of the prime minister was taken in 1989, which suggests that she is referring to the May 1989 events.

In an interview with Peter Boyce, Hawke vigorously denied that Keating's position on CRAMRA had any bearing on his own decision to oppose it, or that mounting NGO agitation influenced his thinking.[37] D'Alpuget argued that the Australian public was unaware of the Convention's existence at the time Hawke reached his decision and that the media were uninterested.[38] Even if media discussion of CRAMRA *had* been limited, and that apart from environmental NGOs the public were not excited by its ramifications, in the five months preceding the May 1989 Cabinet decision sections of the community had become aware of developments and were quite vocal. The then head of the Antarctic Division, Rex Moncur, recalls that something like 20,000 appeals to his minister had been received.[39]

Shockwaves

Environment groups greeted Cabinet's decision with elation. But not so New Zealand, which had a strong investment in CRAMRA following Beeby's role.

Marshall deplored Australia's action and Lange expressed New Zealand's frustration at twice being stymied by Australia: 'New Zealand set out ... in favour of a World Park concept a decade ago and we were actually thwarted in that by Australia'. But his famous sense of humour prevailed when asked whether Australia had a better perception than New Zealand of public attitudes to Antarctica: 'Yes. Five Tasmanian [parliamentary] seats better!'[40] Diplomatic reporting described other Treaty Parties' reactions. Some expressed mild surprise while others were bluntly angry, and with impeccable diplomatic understatement one embassy reported back to Canberra that 'good taste compels us to forbear quoting some of the expressions involved'.[41] Parties pointed to potential destabilisation of the Treaty, the risks of the moratorium collapsing and unregulated mining. While relishing domestic support the government clearly had work to do internationally.

In his response to Lange on 15 June, Hawke refused to back down. He then had to work on France, which had still not formally rejected CRAMRA. Hawke wrote to Rocard proposing a 'Wilderness Park' and arguing that banning mining would greatly reduce pressure on the Treaty. The following day he left for France, the United Kingdom and the United States, accompanied by Richard Woolcott, Australia's most senior diplomat.

In Paris on 19 June, in 30 minutes over coffee, President Mitterand assured Hawke that France would not sign, agreed that mining should be prohibited, and said that France would help pursue an alternative. The ensuing announcement was personally drafted by Mitterand.[42]

The United Kingdom dug in – its objection to a mining ban was 'not negotiable'.[43] On 21 June Evans met his British counterpart, Geoffrey Howe, who argued that the 'perfect' risked being an enemy of the good. Evans reassuringly noted that Australia had only forsworn signature, not subsequent accession, which remained a fallback.[44] In the House of Commons the defence of CRAMRA was curt: 'the world needs not a grand gesture, however superficially attractive it might be, but an example of how environmentally properly [sic] internationally negotiated sustainable development can be pursued'.[45] In Washington on 25 June, Hawke's reception from President George H W Bush was equally unenthusiastic, although Senator Al Gore showed sympathy. Gore's instrumental role would have to wait.

Like Evans, Richardson was sanguine about the chances of success. Asked on 3 July if he could foresee Australia ever signing CRAMRA, he said that Australia would spend six or twelve months canvassing opinions: 'Hopefully by the end of that period we will be winning, and if we are not then we will reconsider'.[46] In New Zealand, Palmer optimistically observed that Rocard, too, had not rejected CRAMRA for all time.

Global diplomacy

Despite widespread lack of support for Australia's position it did appeal to some. Italy, Denmark and Austria were encouraging and then Belgium announced that it too opposed CRAMRA.[47] Nevertheless, more diplomatic effort was needed. The government appointed former governor-general Sir Ninian Stephen as Australia's inaugural Environment Ambassador and charged him with pursuing the initiative. Australia's most highly skilled diplomats were brought in.[48] The challenge confronting them, to persuade their counterparts to accept Australia's proposal and restore consensus diplomacy, was truly daunting. Woolcott recalls that the Department of Foreign Affairs and Trade (DFAT) was handling 'an unusually demanding situation' in 1989, simultaneously pursuing five major additional Hawke government foreign policy initiatives.[49] All diplomatic missions were briefed on the CRAMRA decision, but no additional staff were deployed to the fence-mending assignments.

To this point New Zealand had strongly defended CRAMRA: not only had Beeby led the negotiations, but it was known as the 'Wellington Convention' and New Zealand was to gain the Commission's headquarters. But on 4 August NZ Opposition Leader Jim Bolger announced that a National Party government would reject CRAMRA, noting that New Zealand, previously a leader on environmental issues, was slipping behind world opinion: 'We will not sign the Convention but will instead work with countries like Australia to develop a framework in which no mining is allowed'.[50] The following week Geoffrey Palmer, by then prime minister, tabled his Antarctic White Paper with a more accommodating position than his predecessor. In wistful reference to the failed 1975 World Park idea, he noted that 'the international community has now caught up'.[51] While proposing integrated environmental measures, the paper retained CRAMRA pending consensus on a new approach. The government would, however, legislate to prohibit mining in the Ross Dependency and by New Zealanders anywhere in Antarctica.[52] Palmer rejected accusations of stealing the high ground from Australia. Sadly for Palmer, environment groups dismissed the strategy as inadequate.[53]

In mid-August Hawke widened the effort, writing to counterparts in Argentina, Japan, China, the USSR and India. Further discussions with France followed, this time in Australia, where Hawke and Rocard agreed to a joint initiative. Preparations began on a proposal to October's Treaty meeting.[54]

While some countries were interested, others stood firm. Giving evidence to US Congressional hearings, a State Department official asserted that while Australia might 'slow down' CRAMRA, it would eventually have to capitulate.[55] Perhaps this view reflected limited public engagement on the issue in the United States, where only two NGO groups (Greenpeace and Humane Society International) openly opposed

CRAMRA. In the United Kingdom the Foreign Office quietly fought back, promoting CRAMRA as an environmental regime.[56]

Australia continued working with France on ways to advance the initiative. France was keen to restore consensus. As host of the October Treaty meeting, it feared diplomatic breakdown. Failure would, however, be inevitable if the two parties were not uniformly resolute – it was important for Australia, seen as leading the campaign, to maintain the commitment despite international opposition. DFAT officers, led by Alan Brown, undertook urgent lobbying missions. Australian diplomats were not insensitive to the feelings of their adversaries, many of whom, such as the United Kingdom's John Heap and Tucker Scully in the United States, had invested long years in negotiating CRAMRA. New Zealand's Beeby was a highly regarded senior career diplomat, and in the words of Australia's Treaty specialist, Bill Bush, 'had been so careful and skilled, one felt that the desertion was like an act of vandalism'.[57] Not surprisingly, Heap and Scully were unsympathetic, but the head of the legal division in Chile's foreign ministry, well known to Alan Brown from Law of the Sea negotiations, admitted to being unenthusiastic about CRAMRA.

In the United States a confidence boost was achieved with Gore's resolution calling on the US Administration to put aside CRAMRA and support the negotiation of new agreements.[58] Evans described this as a 'tremendously important breakthrough'.[59]

Congressional interest later turned out to be crucial in tempering US attitudes. Australia needed all the help it could get and Gore's timing was perfect – 10 days later the ATCM opened.

The Paris meeting would be significant – it was the last one before CRAMRA closed for signature, and the last before a party could call a conference to review the Treaty.[60] It was going to be difficult. For the first time the consensus by which the Treaty operated was fractured because a Party had re-neged.[61] Dominating the room were differences over CRAMRA and its alternatives. On the table were two papers by Australia and France: one proposing a Special Antarctic Treaty Consultative Meeting (SATCM) to elaborate an environmental regime, and another outlining the components of a new convention declaring Antarctica a 'Wilderness Reserve'.[62] There were competing proposals by Chile, New Zealand, Sweden, the United States and the United Kingdom. Vigorous debate was assured and France feared a diplomatic crisis. Pressure on Australia was high. While parties agreed to discuss environmental proposals, the sticking point was the link to CRAMRA.[63] The skill and patience of DFAT's Alan Brown and John Burgess were instrumental in keeping Australia's position afloat. Brown recalls in particular 'the rancid reaction' of the British and the Americans, and likened the meetings to four balls being played at once on the squash court.[64] In the meeting's final hour the parties agreed to hold a SATCM in 1990. The price

Australia paid was agreement to also discuss CRAMRA's liability rules.[65] CRAMRA was still alive.

Signs of progress

As 25 November 1989 approached, the option to sign CRAMRA was about to close. Spain, West Germany and France announced that they would not sign, while Japan and Czechoslovakia squeezed in just before the deadline. Nineteen had signed.[66]

At year's end Australia reviewed progress: four ATCPs opposed CRAMRA; 11 favoured an environment regime alongside CRAMRA; four opposed an environment regime outright; the remainder were undecided.[67] Australia still had a long way to go in the 12 months before the November 1990 SATCM. Would it be possible to change the minds of parties that had already signed CRAMRA? The diplomatic campaign stepped up. In January 1990 Australian and French officials met in Canberra to strengthen the environment proposal, and Australia worked hard to maintain unity with France, at that point its only collaborator.

Signs of progress began to emerge with encouraging noises from the US Congress and softer language from the United Kingdom and others. Speaking in Canberra on 14 February, Nikolai Ryzhkov, Chairman of the USSR's Council of Ministers, announced his willingness to 'collaborate with Australia and other countries in implementing those initiatives that cover the survival of the Antarctic'.[68] Hawke's confidence grew. On 25 February he claimed that India, the

Netherlands, Scandinavian countries, Chile and other South American countries would do the same. 'Country after country is responding to public opinion,' he said, and predicted that the United States would change its mind.[69] He was delighted the following day when in New Zealand Palmer decided 'to set aside consideration of the ratification of CRAMRA'. Palmer said that progress on protecting Antarctica was being hampered by the deadlock and that 'the New Zealand Government intends to do what it can to assist'.[70] NGOs criticised Palmer for leaving CRAMRA alive, but with an unusually apposite metaphor Hawke enthused over the 'snowballing' support for Australia and France, and acknowledged that New Zealand's support had 'a very significant psychological impact'.[71] Cousteau, visiting New Zealand, congratulated Palmer and suggested that an environmental regime should be named the Wellington Convention in deference to New Zealand's early advocacy of a 'World Park'.[72]

These developments did not go unnoticed in the United States, and public awareness was growing with Congressional hearings. NGOs mobilised and on 7 February Republican Congressman Silvio Conte tabled an Act providing for a mining ban and urging negotiations on an environmental agreement. 'Saving a continent is a once-in-a-lifetime opportunity,' he said.[73] Others followed and by August 1990 seven Bills and Resolutions on Antarctic conservation had been tabled. The US Administration had not moved, but pressure was mounting.

In March, Australian and French officials finished revising the proposals and on 5 April Australia's overseas missions were instructed to renew representations. This triggered a 'compromise' proposal from the Federal Republic of Germany and a UK proposal that was ultimately to have a decisive impact on the form of regime to be debated – it suggested a protocol rather than a convention.[74] But the United Kingdom would not abandon CRAMRA and NGOs erupted. Cassandra Phillips of the World Wildlife Fund was determined: 'It is never easy to persuade Margaret Thatcher to change her mind, but we are hopeful we can mobilise public opinion'.[75] The Fund's polling showed that 60 per cent of Britons wanted Antarctica protected. An intensive letter-writing campaign was rewarded on 1 June when Gerald Kaufman, Shadow Foreign Secretary, announced that if the increasingly isolated Thatcher government were to ratify CRAMRA, a Labour government would denounce it.[76]

But Australia and France could not relax – evidence of caucusing among Australia's 'opponents' was emerging. Unknown to Australia and France, representatives of nine ATCPs had met in Kiel in mid-July, under cover of a meeting discussing law of the sea issues, to develop a counter-proposal – a framework Protocol to be accompanied by annexes on specific issues.[77] The paper assumed CRAMRA would be set aside, but only for a fixed period. Other parties had not shown their hand with such precision, but many would be happy to run with whatever this bloc could achieve. When they met again in August, Australian and French officials could not be complacent, as the more accommodating attitude of other parties was predicated on CRAMRA's survival.

On 14 August, Cabinet decided to legislate to ban minerals activities in the AAT, including its continental shelf, and by Australians anywhere in Antarctica. This would replace the toothless 1930 Mining Ordinance, remove any doubts about Australia's commitment, and dispel the criticism that Australia rejected CRAMRA to defend sovereign interests.[78] Ironically, the proposal precipitated protests because the legislation was based on the existence of sovereignty. The Foreign Minister defended the action, claiming that Australia was doing what it expected collective international action to achieve.[79]

New Zealand thaws

Encouragingly, on 23 August New Zealand dramatically shifted position. Palmer said, 'We have set it aside – that means we have abandoned it. We are for permanent bans on mining in Antarctica.' Media noted the government's 'chagrin at being led along a six-year path to nothingness ... now the Government is committed to the World or Wilderness Park concept, the very point from which a New Zealand Labour government started in 1975, and for which it found no support'.[80] On 3 September the New Zealand Cabinet decided to draft its own proposal, an all-in-one protocol that would permanently ban mining.[81]

As the proposal developed, New Zealand took Australia into its confidence – there was no doubting the change in position.

In late September, with the SATCM in Chile just two months away, the US State Department's strident opposition to Australia's proposals was being moderated by Curtis Bohlen, Assistant Secretary of State for International Environmental Affairs. As a former WWF vice-president, Bohlen himself was sympathetic to an indefinite mining ban.[82] News that he was to lead the US delegation raised hopes, as did the October passage of Congressional resolutions calling for a ban on mining.[83] The US position for the SATCM was revealed on 5 October in a paper supporting comprehensive environment measures, but in parallel with CRAMRA.[84]

As the SATCM approached, Australia and France secured support from Belgium and Italy. The four countries met in Brussels on 8 October to assess progress. It was recognised that 'had we set our objectives two months ago we would almost certainly have set them too low', but despite signs of CRAMRA dying, they still lacked confidence in achieving the ultimate objective.[85] Some were even wary of the New Zealand proposal lest it be seen as more 'environmental' than the Australian–French proposal. The four parties prepared a 'silhouette' of a convention, this time to ban Antarctic mining in a 'Nature Reserve, Land of Science'. On 9 October they consulted a 'like-minded' group expressing interest in the approach.[86]

One week later the 'Indicative Draft of a Convention for the Comprehensive Protection of the Antarctic Environment' was ready to be launched by the 'Four Powers': Australia, Belgium, France and Italy.[87]

Parties promoted their positions in a flurry of diplomatic exchanges. By the SATCM there was a plethora of options: the 'Four Powers' Convention; New Zealand's 88-page draft Protocol; a UK draft with 13 main articles, all of which were silent on mining, plus 12 articles on dispute settlement; and proposals from the United States, the 'Kiel 5', India, and a dense 90-page offering from the Antarctic and Southern Ocean Coalition.

With the United States apparently softening, the United Kingdom was becoming isolated. Media reported that Britain's Environment Secretary Chris Patten reacted 'angrily to Britain's tag as the "dirty man of Europe", but he risks escalating that reputation worldwide when the United Kingdom leads the pro-mining lobby at the Antarctic Treaty conference in Chile in a few weeks' time'.[88] The United Kingdom took umbrage at NGO campaigning, and 'comfort in the knowledge that among the real Antarctic specialists, scientists and foreign policy experts its position was well understood and indeed favoured'.[89] But its main concerns were consensus and the precedent that Australia's reneging on CRAMRA had set for other agreements. The United Kingdom was determined to 'lead the way back to consensus. If there was unstoppable movement towards Australia's position then the UK would not step in the way'.[90] Further thawing of British attitudes came a week before the SATCM. Foreign Office Minister of State Tristan Garel-Jones said the United Kingdom would 'try to find a new consensus ... the important thing to remember about CRAMRA is that when it came forward it was part of the consensus'.[91]

On 16 November 1990, US President George H W Bush signed Conte's *Antarctic Protection Act 1990,* making it illegal to engage in mining there and asking the Administration to negotiate a new instrument to protect the Antarctic. The sticking point was how long mining would be prevented: a moratorium or an outright ban? According to Conte, 'an indefinite ban means a ban without time limitation, and the Congress certainly did not intend that CRAMRA, or the son of CRAMRA, be part of the agreement establishing an international ban'.[92]

Three Chile weeks

On 19 November, the SATCM opened in Viña del Mar, a major coastal resort in Chile. Competing proposals meant it would not be easy. Australia, again led by Brown, was keen to avoid a re-run of the 1989 tensions. Despite barbed comments about 1989's loss of consensus, the atmosphere was less charged than in Paris. On 29 November a desultory exchange of views was held on CRAMRA's liability rules, delegations instead concentrating on seeking common ground on the environment.[93] Genuine interest emerged in resolving the differences before the end of 1991, the date after which a Party could trigger a Treaty review conference and, importantly, a year before the UN's 1992 First Earth Summit.[94] Divided into two subgroups, the meeting progressed multiple issues simultaneously. The negotiating text prepared by Norway's head of delegation, Rolf Trolle Andersen, was instrumental as it allowed common ground and differences to be isolated. The 'Four Powers' gave ground on the type of instrument as there was no prospect for their stand-alone convention.

Back in Australia the government accepted its proposed mining ban was 'unlikely to succeed in the near future'. Britain, the United States, the USSR and Japan were obstructing progress. Brown was reported as saying that 'the minerals issue was a very hard nut to crack. It may not be possible to resolve it at Viña del Mar'. Evans made no secret of 'the Government's regret that the United Kingdom, in particular, has so far failed to recognise the groundswell of national and international opinion'.[95]

After three weeks of intense negotiation the SATCM concluded on 6 December. The parties had agreed to negotiate a new environment instrument. On the table was the 'Andersen Draft': a protocol to the Treaty with appendices on marine pollution, waste disposal, environmental impact assessment, and the conservation of fauna and flora.[96] The critical prohibition on mining was in, but with a subtle ellipsis flagging that discussion had not closed.[97]

Returning to their capitals, delegations reflected on the next steps before the SATCM reconvened in April 1991 in Madrid. New Zealand conceded that the Andersen Draft would subsume its own proposal – their 'bottom line' had been less flexible than Australia's.[98] Germany, which would be hosting the October ATCM in Bonn, said that it might consider a mining ban. Japan considered the minerals question still open, but recognised it was increasingly isolated.[99] The USSR accepted an unqualified mining ban, provided there was the option for review; and the United States accepted Andersen as the way forward.[100]

United in opposition

The US position was, however, not as flexible as it appeared, since it had an important qualifier on mining – it would insist on a fixed 20–40 year moratorium requiring consensus to be extended, with a fallback as rigorous as CRAMRA to avoid a legal vacuum. Some saw it as taking the debate backwards. Quizzed on this in Congressional hearings, Bohlen conceded that CRAMRA was dead but that it was better to keep all options on the table.[101] Australia, not surprisingly, wanted no departure from the Andersen Draft, which provided a prohibition rather than a moratorium, and no reference to a CRAMRA safety net. All Australia required was to end Article 6 with a full stop.[102] It would not be that simple. The United Kingdom and the United States were united on a fixed moratorium.[103] The 'Four Powers' met in Rome on 25 March to plan their approach to the forthcoming negotiations – they would move to an unqualified ban, lifted only by consensus or a review conference called after 60 years.[104] Clearly the key to consensus would be finding a compromise: would agreement be required to lift a mining ban, or to extend it?

As the Madrid meeting approached, the 'Four Powers' circulated amendments to the Andersen Draft, retaining the unqualified mining ban. The United Kingdom accused Australia of being unwilling to find consensus. It was also reported that British NGOs had been told the Australian and New Zealand positions were based on short-term political considerations and were dishonourable.[105] The President of SCAR weighed in, saying that the rejection of CRAMRA would be regretted: 'the blame for the wrecking of the Convention lies with a number of vociferous, well-financed environmentalist groups'. He went on to dismiss concerns about the environment: 'increasing numbers of fur seals have destroyed vegetation on a number of islands ... human sewage is nothing compared to the runoff of faeces from birds and seals into inshore waters'.[106] NGOs responded by demanding an absolute mining prohibition and no review before 100 years, and in April organised protests in Bonn during the preparatory meeting for the 16th ATCM.

Environmental campaigners in penguin suits outside the ATCM XVI preparatory meeting in Bonn in April 1991. Courtesy Andrew Jackson

Despite the clamour, diplomatic missions reported an emerging mood for early consensus and a prohibition with a review mechanism. On 16 April, a week before the negotiations resumed, Germany and Japan relented and supported a prohibition. The defection of Japan stung CRAMRA's supporters. On 11 April, 16 US Senators wrote to President Bush expressing alarm that the United States might promote a position weaker than the *Antarctic Protection Act* signed the previous November. Australia judged that the United States would be the last holdout. The US paper in Madrid confirmed this, characterising its proposed fixed-term prohibition as a significant concession and arguing that parties advocating a permanent ban had shown no flexibility. The United States saw no reason to alter its position while others adhered rigidly to theirs.[107] There was still some way to go.

Coming together in Madrid

The second session of the SATCM was held from 22–30 April 1991. The two working groups separated the political issues from the practical matters to be covered in the annexes. The Andersen text was the basis. Australia's delegation, led by John McCarthy, came under sustained pressure. The problematic issue of mining was led personally by Rolf Andersen at a dinner on 25 April for the heads of nine key delegations. It was resolved three days later in a further meeting that ran until 4 am on 29 April. Consensus on mining was reached – it would be prohibited. If a party so wished, a review conference could be called after 50 years, but there would be strict provisions regarding how the prohibition could be lifted.[108] The hurdles for mining had been set very high.

Australia's position had been vindicated, but at a price. In Working Group 2, Antarctic Division Director Rex Moncur met an unexpected vulnerability – strict rules on non-indigenous species made it untenable to maintain Australia's much-loved huskies in the AAT. Dogs were prohibited, and there were howls of anguish in Australia's Antarctic community.[109]

The diplomats in Madrid had decided that Antarctica would become a 'Natural Reserve Devoted to Peace and Science'.[110] There would be no mining. In

Australia, ministers applauded the outcome. Environment Minister Ros Kelly said that the agreement was one of the most significant environment agreements ever reached.[111] Later, Bob Hawke was to describe the achievement as 'one of the things I'm proudest of in my career in government'.[112] Environmentalists praised the result. But more important was whether other governments would accept what diplomats had negotiated. The debate was nearly over and Treaty governments moved to signal their support. British Prime Minister John Major personally intervened on 10 May 1991 by outflanking 'strong Whitehall opposition to the proposed 50-year Antarctic mining ban by the simple but bold expedient of declaring his support for it' in an unnoticed parliamentary written answer.[113]

The parties returned to Madrid on 17–22 June to finalise the drafting. Two days later, the 30th anniversary of the entry into force of the Treaty passed. But one party had still not accepted the Protocol. It was not until 3 July that President Bush announced US agreement: 'I strongly support these measures which are based on a US initiative. I also support the restrictions on mining activity in the Antarctic'. Bush welcomed the agreed formula relating to mining because it provided effective protection for Antarctica without foreclosing options for future generations.[114]

Hawke was jubilant:

Ambassador John McCarthy signing the Madrid Protocol for Australia on 4 October 1991. Australian Antarctic Division, © Commonwealth of Australia

I hope that perhaps my letter to George Bush last week may have been one of the factors in bringing the Americans to that point ... You remember when I initiated this process a relatively short time ago we were treated with almost scorn. It was regarded as mission impossible. We've stuck to our guns, that great wilderness in the Antarctic is going to be preserved.[115] Three months later, on 3–4 October, the parties met in Madrid for the

SATCM's concluding session. The text of the Protocol on Environmental Protection to the Antarctic Treaty and its four annexes were adopted, as well as the Final Act committing parties to early ratification and provisional implementation.[116]

Two weeks later in Bonn, at the 16th ATCM, a further annex was adopted, signalling the start of a new period of priority for Antarctica's environment. The Bonn meeting also adopted a declaration, drafted by Australia, to celebrate the 30th anniversary of the Treaty's entry into force. There would be no review conference – the Protocol negotiations had done their job. Consensus was restored.

Who saved Antarctica?

It is entirely appropriate that Bob Hawke should be proud of protecting the Antarctic. But others can also claim credit. Michel Rocard and Jacques Cousteau had instrumental roles in France, including influencing the Australian Government. Promotion of the initiative also came from the environment movement in Australia and around the world.[117] Within Australian domestic politics there were many players, such as Labor's Bob Chynoweth and Opposition Leader John Howard, both of whom aired objections to CRAMRA ahead of the government's decision. Treasurer Paul Keating also directly raised with Hawke the 'World Park' option in his April 1989 letter.[118] But turning the initiative into a viable proposal required the help of key Australian diplomats and officials such as Sir Ninian Stephen, John Burgess, Alan Brown, John Mc-Carthy, Brendan Doran, Bill Bush and Rex Moncur. Even then Australia could not act alone and depended on support from France, Italy, Belgium and a growing coalition of others. Perhaps facetiously, it may be argued that in Alaska the *Exxon Valdez* had a role in protecting the Antarctic. Others have somewhat wistfully observed that CRAMRA itself played its part – had it been given a more sensitive title (along the lines of Convention to Protect the Antarctic from the Effects of Mining) the debate might never have occurred at all.[119]

Ultimately, however, protection of the Antarctic environment was achieved by all Antarctic Treaty Consultative Parties. That required patient diplomacy and timely compromise – witness, for example, the numerous concessions made by Australia from its original proposals, the dramatic shift in New Zealand's support for the Wellington Convention, and the eleventh-hour deal on reviewing the mining ban offered by the United States. Consensus was the objective and all of the Treaty parties can take credit for that.

Notes

[1]   The authors thank the Australian Antarctic Division for facilitating access to its records, and Bill Bush and David Lyons for their helpful suggestions during the drafting of this chapter.

[2]   Law (1964).

[3]   Talboys (1978) 33.

[4]   The delegation comprised officials covering foreign affairs, international law, resources, treasury, science, environment and other interests. A representative of the Tasmanian Government

and environmental groups was also included. Delegations were led by senior DFAT negotiators Ian Nicholson and John Brook.

[5] Antarctic and Southern Ocean Coalition (1988).

[6] *JOIDES Resolution* had discovered rich sediments in Prydz Bay, offshore from Davis and Mawson. Beale (1988).

[7] Antarctic Treaty Special Consultative Meeting on Antarctic Minerals. *Chairman's Plenary Statement.* INF/09. Secretariat/23.5.88.

[8] In AAD file 87/720(6).

[9] On 19 September, New Zealand reported that Greenpeace would campaign against ratification, but not signature.

[10] Transcript of talks with Peak Conservation Organisations, Canberra 11 November 1988, in AAD file 88/893(2).

[11] Keating's letter was no doubt prepared in his Department. He has since maintained that his rationale for opposing CRAMRA was quite different from that of his Department: 'I didn't take any notice of Treasury briefings, which were predictable and pedantic'. Interview with Peter Boyce, 11 October 2010.

[12] Seccombe (1988). The view that Australia failed or was disunited arose from differing expectations of what Australia could realistically achieve in the final negotiations. See also Fewster, Alan (1989) in *Sunday Telegraph* 30 April 1989.

[13]   Minister for Foreign Affairs and Trade. Antarctic minerals convention. News release M200, 22 November 1988.

[14]   Surprise at Keating treaty opposition. *Dominion* (NZ) 23 November 1988.

[15]   Senate Hansard, 23 November 1988, 2580. This was followed a week later by a motion from Democrats Senator Jean Jenkins calling for an 'Antarctic Conservation World Wilderness Park' (Senate Hansard, 30 November 1988, 3141).

[16]   Brazil, Finland, New Zealand, Norway, South Africa, South Korea, Sweden, Uruguay and USSR.

[17]   Senate Hansard, 12 April 1989 1436.

[18]   Transcript of French television TF1 *Questions à Domicile,* 29 April 1988. It was later reported that Rocard's announcement caught French Foreign Ministry officials by surprise: in AAD file 88/893(3).

[19]   Transcript of interview: Radio New Zealand *Good Morning NZ* 24 April 1989.

[20]   Reproduced as document AU27041989 in Bush (1997) Booklet AU88-89, 19–21.

[21]   Joint Press Release, John Howard and Senator Puplick, 2 May 1989.

[22]   Scott (1989).

[23]   Senate Hansard. 3 May 1989, 1645–67.

[24]   Transcript of interview on AAD file 88/893(3).

[25] Antarctic Treaty Preparatory Meeting 1989, paper PREP/WP/1.

[26] In AAD file 89/311(1).

[27] Antarctic Treaty Preparatory Meeting 1989, paper PREP/WP/14.

[28] DASETT minute to Environment Minister 19 May 1989, in AAD file 89/311(1).

[29] Clark (1989), Peake and Milburn (1989).

[30] *Daily Telegraph* 19 May 1989, 14.

[31] Letter to the Editor, *The Australian* 18 May 1989, 12.

[32] Houwelling (1989).

[33] Prime Minister of Australia (1989) *Protection of the Antarctic environment.* Joint Statement with the Minister for Foreign Affairs & Trade, Senator the Hon Gareth Evans QC, and the Minister for Arts, Sport, the Environment, Tourism & Territories, Senator the Hon Graham Richardson.

[34] Annie Rushton interview with Keating for ABC, nd, 1996; also Keating interviewed by Peter Boyce, 11 October 2010.

[35] d'Alpuget (2010) 254.

[36] Emerson is quoted in d'Alpuget (2010).

[37] Bob Hawke interviewed by Peter Boyce, 11 October 2010.

[38] d'Alpuget (2010) 255.

[39] Rex Moncur interviewed by Peter Boyce, 8 December 2010.

[40] NZ would back polar mining veto. *Canberra Times* 30 May 1989, 4. The assessment that Hawke was pursuing the green vote in Tasmania was shared by Richard Woolcott (2003) 214. Lange's legendary wit surfaced again when challenged with Graham Richardson's insistence that claims Australia's decision was driven by Tasmanian politics were rubbish – Lange is reported as replying 'Being Minister for the Environment, he would know all about rubbish!', reported in AAD file 89/311(2).

[41] In AAD file 89/311(2).

[42] Statement agreed between Prime Minister Hawke and President Mitterand, Prime Minister Rocard and Foreign Minister Dumas during talks in Paris on Monday 19 June 1989. Reported in Australia (1989). It was also reported that Mitterand seized the drafting from officials: 'When something is so clear we don't need all this diplomacy!' He then took over the drafting of the final text himself, which was then agreed in a few minutes.

[43] United Kingdom, Foreign and Commonwealth Office (1989) *Antarctic minerals convention: a memorandum.*

[44] In AAD file 89/453(1).

[45] Tim Eggar, Under Secretary of State for Foreign and Commonwealth Affairs. UK House of Commons *Hansard,* 4 July 1989, <www.p

ublications.parliament.uk/pa/cm198889/cmh ansrd/1989-07-04/Debate-11.html> (accessed 24 November 2010).

[46] Transcript of press conference, Wellington, New Zealand, 3 July 1989.

[47] Neither Denmark nor Austria were ATCPs, and Belgium (an ATCP by virtue of being an original signatory) was not active in Antarctica. For these reasons Australia's early coalition of support may not have been taken seriously, and this was compounded by the then environmental concerns about France's Antarctic airstrip.

[48] Leading DFAT officials included John Burgess, Alan Brown, John McCarthy, Bill Bush and Brendan Doran.

[49] Woolcott (2003) 214.

[50] Bolger JB (1989) Address to Environment and Conservation Organisations of New Zealand Conference, 4 August 1989.

[51] New Zealand. Prime Minister. Press statement 9 August 1989.

[52] New Zealand (1989).

[53] White Paper disappoints Greenpeace. *Evening Post* (NZ) 10 August 1989.

[54] Prime Minister of Australia (1989) *Joint statement on environmental issues agreed by Prime Ministers Hawke and Rocard,* Canberra, 18 August 1989.

[55] In AAD file 89/453(2).

[56]   UK Foreign and Commonwealth Office (1989) *The Antarctic Minerals Convention and its role in protecting the Antarctic environment.* Background brief series.

[57]   Bill Bush interviewed by Peter Boyce, 8 October 2010.

[58]   US Senate Resolution 206.

[59]   Transcript of press conference 28 September 1989.

[60]   These dates were critical, even if for symbolic reasons. The option of signing CRAMRA would close on 25 November 1989 (although afterwards it would be open for a State to accede, but not automatically become a permanent member of the Commission – hence the last-minute rush by Sweden and Spain to become recognised as ATCPs). The 30th anniversary of the Treaty held more importance. Article 12.2(a) of the Treaty provides that a review conference can be held 30 years after the Treaty's entry into force, that is, after 23 June 1991. Australia was keen to discourage any thought of a review conference.

[61]   The point was not lost on Australia's Antarctic diplomats: Australia was an original signatory, a keen supporter of the Treaty, and itself a long champion of consensus.

[62]   XV ATCM/WP/2 and XV ATCM/WP/3. Interestingly, the components paper proposed that human activities having an impact on the

environment should be regulated or, where agreed, prohibited. It did not specify mining.

[63] Andrew Jackson (1989) Report on attendance, Antarctic Treaty meetings, October 1989 (unpublished).

[64] Alan Brown interviewed by Peter Boyce, 10 October 2010.

[65] Antarctic Treaty, Recommendation XV-2. The importance of this for the future of CRAMRA should not be understated. The requirement to elaborate the liability rules was embedded in Article 8.7 of CRAMRA and the Convention's Final Act. While prospecting could take place, Article 8.9 of CRAMRA provided that exploration and development could not proceed until the liability rules were in place.

[66] The signatory states were Argentina, Brazil, Chile, China, Czechoslovakia, Denmark, Finland, German Democratic Republic, Japan, New Zealand, Norway, Poland, South Africa, South Korea, Sweden, Union of Soviet Socialist Republics, United Kingdom, United States of America, and Uruguay. See www.mfat.gov t.nz/Treaties-and-International-Law/01-Treat iesfor-which-NZ-is-Depositary/0-Antarctic-Mi neral-Resource.php.

[67] Informal 'running sheet' in AAD file 89/932(1).

[68] In AAD file 89/932(2).

[69] Montgomery (1990).

[70] Transcript of post-Cabinet press conference, 26 February 1990. See also Prime Minister (NZ) *Antarctica.* Press statement, 26 February 1990.

[71] Prime Minister (Aust.) Media release, 26 February 1990; transcript of interview with radio journalists, Sheraton Brisbane, 26 February 1990.

[72] In AAD file 90/932(1).

[73] Conte, Silvio O (1990) Media release, 8 February 1990. See also: *Antarctic Protection and Conservation Act* HR3977.

[74] The difference is significant. A Convention would (like CCAS and CCAMLR) be separate from the Treaty and open to any country in the world to negotiate and sign. A Protocol would be a supplement to the Treaty, open only to Treaty Parties to negotiate, and designed so that all ATCPs had to be part of it.

[75] Transcript of ABC Radio, *Early AM* 10 May 1990.

[76] In AAD file 90/498(2).

[77] The parties that met in Kiel were the US, USSR, India, Brazil, UK, Chile, NZ, Argentina and Norway. Australia and France were not surprised by an emerging alternative, although they did not want arguments over the type of regime to detract from discussion of its substance. In AAD file 90/498(3).

[78] *Australia to legislate to ban on* (sic) *Antarctic mining.* Joint Statement by Senator Gareth

Evans, Minister for Foreign Affairs and Trade, and Mrs Ros Kelly, Minister for the Environment, 17 August 1990. The *Antarctic Mining Prohibition Act 1991* replaced the Australian Capital Territory ordinance, which applied in the AAT, allowed mining and imposed a trivial $20 penalty.

[79] Minister for Foreign Affairs and Trade (1990). *Protecting Antarctica.* Speech by Senator Gareth Evans, Australian Institute of International Affairs.

[80] In AAD file 90/759(2). See also Full circle on Antarctica. Editorial. *Herald* (NZ) 27 August 1990.

[81] Hon Phillip Woolaston. *The Antarctic Environment.* Speech given at University of Auckland, 8 September 1990.

[82] In AAD file 90/759(1).

[83] US House of Representatives Resolution HJR418 and Senate Resolution SJR206.

[84] United States (1990) Comprehensive Measures for the Protection of the Antarctic Environment and Dependent and Associated Ecosystems. Working paper.

[85] In compendium comprising brief and other documents in preparation for discussions with France in Brussells, 10 October 1990 (unpublished).

[86] Greece, India, Sweden, Denmark and the Netherlands.

[87]   This document became meeting document XI ATSCM/1

[88]   Brown (1990).

[89]   In AAD file 90/759(2). This echoed earlier comments by senior Australian scientists about the potential impact on science. The concern had been expressed 'that scientific research is becoming more and more crowded in with reviews and bureaucracy and that the creative spirit, essential in science, can be squeezed to death. We seem further down this track in Australia than elsewhere'; see AAD file 90/888.

[90]   In AAD file 90/759(3).

[91]   Transcript of BBC Radio Four interview, 16 November 1990.

[92]   Statement of Honorable Silvio Conte, 15 November 1990. The Act is at <http://uscode.house.gov/download/pls/16C44B.txt>.

[93]   Antarctic Treaty (1990). *Report to the XVI ATCM on the meeting held pursuant to Recommendation XV-2.* (XVI ATCM/INFO 43)

[94]   Treaty Parties were concerned that lack of consensus could spark UN interest in debating the Antarctic environment. For information on the Summit see <www.un.org/esa/earthsummit/>.

[95]   Peake (1990).

[96]   Chile (1990).

[97]   Draft Article 6 simply provided that 'Any activities relating to mineral resources, other then

scientific research, shall be prohibited...' (the ellipsis was included).

[98] In AAD file 91/55(1).

[99] In AAD file 90/759(3).

[100] In AAD file 91/56(1).

[101] In AAD file 91/55(1).

[102] Australian non-paper. Australian comments on non-paper 'Antarctica: Preparation of the forthcoming round on global protection of the environment' presented by Spanish embassy, Canberra on 5 March 1991 (unpublished).

[103] United Kingdom. Tristan Garel-Jones, Minister of State for Foreign and Commonwealth Affairs. Foreign and Commonwealth Press Release 25 March 1991.

[104] Australia (1991) Antarctica SCM XI. Comprehensive environmental protection instrument. Rome 4P consultations (25–26 March 1991) (unpublished).

[105] In AAD file 91/55(1).

[106] Laws (1991) 4

[107] XI ATSCM/2/INFO.1

[108] Article 7 prohibits mining: 'Any activity relating to mineral resources, other than scientific research, shall be prohibited'. Contrary to popular misconception, this is not a 50-year ban or moratorium. In common with any international convention, including the Antarctic Treaty itself, there are provisions for amendments to be made. Article 25 provides the

mechanisms, and includes special rules relating to the mining ban. In brief, the prohibition can be lifted at any time provided there is consensus. If there is no consensus to lift the ban, a review conference may be called after 50 years if a party so wishes. A change to the ban can take effect only if ratified by 75 per cent of the ATCPs, including all of the ATCPs present at the Protocol's adoption, and a regime to assess and manage minerals activities is in place. The earliest date for a review conference is January 2048.

[109] John Heap of the UK (a country also using dogs) subsequently described this as 'one of the higher absurdities of the negotiations' but one that had to be conceded 'in order to achieve more realistic solutions in other areas'. In AAD file 91/32(2).

[110] Other labels that had been tried included 'Wilderness Reserve', 'World Wilderness Park' and 'Nature Reserve'. Ultimately, Article 3 of the Protocol replaced the 1964 Agreed Measures label of 'Special Conservation Area' and settled on the unique, but hardly euphonious, 'natural reserve, devoted to peace and science'. Some consider the Protocol a step along the way to achieving the 1972 'World Park' concept and the problematic inclusion of Antarctica on the World Heritage List. See, for example, Mosley (2007).

[111]   Seccombe (1991) 9.
[112]   Nonee Walsh (2009) Hawke honoured for Antarctic mining fight, <www.abc.net.au/news/stories/2009/12/14/2771530.htm?section=justin>.
[113]   McCarthy (1991) 10. Major's response is recorded in the House of Commons *Hansard,* <hansard.millbanksystems.com/written_answers/1991/may/10/antarctica S6CV0190P0_19910510_CWA_64>.
[114]   In AAD file 91/55(2).
[115]   Transcript of press conference, Parliament House, 4 July 1991.
[116]   Antarctic Treaty (1991).
[117]   Among the notable players within the non-government organisations were Lyn Goldsworthy, Cath Wallace, David Westlake, Margaret Moore, James Barnes, Beth Marks and Janet Dalziell. It has been suggested that over 200 environmental organisations were involved in the campaign – see Goldsworthy (1990). For an NGO insider's account see Mosley (2009).
[118]   Keating was later to assert an even more significant role by claiming that it was he who had sown in the mind of Michel Rocard the idea of stalling on CRAMRA – see chapter 12 and Bowden (1997) 410–12.
[119]   See, for example, David Lyons quoted in Bowden (1997) 409.

12

Diplomacy

Peter Boyce and Tony Press

Antarctic foreign policy has not often been prominent in the Australian public mind or, surprisingly, even in the minds of historians of Australian foreign policy.[1] However, the Australian Government, keenly interested in Antarctica from the beginning of the twentieth century, recognised its relevance to foreign policy from at least the 1940s, prompted by the expansion of activity on the continent. In the late 1980s the dramatic events surrounding the abandonment of the minerals convention and the subsequent negotiations leading to the adoption of the Madrid Protocol revealed the government's capacity to actively reconsider Australian interests and policy objectives in the Antarctic (see chapter 11 and below).[2] Policy statements at the time and thereafter have described Australia's interest in the region in a mixture of strategic, scientific, environmental and economic terms, all pursued through diplomatic efforts.[3] This chapter provides examples of how Australia conducted its diplomacy during three critical periods and outlines some distinctive features of Australian Antarctic diplomatic style.[4]

Although at Antarctic Treaty Consultative Meetings (ATCMs) the English-speaking delegations form a natural grouping, there are several other discernible 'blocs', overlapping and by no means mutually exclusive. These include the seven claimant states, the 'Latins' (the Spanish-speakers), the southern hemisphere states, and others that form when parties are like-minded on an issue. While four Anglophone states (Australia, the United States, the United Kingdom and New Zealand) have remained very close allies in international politics, within the narrower context of Antarctic diplomacy the British and American viewpoints, especially the latter, have not always accorded with Australia's. This was evident during the 1959 negotiations that produced the Antarctic Treaty and, to varying degrees, in the negotiations described later in this chapter.

Open disputation has been rare. This is partly because of a strong culture of cooperation in Antarctic affairs, and because meetings of the Consultative Parties make decisions by consensus and have generally been spared media attention. The quality of diplomatic communication between the parties has nevertheless been critically important. Antarctic diplomacy has been distinctive on a number of counts, and Australia's exercise of influence within the Antarctic Treaty System (ATS) has exhibited some features of diplomatic engagement which are strikingly different again.

Australian institutions

Australia's earliest political machinery for handling its Antarctic interests was a six-person committee formed in March 1929 to organise the British, Australian and New Zealand Antarctic Research Expedition (BANZARE) (see chapter 1). The committee was chaired by Senator Sir George Pearce, Vice-President of the Executive Council, and included Sir Douglas Mawson and the head of the External Affairs Branch of the Prime Minister's Department, Dr Walter Henderson.

Apart from the few eminent explorers called upon to provide policy advice, Mawson and Edgeworth David especially, the official who exhibited most interest in Antarctic matters during the 1920s and 1930s was Richard Casey. Casey served as Australia's political liaison officer in London from 1924, reporting regularly by confidential letter to Prime Minister Stanley Bruce. He developed a strong interest in Antarctic exploration, especially as a means of securing territorial claims, and forged a close friendship with Australian aviator Sir Hubert Wilkins, whom he persuaded to drop British flags during the pioneering 1928 flight over the Antarctic Peninsula.[5] While helping prepare BANZARE from London, Casey confessed to Bruce that 'it occupies the greater part of my time'. He pressed for a two-season expedition, the aims of which should be 'the strengthening of our claims to the whole area from the Ross Sea to Enderby Land'.[6]

The formal transfer of the bulk of Britain's territorial claim to Australia in May 1933 failed to arouse much public interest, but was welcomed by several members of the national parliament, none more than Casey, who was by then a federal MP and would soon be appointed Treasurer in the Lyons Cabinet. Not until 1947, however, did the administration of Antarctica become a priority within Australia's Department of External Affairs. An Antarctic Division was established within the department, signalling recognition that advancement of Australia's Antarctic ambitions carried implications for foreign policy and the conduct of diplomacy, especially within the context of the Cold War. Nevertheless, the division was located in Melbourne and focused on establishing stations and conducting research. In 1968 the Antarctic Division was detached from the Department of External Affairs and moved to the Department of Supply, then to Science and finally the Environment portfolios. These changes probably had less of an impact on communication between the division and the foreign policy advisers than might have seemed likely, since the division had never been located in Canberra nor employed any professional foreign service officers. The division continued to expand and its senior ranks included officials whose attendance at ATCMs would play an essential role. In 1980–81 the Antarctic Division transferred to Hobart, and in 1985 it established its own policy functions there.

What is not often recognised publicly is that while the Australian Antarctic Division (AAD) controls the Antarctic program and administers the Australian Antarctic Territory (AAT), it plays a technically subordinate role to the Department of Foreign Affairs and Trade (DFAT) in the nation's Antarctic diplomacy. Leadership of Australian ATCM delegations falls to DFAT, which is able to draw from its large pool of experienced diplomats.[7] The delegation leaders have nearly always been drawn from DFAT's legal division and have a special combination of international legal experience and diplomatic skill. Under DFAT leadership Australia has made significant achievements within the ATCM, which, in turn, have led to important developments in the Treaty system more generally. The following three case studies illustrate how Australian diplomatic effort has been expended in Antarctic affairs.

CCAMLR: from Canberra to Hobart

ATCM IX in London in 1977 paved the way for two regimes: one to manage Antarctica's marine living resources and one to manage its mineral resources (discussed in the next section). Although the road to the first agreement, the 1980 Convention on the Conservation of Antarctic Marine Living Resources (CCAMLR), was by far the smoother of the two, there were distinct challenges. Negotiations took place in a decade when tensions between protecting the environment and exploiting its resources were being debated in unprecedented ways. Not long before, there had been a round of Cod Wars between Britain and Iceland over fishing rights in the North Atlantic, followed by an international oil crisis which raised the spectre of Antarctic oil drilling. Agreements had recently been signed to prevent marine pollution, control the trade in endangered species and conserve Antarctic seals, and Greenpeace had launched its campaign to end whaling. The labyrinthine Law of the Sea negotiations were well underway and the United Nations had made declarations on the exploitation of the ocean floor and on the environment in general which called for collaborative scientific research, international cooperation and due regard to be paid to sovereignty concerns. Many of these matters would have been in the mind of the CCAMLR negotiators. Moreover, the parties at the table had very different interests depending on whether they were fishing nations and whether they were Antarctic claimants. Chapter 7 considers the remarkable regime which resulted; here we focus on Australia's part in its negotiation.

An extended preparatory meeting on marine living resources had preceded the London ATCM by a few months. It established a working committee, chaired by Australia's Keith Brennan. The ATCM adopted 'Interim Guidelines for the Conservation of Antarctic Marine Living Resources' and called for a Special Consultative Meeting (SATCM) to draft a definitive regime. Australia offered to host the meeting. In the event, two sessions were held in 1978: the first in

Canberra from 27 February to 16 March and the second in Buenos Aires from 17–28 July. Informal meetings were also held in Washington and Berne.

The Canberra SATCM was attended by 93 delegates. Hosting the meeting in Canberra had heightened interest in Antarctica among Australian parliamentarians, and two were designated as advisers to the delegation.[8] The Minister for Foreign Affairs, Andrew Peacock, opened the first session, expressing confidence that the successful 19-year history of the Antarctic Treaty would enable negotiators of the new instrument to meet the challenges of reconciling increased exploitation and differing views on sovereignty. Brennan, leader of the Australian delegation, emphasised the magnitude of the task of negotiating a conservation instrument which would extend well beyond the Antarctic continent – and the Treaty nations – and which would protect a whole ecosystem, not just individual species.

The meeting saw the introduction of the technique of 'the chairman's draft', pioneered in the Law of the Sea negotiations. Eight draft treaties were presented and Australian officials worked to consolidate them over several evenings. The result was a very large table comparing each of the drafts. The USSR's summary of the main points became the basis for the chairman's draft discussed at the meeting.

The Australian delegation felt that 'a great deal of progress' was made at the meeting.[9] The first session had agreed on an ecosystem approach to management – although this was 'not achieved painlessly', since splits appeared between fishing nations, led by the USSR and Japan, and more conservation-oriented countries, led by Australia and the United States.[10] Another issue was even more challenging. Australian delegates recognised that the failure to achieve a breakthrough at Canberra hinged largely on the inability of consultative parties to come to an accommodation on the sovereignty issue, particularly as it related to sub-Antarctic islands.[11] At the conclusion of the meeting the Chairman's Draft was taken back to governments for consideration, but with a number of matters unresolved. The parties agreed to meet again in Buenos Aires.

Many participants described the Buenos Aires meeting as 'frustrating'.[12] Much of the work completed in Canberra was revisited, with the result that the coherence of the Canberra draft was diminished and Australian delegates were concerned that major commitments were being unravelled. They also noted that 'negotiations failed to resolve the central issue of sovereignty which divides the non-claimant fishing states from the claimant states'.[13] Nor had consensus been reached on the matter of the sub-Antarctic islands. France remained firmly committed to its rights as a coastal state, rights that were being reinforced at the concurrent negotiations at the Third United Nations Conference on the Law of the Sea (UNCLOS III). Argentina also raised its sovereignty interests and insisted on maintaining the principles embodied in Article IV of the Antarctic Treaty.[14] While there were substantial revisions, Australia's concept of an ecosystem approach to management survived. Critically, the Buenos Aires meeting produced agreement on the necessity for a definitive regime. Recognising the challenges remaining, Australia noted that 'there is no realistic possibility that the definitive regime can be concluded before the end of 1978', as originally envisaged.[15]

Consequently, the Australian delegation regarded the informal meeting in Washington held on 1 September 1978 (in conjunction with an UNCLOS III meeting in New York) as an attempt to get the negotiations back on track.[16] Substantial agreement was reached on the sovereignty issue. Consensus on a number of key articles formed the basis of what was termed the 'Gentlemen's Agreement' and resulted in a draft treaty, the Washington Draft, to provide the basis for ongoing discussion.[17]

Recognising that momentum had returned to the deliberations, the Australian Government was concerned that more work was needed before it hosted the final meeting. On 7 December Peacock wrote to all ATCPs suggesting a deferral of the second Canberra meeting, originally proposed for January 1979. He identified a number of issues that needed to be resolved, including the European Community's relationship with the Convention, and the question of the French islands. Australia suggested that diplomatic exchanges continue and that an informal meeting be held at the Australian Embassy in Berne to address these concerns.

The Berne meeting, 12–16 March 1979, was chaired by John Rowland, chair of the first Canberra SATCM and now Australian Ambassador to France, and hosted by Keith Brennan, now Ambassador to Switzerland. This meeting became pivotal. It was attended by all 13 ATCPs and provided an opportunity for parties to discuss the Washington Draft and to agree on a venue and date for the final conference.[18]

In late 1979, the tenth ATCM in Washington provided opportunities for further discussion and informal meetings, mostly directed at 'the French Islands problem'. An annex to the Convention dealing with this issue was proposed, but did not at that stage gain consensus. The Australian Government promoted Hobart as the site for the headquarters of the new convention's Commission and distributed a promotional brochure to all delegates.

A formal meeting was held in Canberra on 5–6 May 1980 to establish rules for the final diplomatic conference (7–20 May). The conference was attended by the European Union, and two non-ATCPs – the German Democratic Republic and the German Federal Republic. Australia's proposal that invitations be extended to South Korea and the Netherlands was rejected by the USSR. The United States sought accreditation for the Antarctic and Southern Ocean Coalition in a move that anticipated action to broaden the observer base to the ATCM in the next decade, but this too was unsuccessful.

During the preparatory meetings the USSR made several unsuccessful attempts to alter the Washington Draft, reflecting its declared interest in harvesting. It wished to restrict the boundary of the convention to the Antarctic Treaty Area and for the text to refer to marine living resources rather than the marine ecosystem.[19] An annex prepared in Washington to address France's concern was accepted without further discussion.[20] It became known as 'The Chairman's Statement' and was appended to the Convention, deftly resolving 'the French Islands problem'. It also applied to other states, including Australia, which had island territories in the Southern Ocean.[21] The remainder of the draft convention was approved virtually unchanged.

The second part of the SATCM was the diplomatic conference responsible for adopting the Final Act. Eager for the convention to take effect, Australia joined the fishing states in opposing measures aimed at preventing a rush of harvesting in the interval between signing the convention and its entry into force. Instead, a compromise was reached whereby the Final Act of 20 May 1980 urged parties to bring the convention into force as soon as possible and in the meantime to bear in mind its principles. Thus a pioneering instrument came into being. The new convention achieved a rapprochement between conservation and harvesting and was a prototype of what became known as the precautionary approach.

Australia had made valuable contributions to this successful outcome. It had hosted two of the three special ATCMs, committed to concluding a convention and worked to maintain the integrity of an ecosystem approach. At the first Canberra meeting the Australian delegation had skilfully collated the various draft treaties and working documents, keeping the scientific principles at the forefront. And by calling the Berne meeting, Australia had intervened at a critical time to maintain momentum. During the final conference, delegation heads were flown to Tasmania to inspect facilities and were entertained for a weekend 'to convince them of Hobart's suitability as the headquarters for the Commission's secretariat'.[22] The effort was successful. CCAMLR was the first international secretariat established in Australia and its meetings have been held in Hobart annually ever since. This and the position of being the convention's depository state recognise Australia's major contribution to establishing the management regime for marine living resources.

From CRAMRA to the Madrid Protocol: politicians enter Antarctic diplomacy

The other negotiations set in motion by the 1977 London ATCM – to manage Antarctica's mineral resources – were to prove far more fraught. Cabinet's shock decision to reject the Convention on the Regulation of Antarctic Mineral Resource Activities (CRAMRA), the result of six years of patient negotiations within the ATS, was taken on 22 May 1989. It was a dramatic policy reversal. The breaking of hard-won consensus threatened to destabilise the ATS, antagonise Australia's closest Treaty partners, and challenge the culture of trust and collaboration which had been successfully nurtured through nearly three decades (see chapter 11). Some ministers involved had decided not to follow the advice of their departments and, unusually for an Antarctic issue, Australia's political leaders deliberately took on the role of diplomats by directly taking the campaign to other governments.

The decision to reject the convention was not made because the development of CRAMRA had taken Cabinet by surprise. Its detailed negotiation had coincided with the term of the Hawke Labor government, and Foreign Minister Bill Hayden had taken keen interest in developments. When negotiations were completed the year before, in June 1988, the acting Foreign Minister, Michael Duffy, had no hesitation in approving the Final Act, and there had been no public hint of any disinclination to sign the convention.

Domestic debate about the wisdom of signing CRAMRA gathered momentum from mid-November 1988. Conservation bodies lobbied government and a letter-writing campaign ensued. Treasurer Paul Keating warned against signing the convention on 20 November, and the new Foreign Minister, Gareth

Evans, tabled the document in parliament on 23 November 'to promote community discussion'.

Who led the political move to change course is a matter for debate. Then Prime Minister, Bob Hawke, has claimed that from the time of his first close reading of the convention text he was firmly opposed to it: 'When I looked at the agreement in detail and discussed it with my staff, particularly Craig Emerson, I decided that it was preposterous for Australia to be associated with such a proposal.'[23] Furthermore, he decided, 'We are going to lead the world on this issue and change the world's thinking on it.'

But Keating's discussions in Paris in October 1988 assume a special significance. He says that at an OECD meeting he seized the opportunity to establish personal links with France's newly appointed Social Democrat Prime Minister, Michel Rocard. Rocard ex-pressed his hope that France could take a major ini-tiative in international environmental protection to mark the bicentenary of the French Revolution. Keat-ing claims to have suggested that Antarctica be de-clared an international wilderness park and encouraged Rocard to seek cooperation from Australia.[24] He warned Rocard that his own views were not shared by the majority of Cabinet and that if Rocard wished to advance the cause he would need to convince Hawke. If Rocard were receptive to the idea, his president, François Mitterand, had not at that time been persuaded that France should abandon CRAMRA. That would be a challenge awaiting Hawke when, some eight months later, he would lead the Australian charge internationally against the minerals convention.

Lobbying by environmentalists intensified in the weeks preceding the critical Cabinet decision. Political determination to lead the issue was also prompted by what appear to have been differences of view within Cabinet. A well-informed journalist reported: 'A major row is brewing in Cabinet over the Government's attitude to the issue.'[25] Hawke had been lobbied by both the French underwater explorer Jacques Cousteau, who had also been pressuring Rocard, and Sir Peter Scott, son of the British polar explorer. Furthermore, on 27 April 1989 Keating informed Hawke by letter of his discussion with Rocard the previous October.[26]

At the Cabinet meeting of 22 May Hawke assumed leadership of the challenge – to take the Treaty in a new direction, that of a prohibition on minerals exploration in Antarctica. Evans promised an all-out attempt to minimise the damage to Australia's standing within the ATS by the government's *volte-face* and to work closely with the French to persuade their treaty partners to accept an entirely new regime of environmental protection for Antarctica.

Having committed himself to the cause, Hawke stepped energetically into the diplomatic arena. Accompanied by Richard Woolcott, newly appointed head of the Department of Foreign Affairs and Trade, and Emerson, the prime minister visited Paris, London and Washington during June 1989. Woolcott's recollections of the Paris meetings with Rocard and President Mitterand are at slight variance from those of Hawke himself, but there is agreement that the prime minister and Woolcott met Cousteau over breakfast on 18 June.[27] Hawke also met with both Rocard and Mitterand, and has claimed that the French president was not fully committed to a rejection of CRAMRA until he, Hawke, challenged him to firmly endorse Rocard's stand. Attended by only two advisors, the two prime ministers shaped a joint declaration. According to Hawke, 'there was a mutual sense of excitement as we joined forces in pledging to take on the world'.[28]

In London, the British Government was unsympathetic, notwithstanding the generally warm personal relationship between Thatcher and Hawke. Hawke also suspected that some senior Australian officials did not support his change of policy, and challenged Evans and Woolcott about their resolve to push Australia's advocacy of a new regime to a successful conclusion.[29]

In Washington, Hawke received a decidedly frosty reception. The administration of George H W Bush had been in office only a few months, and because of this, State Department influence on its attitude to Antarctica was possibly greater than it would otherwise have been. Furthermore, Australia had recently offended the Americans by announcing the formation of the Asia–Pacific Economic Cooperation forum without US membership. For whatever reasons, Secretary of State

James Baker did not wish to discuss Antarctica with Hawke.[30]

Neither the prime minister nor the foreign minister participated personally in the negotiations between diplomats or at the Treaty meetings. This was left to DFAT's lead negotiators, Alan Brown and John Burgess, who flew to Paris for the October ATCM, described by Brown as 'a horror meeting'.[31] Australia formally flagged the proposal for a comprehensive environmental protection convention and confirmed its unwillingness to sign CRAMRA.

No sooner had the Paris meeting concluded than several of the disagreeing delegation leaders embarked on the long flight to Hobart to participate in a conference on Antarctica's future, sponsored by the Australian Institute of International Affairs, where Hawke took the opportunity to address them directly. He acknowledged that 'our decision has caused considerable anxiety amongst those Antarctic Treaty members who believed that the coming into force of the minerals convention was not just a correct outcome but a foregone conclusion', but he challenged them to accept that times had changed since the 1970s.[32] America's Tucker Scully vigorously defended CRAMRA: 'To me the debate around the Antarctic Minerals Convention seems removed from reality.'[33] His like-minded British colleague, John Heap, pursued the theme of 'sovereignty as a source of stress', but his closing remarks were sharply polemic: 'It would be a tragedy if CRAMRA, the flower of 30 years of development of the ATS – not just six years of active negotiation – were now to be lost.'[34]

Chapter 11 describes how the ensuing weeks and months saw the Australian Government's initiatives pursued. When the Treaty Parties finally agreed to the Protocol which decisively set aside CRAMRA, it did not surprise the Australians that Britain and the United States were the last two to agree. There was a key difference, however, between the British locus of resistance and that of the United States. In Britain, Whitehall's opposition to the draft Protocol was over-ruled by Prime Minister John Major, whereas in the United States it was the president who had to be persuaded. Hawke personally wrote to George Bush to press the case at the last minute.

Prime Minister Hawke was understandably jubilant at the outcome, and the combined efforts of his personal involvement and that of Gareth Evans, and the work of the DFAT/AAD negotiating team, yielded more success than many diplomats would have expected when first confronted with the challenge in May 1989. Not since then have Australian ministers had such a high-level personal role in Antarctic negotiations.

Australia, Antarctica and the 'problem' of the continental shelf

Australia would also be responsible for generating another big test of Antarctic diplomacy. When the government decided in 1999 to collect the data necessary to define an extended continental shelf from the AAT, it did so aware that this would pose significant challenges for it and other Antarctic Treaty parties. This brought actions taken under the UN Convention on the Law of the Sea (UNCLOS) into sharp focus within the ATS, highlighting Australia's standing as a claimant state and disturbing the comfortable silence that had developed on the status of Antarctic claims since the end of the CRAMRA negotiations. The norms of Antarctic diplomacy – where all things Antarctic could be dealt within the ATS – were now upset by the risk that a decision about Antarctica could be brought into the UN system.[35]

Minister for the Environment, Robert Hill, who was also responsible for the Antarctic, shepherded through Cabinet the decision to collect the Antarctic data. Bringing forward a government submission which proposed new expenditure was considered a risky proposition at the time, because the government was looking to make significant budget savings and demanding that offsets be identified.[36]

Earlier in the decade the government had begun the process of collecting data for all of Australia and its territories (except Antarctica) in order to meet the 2004 'deadline' for its extended continental shelf submission to the Commission on the Limits of the Continental Shelf (CLCS). Australia had ratified UNCLOS in 1994, and was obliged under the convention to make its submission within ten years of ratification (on or before 16 November 2004).

Ultimately, the government came to the view that a strict reading of UNCLOS required Australia to submit data within 10 years of the convention coming into force – a view which continued to be held despite a later decision by States Parties to the Law of the Sea (SPLOS) in 2001 that the 10-year deadline for parties to make extended continental shelf submissions to the CLCS would begin from 1999. Australia did not want to potentially prejudice any of its rights to an extended continental shelf.

In the lead-up to the 1999 decision to collect the Antarctic data, there was much internal legal and political wrangling – the exercise would be expensive, other Antarctic Treaty parties were likely to object, and the status quo would be disturbed. Since signing UNCLOS, Australia had been aware that Antarctica raised important and difficult diplomatic questions and had been actively exploring options to deal with this 'problem'. Some proposed solutions, such as formally amending UNCLOS, a special resolution by States Parties, or the making of an interpretative instrument, were not feasible as they would bring up exactly the same diplomatic issues that Australia would face by collecting and submitting the Antarctic shelf data, and they were most likely to fail. In making the specific decision to collect Antarctic data, Australia was prepared for strong reactions from other Treaty parties, especially those that did not recognise its territorial claim; but the other six claimants were also expected to take a keen interest in the precedent being set.[37] That precedent would be particularly sensitive for the three claimants that had overlapping claims (the United Kingdom, Argentina and Chile), especially at a time of lingering tensions between the United Kingdom and Argentina over other South Atlantic territories.

Australia was strongly of the view that its rights to an extended continental shelf off the Australian Antarctic Territory were not in conflict with its rights and obligations under the Antarctic Treaty. In the government's judgment an extended continental shelf from the AAT was not a claim to new territory (and therefore not contrary to Article IV of the Antarctic Treaty) but was defining an area where rights could be exercised. In addition, Australia was acting consistently with its obligations under UNCLOS and its high seas rights under Article VI of the Treaty.[38] Further, Australia had declared in 1953, well before the negotiation of the Treaty, that it had an extended continental shelf for all of Australia and its territories (including the AAT).[39] Australia considered that, far from this being in conflict with the Treaty, Article IV protected its rights as a claimant state and, further, that not to take action as a claimant in relation to its Antarctic continental shelf could be seen as a retreat from its longstanding position on its Antarctic territory. These legal and political arguments were significant in bringing together the differing views within government about how to deal with the Antarctic shelf, and helped to coalesce evolving diplomatic strategy.

Aware that the decision would provoke much debate, Australia began to engage with Antarctic Treaty parties to find common ground and minimise threats to the stability of the ATS. Australia's intention was to inform the parties of its decision to collect the Antarctic data and to undertake consultations on a 'no surprises' basis on how it would deal with the material in the lead-up to the 2004 CLCS submission deadline.

Initial discussions on the 'problem' of the Antarctic extended continental shelf were held among the seven claimant states together with the United States and Russia (that is, those states that had asserted Antarctic claims, or that held the basis of a claim, as protected under Article IV of the Antarctic Treaty).[40] These discussions, held in the margins of ATS meetings from 1999 onwards, centred on how to ensure that any actions taken by Australia or other claimants in the future, and any reactions to them, would not undermine the Antarctic Treaty, the protection provided by Article IV and the cohesion between the parties. While the claimants were focused on how they would each deal with their own Antarctic territories, the United States concentrated on dissuading Australia from making any submission under UNCLOS, at one stage arguing the case for a resolution on Antarctica from SPLOS, even though the United States was not (and still is not) a signatory to UNCLOS. Although the matter of Australia's potential submission of Antarctic data to the CLCS provided a certain level of diplomatic friction, strong working relationships among officials across the ATS ensured that normal Antarctic practical and diplomatic collaborations continued in a strong spirit of cooperation. And while a great deal of communication among Antarctic Treaty parties on the 'problem' was conducted through conventional channels, much of the practical resolution was developed in conversations between individuals who had built strong working relationships over many years. Trust was an important factor in resolving tensions and in finding common ground among the different perspectives.

Early in 2004 the Australian Government decided that it would submit data for all its shelf areas to the CLCS in time for the 16 November 2004 'deadline', but that it would ask the CLCS (in an accompanying note) 'not to consider' the data for Antarctica for the time being. Faced with a very short timeline between the government's decision, the Antarctic Treaty meeting in June, and the 16 November CLCS deadline, Australian Antarctic officials undertook a rapid round of face-to-face meetings with counterparts in Buenos Aires, Santiago, Washington, Paris, London, Oslo and Moscow (discussions having previously been held in New Zealand).[41] The reactions they faced at these meetings were no surprise. The claimants understood the Australian standpoint and, although they were developing their own positions, were keenly aware of the precedent the decision would create. The United Kingdom was perhaps the most shocked. The then director of the Australian Antarctic Division, Tony

Press, recalls that Mike Richardson of the Foreign and Commonwealth Office was lost for words on being told that Australia would include the Antarctic data in its 2004 submission to the CLCS. The UK officials left the room for further consultation; they appear to have expected that Australia would at least delay submitting its data until 2009. The United States, while formally opposed to the decision, was keen to work with Australia to find a solution that would satisfy all interests and maintain the stability of the Antarctic Treaty.

The United States was particularly concerned that any submission to the CLCS should include a statement about the unique position of Antarctica and the operation of Article IV of the Treaty. During informal discussions between Press and Ray Arnaudo of the US State Department, Arnaudo also expressed concern that the NGOs might take Australia's submission as opening the lid again on mining in the Antarctic. Press responded by emphasising Australia's unswerving commitment to the Madrid Protocol, and the fact that, under Australian law, the provisions of the Protocol applied to the entire Treaty area, including the continental shelf and sea bed. Russia, while also formally opposed to Australia's position, was keen to continue discussions with Australian officials on the technical aspects of its submission, as Russia was the first UNCLOS party to submit its extended continental shelf data (relating to northern hemisphere waters) to the CLCS.

In March 2004, Norway hosted an Antarctic Treaty meeting of experts on Antarctic tourism and non-governmental activities aboard a cruise ship sailing from Tromsø to Trondheim. The meeting, also attended by Antarctic officials, provided the backdrop for much quiet, informal discussion between Australian officials and those of other parties on Australia's decision regarding its Antarctic continental shelf, and on how to proceed. These informal discussions, and others held during the remainder of 2004, contributed significantly to the eventual architecture of Australia's submission of its Antarctic data to the CLCS and to the subsequent diplomatic responses.[42] The wording of the submission was carefully crafted. It specifically noted the objectives of the Antarctic Treaty and the 'continuing peaceful cooperation, security and stability in the Antarctic area [and] ... the special legal and political status of Antarctica under the provisions of the Antarctic Treaty, including its article IV'.[43] Australia requested 'the Commission in accordance with its rules not to take any action for the time being with regard to ... the continental shelf appurtenant to Antarctica'.[44]

Australia's submission of its Antarctic extended continental shelf data to the CLCS did not provoke a crisis in the ATS, as had been predicted by some casual observers. The issue never found its way onto the ATCM agenda, and the diplomacy of what was potentially a great challenge to the Treaty system was handled outside the established bodies of the ATS.

The lead-up to Australia's CLCS 'deadline' provided rich grounds for formal and informal diplomatic engagement on the fundamental underpinnings of the Antarctic Treaty, and reaffirmed the importance of strong and effective personal and institutional relationships within the ATS.

Australian style

The Australian ATCM delegations have generally been among the largest, and their members are encouraged to employ a range of techniques in negotiation that might not seem to conform to traditional diplomatic practice.[45] This section explores some of the characteristics of Australian Antarctic diplomacy.

For some Treaty parties, Antarctic policy development has been the responsibility of small cadres of government officials who have acquired expertise by virtue of lengthy tenure. Such stability has enabled these parties to rely heavily on a few long-serving officials to lead their ATCM delegations and, accordingly, their personalities have assumed special significance. The influence of an individual's character and willingness to negotiate can have has much force as the substance of their government's position. During the past half century the reliance on individuals has been particularly the case for Britain, the United States, Norway, New Zealand, Chile and Argentina – all original signatories.[46] Because of the rotating appointments within the Canberra foreign ministry,

Australian delegation leaders, by contrast, have generally not had the benefit of longevity, although in some cases diplomats have rotated back into Antarctic affairs with great effect. Longevity has, however, been provided by delegations' AAD members, who are not trained as diplomats but participate as advisers.[47] They provide great strength to the Australian delegation from their experience in Antarctic politics over many years, combined with on-the-ground responsibility for implementing ATCM measures.

Australian delegations have always been particularly well prepared for ATCMs, and many other delegations have remarked on the fact that they carry comprehensive briefs – which explore options, set objectives and analyse likely negotiating hurdles. The value of such preparation is that the delegates arrive with a whole-of-government position agreed through an interdepartmental committee. Stakeholders such as environment groups and industry representatives have also been consulted. Meeting papers are carefully prepared on initiatives for which the Australian delegation will seek support, and there is seldom a situation where it needs to reserve its position while seeking instructions from Canberra. By contrast, some delegations arrive without internally agreed positions or with such rigid objectives that they need to refer to their governments for guidance. Australia will normally ensure some flexibility in its objectives so that there is scope for compromise to achieve consensus.

Australian negotiators

Andrew Jackson

The 'heroes' of international Antarctic diplomacy are not as visible as the well-known Antarctic explorers. The contributions of diplomats and other officials to negotiations and policy advising were made over many years, and sometimes subtly: serving long-term objectives, or in cameo roles demanding a brief intervention or specific skills. But when measured in terms of pursuit of the wider good in Antarctic affairs and support for Australia's national interest, theirs is a story equal to that of the big names. They can be seen as the people who invested the capital established by their more famous predecessors.

Before mentioning the Australians, we should acknowledge some of their memorable counterparts overseas. Brian Roberts, John Heap and Mike Richardson successively led the UK delegations for a remarkable total of more than 45 years – a record hardly likely to be beaten. Others whose engagement spanned long periods include Tucker Scully and Ray Arnaudo from the United States, Chris Beeby and Don Mackay from New Zealand, Oscar Pinochet de la Barra and Jorge Berguño from Chile, Roberto

Guyer and Juan Carlos Beltramino from Argentina, and Rolf Trolle Andersen from Norway.

Of course, it is not possible to list everyone, either from other countries or from Australia, but the following Australians deserve particular mention:

Malcolm Booker–

the Australian representative at the negotiation of the Treaty, an outspoken voice of conscience in Australian foreign policy

Keith Brennan–

guardian of the ATS and Head of Delegation during the first serious forays into marine living resources and minerals

Alan Brown–

leader in high-pressure Protocol negotiations

John Burgess–

first head of the Foreign Affairs Antarctic and Environment Branch

Bill Bush–

legendary Foreign Affairs lawyer and architect of Australian environmental proposals

Brendan Doran–

member of Australian delegations and awarded a Public Service Medal for involvement in the minerals and Protocol negotiations

Rex Moncur–

Antarctic Division Director and Deputy Head of Delegation for many meetings

Tony Press–

Antarctic Division Director, Chair of the Committee for Environment Protection and leader of Australian delegations to CCAMLR

John Rowland–

had a major role in chairing the first special meeting negotiating CCAMLR

Richard Woolcott–

made famous in Antarctic affairs defending the Treaty in the United Nations; as Foreign Affairs Secretary, recalled to Antarctic business supporting Hawke's no-mining campaign

Hugh Wyndham–

long-serving Foreign Affairs desk officer, who rotated back into Antarctic Affairs to lead Australian Treaty and CCAMLR delegations

Among the large group supporting the diplomatic effort with specialist skills were many other Australian officials from Foreign Affairs, the Attorney-General's Department, the Antarctic Division and other agencies who made important contributions. John Brook was influential in CCAMLR and the minerals debates; Henry Burmester was an Attorney-General's Department adviser on complex issues of international law; Marie Kawaja was one of the longest-serving Foreign Affairs Antarctic desk officers; Knowles Kerry was an Antarctic Division scientist and stalwart in CCAMLR; Tom Maggs was a long-serving Antarctic Division adviser in the Committee for Environmental Protection; John Mc-

Carthy, leading the Australian delegation, was a troubleshooter in the final Protocol debate; Ian Nicholson championed Australia's interests in the minerals negotiations; Darry Powell was a Department of Science official who went on to become the first executive secretary of CCAMLR; and Phil Sulzberger drove policy interests in the Antarctic Division while it was in Melbourne. And it was not just officials – Lyn Goldsworthy represented environment groups on Australian delegations over many years and was made a Member of the Order of Australia for services to conservation and the environment.

Many others have represented Australia behind the microphone, in numerous meetings of experts and intersessional discussions, and built relationships with their foreign counterparts. Sometimes they have done this over many years and without external recognition.

It can be confidently said that Australia's achievements and reputation within the Antarctic Treaty System over 50 years depend completely on the wisdom and insight of these men and women, their commitment to pursuing the national interest, and their convictions about strengthening the Antarctic Treaty system. They have left an enviable record for the current generation to follow.

A further technique employed by Australia is to ensure a good relationship with the chairs of the meeting or its working groups by, for example, undertaking to convene informal contact groups, drafting resolutions and compiling parts of the meeting report. But these relationships can also be subtle – a proposal slipped anonymously under the door of the chair's hotel room can have the desired effect. Australian delegations are also used to facilitating intersessional discussions to prepare the way for debate at the following ATCM.

Despite the ATCM being an intergovernmental forum, much of Australia's success in Antarctic affairs has been achieved by not relying solely on conventional channels of diplomatic communication. Australian delegations encourage personal relationships to develop and a degree of informality to be adopted. Australia's approach can be described as not taking itself too seriously, not taking setbacks personally, and using well-timed and respectful levity when necessary to reduce the pressure during negotiation. The development of connections with other delegations is particularly effective, as it allows personal contact to be maintained between the more formal meetings and for initiatives to be tested without commitment. A timely email or telephone exchange can maintain good relationships and achieve very quickly what otherwise might require days of patient diplomatic process. Within a meeting, a whispered aside to a nearby delegation or a discreet text message across the room can achieve remarkable results. Creating the environment during the ATCM for frank exchange is an important part of the Australian approach, and in recent years this has been achieved in a variety of ways. These include hosting dinners between delegations, where relationships can be strengthened, and receptions, where informal discussions can proceed in a non-threatening environment. In essence, Australian delegations see themselves as dealing not with governments but with people. The result is that they make friends out of opponents and help build within the ATCM a sense of cooperation – a direct expression of the Treaty's objective.

Part of the Australian delegation at the CEP and the ATCM in Kiev in 2008: (from right) Australian Antarctic Division Director, Tony Press; Penny Richards, Department of Foreign Affairs and Trade (head of delegation); and Ewan McIvor, Australian Antarctic Division. Andrew Jackson, Australian Antarctic Division, © Commonwealth of Australia

In the relatively rare periods of serious disagreement, such as that arising from Australia's rejection of the minerals convention, highly skilled Australian diplomats have been brought in, complemented effectively by long-serving AAD advisers. Overall, however, the distinctive collegial culture which has emerged over time among ATCPs could be described as somewhat conservative. Moreover, because of the consensus requirement, agreement has sometimes been deliberately shrouded in ambiguity. While lawyers would normally find such outcomes uncomfortable, Australian delegation leaders, usually lawyers by training, have generally allowed their diplomatic instincts to prevail. An enduring element of the Australian style in the Treaty forums is pragmatism: the ability to avoid an overly legalistic approach that can lose sight of the practical objective.[48] In a consensus system, there really is little alternative.

***

As an original signatory to the Treaty, Australia has successfully and with its own distinctive style pursued policy objectives through 50 years of the Antarctic Treaty System. It has sought to consolidate the continent's demilitarised status, protect its environment, maximise opportunities for scientific research, and reinforce the uniquely collegial framework of decision making among the Treaty partners, while ensuring that Australia's longstanding claim to

Antarctic territory is not forfeited. It was a key player in the protracted negotiations which produced CCAMLR, whose secretariat and annual meetings it was to host. In two later episodes of Antarctic diplomacy – in abandoning CRAMRA and in daring to submit its data for an extended continental shelf – Australia sorely tested, but ultimately retained, the trust of its Treaty partners.

Notes

[1]   Most surprising perhaps was the neglect in Watt (1967), since the author had been secretary of the Department of External Affairs, and in the influential text of Millar (1978).

[2]   Orheim, Press and Gilbert (2011); and *The Protocol on Environmental Protection to the Antarctic Treaty,* <www.ats.aq>.

[3]   For an early statement, see Parliament of Australia (1992).

[4]   Other examples of diplomacy are mentioned in passing throughout this book and chapter 9 deals with another critical period in detail.

[5]   Kerr (2009) 226.

[6]   Hudson and North (1980). See letters of 6 June 1929 at 519, and of 4 July 1929 at 534.

[7]   While DFAT leads the ATCM delegation, in recent years the Antarctic Division has led the delegation to CCAMLR meetings.

[8]   Australian Antarctic Division (1978a).

[9]   Australian Antarctic Division (1978a) 8 (para 3) and 14 (para 15).
[10] Johanson (1998) 77.
[11] Australian Antarctic Division (1978a) 8 (para 4).
[12] Australian Antarctic Division (1978b).
[13] Australian Antarctic Division (1978b) 8.
[14] Johanson (1998) 79.
[15] Australian Antarctic Division (1978b) 14.
[16] Johanson (1998) 83.
[17] The Gentlemen's Agreement centred on, *inter alia,* recognising the core of the draft agreement and particularly the focus of management contained in Article II.
[18] Johanson (1998) 84.
[19] Johanson (1998) 87.
[20] Johanson (1998) 87.
[21] The statement retained French measures relating to the management of marine living resources which had applied prior to the entry into force of the Convention. It also enabled France to make reservations regarding the application of Conservation Measures to the waters around Crozet and Kerguelen islands. France would be bound by Conservation Measures 'adopted by consensus with its participation', but in the absence of consensus 'could promulgate any national measures which it might deem appropriate'.
[22] Johanson (1998) 89.

[23]   Hawke (1994) 467–68; see also d'Alpuget (2010) 254–58. This interpretation of events was forcefully reiterated by Hawke in an interview with Peter Boyce on 11 October 2010.

[24]   Boyce interview with Keating, 11 October 2010; see also the report by Alan Fewster in *Sunday Telegraph* (Sydney), 30 April 1989.

[25]   Fewster, *Sunday Telegraph* (Sydney), 30 April 1989.

[26]   Boyce interview with Bush, 8 October 2010; and Fewster, *Sunday Telegraph* (Sydney), 30 April 1989.

[27]   Boyce interview with Woolcott, 11 October 2010.

[28]   Hawke (1994) 470.

[29]   Woolcott (2003) 214.

[30]   Boyce interview with Woolcott, 11 October 2010.

[31]   Boyce interview with Brown, 10 October 2010.

[32]   Herr, Hall and Haward (1990) 19.

[33]   Herr, Hall and Haward (1990) 100.

[34]   Herr, Hall and Haward (1990) 187.

[35]   By this time the UN discussions on the 'Question of Antarctica' had become essentially ritualistic.

[36]   Ultimately the government decided to fund the collection of the data without Hill's portfolio being required to make the equivalent savings (of over $30m), and the budget for the collec-

tion of the Antarctic data was administered by the Department of Finance and Administration.

[37]   In 1994 Australia had proclaimed an EEZ off the AAT and this resulted in reactions from a number of Antarctic Treaty Parties which did not recognise Australia's claim to the AAT.

[385]   Article VI of the Treaty provides that the Treaty applies to the area south of 60° S, but that 'nothing shall prejudice the rights, or the exercise of rights, of any state under international law with regard to the high seas in the Treaty area'. Furthermore, under UNCLOS the extended continental shelf does not itself constitute territory but is an area where certain rights can be exercised because of the coastal state's existing terrestrial claim.

[39]   *Commonwealth of Australia Gazette,* 1953, No 56, 2563, cited in Bush (1982) vol2, 173.

[40]   Jacobsson (2007) 1–16.

[41]   Tony Press, who was the Director of the Australian Antarctic Division from 1998 to 2008, attended each of these meetings, thus providing the AAD with a significant tactical role in these negotiations.

[42]   <www.un.org/Depts/los/clcs_new/submissions _files/submission_aus.htm> (accessed 7 December 2010).

[43]   ibid, note no 89/2004.

[44]   ibid.

[45]   Those who have assisted in identifying key aspects include Alan Brown, Bill Bush, Andrew Jackson, Rex Moncur and Tony Press.

[46]   The UK delegation has a particularly impressive record in longevity of its delegation leaders – the first 50 years of the Treaty had seen just four: Brian Roberts, John Heap, Michael Richardson and Jane Rumble.

[47]   The Director of the AAD typically acts as Deputy Head of Delegation.

[48]   For example, Australia cut through hours of debate on the Treaty Secretariat with an effective, if inelegant, funding formula that balanced the objectives of those seeking equal contributions and those insisting on a UN sliding scale.

13

The Protocol in action,1991–2010

Andrew Jackson and Lorne Kriwoken[1]

This chapter commences in October 1991, when the Protocol on Environmental Protection to the Antarctic Treaty was adopted. The parties justifiably took pride in the Protocol, which created a systematic approach to Antarctic environment protection. It expanded the Antarctic Treaty System's (ATS) governance and institutional arrangements, and this precipitated a raft of changes to the way parties worked and opened up opportunities for many new initiatives. In Australia's view, its own role in the transition from a minerals regime to an environmental regime created an obligation to constructively engage in ensuring effective application of the Protocol through its institutional mechanisms. But early entry into force was the essential first step. Australia's initial priorities were to achieve this, to promote consistent implementation of the Protocol's requirements, and to capitalise on the momentum created by its adoption. This included assisting with the critical task of modernising the institutional framework of the ATS. There was also work to be done in addressing matters not covered by the

Protocol, such as better arrangements for area protection and liability for environmental damage. This chapter examines how Australia responded to these issues and other challenges that emerged, including environmental impact assessment and tourism.

Next steps

The 1991 adoption of the Protocol represented a landmark in the evolution of the Treaty system. In terms of international law, binding rules had been agreed upon to provide for wide-ranging protection of the Antarctic. Pre-existing commitments were updated and codified in a unified way, and new obligations introduced to complement them.[2] In policy terms, a new priority for Antarctic decision making had been agreed to – Article 3 of the Protocol made protection of the environment a 'fundamental consideration in the planning and conduct of all activities'. In political terms, international criticism of the Treaty system had largely been defused by resolving the vexed issue of mining and by demonstrating that it was capable of managing this vast part of the globe. On the ground, improvements were evident in the conduct of Antarctic activities. Within the Treaty, the conduct of meetings would change, with fuller agendas and increased frequency of consultative meetings. This in turn led to structural modernisation of the system, including the establishment of much-needed institutional support for the Treaty and refinement of the decision-making processes of the Antarctic Treaty Consultative Meetings (ATCMs).[3]

Despite the particular pride that it felt in the Protocol, Australia now trod carefully within the Treaty system. Promoting an alternative to the Convention on the Regulation of Antarctic Mineral Resource Activities (CRAMRA) had signalled leadership in environmental issues but, having 'broken ranks' over mining, its relationship with a number of Antarctic Treaty Consultative Parties (ATCPs) had changed. The period of the negotiations had been stressful for the Treaty system, the parties and the individuals involved. After adoption of the Protocol there was a risk that Australia might be regarded as unpredictable and demanding. Recognising that there was a national reputation to protect, Australian diplomats admitted that 'it might take some time for all the wounds to heal'.[4] That said, John Heap, head of the UK delegation, was building bridges by resurrecting the so-called 'correspondents group' (a series of informal exchanges of ideas between a number of like-minded counterparts, including Australia) which had disbanded in the heat of the CRAMRA debate because 'it [had] seemed no longer possible to assume, give or take a bit here and there, that we were all pushing the same barrow'.[5]

Like other parties, Australia was conscious of the limitations and ambiguities in the Protocol and its annexes but chose to defer action on these until another day.[6] It wanted to be seen as a reliable party, focused on implementing the arrangements that had been agreed. It decided to take a low profile on new initiatives, at least for the time being.

Australia was particularly sensitive to the risk that proposing new environmental initiatives or amendments to the Protocol before its entry into force could prompt other parties to delay development of implementing legislation. Early entry into force was therefore a priority. Australia was conscious that the 12 parties to the 1964 Agreed Measures had taken 18 years to make it effective. There was no way of knowing how long it would take for 26 parties to bring the Protocol into force. If momentum was lost, or even one party faltered, the system could end up in a legal vacuum. Satisfyingly, just over six years from its adoption, the Protocol entered into force on 14 January 1998. Australia had moved early to enact its implementing legislation: for good reasons, it wanted to be among the first to ratify.[7] The Australian Antarctic Division (AAD) established the Protocol Implementation Group to ensure its activities fully complied with Protocol requirements and, importantly, sought to set an example for other operators in its own practices. In this it was successful, although other Parties went on to exceed Protocol requirements. Waste management was an example – an area in which, as discussed later, Australia would face a protracted challenge.

The last huskies returning to Australia from Mawson Station – shown here on board the Aurora Australis after arrival in Hobart. The dogs were then flown to Los Angeles before being taken by road to Minnesota. Jan Dallas, Australian Antarctic Division, © Commonwealth of Australia

Doggone

One matter demanding the Division's immediate attention was the obligation under Article 4 of Annex II to remove dogs from Antarctica by 1 April 1994. Seemingly straightforward, the exercise generated considerable anguish because of the long-established heritage of Antarctic sled dogs. By the time the Protocol was adopted, Australia maintained huskies only at Mawson, where dog teams had been used since 1954 for field journeys on the region's stable sea ice. The ANARE Club, an association of past expedition members, argued vigorously against the dogs' removal and launched an ultimately unsuccessful petition and a letter-writing campaign to the Environment Minister, Ros Kelly. Pat Moonie, a former Antarctic dog handler, reported that the minister received more mail on the Mawson huskies than on any other issue.[8] Twenty-six dogs had to be removed. Most went aboard *Aurora Australis* in November 1992 for the start of a long journey to northern Minnesota in the United States, where arrangements had been made for an outdoor education program to take them into existing working teams. A number of older dogs found foster homes in Australia with members of the Antarctic community. With the dog issue solved, attention turned to the more substantial environmental agenda.

Institutional modernisation

Major changes introduced by the Protocol raised concerns about the effectiveness of the Treaty's organisational arrangements. Until the adoption of the Protocol, ATCMs had been held biennially. From ATCM XVI this changed to annual meetings, primarily because of the effect of the procedures relating to comprehensive environmental evaluations.[9] A further critical need was for a secretariat. There was no effective mechanism for supporting those governments hosting meetings, and the proliferation of documents emanating from the meetings mirrored the size and complexity of the environmental agenda.

Australia had argued the case at the first ATCM in Canberra in 1961 for a permanent administrative headquarters.[10] But the proposition faced vigorous objections from Parties concerned that creation of institutional support could 'internationalise' Antarctica, with decision making removed from the consultative mechanism established by Article IX of the Treaty. Australia offered to host a secretariat in Canberra, but to no avail.[11] It was not until 1992 that there was finally consensus on the establishment of a secretariat, when Argentina, the last hold-out, finally conceded its necessity.[12] However, the celebration was short-lived – Argentina's acceptance was conditional on being the host nation, a position that met with objection from the United Kingdom and exasperation from others. As the depository government for the Treaty, the United States offered to host the office in Washington, DC. Australia optimistically resurrected its offer, this time for Hobart, where the secretariat could benefit from synergies with the secretariats of CCAMLR and the Council of Managers of National Antarctic Programs.[13] The pressure to establish a permanent office eventually became overwhelming and Buenos Aires was finally agreed on as the location in 2001, some 40 years after Australia first put forward the idea.[14] Finalising the legal instruments and practical arrangements required further negotiations, in which Australia took a strong lead.[15] When the secretariat opened for business in 2005, the Treaty's operation and its ability to deal with environmental issues immediately improved.

An equally important institutional development came from within the Protocol, changing the way the ATCM received advice on environmental issues and requiring the creation of the Committee for Environmental Protection (CEP).[16] With parties keen for the CEP to be functioning, a Transitional Environmental Working Group under the leadership of Norway's Olav Orheim was set up to build momentum on the practical issues involved in making the Protocol work. When the Protocol entered into force in 1998, the CEP was formally constituted and Orheim was elected its inaugural chair, thus maintaining vital continuity with the working group.

A critical task was to give Orheim the support he needed. AAD environment manager Tom Maggs worked closely with his Norwegian counterpart, Birgit Njaastad, to underpin the environmental function until the Treaty secretariat was established, and Norway and Australia hosted a CEP website and document archive for the Parties well before the secretariat provided this service. In 2002 Orheim's term as CEP chair came to an end at the Warsaw meeting and the position was opened for election. After two tied votes in a close contest between the Australian and New Zealand candidates, the result was determined in favour of AAD director Tony Press by the toss of a zloty.

With Press in the chair, Australia established the CEP's online discussion forum, which went on to become the parties' main tool for intersessional work.

Australia introduced other important initiatives as well, such as the CEP handbook and annotated CEP agendas. A further important step in developing a strategic approach to the committee's work was Australia's convening, with the United Kingdom, of the 2006 Workshop on Antarctica's Future Environmental Challenges, which flowed into intersessional discussion on a five-year CEP work plan. Australia's advocacy of the need to prioritise work on the basis of environmental risk and institutional improvement was rewarded with a work plan that became a key reference for the CEP's strategic planning.

Press's tenure concluded in 2006 and New Zealand's Neil Gilbert, who had lost the coin toss in 2002, was elected unopposed as the third chair of the CEP. Recognition of Australia's continuing leadership role in the CEP came again in 2008, when Ewan McIvor, AAD senior environmental policy adviser, was elected a vice-chair.

Environmental impact assessment

The requirement for assessment of the environmental impacts of Antarctic activities had been a major component of Australia's proposals for an environmental regime. This was reflected in Article 3 of the Protocol, which established the principle that all activities in Antarctica must be subject to prior assessment of the possible impacts. Article 8 identifies the three levels of assessment that may be required, depending on the impacts likely to be caused, and Annex I identifies the procedures that must be followed in undertaking the assessments.

The assessment system hinges on the threshold level of 'minor or transitory impact', and defining these terms was an important element in the practical application of Annex I. In Tromsø in 1998 Australia tabled a working paper on the issue, proposing that the ATCM establish a working group to develop environmental impact assessment guidelines and common understandings on the thresholds of initial and comprehensive environmental evaluations.[17] The CEP and the ATCM are required to examine activities subject to a comprehensive environmental evaluation: that is, any activity that a proponent considers likely to have more than a minor or transitory impact. Whether or not an activity is subject to this evaluation depends on a national process – and there was considerable scope for differences of interpretation of the requirements. Debate among the Treaty parties raised issues about achieving consistency, triggering Australia's concern that a mechanism be found to standardise the processes.[18]

Since the Protocol was adopted, some 19 comprehensive environmental evaluations had been prepared by the parties. The fact that none of these assessments had been prepared by Australia left it vulnerable to the accusation that it was not meeting its obligations. The alternative view was that a low number of comprehensive environmental evaluations demonstrated that the Protocol was having the desired effect of parties planning their activities to *avoid* having more than minor or transitory impacts. Australia's establishment of an intercontinental air link between Hobart and Antarctica was a good example. The construction of an all-weather, year-round rock runway had been rejected on environmental grounds, and a glacialice runway serviced by sledge-mounted accommodation was chosen instead. This meant that the facility could be removed in its entirety at any time and leave no evidence of its presence. In addition, the decision to use an aircraft able to make the return trip without refuelling avoided the suite of issues associated with transporting, handling and storing bulk fuel. The approach chosen would have only a minor or transitory impact and therefore did not require a comprehensive environmental evaluation.

Consideration of comprehensive environmental evaluations is a significant role of the CEP and Australia became a key player in the process, and in the CEP's intersessional contact groups. In 2007 Australia joined with France to secure the Committee's agreement that all draft comprehensive environmental evaluations should automatically be subject to review by an intersessional contact group. This replaced the previous arrangement, where review occurred only if requested by a party. The result was a robust process and significant progress in minimising the impacts of activities in Antarctica.

Tourism and non-government expeditions

When the Treaty was negotiated, Antarctica was essentially the exclusive domain of national governments, although a 1956 Chilean tourist overflight and a 1958 Argentinean cruise had alerted the parties that exclusive use of the continent could no longer be assumed.[19] US-based Lindblad Travel Inc., with a visit to the Antarctic Peninsula in 1966, is credited with initiating modern Antarctic expedition cruising. The Treaty parties' initial response to this new activity was to adopt a recommendation dealing with visits to stations.[20] In other respects, they reacted cautiously, in part because of the perennial jurisdictional issues.[21] However, Australia's first concerns were not about jurisdiction or the environment (the Australian Antarctic Territory (AAT) was not then a destination for tourists, and would not be for many years), but about the potential disruption to its scientific program if search and rescue was required.[22] The growth of the industry triggered the Treaty parties' first measure to address environmental issues in 1975.[23]

Tourist interest faltered only momentarily after the disastrous 1979 collision of an Air New Zealand sightseeing aircraft with Mount Erebus. As new interests emerged Australia became involved – Sydney architects Helmut Rohde & Partners optimistically proposed 'Project Oasis', a combined tourist and science facility in the Vestfold Hills, to be accessed by air. Adventurers headed to the South Pole, climbed virgin peaks or wintered in tiny yachts. Environment organisations mounted expeditions, including the installation of World Park Base on Ross Island and protests during construction of France's Dumont d'Urville airstrip. The Treaty parties could not ignore developments but they still continued to move cautiously.

Despite growing interest, the numbers involved were very low, by 1991, when the Protocol was adopted, reaching just 4000 passengers a season.[24] Australia's involvement at that time was a small fraction of that total and there were few visits to the AAT. Nevertheless, Australia sought to have a role in defining how tourism was managed. Its approach had, in part, been informed by the report of a 1988 parliamentary inquiry into Antarctic tourism which had echoed the community's strong environmental concern and recommended that the government develop a conservation strategy for the AAT. The report also recommended that there be no approval for on-shore tourist accommodation in the AAT until such a strategy was in place and that Australia initiate negotiation of a convention to regulate tourism.[25] However, these initiatives were overtaken by the Protocol, which sought to regulate the environmental aspects of all Antarctic activities.

At the 1991 and 1992 Treaty meetings vigorous arguments were mounted for the negotiation of an additional Protocol annex specifically to regulate tourism. The chief proponent was France which, referring to its proud history of collaboration in overturning CRAMRA, was understandably keen to secure Australia's support. But on this issue France and Australia did not see eye to eye. Not only did Australia want to avoid burdening parties with new legal obligations before the Protocol was in force, it also rejected a tourism annex on principle, believing that developing special rules for tourism would undermine the principle that the Protocol applied uniformly to *all* activities in Antarctica. Furthermore, the Protocol could only regulate environmental impacts, not matters of safety and self-sufficiency.

Tourism remained on the ATCM agenda but there were marked differences of approach, with some arguing for measures even stronger than those applying to national programs while others advocated self-regulation. In 1992 Australia proposed the adoption of a statement of principles by which tourism should be conducted. This was timely, as significant industry actors were emerging, including Greg Mortimer, who that year set up Aurora Expeditions. But these principles were developed without the knowledge that another Australian venture would soon take off – in 1994 Croydon Travel reintroduced tourist overflights.[26] By the end of Croydon's first season Australian operators accounted for some 25 per cent of Antarctic tourists. Other Australian operators started business, while elsewhere the industry was expanding and new activities contemplated. Private adventure expeditions became increasingly audacious.[27] The AAD began to track developments and between 1999 and 2003 published its findings in the widely-praised electronic newsletter *Antarctic Non-Government Activity News.* The AAD commenced a practice of regular consultation with the industry to inform policy responses and developed a website to capture tourism data that allowed information relevant to monitoring major developments to be found in one place. This presaged the electronic information exchange system later developed by the Treaty secretariat, and thus the discussion of tourism regulation became more than just a debate about numbers.[28]

Australia was later to lead an initiative on centralised accreditation of tour operators, although the Parties ultimately settled on continuing industry self-regulation. The Treaty did, however, adopt a measure relating to self-sufficiency.[29] Concern about safety and self-sufficiency had become significant. Activities by Australians had contributed to this debate, including an attempt in 2001 by a private ski expedition to cross the Antarctic Peninsula that ended in a crevasse and necessitated rescue by the Chilean Antarctic program, and another adventurer's unplanned landing at McMurdo Station in 2003 after flying his home-built light aircraft over the South Pole.[30] The larger operators were likewise not immune from trouble: a run of potentially disastrous accidents, such as the 2007 grounding of MS *Nordkapp* and the sinking of MS *Explorer,* focused Treaty parties' thinking on issues of ship safety. Australia maintained a close engagement in the work of the ATCM and International Maritime Organization (IMO) on Antarctic passenger vessel safety, was very active in the Antarctic Treaty Meeting of Experts on ship-borne tourism in 2009, and proposed the 2010 resolution on the relationship between the IMO and the ATCM.[31] Australia was also active in improving understanding of the environmental aspects of tourism by, for example, conducting research into the behavioural response of Antarctic wildlife to human visitors; supporting efforts to improve environmental monitoring; developing measures to prevent the introduction of nonnative species; and participating in the preparation of the first tranche of site-specific guidelines for areas frequently visited by tourists.

The dormant issue of whether or not to prohibit permanent tourist infrastructure arose at the 2004 Antarctic Treaty Meeting of Experts on Tourism – a conference held, ironically, at the other end of the world on a cruise vessel traversing Norway's fjord coastline. Tourist infrastructure brought together historical and contemporary issues: the traditional concerns of sovereignty and the emerging industry in Antarctica. At the heart of the question was speculation that in the future hotels might be proposed. Australia's policy was that tourism should have no more than a minor or transitory impact on the environment, which negated the possibility of permanent hotels by implication (and was an apparent discrimination against tourism, as Australia accepted other activities with larger impacts). Other parties stated opposition with much more passion, while some defended vigorously the principle that, ultimately, each party individually decides whether an activity can proceed. No hotel was in fact proposed, but some Treaty parties continued to advocate pre-emptive action to explicitly rule out the possibility. The discussion surfaced again in 2007 at the New Delhi meeting. Following a proposal by New Zealand, AAD's Phillip Tracey, an expert in Antarctic tourism policy, convened the small group that hammered out agreement, at least for the time being, on the vexed issue of hotels. It was a fine example of the Treaty's bifocalism – its way of accommodating the perspectives of both claimants and non-claimants. A resolution was agreed on with just one operative paragraph, discouraging 'any tourism activities which may substantially contribute to the long-term degradation of the Antarctic environment and its dependent and associated ecosystems'.[32] Fifty years of the Treaty had not diminished the capacity of parties to find consensus in artful minimalism.

Protected areas

The Antarctic protected area system had its roots in Article VIII of the 1964 Agreed Measures, which provided for the designation of Specially Protected Areas. As knowledge of Antarctic values increased, the mechanisms for protecting particular areas evolved. By the time Protocol negotiations began in

1990 there was already a plethora of protected area categories, including the long-established Specially Protected Areas, Sites of Special Scientific Interest and Historic Monuments, and the more recent Areas of Special Tourist Interest, Specially Reserved Areas and Multiple Use Planning Areas. Negotiations did not cover the protected area system, but immediately upon adoption of the Protocol rationalisation of the system was proposed. This resulted in agreement in October 1991 to Annex V to the Protocol: Area Protection and Management.[33]

Under the Protocol's Article 12 and Annex V, the Committee for Environmental Protection is mandated to develop the protected area system, including the elaboration of site management plans. Australia had long held a strong interest in the protected areas system and was keen for the Annex to come into effect quickly (a process separate from that applying to the Protocol). The Annex came into effect four years after the Protocol entered into force.[34]

Like other parties, Australia commenced the process of reviewing and updating management plans for the suite of protected areas that it had previously nominated, and made successful proposals for new areas: an Antarctic Specially Managed Area (ASMA) at Cape Denison, and Antarctic Specially Protected Areas at Mawson's Hut, Hawker Island, Amanda Bay, and the Scullin and Murray monoliths. In 2000, concerted work started on the development of a management plan for the Larsemann Hills area in the

AAT. This followed agreement in 1997 by the Australian, Russian and Chinese Antarctic programs to manage cooperatively a region undergoing expansion of scientific activities and proposals for new or upgraded stations. Australia led the development of a draft management plan that recognised the existence of three stations (Russia's Progress II, China's Zhongshan, and Law-Racovita, an Australian field base occupied by Romanian summer scientists) which were accommodated in a proposed 'facilities zone'. The draft management plan was submitted for adoption at the 2005 meeting. Just at this time, India announced plans to establish a new Antarctic station, probably in the Larsemann Hills and outside the proposed facilities zone. This precipitated concern from some parties about arrangements for environmental management and regional cooperation. Following two further years of negotiations among regional stakeholders, the facilities zone became an ASMA when the management plan was adopted by the parties in 2007.[35]

Australia also advocated strategic development of the protected area system, including, as envisaged in Article 3(2) of Annex V, making it more representative of the scope of values in the Antarctic.[36] The CEP also agreed to Australia's proposal to establish its first subordinate body, the Subsidiary Group on Management Plans, which Australia convened. This latter development brought the welcome prospect of further institutional evolution within the Treaty system.

Inspections

Article VII of the Antarctic Treaty provided parties with an important right: the ability to appoint observers to conduct inspections of other parties' facilities. This was a strong incentive for parties to comply with their obligations, especially demilitarisation at a time of heightened Cold War sensitivities. In promoting the environmental regime, Australia argued that to encourage compliance on environmental issues it would be desirable to have an independent inspectorate. That idea was not successful, although it was reflected in the Protocol's Article 14, which placed a positive obligation on parties to arrange inspections and allowed them to be undertaken individually or collectively. Several parties took up this opportunity with enthusiasm, although competing priorities limited Australia's ability to participate. The number of inspections ultimately increased, including those done collaboratively. Australia recognised that it was essential to become engaged in the inspection system and applied a strong environmental focus when it was able to reinstate its own inspection program in 2004–05 (two stations on Ross Island, and 23 on the Antarctic Peninsula in conjunction with Peru and the United Kingdom) and 2010 (three stations in East Antarctica). Some of the stations had not been inspected for many years.

Liability

Encouraged by the speedy negotiation of Annex V in 1991, the parties turned their attention to another area where they had agreed work was required. Article 16 of the Protocol obliged the development of rules and procedures relating to liability for damage from Antarctic activities. When the Protocol was adopted the parties had agreed that work on the liability rules should begin promptly.[37] Australia took a keen interest in this work – of necessity, as the inclusion of liability rules was a key component of Australia's proposed environmental regime, reflecting the importance that had been placed on liability in CRAMRA.

Initial discussions were referred to a group of legal experts in 1993. The group met twice each year, in conjunction with the ATCM and in separate sessions hosted by various parties. Nine meetings were held. Australia's objective was the negotiation of an annex that would provide a comprehensive system of liability for environmental damage in Antarctica. It would be a strict regime. Australia had argued there should be liability for damage caused by all forms of activity, including science and tourism – an ambitious objective. At the other end of the spectrum was a US proposal to start with an annex dealing with obligations for response action, a matter covered by Article 15 of the Protocol.[38] The Australian and US proposals were polarised. So were the lawyers. The legal experts examined the options in fine detail and exhausted all avenues for finding common ground. In 1997 it was decided there was no prospect for progress without policy direction from the ATCM.[39] In 1998 negotiations were shifted to the ATCM's Working Group I, which handled legal matters.

To assist the debate, in 1999 Australia circulated a working paper on principles for an Antarctic liability regime.[40] This was in equal measure optimistic and futile – optimistic because it suggested that the liability annex be concluded in 2001 (the 40th anniversary of the entry into force of the Treaty and the tenth anniversary of the adoption of the Protocol), futile because it completely misread the mood of the other parties. Over the ensuing six years progress towards consensus would be possible only through Australia (and the other parties which were seeking comprehensive liability measures) conceding all contentious points and accepting that Article 16 had indeed provided for the objective to be achieved in 'one or more annexes'.

Ironically, when Annex VI was adopted in Stockholm in 2005, the negotiation of an annex of very limited scope had taken 16 negotiating sessions over 13 years – some five times the effort involved in negotiating the entire Protocol and its five other annexes. Yet Australia, like others, celebrated the achievement of consensus on the grounds that 'something is better than nothing'.

Annex II revisited

The deliberations on Annex VI had been significantly more difficult than those required for Annex V. If negotiating any other new annex threatened to be just as protracted a process, perhaps it might be easier to update an existing one. Each annex to the Protocol provides that it may be amended by a simplified process – adoption of a Measure under Article IX of the Treaty – so that an individual annex can be readily updated in keeping with contemporary practice or if circumstances change. In 2001 the ATCM agreed to the CEP proposal to commence a rolling review of the annexes, commencing with Annex II on the Conservation of Antarctic Fauna and Flora, the provisions of which had been largely carried over from the 1964 Agreed Measures. The process was initiated that year and, following concentrated intersessional work, the CEP provided its advice in 2004. Progress then stalled. Recognising the importance of enhancing the provisions for conserving fauna and flora and, importantly, of continuing the rolling review of annexes, Australia reinvigorated the negotiations with annotated texts providing background for proposed changes and enabling direct comparison between different options. Australia was congratulated on its role when the amendments were finally adopted in Baltimore in 2009.

***

In keeping with its lead role in developing the Protocol and its annexes, Australia took a conscious decision to be constructive in its implementation and improvement. That engagement was directed to ensuring sound institutional support for the Treaty system through the permanent secretariat and the formative years of the CEP. Healthy institutions achieve meaningful outcomes, hence Australia's attention to improving the way the parties consult and make decisions on the environment. The result is that institutions in the Treaty system now facilitate improved governance in Antarctica in a field of activity which, over 20 years, became its dominant business – protecting the unique environment. The Protocol had indeed made a lasting difference.

Notes

[1]   The authors gratefully acknowledge the contributions to this chapter by Tom Maggs, Phillip Tracey and Ewan McIvor of the Policy Coordination Branch of the Australian Antarctic Division.

[2]   Many Protocol provisions were drawn from existing measures. Key examples include Annex I which was based on the 1987 guidelines forming the operative part of Recommendation XIV-2; and Annex II was based on the 1964 Agreed Measures for the Conservation of Antarctic Fauna and Flora.

[3] In 1995 the Treaty Parties agreed to refine the outcomes of Treaty meetings by replacing the ubiquitous system of adopting Recommendations and replacing it with a hierarchy of measures: Decisions (which relate to internal organisational matters); Resolutions (which are hortatory, with a strong expectation that their provisions will be honoured); and Measures (which contain provisions intended to be legally binding on the Parties).

[4] Australia (1991).

[5] Australia (1991) 210–29.

[6] It was recognised almost immediately after its adoption that the Protocol's annexes incorporated flaws, inconsistencies and ambiguities. Many of these were artefacts of the haste with which the Protocol was negotiated and resulted from the importation into the Protocol of provisions from preexisting instruments.

[7] Australia ratified on 6 April 1994, the seventh Party to do so.

[8] Moonie (1991).

[9] Paragraph 5 of Article 3 of the Annex provided that an activity subject to a CEE should not be delayed by more than 15 months because of the requirement for a CEE to be considered by the CEP and the ATCM. Accordingly, if all CEEs were to be considered by an ATCM it was desirable for there to be no more than 15 months between meetings. This was taken

seriously – in 2000 it appeared that the Russian Federation would not be able to host the ATCM as had been anticipated. Accordingly, The Netherlands offered to host a special meeting essentially to allow the CEP to convene and a short ATCM held to consider its advice. A further effect of the provisions relating to CEEs was that ATCMs were moved towards the first half of the year so that activities which had been subject to a CEE could be commenced in the following summer.

[10] Phillip Law, Director of the Antarctic Division, was particularly concerned about the inefficiencies of meeting the information exchange obligations by each Party sending the data to every other Party, rather than having a central clearing house. His concern was prescient – if the difficulties were obvious with just 12 Parties, how much worse would it be with the current 28 ATCPs and the vastly more complicated programs they run.

[11] In AAD file 89/365.

[12] Antarctic Treaty (1992) 21–23.

[13] Antarctic Treaty (1998) 26–27.

[14] Achievement of consensus on this longstanding issue required the capitulation of Argentina to demands from the United Kingdom that, among other things, Argentina's Antarctic program give stronger emphasis to science and reduce dependence on military support. See Antarctic

Treaty (2001) pp 10 and 45 and Appendixes 2 and 3.

[15] Australia was credited with a number of initiatives that allowed the secretariat to commence work. These included the funding formula which had proved a major stumbling block in negotiations, the provisions of surplus computer equipment to get the headquarters going, and provision of copies of numerous key documents from the AAD's own collection of Treaty records which had been assembled over many years.

[16] The CEP was established by Article 11 of the Protocol. Its functions, which are elaborated in Article 12, are broadly to advise the ATCM on matters relating to implementation of the Protocol. The CEP meets each year at the same time as the ATCM, and provides its advice directly to the ATCM so that its recommendations can be considered immediately. Creation of the CEP diminished the influence of SCAR's Group of Specialists on Environmental Affairs and Conservation (GOSEAC).

[17] Later, when proposals were made to formally define 'minor or transitory' as meaning 'significant', Australia pointed out the circular argument – 'minor and transitory' had originally been adopted as a means to give clarity to 'significant'!

[18] Hemmings and Kriwoken (2010).

[19] Headland (1994b).

470

[20] Antarctic Treaty (1966) *Effects of Antarctic tourism,* Recommendation IV-27.

[21] AAD file 89/366 provides an example of just how cautiously the Parties reacted: an inexplicably coy early-career British diplomat wrote to Lindblad from a private address and under the pseudonym of 'Mr John D Spicer' to find out whether Lindblad intended a repeat visit – presumably this was to inform any diplomatic response that might have been required.

[22] In AAD file 91/640.

[23] Antarctic Treaty (1975) *Effects of tourists and non-governmental expeditions in the Antarctic Treaty Area,* Recommendation VIII-9.

[24] Although the numbers were low in 1991, the potential for growth was evident, as was the potential for increased regulation. That same year the International Association of Antarctica Tour Operators (IAATO) was established by seven operators to advocate, promote and practise safe and environmentally responsible private-sector travel to the Antarctic. By 2010 the number of IAATO members had grown to 100 and the number of passengers to 36 881 – still small by world standards but, in Antarctica, dwarfing the number of people involved in national programs.

[25] Parliament of Australia (1989). Note that the Committee included Bob Chynoweth, who in 1989 led the Labor Caucus opposition to

CRAMRA (see chapter 11). The government's response is recorded in Kovalskis (1993).

[26] Sightseeing flights from Sydney and Melbourne were started in 1977 using aircraft chartered by Dick Smith, Wandana Travel and others. These flights ceased after the November 1979 crash involving an Air New Zealand flight from Christchurch. See Anon (1978).

[27] Australian examples include Alfred Winklmayr's 1997 solo winter at Cape Denison, the world's windiest place at sea level, using a small shelter established by Don and Margie McIntyre for their winter in 1995. For this latter expedition see McIntyre (1996).

[28] Like some other Parties, Australia was concerned that the tourism debate could be distorted by an argument based solely on the numbers of passengers involved. More recently Australia co-sponsored with New Zealand and France a CEP study to better understand the interactions between tourism and the Antarctic environment and provide a much-needed objective basis for discussions about the possible need for further regulation.

[29] Antarctic Treaty (2004) *Insurance and contingency planning for tourism and non-governmental activities in the Antarctic Treaty Area*, Measure 4 (2004).

[30] For a discussion of non-government expeditions at this time, see Murray and Jabour (2004).

472

[31] Antarctic Treaty (2010) *Co-ordination among Antarctic Treaty Parties on Antarctic proposals under consideration in the IMO,* Resolution 5 (2010).

[32] Antarctic Treaty (2007) *Long-term effects of tourism,* Resolution 5 (2007). It should be re-called that a Resolution is not legally binding but has a strong expectation of compliance, notwithstanding the exhortation to 'discourage'. The language of the Resolution substitutes 'more than minor or transitory' with 'long-term degradation' to avoid a direct link to the CEE process. So some Parties may see this as a prevention of hotels – others may see it as a general exhortation to minimise tourism's cumulative impacts.

[33] Antarctic Treaty (1991) *Annex V to the Protocol on Environmental Protection to the Antarctic Treaty – Area Protection and Management,* Recommendation XVI-10. The new protected area system embodied Antarctic Specially Protected Areas (ASPAs), Antarctic Specially Managed Areas (ASMAs) and Historic Sites and Monuments.

[34] Annex V came into effect on 24 May 2002.

[35] Antarctic Treaty (2007) *Management Plan for Antarctic Specially Managed Area No 6, Larsemann Hills, East Antarctica,* Measure 2 (2007).

[36] This work was complemented by the Environmental Domains Analysis for Antarctica. See

Antarctic Treaty (2008) *Environmental Domains Analysis for the Antarctic continent as a dynamic model for a systematic environmental geographic framework,* Resolution 3 (2008).

[37] Final Act of the 11th Special Antarctic Treaty Consultative Meeting, in Antarctic Treaty (1991) 107–10.

[38] The distinction is significant: a regime based on Article 15 would limit liability to any failure to respond to an environmental emergency, and exclude liability for the damage that might be caused by the emergency – that would be addressed by a regime based on Article 16.

[39] Antarctic Treaty (1998) *Liability – Report of the Group of Legal Experts,* XXII ATCM/WP1.

[40] Antarctic Treaty (1999) *Principles for an Antarctic Liability Regime,* XXIII ATCM/WP15 (submitted by Australia).

14

Environment

Lorne Kriwoken and Tom Maggs[1]

When the Antarctic Treaty came into force on 23 June 1961, environmental planning of Antarctic programs was not a priority. Australia was not alone in the long-standing tradition of dumping station waste on sea ice, killing seals to feed huskies and burning waste in open-air pits, practices now considered abhorrent. With the expansion of Antarctic programs over subsequent decades, growing summer and winter populations, and the greater ability to undertake field work, the effects of human activities became an increasing concern at the same time as major changes in worldwide concern for the environment were taking place.

This chapter discusses Australia's expanding environmental footprint – a scenario largely repeated by other Antarctic parties – and examines governance related to Antarctic environmental management. Waste management provides a prime example of changes in expectations and practices.

Australia's expanding Antarctic operational effect

When Douglas Mawson walked away from the 1911–14 Australasian Antarctic Expedition (AAE) winter quarters he left behind a timber hut and two years of accumulated human waste. He fully expected it to disappear out to sea. Like the AAE, the early period of the Australian National Antarctic Research Expeditions (ANARE) was characterised by localised human impacts, whereby waste was typically dumped on land, on sea ice along the coast or in crevasses close to stations. 'Sea-icing' was a common approach: waste was stockpiled on sea ice over winter, and the problem was solved when the ice broke up and floated away.[2] Occasionally, waste dumps were burned off or dynamited. The rubbish tips used over several decades at each station also resulted in significant pollution.

Australia's first stations were intentionally designed to be cheap and quick to build. The buildings were humble in scale and caused little disturbance. Most were levelled on wooden railway sleepers and guyed to the ground with cables. But these frail structures were neither safe nor sustainable. The Australian Government had visions of a grander Antarctic program.

In 1977 Cabinet approved $74.7 million over 10 years to rebuild the continental stations, employ additional staff and commence a marine research program.[3] The rebuilding involved many thousands of cubic metres of building materials, prefabricated panels, steel portal frames, concrete pre-mix, as well as heavy plant, equipment and fuel to meet increased power demands. Substantial earthworks and blasting were required to establish the footings of the new buildings. The result was far larger buildings, which were well spread out and connected by a network of roads and above-ground ducted 'site services' for power, sewerage and water systems, and communications.

Old Casey (1969–89) was located on a peninsula bounded by the waters of Newcomb Bay and by the Thala Valley. It had a population of about 28 in winter and 45 in summer, and covered an area of 2 hectares, with 400 metres of roads and an annual fuel consumption of 410,000 litres.[4] In 2010, the new station one kilometre to the south had a summer population of over 100, covered an area of 4 hectares, and had 3.2 kilometres of roads and an annual fuel consumption of one million litres.

Rebuilding the stations required concrete. At Casey this entailed establishing a concrete-batching plant downwind of the building zone. The absence of protocols to control the spread of dust came to the attention of the 1985 Senate Standing Committee on National Resources, which heard evidence that a lake beside Casey had been dramatically altered by cement dust and that plastic cement bags and other construction waste had been blown out to sea.[5] A study by the Australian Antarctic Division (AAD) showed that highly alkaline cement dust from the batching plant had damaged nearby lichens.[6] This was significant as the shores of Newcomb Bay have some of the most extensively vegetated ice-free land in Antarctica. Protocols were introduced to restrict concrete batching to calm days and to monitor lichen health in the area.

Environmental problems continued. In 1990 approximately 91,000 litres of fuel leaked from a storage tank that was unbunded (lacking a containing wall) adjacent to the wharf. Two years later, another 38,000 litres of fuel drained into Newcomb Bay. The Casey experience was not unique: the proliferation of national programs undeniably increased environmental impacts around the continent.[7] The Treaty parties responded with a number of environmental measures, including waste management guidelines and environmental impact assessment procedures.[8]

The expanding programs required increased logistic support. The Australian stations, as just one example, initially received a single annual resupply voyage using vessels of generally less than 2000 tonnes deadweight (carrying capacity) that included around 50 passengers. The rebuilding program required extra cargo capacity. In 1981, the AAD chartered *Nanok S* (3000 tonnes and up to 20 passengers) and in 1984 *Ice Bird* (6433 tonnes and up to 96 passengers). Commissioned in 1990 and still in operation, RV *Aurora Australis* (3893 tonnes) carries up to 116 passengers and makes an average of five voyages each summer, covering a total of some 25,000 nautical miles to conduct marine science and to convey expeditioners, fuel and supplies.

Fixed-wing aircraft and helicopters used by the Australian Antarctic program in the first few decades after World War II were small and single-engine.[9] In 1994 the AAD changed to Sikorsky S76 twin-engine long-range helicopters, substantially increasing its ability to operate remotely from the three coastal stations of Casey, Davis and Mawson.[10] After several investigations and aborted attempts during the preceding 30 years, Australia started intercontinental air transport direct to Casey in 2008, flying an Airbus A319 from Hobart to the compacted-snow Wilkins airfield, some 80 kilometres south of Casey. The use of ground vehicles also substantially increased, from Caterpillar D4 and Ferguson petrol tractors in the first decades after the war to D6 and D9 tractors, cranes, loaders and excavators and all-terrain vehicles.

The expanded stations and vehicle fleets meant progressively greater energy demands. Station power supplies were upgraded from, for example, 125 kW at Mawson in 1954 to 375 kW generators in 2010. Each station now has bulk fuel storage capacity of approximately one million litres of fuel, which provides supply for a year and a limited but sufficient reserve in case resupply the following year is not possible.

Frameworks for governance

At the sixth Antarctic Treaty Consultative Meeting (ATCM) in Tokyo in 1970, Treaty Parties asked the Scientific Committee on Antarctic Research (SCAR) to advise on measures to protect the environment. In response, the committee presented the Code of Conduct for Antarctic Expeditions and Station Activities, adopted under Recommendation VIII-11 in 1975 (Oslo). The code included a clear expression of the importance of environmental impact assessment and provided guidance on waste handling. Meanwhile, Australia passed the *Environmental Protection Impact of Proposals Act 1974* (Cwth), which extended broad assessment requirements to Australia and its external territories.[11] The commitment of Treaty parties to the code was reiterated through the Declaration on the Protection of the Antarctic Environment, made under ATCM Recommendation IX-5 in 1977 (London), which strengthened the emphasis on prior assessment and mitigation of environmental impacts. Detailed environmental assessment obligations were put in place by the Treaty system in 1987 with the adoption of Recommendation XIV-2.

The 1964 Agreed Measures for the Conservation of Antarctic Fauna and Flora (the Agreed Measures), were brought into Australian law through the *Antarctic Treaty (Environmental Protection) Act 1980* (Cwth). Introducing the Bill, Senator John Carrick,

Minister for National Development and Energy, noted:
> The agreed measures have, until now, been implemented by means of administrative action by the Department of Science and the Environment. The Bill now before the Senate will give the agreed measures force of law ... The Bill also provides for the making of regulations to cover the control of pollution, the use of motor vehicles and other issues relating to environmental protection. As a consequence of Australian sovereignty over the Australian Antarctic Territory, we have a special responsibility to ensure that the Antarctic environment remains protected from any adverse effects of human occupation ... These provisions embodied in the Bill represent the culmination of long and carefully considered efforts by many nations including Australia.[12]

The 'administrative action' referred to also included phasing out the killing of Weddell seals for dog food, from 30 in 1977 to zero in 1980 and subsequent years. This went beyond the requirements of the 1978 Convention on the Conservation of Antarctic Seals, which allowed the killing of a limited numbers of seals 'to provide indispensable food for men or dogs'. While it had been routine practice to feed the huskies kitchen scraps and old tinned food as a supplement to pemmican blocks and seal meat, the dog-food provision of the Convention on the Conservation of Antarctic Seals was specifically omitted from Australia's 1986 Antarctic Seals Conservation Regulations.[13] By the time killing seals for dog food became illegal under Australian law, it had been stopped voluntarily for several years.

In response to ATCM Recommendation XIII-4, in 1986 SCAR formed a panel of experts on waste disposal to advise the ATCM on waste management procedures. The panel was chaired by Jim Bleasel, then director of the AAD. The panel's report, published by the AAD in 1989, described the extent of the waste management challenge across the national Antarctic programs and formed the basis of proposals that were ultimately adopted by the Treaty and translated into Annex III of the Environmental Protocol.[14]

The success in 1991 of Australia's vigorous campaign with France and others to comprehensively protect the Antarctic environment through the adoption of the Protocol yielded high expectations of Australia's ability to meet the standards it had so energetically fought for. The same success energised Australia's determination to implement the Protocol measures domestically.

In 1992, one year after the Protocol was opened for signing, there was a flurry of legislative and administrative activity in Australia to give effect to it. On 11 December 1992, Parliament passed the *Antarctic Treaty (Environmental Protection) Act* (Cwth), incorporating all the requirements of the Protocol, except those contained in Annex IV that had earlier been implemented through amendments to the *Protection of the Sea (Prevention of Pollution from Ships) Act*

1983. Regulations for environmental impact assessment and waste management were introduced over the next two years.[15]

But all these initiatives in the Antarctic Treaty System, reflected in Australian law, did not mean that it would be easy to solve the environmental challenges. The waste dumped around the stations in preceding years remained, and waste was still being generated.

Waste management

In 1984 the AAD commissioned high-temperature dual-chamber incinerators at all its Antarctic stations and ceased the open-air burning and disposal of waste. Operation of the incinerators required specialist training and close attention to waste sorting to avoid noxious emissions and unacceptable levels of heavy metal in incinerator ash, with consequent expensive handling and disposal costs in Australia. But even high-temperature incineration was not without its problems. Heavy metal concentrations in the ash were linked to the incineration of the timber treated with copper, chrome and arsenic that was commonly used in suppliers' packing crates.

In response, the AAD added environmental requirements to the wording of suppliers' contracts. It routinely checked and repacked items received for shipment to Antarctica that contained potentially harmful materials such as polychlorinated biphenyls, polystyrene beads and non-sterile soil so they did not enter the environment or the waste stream. In 1993 the AAD produced a waste management strategy for Australia's Antarctic program in response to the requirements of Annex III.[16] The strategy included specific steps for waste minimisation, reuse, recycling, disposal, contaminated sites, clean-up and monitoring. This was followed in March 1994 by the commencement of the Waste Management Regulations that gave effect to Annex III of the Protocol.

Early resistance in the 1980s among station personnel to more stringent waste management standards imposed administratively from AAD headquarters at Kingston gave way over several years to a zealous uptake of many environmental issues. For example, photographic waste was returned to Australia for silver recovery, and station staff modified mechanical plant to produce 'elephant foot' waste crushers, compacting waste into used 200-litre fuel drums for transport. Attempts to improve the draining and cleaning of the drums before they were used for this purpose proved ineffective, so purpose-built containers were later provided for sewage sludge, photographic and other liquid wastes, and the empty fuel drums were crushed. In 2010 the AAD tested fuel-drum washing, oil-separating equipment and industrial drum crushers at Davis, with a view to operating them at all stations.

To complement improvements to the handling of solid wastes, in the 1980s sewage treatment plants were commissioned as the new stations came on line. Until then, Casey had discharged directly into the sea and Davis had experimented with gas-fired toilets. Mawson had continued to burn solid human waste with waste timber and coal in used fuel drums.[17] The new rotating biological contactor secondary treatment facilities were to discharge effluent through heated pipes to the sea, with sludge and scum periodically removed and disposed on the sea-ice offshore where it was intended to be sterilised by salt and ultra-violet radiation before dispersing broadly into the sea as the ice decayed through summer.

Waste being returned to Australia on board the ship Polar Queen in 1999. Note 'RTA' (Return to Australia) labels. Courtesy Sandra Potter, Australian Antarctic Division

These systems were an advance on direct disposal of raw sewage in that they reduced turbidity, exhausted bacterial activity and reduced biological oxygen demand. However, attention shifted in the late 1990s to the fact that rotating biological contactor systems did little to reduce heavy metals, nutrients, viruses or other persistent pathogens. Partly out of environmental concern and partly because handling it was a safety hazard, depositing sludge on the sea ice was discontinued in the early 1990s.

While Australia continued with some success to improve its management of contemporary wastes, the legacy of waste dumps from the first 30 years remained largely unaddressed until the late 1980s. Following the cessation of dumping, open burning and sea-icing, several attempts were made to clean up and remove waste from the Mawson tip sites on the bare rock of East Arm. In the summers from 1989–90 to 1995–96, when the thaw released waste from ice and snow, station common-duties rosters included work on the tip sites. But much of the tip material had been pushed onto the shoreline sea-ice over the preceding decades, and a substantial amount remains in the water.

Although Wilkes was abandoned in 1969 because of successive heavy winter snow accumulation, in some succeeding seasons extensive thawing exposed much of the station and the associated waste. This allowed for opportunistic clean-ups, according to the availability of personnel, time and equipment. In 1988 the rubber fuel bladders were drained, rolled and removed, along with much surface litter and building debris.[18]

In 1993 the AAD commissioned the Australian Army's Corps of Engineers to render safe the hazardous materials around Wilkes and its tip sites, in particular explosives, detonators and unidentified compressed gases and liquids. While the primary impetus was human safety, the operation also decanted and removed many thousands of litres of liquid, mostly hydrocarbons, from corroded fuel drums exposed by the summer thaw.[19] The high variability of snow deposition and summer thaw at Wilkes makes it economically risky to plan major efforts on the expansive waste dumps, because shipping capacity, specialised plant and equipment and personnel must all be engaged well in advance. A commitment of many hundreds of thousands of dollars could prove futile if seasonal thaw did not allow access.

As a pilot exercise to test remediation techniques for dealing with the Wilkes problem, the AAD began removing waste from Thala Valley in 1996. Australia took seriously the approach of Annex III (Waste Disposal and Waste Management) that clean-up should occur only when it did not cause more environmental harm than it sought to correct.[20] To be able to make that assessment with any degree of certainty, the AAD's Human Impacts science program began to investigate contamination in the Thala Valley tip site, and to map dispersal pathways when meltwater flowed into adjacent Newcomb Bay. The effect of heavy metals and particulates in the marine environment was investigated for ten years to assess the likely effects on marine life before a pilot waste extraction and contaminant containment project commenced in 2000–01.[21]

Following the pilot study, the AAD began to excavate waste at the Thala Valley tip site in 2003. Veolia, the AAD's waste management contractor, provided 240 purpose-built shipping containers and a cargo ship was chartered to transport 1000 cubic metres of waste (approximately two-thirds of the material) to Australia. However, a hiccup in coordination between the AAD and the quarantine authorities meant the waste had to be expensively stored and treated in a temporary secure space on the Hobart waterfront before it could be released to a local controlled landfill site. With quarantine authorities eventually granting an import permit in 2009, the AAD scheduled the containerisation and removal of the remaining 465 cubic metres of waste for the 2010–11 season, and follow-up site monitoring, to complete the project at a total cost of $2.5 million.

Most of the larger waste material at Casey tip was removed, leaving behind the finer material infused in permafrost. In 2004 a cleanup program removed 1000 tonnes of this from Casey. Experiments with permeable reactive barriers across melt-streams below the tip site sought to answer the question 'How clean is clean enough?' Research priorities include understanding the physical and chemical processes of dispersion, the persistence of contaminants and determining the environmental impacts of waste removal.[22] Marine sediments and soft-sediment assemblages are also being investigated.[23]

While Annex III requires operators to clean up sites of previous occupation, very few substantial clean-ups have been undertaken by any party. The many abandoned or long-term unoccupied stations and camps in Antarctica contain infrastructure such as tanks, drums, pipelines and buildings that are increasingly likely to fail due to corrosion, ice movement or wind damage. The knowledge gained from research into the environmental impacts of work at Thala Valley will inform other national operators as they address their own challenges. The contaminated sites research will also inform future development of rules relating to liability for environmental harm under Article 16 of the Protocol.

Protecting the Antarctic environment

The growth in visitors to Antarctica has raised important questions about how best to protect the environment and reduce impact. Tourist numbers now exceed 30,000 in summer (2009–10), and Australian expeditioners number around 200 each year. One of the major attractions for these visitors is interaction with wildlife. However, visits to breeding colonies of seals, penguins and other birds are strictly controlled, and visitors are forbidden to touch or interfere with any wildlife. Tourist operators and national science programs have codes of conduct to manage visitor interactions with wildlife which include prescriptive guidelines on distances. While guidelines for the minimum approach distance establish a buffer between breeding animals and human activity, they are often not based on empirical research.[24]

The AAD has undertaken research into the effects of human activity on Antarctic wildlife since 1992. One study investigated the effects on Adélie penguin breeding success.[25] The penguins were exposed to nest checking for scientific purposes and recreational visits. Control colonies were found to have the highest hatching success and chick survival. The lowest rates were found at colonies subjected to recreational visits. This research was instrumental in developing guidelines for visitors approaching breeding groups of Adélie penguins.[26] The disturbance to emperor penguin chicks when exposed to helicopter overflights has also been examined.[27] The results suggested that 1500 metres would be an adequate buffer around emperor penguin breeding sites. Manipulative experiments conducted on sub-Antarctic Macquarie Island for royal and gentoo penguins showed that guidelines should be based on the distance that allows the birds to undertake normal activity, rather than on the distance to which visitors can approach before they flee.[28] Australia's guidelines were endorsed by Antarctic Treaty parties and now form the basis of currently accepted best practice.

One of the most successful recent Australian initiatives has been the implementation of an environmental management system (EMS) certified to the international standard ISO14000. The system provides a procedure for a strategic approach to the AAD's environmental policy, plans and actions. The process was commenced in 2000 and took three years to complete to certification standard, the first such system to be developed by any party for its entire Antarctic operation. The EMS standard helps the AAD to reduce its environmental impact, improve environmental performance, help in identifying risk associated with AAD operations and guide the organisation in risk reduction.

***

Attitudes to human impact on the Antarctic environment have changed vastly since Australians first visited the continent, and Antarctic environmental planning and management is now a very complex and challenging activity. While Australia has addressed many environmental issues in Antarctica, significant challenges remain. In some cases Australia has led by adopting procedures supporting best practice environmental management; in other cases it has had difficulty in meeting best practice. Of necessity, these challenges must be assessed at various spatial and temporal scales. At a global scale there are the longer term challenges associated with climate change and adaptation to environmental change which require strategic and fundamental research. A central feature of the ATS is its encouragement of international cooperation, and one of the benefits of this is the potential for reducing environmental impact through the shared use of logistics and infrastructure. At a regional scale there are opportunities for greater cooperation between countries to minimise environmental impact. At a local scale there are opportunities for sustainably managing human activities in all Antarctic operations, including the use of new techniques and technologies for energy production, such as wind generators. At both the regional and local scales, highly focused, targeted research is used to mitigate environmental threats. Australian engagement in Antarctic environmental protection now plays a vital role in all future research and operations and, through them, in the improvement of practices by other operators and in measures adopted by the Treaty system. National Antarctic programs can no longer walk away from their environmental responsibilities.

Notes

[1]	The authors gratefully acknowledge the contribution to this chapter by Andrew Jackson.

[2]	Potter (2003).

[3]	Bowden (1997).

[4]	Australian Antarctic Division, 2010. Engineering Division files.

[5]	Australia (1985) *The natural resources of the Australian Antarctic Territory,* Senate Standing

Committee on Natural Resources, Parliament of Australia, Canberra, p 75.

[6] Adamson and Seppelt (1990).

[7] Kriwoken (1991).

[8] See, for example, Recommendation XIV-2.

[9] The exception was a Douglas Dakota wrecked in a blizzard at Mawson in 1960 after only two sorties.

[10] Approved under an Initial Environmental Evaluation, operation of S76 helicopters was the first Australian logistics activity to undergo formal assessment under the 1993 environmental impact assessment regulations of the *Antarctic Treaty (Environment Protection) Act.*

[11] Except for the (then) Territory of Papua-New Guinea.

[12] Hansard of the Australian Senate, 23 May 1980: Antarctic Treaty (Environment Protection) Bill 1980, Second reading speech.

[13] Convention for the Conservation of Antarctic Seals, Article 4(1)(a). Note that the Antarctic Seals Conservation Regulations (1986) specifically omitted reference to this Article, although they did provide for the Minister to grant permits to take 'specimens ... for such other purposes as the Minister sees fit' (section 2E(b)).

[14] Scientific Committee on Antarctic Research (1989).

[15] The Antarctic Treaty (Environmental Protection) (Environmental Impact Assessment) Regula-

tions commenced 11 June 1993. On 11 March 1994 the Antarctic Treaty (Environmental Protection) (Waste Management) Regulations entered into force.

[16] Australian Antarctic Division (1994).

[17] In 'Law Hut', the Mawson toilet block named after the AAD's first director, Dr Phillip Law.

[18] Australian Antarctic Division (1987) file 87/762: Station operation and infrastructure – Wilkes station – Operational Management Plan. Australian Antarctic Division, Kingston.

[19] Australian Antarctic Division (1992) file 92/684: Environmental management – environmental assessments – IEE Wilkes cleanup 1990–1991. Australian Antarctic Division, Kingston.

[20] Annex III, Article 1(5) 'Past and present waste disposal sites on land and abandoned work sites of Antarctic activities shall be cleaned up by the generator of such wastes and the user of such sites. This obligation shall not be interpreted as requiring: (a) the removal of any structure designated as a historic site or monument; or (b) the removal of any structure or waste material in circumstances where the removal by any practical option would result in greater adverse environmental impact than leaving the structure or waste material in its existing location.'

[21] Snape et al. (2001).

[22] Australian Antarctic Division (2010) Australian Antarctic climate change research, Antarctic Treaty Meeting of Experts, Agenda Item ATME3, 6–9 April, Norway.

[23] Stark et al. (2003).

[24] Holmes et al. (2008).

[25] Giese (1996).

[26] Giese (1997).

[27] Giese and Riddle (1999).

[28] Holmes et al. (2005, 2006).

15

Australia's Antarctic future

Marcus Haward and Andrew Jackson

This volume has reflected on a century of Australian engagement in Antarctica, with a particular focus on the past 50 years, during which the nation has pursued its interests within the framework of the Antarctic Treaty System (ATS). Antarctica has had a continuing influence on Australia's climate, environment, economy, culture and security. As discussed in chapters 1 and 3, the negotiation of the Antarctic Treaty addressed a matter 'of close and immediate concern' to Australia, a matter with implications for both domestic and foreign policy. Domestic political interest in the region, while naturally variable in intensity, has been continuous, and there has been remarkable consistency in the way Australia has approached opportunities and challenges within the framework provided by the ATS. Australia has demonstrated a strong ongoing commitment to the Treaty, to consensus diplomacy and to international cooperation, albeit punctuated, as we have seen, by some dramatic developments. This chapter reviews the history related in this volume as a basis for considering Australia's future in Antarctica and thereby, almost inevitably, in the ATS.

Continuity and change

Within the continuity already alluded to, the emphases that Australia has placed on particular policy interests in the Antarctic, and the initiatives it has taken to pursue them, have changed over time. It seems that every decade or so the opportunity has been taken to reflect on what Australia is hoping to achieve in Antarctica. Often, that reflection has focused on the scientific objectives of the Australian program and, as explained in chapter 6, there have been numerous reviews that have reset research priorities to match the needs of government or the inclination of scientists. The 2010 science strategic plan is just the latest, and its review date of 2021 recognises that such goals evolve.

Australian Antarctic policy thinking comes in cycles. It could be argued, for example, that sovereignty has emerged again as a priority, as evidenced by Australia's 2004 submission of Antarctic data to the Commission on the Limits of the Continental Shelf, or suggestions by the Australian Strategic Policy Institute in 2007 that Australia's presence not be drawn down lest it be 'interpreted by others as reducing our commitment to our sovereign interests'.[1] Others have suggested that these interests are overplayed and characterised them as 'frontier vigilantism'.[2] A century after Mawson's pioneering Australasian Antarctic Expedition, and 50 years after the entry into force of the Antarctic Treaty, there is evidently still scope for a robust debate about the things that connect Australia and Antarctica.[3]

Such considerations provide an opportunity for reflection on where Australian emphasis should be placed in pursuing its interests. It is clear that in the immediate post-war years the concern was to establish a permanent Antarctic presence, and this was achieved in February 1954 with the opening of Mawson, the first permanent station south of the Antarctic Circle. This was soon followed by Davis, at a time when several nations were installing facilities in preparation for the International Geophysical Year. Australia subsequently took administrative control of the US station Wilkes, and shortly afterwards replaced it with Casey, distinctively Australian in style and on a more suitable site. Occupying real estate seemed to be the main concern and Australia was staunchly protective of its territorial interests. By the mid-1970s Australia was contemplating a complete rebuild of its permanent stations, to make them even more enduring. The priority was still to maintain a presence, but this was followed closely by the pursuit of the basic science which that presence made possible.

Phillip Law's 1964 vision of where Australia would be in Antarctica 20 years on, in the prophetic year of 1984 (chapters 10 and 11), tried to break the mould by describing a quite different future. Law may have been wide of the mark, but he cannot be criticised for lack of imagination. His was very much a resources view of Antarctica, especially of the future exploitation of its minerals.[4] However, the trigger for a policy rethink was not Law's ambitious predictions, but rather the agenda for the 1977 Antarctic Treaty Consultative Meeting. That meeting opened the lid on the question of regulating Antarctic resource exploitation – living and non-living resources – an issue that had not been confronted head-on during the Treaty negotiations. In the lead-up to the meeting, Australia's Antarctic Inter-Departmental Committee met to consider the scope of a submission to be placed before the Australian Government on Antarctic policy. The sovereignty interest remained acute, possibly reflecting the potential challenges a discussion of resources had for claimants, or perhaps revealing a lack of confidence in the durability of the Treaty so early in its life. Nevertheless, a plea was made to shift the balance:

> Perhaps the greatest disadvantage of our claim is that preoccupation with it tends to lead to emphasizing the continuing occupation of a number of permanent stations, thus absorbing resources that might be applied to scientific investigation ... scientific research should be properly and fully recognized as a prime reason for our involvement in Antarctica. It should not be approached as an excuse, as something secondary to occupation, or merely as a means of maintaining a presence.

It could surpass in value and durability any other Antarctic resource.[5]

Australia and the Antarctic Treaty System

Australian participants at the early Antarctic Treaty consultative meetings made cautious assessments of the Treaty's future. Chapters 3 and 5 have discussed the consequences of Australia's role as an original signatory and as host of the first consultative meeting. In the 1960s, all parties deliberately avoided issues that could overturn the accommodation articulated in Article IV. Resource issues were, however, to bring these tensions into sharp focus. Chapters 7 and 11 have told how marine living resources and minerals brought Australia into the centre of debate and, in turn, locked it into policy directions that placed regulation of resource activities under the direction of the ATS. The provisions that had been agreed in CCAMLR and CRAMRA meant that the dogged pursuit of special benefits for claimants was moderated by cooperative approaches to resource management.

Of course, Australia's decision to reject CRAMRA was to dramatically change its policy approach to Antarctica, although this was not without its critics. Phillip Law, buying back into predictions of the future as the Treaty reached its 30th year, took the view that the government's action would ultimately weaken the Treaty.[6] A decade later, the Antarctic Division's director, Tony Press, put a contrary view, asserting that the Antarctic Treaty represented the 'political reunification of Gondwana' and that for activities in Antarctica 'the overarching framework will continue to be a robust and effective regime centred on the Antarctic Treaty'.[7]

As this book has shown, Australia has fought hard to maintain and strengthen the ATS, and to defend it from external challenges – for example, by leading its defence in the United Nations debate on the 'Question of Antarctica' (chapter 9). Australia has continued to contribute, notably through its role as depository state for CCAMLR (chapter 7) and its contribution to the development of the Environmental Protocol and the Secretariat (chapter 13).

Australia's Antarctic policy

What is Australia's Antarctic policy? Although there are hints in government publications and announcements – and perhaps it can be deduced from the various statements of priorities, goals, charters, visions and values, and White Papers, budget papers and political platforms – there is no single statement of Australia's Antarctic policy.[8] In 2010 the government released a 10-year Antarctic science strategic plan that, for context, described a number of the government's priorities. They included 'maintaining

Australia's diplomatic presence and increasing Australia's influence in Antarctica through actively engaging internationally in matters affecting Antarctic governance arrangements, including under the Antarctic Treaty and other international instruments'.[9] This echoed the government's Antarctic program goal of 'maintaining the Antarctic Treaty system and enhancing Australia's influence within it'.[10]

But the best guidance for Australia's Antarctic policy comes from a 1989 statement of policy interests which has survived various governments and administrative arrangements over many years. Strangely, it is seldom published, so it is timely to present it here:

Australia's Antarctic policy interests are:

- to preserve our sovereignty over the Australian Antarctic Territory, including our sovereign rights over the adjacent offshore areas
- to maintain Antarctica free from strategic and/or political confrontation
- to protect the Antarctic environment, having regard to its special qualities and effects on our region
- to take advantage of the special opportunities Antarctica offers for scientific research
- to be informed about and able to influence developments in a region geographically proximate to Australia
- to derive any reasonable economic benefits from the living and non-living resources of the Antarctic

(excluding the deriving of such benefits from mining and oil drilling).[11]

It is possible to track the evolution of this statement of interests. Its genesis can be traced back to 1959, before the Treaty was signed, when the Department of External Affairs articulated the fundamentals of peace, science, sovereignty and economic benefit.[12] It appeared again in 1975 as preparation for Cabinet's consideration of Antarctic issues.[13] The statement has proven to be remarkably durable, although there have been adjustments in language from time to time as circumstances required. For example, when the Department of Foreign Affairs reflected on the statement in 1981, it dealt with the interest relating to resources in two different ways – in January referring only obliquely to resources and in March specifically including them.[14] And in 1989 an important qualification appeared in the form of the important parenthetical exclusion of mining in the final sentence of the quotation above. This was made to avoid any misinterpretation of the government's refusal to sign the Antarctic minerals convention. But such modifications aside, as the thematic chapters of this book have shown, the core components of Australian Antarctic policy and culture have endured: sovereignty, peace, environment, science, influence and benefit.

Coming full circle: Australia's future policy interests

Successive Australian governments have taken the view that support for the Antarctic Treaty System is the best way to advance Australia's policy interests. Accordingly, Australia has been active within the system and at the vanguard of initiatives that have been pivotal in its evolution. While at times Australia has not shied away from challenging the status quo, it has strongly defended the values of collaboration and consensus embedded in the Treaty. The preceding chapters have shown successful efforts to build consensus (for example in the response to the 'Question of Antarctica' and in the development of an alternative to the minerals convention), but also occasions where Australia was unable to gain that consensus in support of its initiatives (most notably within CCAMLR over the proposed listing of Patagonian toothfish on the Convention on International Trade in Endangered Species of Wild Fauna and Flora).

All the original signatories worked hard to ensure that the Antarctic Treaty would succeed. Small steps were taken in the early years, with all parties aware of the consequences of misstepping or overreaching. At the same time Australia maintained its own policy interests as the basis of engagement. We argue that these interests will endure, although emphases will continue to change in response to circumstances within the Treaty system or domestic politics, as they have over the past 50 years.

Security was a major Australian concern in the negotiation of the Treaty, but has now diminished in importance due to the effectiveness of the Treaty's commitments to peace and demilitarisation. Sovereignty will be an enduring interest, albeit advanced within the rights and obligations provided by Article IV. As previously mentioned, some commentators dismiss the protection of sovereign interests as anachronistic, and argue that discussing sovereignty within the Antarctic Treaty system is dangerous or, at best, irrelevant. Others misrepresent Article IV with the cliché that the claims are frozen, suggesting that they are in some way suspended. What is suspended is not the claims, but arguments about them. The fact is, the territorial claims exist and the Treaty recognises that reality. The sovereign perspective, in various ways, is fundamental to the interests of one-third of the current ATCPs, and an inescapable reality for many others. It can be argued that the two-thirds of states which are ambivalent about or do not accept the sovereign claims take comfort in the status quo, rather than the uncertainties of a completely different regime. Certainly, there are no proposals for a new approach to Antarctic governance. As stated in chapter 2, Australia can be quietly confident about its sovereignty: it has never been disputed and no other state has a superior claim in that part of Antarctica. There is no national interest to be served by Australia retreating from its position, and support for Article IV is an essential element of Australia's strategic approach to Antarctica.

Science will also be an enduring interest. As a remarkably prescient Antarctic Division scientist noted four decades ago:

> the rewards to be had from science are immense. Antarctica, for example, is a key factor in global atmospheric and oceanic circulation, hence also in global climate and marine resources. It is yielding theories and predictions of glaciation and climate change that may be very important to our economy. Further, there can be little rational exploitation or conservation of resources without scientific investigation.[15]

A modern commentator could not put it better. Australian Antarctic science will continue to evolve, and greater use of remote sensing and innovative means of data recording will bring new opportunities and an increased focus on environmental management. Research that unlocks the climate and weather connections between Australia and Antarctica continues the work begun by Mawson a century ago, and is an area of ongoing direct national benefit. Australian Antarctic science also benefits global efforts to understand the scope and extent of future climate change and the factors which contribute to climatic variability. Support for the scientific freedoms facilitated by Article II will continue to fundamentally benefit Australia as well as global understanding of the Antarctic region.

Australia benefits economically from access to fishery resources within the Southern Ocean. Its commitment to the conservation and rational use values of CCAMLR is reinforced by the engagement in Southern Ocean fishing of Australian companies which support sustainable management. Australia will also continue to benefit from use of the Antarctic as a destination for tourists.

Australia has supported development within the Treaty's subordinate instruments of a number of environmental initiatives which have created a comprehensive suite of measures to protect the Antarctic and the Southern Ocean. As shown in earlier chapters, environmental decision making within the Treaty system was initially tentative, but by the mid-1980s the parties had established a number of environmental provisions that became the basis for the Protocol and what has now become the Treaty parties' biggest annual focus. In the last two decades the Committee for Environmental Protection, established under the Madrid Protocol, has provided an important forum for advancing Australia's interests in protecting the Antarctic environment. Without the Protocol and the CEP, Australia would find it very difficult to advance its own environmental agenda.

Australia and the Treaty's future

There is an inseparable connection between the Treaty's principles and the national interest – hence the Australian Government's support for the Treaty system.[16] It is therefore perhaps surprising that Australia's 1989 published statement of policy interests makes no reference to the Antarctic Treaty. One explanation is that the system is seen as a means rather than an end in itself.[17] Sometimes support for the Treaty has been implied – for example, the 2009 Defence White Paper assesses that there is no credible risk that Australia's national interests in the Southern Ocean and the Australian Antarctic Territory will be challenged in a way that would require a substantial military response.[18] This recognises that the Treaty continues to provide an assurance of peaceful usage of the region. Elsewhere the support for the Treaty is overt, such as in the government's 2010 statement of science priorities.

As this volume has shown, the Treaty has clearly served Australia well, just as it has served well the interests of all nations active in the region. But making assumptions about the longevity of governance under the Treaty system and complacency about its responsiveness carries risks. A recent study has shown that the system is robust, particularly with respect to possible future challenges relating to resource interests.[19] But the machinery of governance requires maintenance and lubrication, and even the best-oiled machinery can reach breaking point without regular attention to its performance. Perhaps, too, without occasionally testing its limits we cannot tell whether the Treaty system really has the strength to continue.

What are the likely pressures for change? It could be hypothesised that the biggest threats to stability would come from 'rogue states' becoming active in Antarctica and eschewing the Treaty system, and that such a scenario would inevitably involve unregulated seafloor oil drilling. This event would trigger concerns about sovereignty, high-seas rights and environmental issues. Rogue oil drilling is plausible, but such an 'assault' is likely to remain uneconomical for decades, despite growing uncertainty over the sustainability of global oil reserves. Illegal exploitation of hard minerals is probably even less likely, given the globalised market for what are still readily winnable materials. In either case, however, the response would be diplomatic and, if effective, would probably serve to further strengthen the Treaty system.

More plausible is the incremental erosion of the Treaty system's international credibility. There are three vital components to this: legitimacy, compliance and consensus. International acceptance of the system's legitimacy depends on the regime's continuing effectiveness, supported in turn by the transparency of its decision-making processes and by its engagement with stakeholder nations. There is nothing new in this – witness the response of Treaty parties to the 'Question of Antarctica' in the United Nations. The point, however, is that the system cannot be complacent and adopt the attitude that because the Malaysian challenge was met, the system's legitimacy has been proven. It could easily unravel through the Treaty parties failing to comply with the obligations they have imposed on themselves through numerous measures and resolutions. The final component of legitimacy is consensus, and while the parties remain united in their approach to governing Antarctica the strength of the Treaty is unassailable.

The Treaty parties have taken upon themselves a special responsibility for managing Antarctica in the interests of all mankind.[20] Their ongoing recognition as the custodians of Antarctica requires considerable maintenance of the machine. As national economies are rebalanced and developing states pursue economic strength it will be increasingly important for the Treaty system to engage others and to be responsive to external interest. Never again can the ATCPs take comfort in an insular regime serving only their own interests. A repeat of the 2008–09 global financial crisis could readily see dramatic shifts in national fortunes and in the balance of power in global affairs. The parties maintained their Antarctic programs during the last downturn and the ATCM continued unaffected, but there is no reason to assume that Antarctica will forever be immune from economic disruptions.

Possibly even more worrying is the potential for loss of confidence in the Treaty system in the general community. Mass communication can now generate instant protest and mobilise community passion on governance issues. While in Australia Antarctic issues generally enjoy broad political support, and internationally they are seldom controversial, it is not hard to imagine a grass roots campaign precipitating significant change of policy on Antarctica. The campaign to overturn CRAMRA described in chapter 11 would have been vastly different, and possibly a lot shorter, had contemporary communication media been used. Accordingly, the public reputation of the Treaty system as a trusted and reliable governance regime is a highly valuable asset which needs to be safeguarded in the future.

Protection of the fundamentals of the Treaty is critical for its continuing health; responsiveness to new pressures and new opportunities is equally important. While it may be argued that that the Treaty is an artefact of Cold War rivalry and global posturing after the Second World War, this does not mean that it is of waning relevance. On the contrary, the issues that drew nations to Antarctica and united them within the Antarctic Treaty System are as relevant today as ever. There is little prospect of those fundamentals changing – or reason for them to. Previous challenges to the Treaty have ended up strengthening it, and it is difficult to imagine circumstances in the future where it would be possible to negotiate a more effective regime. So Australia will continue to support the Treaty system, conscious of its importance to all for the sound governance of this remarkable part of the world.

Notes

[1]   Bergin and Haward (2007).

[2]   Dodds and Hemmings (2009).
[3]   Haward and Bergin (2010).
[4]   Cited in Press (2001). See also Law (1964), in which Law also postulated a never-ending krill harvest.
[5]   Sulzberger (1975) paras 10 and 27.
[6]   Law (1990).
[7]   Press (2001).
[8]   See, for example, <www.antarctica.gov.au/about-us> and <www.antarctica.gov.au/about-us/statement-of-purpose-and-values> (accessed 1 February 2011).
[9]   <www.antarctica.gov.au/__data/assets/pdf_file/0019/27307/Australian-Antarctic-science-strategic-plan-2011-12-to-2020-21_14-Oct.pdf> (accessed 1 February 2011).
[10]   Australian Government (1998) 4.
[11]   Jackson (1989).
[12]   Morgan (1996) 20–21.
[13]   Sulzberger (1975).
[14]   Australian Government (1981); Australian Parliament (1981).
[15]   Sulzberger (1975) para 26.
[16]   Brook (1984).
[17]   Powell and Jackson (2007).
[18]   Australian Government (2009) 52.
[19]   Weber (2011).
[20]   Wolfrum (1995).

16

Culture

Tom Griffiths and Sir Guy Green

How should you behave when arriving at an Antarctic station at the end of the polar winter? What is 'the changeover'? Whose ghostly footfalls do you hear when you enter the heroic-era huts? What does it mean to 'pont'?[1] How close should you get to an Adélie penguin? Where is Skua Central and what can you get there? What is a true wilderness? What could the gift of a pebble imply? How exactly might one claim a tract of ice for one's country? Is it dangerous to be alone? What is a ventifact? Is it wise to disagree openly in a small community? How do you feel when you see green? When should you – and when shouldn't you – use the word 'sovereignty'?

Navigating your way through these delicate questions, and countless others, requires immersion in Antarctic culture, which is not confined to the ice. 'Culture' is a famously elusive and all-embracing concept, and anthropologists happily argue over its many definitions. In this chapter, we are going to explore 'Antarctic culture' from four angles. First we will discuss the way human culture on the ice sheet is shaped by its humbling confrontation with an awesome nature. Secondly, we will study some of the peculiarities of Antarctic society generally. Then we will turn to national culture, especially Australia's relationship with Antarctica, and the persistent colonialism of the ice. Finally, we will analyse the special international political culture that has grown up in and around Antarctica, and which we suggest draws some of its strength from the character of life on the continent itself.[2]

Encountering Antarctic nature

What kind of culture is shaped by an extreme environment, a nature that is lethal to humans? Antarctica is a landscape in which the laws of chemistry and physics – and indeed the power of metaphysics – predominate, and terrestrial biology looks very marginal indeed. The ocean is where the life is: the largest exclusively land animal is a mite. A small growth of lichen on rocks at Australia's Casey Station has been described as 'the Daintree of Antarctica', ironically invoking the exuberant rainforest of North Queensland.[3] On a continent of ice, nature is both more dominant and less complex. It is impossible to ignore and impossible to engage with. When humans visit Antarctica, they are extremely vulnerable to nature and yet curiously outside it. They dream of the colour green. The American nature writer, Barry Lopez, who wrote a superbly lyrical book about the Arctic called *Arctic dreams,* was shocked by Antarctica. It was, he said, 'a terrifyingly abiotic' landscape, one where humans feel not so much insignificant as superfluous, and the elements are worse than hostile; they are indifferent.[4] Charles Laseron, a biologist on Mawson's 1911–14 expedition, found the vast ice plateau 'too big, never-ending', and felt it 'a great relief to get inside the tent and get some finality of vision'.[5] The ice is massive, deadly and – in spite of its own variety – reductionist. Historian Stephen Pyne calls Antarctica 'the most intellectual landscape on Earth'.[6]

One view of Antarctic culture is that it has all been about coming to terms with the immensity and meaning of that vast icy outback. Antarctic voyagers of the nineteenth century had originally wanted rock. They wanted rock and soil they could plant a flag in and claim for their country. The ice was in the way: it was a nuisance, an obstacle. Later, the ice became a testing ground for physical endeavour, a source of beauty and fear, but still essentially an obstruction stopping them from reaching, studying and claiming the land beneath. But by the mid-twentieth century, the ice itself had become a primary scientific focus and was no longer regarded just as an obscuring and frustrating 'barrier' between visitors and the much-desired land. Scientists began to see ice as a mineral of interest in itself; they began to see glaciers as geological and Antarctica as a vestigial landscape, a giant white fossil.

In the early 1950s it was discovered that the ice sheets were not just a few hundred metres thick but actually kilometres deep, and so the driest of all continents was actually a vast elevated plateau of frozen water. This startling discovery revealed that world sea level is principally controlled by the state of the Antarctic ice sheet. Questions about the ice changed from how frustrating, to how vast, how continental, how deep, how old, and then to how stable? Recent observable changes in the ice cap became anxiously assessed. The confirmation of global warming due to human influence came not only from the behaviour of the ice sheet, but also from the air bubbles trapped within it. Before Antarctica was even seen by humans, it was recording our impact.

If 100 years ago the defining Antarctic journey was the sledging expedition across the surface of the ice, and 50 years ago it was the tractor traverse that, with seismic soundings, measured the volume of the ice sheet, then the defining Antarctic journey of our own era goes straight down, with the help of a drill, from the top of the ice dome to the continental bedrock, a vertical journey back through time. And the ice core thus extracted enables us to see our civilisation in the humbling context of hundreds of thousands of years of climate history. Right now in Antarctica, the international race is on again – not for the South Pole, not for the first trans-Antarctic traverse, but for the first million-year ice core.[7]

So the great ice cap has reflected and shaped the history of human physical and intellectual endeavour. And space and time take on new dimensions in

Antarctica. The clear polar air is famously illusive, and there are few shadows to provide perspective. Light and looming can reveal features beyond the horizon. Time, too, is warped. It can feel as if time has not only skipped a beat, but has lost the beat altogether. The extremes of climate and geography, and the distortions of high latitudes and compressed longitudes, make a weird nonsense of the passage of a day. Writing in the dark of midwinter at Mawson Station in 1959, John Béchervaise tried to evoke the fabric of polar time:

> whose stuff is with me now: great, slow halyards of it passing through an Antarctic night where ordinary time does not exist. Here is always the time of watching, the time of waiting, the time of contemplation, the time of the little child, time that has not been impoverished by being thought valuable.[8]

Time has contours; it has a geography that resists rationalisation. This is a peculiarity of Antarctic culture: the task orientation of peasant societies endures there in surprising company with technology and modernity.

There were, of course, some dimensions of Antarctic nature to which humans could relate with affection or recognition. The indigenous residents were always very well dressed. They generally greeted the first colonists in what looked like formal delegations. They nearly always approached visiting parties and exuded an air of confident ownership. From a distance, in the deceptive Antarctic light, they looked like a troop of uniformed men. Early voyagers kidnapped them and carried them home as trophies of territorial possession. The crew of the first ship to winter in Antarctica, the *Belgica,* trapped in the ice in 1898 and as far away from civilisation as any humans could be, thought that a posse of marching figures on the winter horizon was a visiting mission and hurriedly got dressed.[9] The Scottish Antarctic Expedition played the bagpipes to an impassive local audience in 1903. Shackleton's 1907–09 expedition entertained a group of residents with a gramophone on the ice, and Scott's men regularly sang to them. A Nazi from the German Antarctic Expedition saluted a particularly impressive Antarctic representative (an 'emperor' no less) with chants of 'Heil Hitler' in 1938.

Every culture defines itself against some *other.* Although the 'humanity' of the penguins enchanted the visitors, it also exposed them to the kind of bullying and violence often perpetrated by voyagers on indigenous inhabitants. The very passivity of a penguin was provocative. It literally stood up to you. During the Dundee Antarctic Expedition of 1892–93, the emperor penguins, in spite of their size, were found to be hard to catch. The artist on board the *Balaena,* W G Burn Murdoch, put it simply and brutally: 'We crept up to them, partly surrounded them, and let drive with our picks...'[10] Like many indigenous peoples encountered by voyagers around the world, the emperors were first seen to be 'primitive', a 'doomed race', noble savages of a kind, destined to die out because they were an unchanging relic of past ages. But as the humans came to know the birds better, and lived with them through the polar winters, they began to see how the life cycle of the emperors was subject to change and contingency – not just over millions of years but from year to year. The birds now seemed to offer a parable of evolutionary adaptation, or even a model of social behaviour.[11] Soon the intruding people came to realise that their own presence on the ice and, indeed, on the planet – as scientists, as humans – might change the life and prospects of the penguins in devastating ways. Antarctic nature, it emerged, was much more vulnerable than we thought. Even the future of the awesome ice cap, which so dwarfs and humbles us, is in our hands.

The peculiarities of Antarctic society

Human culture first came to the ice in ships, and for quite a while it stayed in them. Occasionally it came ashore and expressed itself in flags and anthems, and it constantly packed and unpacked itself into sledges and tents and measured its geographical progress by sun and sextant. Civilisation found some enduring presence in lonely huts warmed with blubber and books, buildings that have since been worn to a splinter by the wind or eaten by the ice; some of them remain today, transformed by the passing of the years from shelters into shrines. The Ross Island huts of

Scott and Shackleton today offer tableaux of an Edwardian frontier. In their darkened interiors you will find still lifes with rope, harness, biscuit, wood and tin. Visitors have heard footfalls, voices, whispers, shouting in the night. Robert Falcon Scott's inspiring letters and diary entries, written from the tent that would become his tomb in early 1912, have become the sacred texts of Antarctic history. The Australian writer, Douglas Stewart, read Scott's diary 'time and time again' every Australian winter and memorably dramatised his tragic struggle for survival in the radio play *The fire on the snow* (1944). Scott, Shackleton, Amundsen, Mawson and Byrd have forever shaped the patterns of history, memory and language in Antarctica. When the American scientist Bill Green was camped in the McMurdo dry valleys at the end of the twentieth century, he dreamt of Edwardian figures sledging, and the wind that he heard was 'the wind of Scott's death'.[12]

In early 1954, the permanent colonisation of Antarctica began. A small group of Australians led by Phillip Law landed at Horseshoe Harbour and, on 13 February, an Antarctic ceremony was inserted into a hectic schedule of clearing cargo heaps. Fumbling the flag with cold hands and self-consciously singing 'God Save the Queen', the men acted out the seriousness of their government's political purpose.[13] Mawson Station's crude huts of the 1950s now cluster below the bigger, colourful modules of the building program of the 1980s. The preservation at Mawson of the

520

architectural sequence of colonial history deliberately strengthens the cultural narrative of Australian sovereignty.[14] In 1988 the Australian artist Jan Senbergs depicted this historical layering of the station by presenting a view from the 'old quarter' looking up towards 'Mawson Heights' where, as he put it, the Red Shed 'towers over the settlement like a modern castle over an old village'. He was interested to find that, in Antarctica, 'we see suburbia and its values more evident there, huddled on the edge of yet another continent'. He observed that, whereas perceptions of Antarctica once emphasised the heroic battle against nature, now 'it seems that survival ... is more to do with the cocoon of one's mind in heated and close quarters'.[15]

Mawson Station, February 1956. Kista Dan in Horseshoe Harbour. Phillip Law, Australian Antarctic Division, © Commonwealth of Australia

Antarctica has developed a peculiar, intense and ephemeral society. It is a place where the human generations are mostly annual. No one lives their whole life down there; no one comes home to Antarctica. 'The changeover' of personnel and the resupply of stations is the crucial operational exchange, a period of urgent refuelling in every sense, a passing on of learning and wisdom in a matter of days. It is the frantic turnover of generations in Antarctica. What other societies may do in years, Antarctica has to achieve in hours. Anticipation, experience, memory and history are telescoped into one frenetic moment and become indistinguishable.

But these Antarctic stations have distinctive histories, and not just those of discontinuity or eternal changeover. An intriguing local culture tenaciously takes root. There is even a recognisable kind of urban history in Antarctica's biggest town, the main US base at McMurdo Sound, known as 'MacTown', where there are more than 100 buildings, including a church, bowling alley, barber shop, video store, gym, three bars, a coffee house and an aquarium. You will even find automatic teller machines. The place where you pick up recycled gear is called Skua Central. A weekly newspaper, the *Antarctic Sun,* is published throughout the summer, and Radio McMurdo broadcasts on 104.5 FM. By 1970, McMurdo in summer was described as 'a dry, dusty, American frontier town, with saloons containing full-length nudes in the best Wild West tradition'. The official language was English but the dialect, as one resident put it in the 1950s and 1960s, 'was expletive'.[16] Antarctic bases are often compared to shabby mining towns: there is a brutal practicality about them and an abrupt disconnection with the landscape. MacTown tells us that, in Antarctica, no matter how substantial the installation, it always remains a camp – but a camp with its own culture.

There are rhythms to the year, and to the Antarctic experience. Seeing the ice for the first time is a great adrenaline burst – the sea becomes calmer and one's soul exults. You watch the ship leave in late summer and the real adventure begins. Midwinter comes more quickly than you think because you forget that you have not yet reached the thermic depths of the year. There is the excitement and release of the midwinter dinner and pantomime, the mirror moment of the year when you play at opposites, cross-dressing and subverting authority for a day. On Australian stations, *Cinderella* is the traditional pantomime. Whether the station leader is cast as Cinderella or an ugly sister may be significant. Midwinter is a moment of celebration because the sun begins its long journey back to you. But the worst is yet to come. The polar winter deepens, the hours seem to move more slowly, night is indistinguishable from day, the blizzards enclose you, the cold enters your bones, there is the weird scintillation of the aurora, and you hear the sighing and sobbing of the ice pack. The inertness of Antarctica begins to claim you. August to October are the danger months – the post-midwinter blues can set in. In late spring there is the excitement of returning penguins and of quickening summer activities and plans, but also the gnawing anxiety about release ... will the ship come? When will it come? The ship brings the flu, and the invasion.

Tasmania's Antarctic culture

Sir Guy Green
Tasmanians commonly refer to the continent of Australia as 'the mainland'. But given that Tasmania and Antarctica were once adjoining parts of the ancient continent of Gondwanaland and that the most southerly part of Tasmania, Macquarie Island, a sub-Antarctic outlier of the Municipality of Huon, is closer to Antarctica than it is to the continent of Australia, it might be just as apt for Tasmanians to call Antarctica the mainland. An even stronger reason for adopting that perspective is that today Tasmania has emerged as an example of a remarkably exten-sive Antarctic community not actually located in Antarctica.

This community comprises many major insti-tutions engaged in Antarctic activities, including the University of Tasmania, the Australian Antarctic Division, the CSIRO Division of Marine and Atmospheric Research, the Antarctic Climate and Ecosystems Cooperative Research Centre, the Institute for Marine and Antarctic Studies, the Integrated Marine Observing System, the Tasmanian Polar Network and the International Antarctic Institute, together with some 60 companies, government departments and other organisations involved in the Antarctic sector. Supporting those institutions is a diverse group of people teaching, undertaking scientific investigations, developing technology, engaging in business or providing myriad services in virtually every Antarctic field. It is said that everyone in Hobart has, or at least knows someone who has, an Antarctic connection.

Tasmania's Antarctic community had its origins in Hobart's history of serving ships carrying explorers and expeditioners on voyages to the Southern Ocean and Antarctica. The influence of Tasmania's maritime heritage on the development of its Antarctic culture is epitomised by the visit to Hobart in 1839 of the French corvettes *l'Astrolabe* and *La Zélée* on their voyage to Antarctica. Unhappily, before their arrival an epidemic of dysentery had broken out on both ships. The ships remained in Hobart for several months and in his journal Captain Jules Sébastien César Dumont d'Urville writes repeatedly of his gratitude for the way his sick crew members were looked after and for the overwhelming kindnesses, help and hospitality which were extended to them. Many members of Dumont d'Urville's crews died during the course of the expedition: some were buried at sea and the others with full naval honours in Hobart. In the city's Cornelian Bay cemetery a memorial listing their names stands in a garden with the French tricolour flying.

A lithograph of Hobart Town from a drawing by 'LeBreton' during the visit of the French expedition under Dumont d'Urville in 1839. Allport Library and Museum of Fine Arts, Tasmanian Archive and Heritage Office

Dumont d'Urville and his crew became actively involved in the life of the colony, climbing Mount Wellington, setting up a magnetic observatory, helping to fight a fire in one of the wharf buildings, painting scenes of Hobart Town and, as far as their impaired intestinal systems permitted, joining enthusiastically in the convivial gatherings held in their honour, which culminated in a great ball at Government House.

The memorial in Hobart's Cornelian Bay cemetery to those who died on Dumont d'Urville's Antarctic expedition (1837–40) and to later French explorers and expeditioners. Courtesy C Murray

That early encounter engendered a special relationship between France and Tasmania in the Antarctic sphere which has endured ever since. In 1972 in the Royal Tasmanian Botanical Gardens, the Ambassador of France unveiled a fountain sculpted from Huon pine which commemorates French exploration in Tasmanian and southern waters and, remarkably, is depicted in a French postage stamp. The names of French explorers from other ships since lost in Tasmanian waters have been added to the Cornelian Bay memorial. In 2000 a moving ceremony was held there, when representatives of the French and Tasmanian governments honoured the memory of three French expeditioners who had died in a helicopter accident in Antarctica the previous year. And today Hobart is the home port of the French Antarctic ship, a modern-day *l'Astrolabe.*

In recent decades Tasmania's Antarctic culture has developed far beyond that arising merely from its maritime links. Tasmania now provides Australian and other Antarctic visitors with an air link between Hobart and the Wilkins ice aerodrome in Antarctica near Casey Station. Emphasising Hobart's proximity to Antarctica, this service brands itself with as much flair as any of the better known international airlines. It publishes full-page colour advertisements showing an aircraft poised on an ice runway, bathed in the golden glow of an Antarctic sun hanging low on the horizon. The text simply announces: 'HOBART 0700 WILKINS 1130 – THAT'S PLANE SAILING'.

One block from the centre of Hobart, the flags of 24 nations and the European Union flutter in southern oceanic breezes. They mark the location of the Commission for the Conservation of Antarctic Marine Living Resources, one of the most significant components of the arrangements and treaties which collectively comprise the Antarctic Treaty System. Housed in a historic sandstone building previously home to one of the oldest schools in Australia, the Commission is literally integrated into the built heritage of Tasmania. More importantly, although they are international public servants, the Executive Secretary of CCAMLR and his staff are actively involved in Tasmanian affairs, and the delegates who meet here socialise with their Tasmanian professional colleagues and the wider community. Many regard Tasmania as a second home – in fact, one of the Swedish delegates has stayed in the same room in the same hotel every year for 20 years. Continuing a long gubernatorial tradition, the meetings of CCAMLR include a concert and a dinner at Government House – an event every bit as convivial as the ball held for Dumont d'Urville.

Antarctica has a ubiquitous physical presence in Hobart. As well as the sites of its Antarctic institutions, pilgrims can follow a polar pathway which links some 30 stations around the city. These include the Cornelian Bay memorial and Hadley's Hotel, which accommodated Carsten Borchgrevink and his men before their departure for Antarctica in 1898 and, 13 years later, Roald Amundsen, following his expedition to the South Pole. The 'cold house' at the Royal Tasmanian Botanical Gardens envelops visitors in the icy, damp, windy atmosphere of Macquarie Island and is the only place on earth where the living flora of a sub-Antarctic island can be seen without the inconvenience of actually having to voyage there. There is the weatherboard building on the Hobart Domain housing the transmitter which relayed the first radio communications between Antarctica and the rest of the world and is now, fittingly, the home of the Radio and Electronics Association of Southern Tasmania. And nearby, in the grounds of what is now Government House, is the site of the magnetic observatory Rossbank, built in 1840 by the Lieutenant-Governor, Sir John Franklin, for James Clark Ross on his voyage to Antarctica to search for the South Magnetic Pole.

The significance of the place which Antarctica occupies in Tasmanian culture was recognised when, between 1996 and 2003, I held four forums at Government House to promote the development of Tasmania's Antarctic community. The state's Antarctic culture has also been recognised by the establishment at the Tasmanian Museum and Art Gallery of an extensive permanent Antarctic and sub-Antarctic exhibition, which attracted over a million visitors during the four years after its opening in 2006. The Tasmanian quarterly magazine, *Ice Breaker,* has for ten years been publishing Antarctic news stories and been a forum for the discussion of Antarctic issues. In 2006 the literary magazine *Island* devoted an entire issue to Antarctic-related poetry, essays, short stories and articles. This built on a Tasmanian Antarctic arts and literary heritage which goes back at least to 1841, when an *Antarctic drama,* which portrayed real Antarctic and Arctic explorers and less real giant penguins and was probably the first Antarctic play produced anywhere in the world, attracted a full house at Hobart's Theatre Royal.

Although Australia has now established an air link with the continent, for most of its history the Australian encounter with Antarctica has been through voyaging. Because ships cannot reach the stations between early autumn and late spring, Australian expeditioners have experienced especially isolated winters. There, in the howling wilderness, people learn to suppress conflict if they can, and to look constructively for common ground. When out sledging, the heroic-era polar explorer Raymond Priestley knew 'to confine your remarks to the afternoon [and to] avoid controversial subjects like you would the devil'.[17] Open conflict is too damaging. On the ice, minor disagreements can easily snowball. The never-ending polar night, the claustrophobia of a small community, the boredom of isolation – an environment of such forced intimacy can make the politics or personalities of your companions irritating and unbearable. The physical, mental and social dimensions of living become dangerously seamless in small, isolated communities of people outside nature. The storm in one's soul might well be more destabilising to an expedition than the blizzard outside.

Antarctica was the twentieth century's prime site for 'boys' own' adventures, and they were very much their own. The ice was a masculine place, to be defended, where women might be imagined and missed but never seen or held. The polar explorer emerged as an international icon of manliness at a time when the politics of 'the new woman' was gathering momentum. Men battled not only the elements but also their weaker selves to establish their manliness. There was resistance to women visiting Antarctica, and then there was resistance to women wintering, and then there was resistance to women getting beyond the coastline and working in the interior.[18] The last male bastion was continually rebuilt and defended. The media reported the arrival of women on the ice as 'invasions' and 'incursions'. A list of firsts gradually accumulated: first woman on the continent (Caroline Mikkelsen, wife of a Norwegian whaling captain, 1935); first women to winter (Jackie Ronne and Jennie Darlington, 1946–47); first woman to visit an Australian Antarctic base (Nel Law, 1961); first women at the South Pole (six Americans jumped hand in hand from the ramp of a transport plane, 1969). But the real challenge was to have women accepted as normal members of expedition parties.

The senior male resistance was tenacious and ingenious. Rear-Admiral George Dufek, commander of US Antarctic operations, was quoted in 1957 as saying: 'Women will not be allowed in the Antarctic until we can provide one woman for every man'. Two years later, he described the women who wanted to go south as 'the do-gooders and newspaper girls'. He continued: 'I felt the men themselves didn't want women there. It was a pioneering job. I think the presence of women would wreck the illusion of the frontiersman – the illusion of being a hero.'[19] To avoid discussion of the emotional and psychological dimensions of having women in Antarctica, male managers offered a simple logistical excuse: 'There are no facilities for women provided in Antarctica.' It all came down to bathrooms – as if women were a different species and 'all-male facilities' were a natural, inviolable feature of the ice.

When the first women went ashore at Casey Station in the summer of 1975–76, the men awaiting them sent a welcoming message by teleprinter: 'Men of Casey 1975 delighted to hear you visiting us next changeover stop few only mumbles about invasion of man's last domain but grins give them away and know deep in their stoney [sic] hearts they happy to embrace you all on arrival stop'.[20] By the 1990s, husband and wife teams were wintering at Australian stations and double beds were available for people who unexpectedly fell in love on the ice. In his book *Terra Antarctica,* Bill Fox tells of a man who fell in love with a woman who worked in a McMurdo lab and brought her tokens of affection from his fieldwork: ventifacts (wind-sculpted stones) from the dry valleys and specimens of sedimentary layers from the Transantarctics. Another woman at the station, experienced in Antarctic ways, observed: 'Just like any good [Adélie] penguin, he brought her stones every day to prove his devotion'.[21]

Assertions of nationalism on the ice fairly quickly enlisted women. In 1978, Argentina flew a woman in the late stages of pregnancy to the continent so that an Argentine baby could be 'indigenous', and Emilio Marcos Palma was born at Argentina's Esperanza Station. By 1984, the Chileans had matched the accomplishment and had even established a school.[22] Babies joined flags, postage stamps, Cabinet meetings, lusty singing, proclamations and science as assertions of territorial ambition.

Nationalism and colonialism

The dominant historical narratives of this international continent are nationalist. Nationalism is not contrary to the spirit of the Antarctic Treaty, for national endeavour is the means of contributing to the treaty system and there is national pride in becoming an influential party. But, as well as being a site of international cooperation, Antarctica has generated patriotism and competition, and sectors of the ice sheet have been integrated in distinctive and exclusive ways into dozens of national histories. Argentine and Chilean Antarctic territories appear on those nations' domestic maps; Richard Byrd established a 'colony' at what he called 'Little America'; Amundsen's triumph consolidated early twentieth-century Norwegian nationhood; and in Australia, Mawson's huts have been seen to be 'as much a part of the national psyche as the Hills Hoist, Uluru, [and] the Eureka Stockade'.[23] Marie Kawaja's recent work has revealed that, with respect to Antarctica, the new Commonwealth of Australia pursued an unusually assertive and independent foreign policy within the British Empire (see chapter 1).[24] Antarctic scholars have been wary of embracing post-colonial perspectives of Antarctic history and geography because of the continent's lack of indigenous people and its extreme environment, but as Klaus Dodds, Sanjay Chaturvedi and Christy Collis have argued, these factors make Antarctic colonialism a fascinating special case.[25]

What are some of the distinctive characteristics of Australia's cultural relationship with its 'Great Frozen Neighbour'? As chapter 1 explored, Antarctica became a significant part of the Australian scientific imagination from the late nineteenth century. For adventurous and scientific Australians, two frontiers beckoned: the white ice and the red heart, the south and the outback. Mawson, Cecil T Madigan, Charles Laseron, Edgeworth David, Griffith Taylor and Syd Kirkby ventured in both directions. Baldwin Spencer and J W Gregory went inland after almost going south. Adelaide, where Mawson gained a lecturing post in his twenties, was sandwiched between these frontiers; it was a city exposed to the winds of both deserts.

Although inhabitants of an arid land may seem strange colonisers of the ice, Australians *do* know something about deserts. Christy Collis has argued that, in the twentieth century, the Australian desert of the imagination – the place of imperial opportunity and continental conquest – effectively moved to Antarctica.[26] Certainly there is a fascinating parallel cultural history of the two deserts to be teased out. Part of the sustained power for Australians of *The fire on the snow* must lie in this correspondence. Literary scholars have suggested that Australian writers like Stewart and Thomas Keneally (who wrote two novels inspired by heroic-era expeditions) use Antarctica as 'a surrogate land for Australia', as an alternative template for imagining a continental colonisation.[27] Sidney Nolan, one of Australia's great artists of the mythic outback, relished the opportunity he gained in 1964 to paint the white desert. In the same year that he was working on his paintings of the lost inland explorers, Burke and Wills, Nolan visited Antarctica and found it provided 'an intensification' of what he had experienced in the heart of his own country.[28]

It is not just a matter of Australians learning to look south and to secure their national interest there; it is also a story of Gondwanan cousins – one claimed by fire and the other by ice – providing vital, formative experiences of the frontier in a settler nation.

Mawson thought Antarctica might become an 'Alaska' to Australia's United States, a new frontier for a 'young' nation.[29] Brigid Hains, in *The ice and the inland,* studies the lives of Douglas Mawson and John Flynn (of the Inland) to explore the myth of the frontier in a rapidly modernising Australian nation. She argues that for settler Australians of the early twentieth century, anxious to assert a national identity and worried about the mental and physical effects of an urbanising population, the Antarctic frontier, like the outback, was a place of both anxiety and opportunity. There were concerns about the organic vitality of the race (especially in a young nation founded as a penal colony) and about the invigorating potential – but also degenerate effects – of the frontier. The harsh desert environments threatened regression but also offered renewal. 'To the white Australian imagination,' writes Hains, 'the frontier was the place where civilization unravelled into wilderness – for good or ill.'[30]

There was a cultural as well as a political theatre in Antarctic life: when British, Australian and New Zealand Antarctic Research Expedition (BANZARE) members had their group photo taken at Commonwealth Bay, Mawson insisted that they 'all dress up for it and make it look cold'. Australians down south were journeying into the heart of another 'unclaimed' space and testing and proving their national and racial qualities.

To settler Australians, there was also an attractive moral simplicity about colonising an uninhabited continent. Australia's Aboriginal lands had been appropriated under the doctrine of *terra nullius,* because they had been regarded as belonging to no one, and a 'Great Australian Silence' had grown around the experience of frontier war and dispossession. There was something redemptive about Antarctica's unalloyed whiteness. Collis reminds us that a shocking massacre of Aboriginal people took place at Coniston in central Australia in 1928, just as BANZARE was preparing to go south to claim genuinely uninhabited lands.[31] The *Discovery* sailed with a plain white flag. The expedition was securing for Australia a polar empire where any contests over ownership would be international, public and negotiable.

There is a delicate balance in Antarctic culture between assertive nationalism and cooperative internationalism, one that is sometimes expressed in the tension between sovereignty and science. Occasionally the balance tips and the resulting instability can be manifest in everyday station life as well as in diplomatic exchanges. In 1985 there was a coup at Australia's Casey Station. The officer-in-charge was isolated by his fellow expeditioners and there was an 'effective takeover' of the base during the winter. Authority crumbled, morale plummeted, and portraits of the Queen and Lord Casey were damaged and taken down. It was a result of tensions let loose by Australia's big Antarctic rebuilding program of the 1980s, which was itself prompted partly by anticipation of a possible new minerals regime down south. In this same period of political uncertainty, Australians began to revisit and maintain Mawson's original huts at Commonwealth Bay.

When the historian Stephen Murray-Smith stepped ashore at Casey in 1985, he found himself in the middle of a dysfunctional community. He was dismayed by the scale of the building going on around him: 'what we saw could only be interpreted one way, as a massive statement by Australia that it was in Antarctica in a big way, and there to stay'. In securing sovereignty at a time of international uncertainty, it seemed that science had taken a back seat. It was not just that builders outnumbered boffins, but also that they no longer shared a mission. The old fabric of Antarctic culture had been stretched to breaking point. Murray-Smith said of this period that Australians in Antarctica had become 'the ultimate existentialists'. He was shocked by the rupture of 'the changeover', the poverty of the bureaucracy's historical imagination, and the severity of the annual discontinuity between past and present.[32]

In some ways, the 1980s recalled the disabling tensions of the BANZARE era 50 years earlier, when the open conflict of science and sovereignty corroded even the old friendship between Mawson and J K Davis as they went about their flag-planting. In the 1950s, as international cooperation grew, Keith Waller of the Australian Department of External Affairs nevertheless reminded Phillip Law: 'I do not think of our Antarctic effort as a scientific expedition. To me the scientific work is secondary to the political consideration of maintaining our claim to this territory.'[33] These anxieties and tensions are endemic to Antarctic culture, but they can be observed especially in the culture of a small nation defending the largest Antarctic claim. There is currently a vigorous scholarly debate about whether Australia is 'in the vanguard of Antarctic nationalism right now'.[34]

The international political culture of Antarctica

Much of this book has analysed the evolving international political culture of Antarctica and Australia's engagement with it. This modern political culture was not simply imposed on the continent by high-level international negotiations, but grew also out of the surprising reality of life on the ice. The signing of the Antarctic Treaty in 1959, for example, was made possible by the radical social, political and intellectual experience in Antarctica itself of the International Geophysical Year. The IGY showed the political power of scientific cooperation; it was such a resounding success that it cried out to be institutionalised. The

Soviet Antarctic leader of the 1950s and 1960s, Mikhail Mikhailovich Somov, observed that 'Antarctica remains the paradox of our globe; in the most under-developed continent are practised the most advanced ideas in the world regarding friendship between nations. In the coldest continent are to be found the warmest human relationships.'[35] 'How absolutely spontaneous in the Antarctic is goodwill towards strangers!' declared John Béchervaise when he first made contact with Russians at Mirny in 1959.[36] Meanwhile, in Washington, preparations were well underway for a meeting of the 12 nations that had participated in IGY in Antarctica to discuss a treaty. 'United in diversity,' Ambassador Oscar Pinochet de la Barra from Chile later wrote of the Treaty negotiations, 'we created in those autumn days in Washington a product of simple commonsense, helped by a secret key: consensus.'[37]

The Treaty has proved to be what is arguably the most successful and creative international regime in history. Not only has it been faithfully observed but it has given rise to a coherent complex of institutions, practices and values which collectively comprise an identifiable and distinct international political culture. One of its hallmarks is that, as with the achievement of creating the Treaty itself, Antarctic governance is conducted through decisions arrived at by consensus. Relations on the ice have long evolved to minimise open conflict and to favour diplomacy. Antarctic culture at all levels, from the station to the ATCM, strives watchfully for consensus – inspired not only by political idealism and strategic pragmatism, but also by an awareness that the costs of division are too high. In some spheres consensus decision making has made institutions vulnerable to what has been described as 'consensus paralysis' or, at best, the law of the least ambitious proposal. That has generally not been the case with the Antarctic Treaty System (ATS), which has produced a large number of effective agreements governing fields as diverse as scientific cooperation, the protection of the Antarctic environment and historic sites, logistics, communications, transport and safety, the conservation of plants and animals, the management of tourism, the organisation and sharing of meteorological data, fisheries management and much else.

The special nature of the Antarctic political culture is also apparent in the character of the institutions and organisations which have been created within the ATS. The Commission for the Conservation of Antarctic Marine Living Resources (CCAMLR), for example, is the largest international organisation domiciled in Australia and is widely acknowledged to be a model of civilised international regulation and environmental management. CCAMLR is 'a very fine manifestation of the philosophy [of the ATS] in action' observed the executive secretary of CCAMLR. 'Its work,' he went on, 'is informed neither by the greed of those who would excessively exploit the Southern Ocean nor by the zealotry of the uncompromising conservationist but by rational, civilized discussion based upon the results of sound scientific research.'[38]

Another organisation which manifests the special qualities of the Antarctic culture is the Council of Managers of National Antarctic Programs (COMNAP). While its members are appointed by national governments, the council's objectives and work are not nationally oriented but reflect a commitment to advancing the mission of the whole international Antarctic community. It is a hardworking body which promotes and facilitates partnerships, operational arrangements and the sharing of information between countries throughout the continent as well as providing advice to the Antarctic Treaty System.[39] What is more, it is widely acknowledged by the operators and managers involved that COMNAP does a good deal more than just coordinate the contributions made by national programs: it adds significant value to them and achieves more than any one country could accomplish alone. An example has been the emergence of groupings within COMNAP to coordinate activities in regional areas. Of particular significance for Australia is the development by the East Antarctic nations, particularly the group at Prydz Bay, of coordinated responses to emergencies and the collaborative use of national shipping and air assets.

The Scientific Committee on Antarctic Research (SCAR) provides a further instance of the special character of the Antarctic culture. Since the inception of the Antarctic Treaty, SCAR has had official observer status and been one of the principal sources of scientific advice at Treaty meetings. It has played a major role in promoting cooperative scientific programs and made numerous recommendations on a large variety of matters, most of which have been incorporated into Antarctic Treaty instruments. Remembering that the ATS and its institutions are international arrangements or entities which were created by national governments, it is surprising to find that SCAR was not set up by the ATS but is a committee of the International Council for Science, a non-government association of national and international scientific bodies whose mission is to 'strengthen international science for the benefit of society'. The fact that such an influential source of advice to the Treaty parties on the primary activity which they undertake – science – is a committee of a non-government organisation is another illustration of the unique character of the Antarctic culture.

From the private sector, the International Association of Antarctica Tour Operators (IAATO) provides another example of an organisation whose work is strongly informed by the Antarctic ethos. While tourism raises important issues, there is no significant body of opinion that Antarctic tourism should not occur at all, and at least since the 1970s the policies of the Treaty parties and the Australian Government have been to recognise tourism as an acceptable Antarctic activity. The only real issue is how tourism should be regulated.

A distinguished authority on Antarctic tourism, Greg Mortimer, takes a positive view about its management. He regards it as 'a remarkable model – [because] Antarctica is the first continent where ... a set of rules were in place before significant tourism came along. Luckily enough, the people developing Antarctic tourism were environmentally aware and were driven by a love of the place rather than the buck.'[40] The policies and work of IAATO amply vindicate this assessment. IAATO's objectives, which include operating within the parameters of the ATS and the Madrid Protocol, enhancing public understanding and concern for conservation in the Antarctic, creating ambassadors for Antarctica and giving direct practical support to Antarctic science, are overwhelmingly directed to serving the wider public interest rather than merely the interests of its members.[41] Such is its commitment that IAATO has even made rules of its own which have gone further than the Treaty regulations require.[42]

These four organisations illustrate well the reach of the Antarctic political and management culture. CCAMLR is an international organisation created under the Antarctic Treaty; COMNAP is a committee of representatives of national governments; SCAR is a committee of a non-government organisation; while IAATO is an association of companies from the private sector. In other societies organisations with such very different foundations and functions would have correspondingly very different cultures, but in the Antarctic world all four share the commitment to the core values which collectively comprise an Antarctic ethos.

Antarctic political culture also makes an important contribution to the international community through the benign, civilising influence it seems to have upon those who come within its purview. An impressive demonstration was provided during the first meeting of CCAMLR, which was held in Hobart from 25 May to 11 June 1982.[43] Although taking place during the height of the Falklands War, the meeting was attended by full delegations from Argentina and the United Kingdom, who actively participated in the proceedings. We are not aware of any precedent in modern times when countries who were engaged in actual warfare with each other in one part of the world managed to sit down together in another part of the world and engage in open, productive international discussions. And yet such is the power of the Antarctic culture that that is exactly what happened in Hobart in the winter of 1982.

***

In the year the Antarctic Treaty was signed, the US exchange scientist Gilbert Dewart joined the Fifth Soviet Antarctic Expedition. While on an over-snow traverse from Mirny to Vostok in the summer of 1960–61, Dewart and his companions conducted what he called 'the Great Trans-Antarctic Russian-American Seminar'. Hunched together in their tractors on the great white plateau, they pondered their place in the world. They heard of the ratification of the Antarctic Treaty when they arrived at Komsomolskaya, and they talked about its implications for a long time. Could Antarctica avoid the destructive national rivalries that were tearing the rest of the world apart, they wondered? One of the Russians voiced their doubts: 'The Antarctic Treaty should work very well, at least until something of real commercial value is found down here to set us at loggerheads again', he declared.[44] Outside, a crystal desert surrounded them, as dead in high summer as it would have been in deepest winter. What had brought them here? This 'vast, cold, white country' had somehow seduced them into making this scientific pilgrimage. 'But was it the wasteland that we really sought', they wondered, 'or was it the integrating effect that this menacing environment had upon the social consciousness of our little community?' Did they, in other words, cherish the peculiar society of Antarctica even more than the remarkable environment? Perhaps, in coming to Antarctica, they were really seeking 'the heightened sense of humanity that grows from a communal struggle against hardship and peril'.[45]

Australia and Antarctica have developed a distinctive relationship. A geographical, historical and cultural kinship has grown between these two Gondwanan fragments and twin Great South Lands, these neighbouring continents and contrasting deserts, one a New World within the other. A fundamental part of that relationship in the Treaty era has been Australia's investment, itself also distinctive, in the unique international culture that has developed around, and on, the continent. We suggest that this global political achievement draws strength from the fact that not only is it idealistic; it is also organic and practical. It has grown from instincts and inclinations deep within the history of Antarctic culture itself: from humility in the face of truly wild nature, from the romantic idealism of the heroic era, from Antarctica's constant revelation of a common humanity, from the irrelevance of national boundaries to the doing of science and the sheer excitement of that science, from the need to avoid open division and to seek consensus within isolated communities. Ideas and idealism keep drawing people south and sustaining them there. A hunger for knowledge – a sense of wonder and curiosity about an extraordinary place – remains the substance of community in Antarctica. This is what people feel when they voyage across the Southern Ocean or find themselves face to face with the ice – and it is present even in the highest levels of Antarctic politics.

Notes

[1]   The verb 'to pont' means to pose, in polar discomfort, for a photograph, and is drawn from the name of Herbert George Ponting, photographer on Scott's last expedition. See Hince (2000).

[2]   In this chapter we draw upon our public lectures in the series entitled 'Antarctica: the Cultural Challenge', organised by the School of History and Classics, Faculty of Arts, at the University of Tasmania in 2009, and also on Griffiths (2007).

[3]   John Rich, Casey Station Leader in 2002, made this observation when giving a station tour to the latest arrivals, 27 December 2002.

[4]   Lopez (1998) 68.

[5]   Quoted in Hains (2002a).

[6]   Pyne (1986) 150.

[7]   For an elaboration of these paragraphs and for the meaning of ice in the climate crisis, see Griffiths (2010).

[8]   Béchervaise (1963) 19, 47, 62–63.

[9]   Cook (1900) 286.

[10]   Burn Murdoch (1984) 238–39.

[11]   See Griffiths (2007) chapter 11.

[12]   Green (1995).

[13]   Law (1983) chapter 9; Fred Elliott, 'Establishment of Mawson Base 1954', typescript of original diary with later comments in parentheses, MS 9443/1, and 'Diary', MS 9442/2, National Library of Australia.

[14]   Collis and Stevens (2007).

[15]   Jan Senbergs (1988) *Voyage Six – Antarctica,* Powell Street Gallery, Melbourne, and Boyer (1988) 30.

[16] Swithinbank(1997) 21, 24; *Polar Times,* June 1970, 6.
[17] Priestley (1914) 354.
[18] Rothblum et al. (1998) 213.
[19] Chipman (1986) 86–87, Burns (2005).
[20] Chipman (1986) 114.
[21] Fox (2005) 79.
[22] Wheeler (1997) 204.
[23] *Sydney Morning Herald* article (1997) quoted in Collis (2000) 22.
[24] Kawaja (2010).
[25] Dodds (2006), Chaturvedi (1996), Collis (2000), Collis and Stevens (2007).
[26] Collis (2000) 24.
[27] Leane (2007) 261–89, Hassall (1988).
[28] James (2006).
[29] Hains (2002a) 124–39.
[30] Hains (2002b) 5.
[31] Collis (2004).
[32] Murray-Smith (1988) 90–92, 225, and Griffiths (2007) chapter 12. For an excellent account of Australians in Antarctica in the 50 years after World War II, see Bowden (1997).
[33] Letter K Waller to P Law, 24 March 1955, quoted in Bowden (1997) 169.
[34] Dodds and Hemmings (2009), Haward and Bergin (2010), and Dodds and Hemmings (2010).
[35] Somov (1966).

[36]   Béchervaise (1963) 195.
[37]   Jackson (1995) 7.
[38]   Denzil G Miller, Executive Secretary of CCAMLR 2002 to 2010.
[39]   Fowler (2000).
[40]   Mortimer (2006).
[41]   For example, IAATO has promoted the fundamental principle that Antarctic tourism should have no more than a transitory impact on the environment, Mortimer (2006) 47.
[42]   For a discussion of the role of IAATO, see Johnson and Kriwoken (2007) 85.
[43]   *Report of the First Meeting of the Commission for the Conservation of Antarctic Marine Living Resources, Hobart, Australia 25 May – 11 June 1982.*
[44]   Dewart (1989) 166.
[45]   Dewart (1989) 155–56.

Australian Antarctic timeline

1642   Abel Tasman discovers and charts Tasmania [Van Diemen's Land], separating Australia from the Unknown Southern Continent on traditional maps.

1773   James Cook crosses the Antarctic Circle on his second voyage and visits Tasmania.

1788   The First Fleet arrives at Sydney Cove on 26 January and European settlement of Australia begins.

1789   HMS *Guardian,* carrying plants, animals, farm machinery and convicts to the colony in New South Wales, nearly founders after hitting a 'floating island of ice' in the south Indian Ocean.

1791   Whale hunting in Australian waters begins.

1801   A mercantile voyage from Sydney to Cape Town rounds Cape Horn and visits the Falkland Islands.

1804   Hobart [Town] is founded.

1805   The first sealing voyage of many in the next three decades leaves Sydney: Owen Smith on the *Independence;* Alexander McAskill takes the first cargo of elephant seal oil and fur seal skins entirely caught by NSW colonists to London on the *Lady Barlow* – British whaling interests have it declared contraband.

1810 Frederick Hasselborough discovers Campbell and Macquarie islands during sealing expeditions from Sydney in the brig *Perseverance.*

1820 Fabian von Bellingshausen's Russian expedition makes the first of two visits to Sydney in the *Vostok* and *Mirny,* after having been the first to cross the Antarctic Circle since James Cook and having sighted the Antarctic mainland.

1821 Daniel Taylor on the *Caroline* departs for the South Shetland Islands on the first sealing voyage out of Tasmania.

1831 John Biscoe's disabled Southern Ocean expedition overwinters in Hobart *(Tula)* and Melbourne *(Lively).* (Biscoe returns to live in Australia from 1837 to 1843.) James Weddell, also in Hobart, helps *Tula* to moor.

1837 John Franklin is appointed Lieutenant-Governor of Tasmania.

1839 Charles Wilkes' United States Exploring Expedition makes the first of three visits to Sydney.

1839 Jules Sébastien César Dumont d'Urville arrives in Hobart and is entertained by John Franklin; departs January 1840 on his third and successful attempt to reach mainland Antarctica.

1840 James Ross and Francis Crozier arrive in Hobart in the *Erebus* and *Terror,* construct a magnetic observatory with Franklin's assistance, depart for the Antarctic, and return the following year.

1842 A Tasmanian scientific journal promotes Australian research in the Antarctic for the first time. The call is not taken up until after the highly successful *Challenger* expedition concludes in 1876 and the studies of the International Polar Year are completed in 1883.

1853 American sealer John Heard on the *Oriental* sights Heard Island while sailing from Melbourne to Boston.

1862 Georg von Neumayer, noted German polar explorer and scientist resident in Melbourne, gives a series of public lectures promoting Arctic and Antarctic exploration.

1884 Ferdinand von Mueller, Victorian Government Botanist and an internationally recognised scientist, promotes Antarctic exploration at an address to the Victorian branch of the Royal Geographical Society of Australasia.

1886 The Antarctic Exploration Committee established by the Royal Society of Victoria and the Victorian branch of the Royal Geographical Society of Australasia to promote and pursue Antarctic research. Seeks partnerships with whalers, colonial and imperial governments and with famous Arctic explorer Adolf Nordenskiöld; ultimately unable to secure funding for an expedition but continues vigorously to promote Antarctic exploration.

1894 A proposal to include two Australian scientists having failed, Carsten Borchgrevink joins Henrik Bull's whaling expedition to the Antarctic (both are Norwegian residents of Australia). The expedition visits Melbourne and Hobart and claims the first landing on continental Antarctica, at Cape Adare in January 1895.

1898　Tasmanian Louis Bernacchi joins Carsten Borchgrevink's *Southern Cross* expedition as physicist and astronomer. The expedition sails south via Hobart and the following year Bernacchi becomes the first Australian to overwinter in Antarctica.

1901　Federation of Australian colonies – Commonwealth of Australia proclaimed on 1 January. Bernacchi is physicist on Robert Scott's National Antarctic *(Discovery)* Expedition (1901–04).

1907　Ernest Shackleton visits Adelaide and the Australian Government donates £5000 to his *Nimrod* expedition (1907–09).

1909　Australian geologists Edgeworth David *(Nimrod'*s chief scientific officer) and Douglas Mawson (with Scottish doctor Alistair Mackay) are first to reach the vicinity of the South Magnetic Pole and in first party to climb Mount Erebus (Edgeworth David leading). Australians Bertram Armytage and Leo Cotton are also members of expedition, which visits Sydney. *Nimrod* is repaired with assistance from the Navy on its return. *Nimrod'* s master, John King Davis, later commands *Aurora* on Australasian Antarctic Expedition and *Discovery* on the first of the two British, Australian and New Zealand

Antarctic Research Expedition (BANZARE) voyages.

1910   Australians Thomas Griffith Taylor and Frank Debenham join Robert Scott's *Terra Nova* expedition (1910–13) as geologists. *Terra Nova* calls at Melbourne and Scott also visits Sydney, where businessman Samuel Hordern matches the Australian government's donation of £2500 to the expedition.

1911   Douglas Mawson's Australasian Antarctic Expedition (1911–14) explores and claims for the Crown a new section of coast and achieves first successful radio communication between Antarctica and outside world, via relay station on Macquarie Island.

1912   Roald Amundsen announces achievement of the South Pole from Hobart.

1913   Hubert Wilkins second in command on Vilhjalmur Stefansson's Arctic expedition. Frank Hurley's Antarctic film released in Sydney cinemas.

1914   Return of Australasian Antarctic Expedition. Australians Ivan Gaze, Frank Hurley, Owen Jack and Richard Richards join Shackleton's British Imperial Trans-Antarctic *(Endurance)* Expedition. The expedition's Ross Sea party departs from Hobart on *Aurora.*

1916   John King Davis commands British, Australian and New Zealand governments' Ross Sea Relief Expedition for *Endurance* expedition.

1925   Hubert Wilkins proposes Australasian Pacific Polar Expedition but unable to find sufficient support. Frank Debenham appointed first director of Scott Polar Research Institute.

1928   Hubert Wilkins with American pilot Carl Ben Eielson makes first exploratory flight in Antarctic region, from Deception Island along the Antarctic Peninsula and back on 20 December, photographing, filming, charting and making territorial claims on behalf of the Crown.

1929   Departure of Douglas Mawson's British, Australian and New Zealand Antarctic Research Expedition (BANZARE 1929–31) with John King Davis commanding *Discovery.* Extensive new sovereignty claims and mapping. Flights over BANZARE coast and Princess Elizabeth Land; detailed scientific work. Heard Island visited.

1929   Hubert Wilkins, based on *William Scoresby,* makes more flights and territorial claims in Bellingshausen Sea region (following year also).

1933   The *Australian Antarctic Territory Acceptance Act* formalises transfer to Australia of sovereignty over territory formerly claimed in the Australian Antarctic Sector for the British Crown. Tasmanian Government declares Macquarie Island a wildlife sanctuary.

1934   Australian John Rymill leads British Graham Land Expedition (1934–37) with an integrated approach to mapping and exploration. Sir Raymond Priestley, geographer on Scott's *Terra Nova* expedition, appointed Vice-Chancellor of the University of Melbourne.

1935 Following ratification of the Convention for the Regulation of Whaling signed in Geneva in 1931, the Commonwealth Government passes *Whaling Act* (potential application includes AAT waters) to enforce its provisions. With American Lincoln Ellsworth, Hubert Wilkins completes the first flight across the Antarctic continent on 22 November.

1936 Entry into force of 1933 Act placing the Australian Antarctic Territory under Australian control.

1937 Australian representative on board for part of circumpolar cruise of oceanographic research ship *Discovery II,* 1937–38.

1939 Bayliss and Cumpston prepare their landmark map of Antarctica.

1947 Australian National Antarctic Research Expeditions (ANARE) formed. Stations established on Macquarie and Heard Islands, beginning continuous Australian operations in the sub-Antarctic.

1948 Antarctic Division (of the Department of External Affairs) created to administer ANARE. Phillip Law, ANARE's senior scientific officer, sails south on an old wooden ship, *Wyatt Earp,* in unsuccessful attempt to find site for future Australian Antarctic continental station. French ship *Commander Charcot* visits Hobart on first attempt to establish base in Adélie Land.

1949 Phillip Law appointed head of the Antarctic Division.

1950 Two years of design work begin for Australian Antarctic vessel.

1953 In the absence of Australian vessel, ice-strengthened *Kista Dan* chartered from Danish company. Australian Government announces expedition to establish continental scientific research station.

1954 Establishment of Mawson, the longest continually operating station south of the Antarctic Circle; beginning of continuous Australian occupation of Antarctica and of wide-ranging surveying, mapping and scientific investigation of surrounding regions.

1957 Davis Station (named after John King Davis, captain of Australasian Antarctic Expedition, BANZARE and other expedition ships) established during the International Geophysical Year. Hubert Wilkins's last voyage to the Antarctic, with US Operation Deep Freeze.

1959 Robert Casey, Australian Minister for External Affairs, persuades Soviet Deputy Foreign Minister Nicolai Firubin to accept crucial Article IV of proposed Treaty. Antarctic Treaty signed on 1 December. Australia takes over Wilkes Station, built by the United States in 1957.

1961   Antarctic Treaty enters into force on 23 June. First Antarctic Treaty Consultative Meeting (ATCM), Canberra.

1965   Davis Station closed for four years during construction of new station to replace snow-covered Wilkes.

1969   Opening of Casey Station near site of former Wilkes. Davis Station reopens.

1970   First recorded landing on McDonald Island.

1974   Federal government decides to move Antarctic Division headquarters from Melbourne to Hobart.

1978   Special ATCM II-1, Canberra.

1980   Special ATCM II-3, Canberra. Conference on the Conservation of Antarctic Marine Living Resources (CCAMLR), Canberra.

1981   Antarctic Division moves into new headquarters in Kingston, near Hobart.

1982   CCAMLR enters into force. Commission headquarters and venue for annual meetings established in Hobart. Malaysian Prime Minister Mahathir criticises the Antarctic Treaty System in the UN General Assembly.

1983   Special ATCM V, Canberra. ATCM XII, Canberra.

1986   Special ATCM IV-8, Hobart.

1988   Institute of Antarctic and Southern Ocean Studies established, University of Tasmania. Dick Smith and Giles Kershaw fly Twin Otter from Hobart to Casey to demonstrate potential of aircraft for Antarctic work. Twentieth meeting of the Scientific Committee on Antarctic Research, Hobart. Convention on the Regulation of Antarctic Mineral Resources (CRAMRA) adopted.

1989 At meetings in France and Australia, French Prime Minister Michel Rocard and Australian Prime Minister Bob Hawke agree not to sign CRAMRA but to push for comprehensive environmental protection agreement. Two years of intense diplomatic activity follow.

1990 After many years of chartering foreign vessels, the Antarctic Division starts using an Australian designed and built research and supply ship, *Aurora Australis.*

1991 Australia institutes *Antarctic Mining Prohibition Act,* prohibiting mining in the Australian Antarctic Territory and by Australians anywhere in Antarctica. In October, Treaty parties adopt Protocol on Environmental Protection to the Antarctic Treaty ('Madrid Protocol') and agree to observe its requirements pending entry into force. Australian Science Council establishes Cooperative Research Centre for the Antarctic and Southern Ocean Environment at the University of Tasmania to coordinate Australian Antarctic research. Australian Antarctic Foundation begins operation in Hobart.

1997 Antarctic Cooperative Research Centre refunded.

1998   Madrid Protocol enters into force.

2003   Antarctic Climate & Ecosystems Cooperative Research Centre (ACE CRC) succeeds Antarctic CRC.

2004   Australia submits data to Commission on the Limits of the Continental Shelf.

2006   International Antarctic Institute created with secretariat at University of Tasmania.

2009   50th anniversary of signing of Antarctic Treaty celebrated at Old Parliament House, Canberra.

2010   ACE CRC re-funded to 2014. Institute of Antarctic and Southern Ocean Studies expands to become Institute for Marine and Antarctic Studies.

2012   ATCM XXXV, Hobart.

Acronyms

Antarctic activities are renowned for the plethora of acronyms they produce. This is particularly evident in the work of COMNAP which, among others, has spawned AFIM, AINMR, AIROPS, ENMANET, EXCOM, INFONET, MOLIBA, SCALOP, SHIPOPS and TRAINET. It has even been suggested that COMNAP itself stands for Committee on the Management of New Acronym Proliferation! Antarctic officials are not immune from acronyms and many creep into daily language. Some are particularly elegant (BIOMASS is a fine example), others less euphonious (SCAR or ASAC, for instance), and still others intriguingly ambiguous (BROKE: Baseline Research on Oceanography, Krill and the Environment). This volume has sought to minimise the use of acronyms – below are some that were un-avoidable.

AAD	Australian Antarctic Division
AAE	Australasian Antarctic Expedition
AAT	Australian Antarctic Territory
ACAP	Agreement on the Conservation of Albatrosses and Petrels
ACT	Australian Capital Territory
AFZ	Australian Fishing Zone
ANARE	Australian National Antarctic Research Expeditions
ANZUS	Australia, New Zealand and the United States
ASAC	Antarctic Science Advisory Committee

ASMA	Antarctic Specially Managed Area
ATCM	Antarctic Treaty Consultative Meeting
ATCP	Antarctic Treaty Consultative Party
ATS	Antarctic Treaty System
BANZARE	British, Australian and New Zealand Antarctic Research Expedition
BIOMASS	Biological Investigations of Marine Antarctic Systems and Stocks
CCAMLR	Commission for the Conservation of Antarctic Marine Living Resources *and also*
CCAMLR	Convention on the Conservation of Antarctic Marine Living Resources
CCAS	Convention for the Conservation of Antarctic Seals
CEP	Committee for Environmental Protection
CITES	Convention on International Trade in Endangered Species of Wild Flora and Fauna
CLCS	Commission on the Limits of the Continental Shelf
COMNAP	Council of Managers of National Antarctic Programs
CRAMRA	Convention on the Regulation of Antarctic Mineral Resource Activities
CSIRO	Commonwealth Scientific and Industrial Research Organisation
DFAT	Department of Foreign Affairs and Trade
EEZ	Exclusive Economic Zone
EMS	environmental management system

EPBC Act   *Environmental Protection and Biological Diversity (EPBC) Act 1999*
G77 Group of 77
GPS   global positioning system
IAATO   International Association of Antarctica Tour Operators
ICRW   International Convention for the Regulation of Whaling
ICSU   International Council of Scientific Unions
IGY   International Geophysical Year
IUU   illegal, unreported and unregulated (fishing)
IMO   International Maritime Organization
NAM   non-aligned movement
NGO   non-government organisation
SATCM   Special Antarctic Treaty Consultative Meeting
SCAR   Scientific Committee on Antarctic Research
SPLOS   Meeting of States Parties to the United Nations Convention on the Law of the Sea
UNCLOS   United Nations Convention on the Law of the Sea
UNGA   UN General Assembly

References

Adamson E and RD Seppelt (1990) 'A comparison of airborne alkaline pollution damage in selected lichen and mosses at Casey Station, Wilkes Land, Antarctica', in KR Kerry and G Hempel (eds) *Antarctic ecosystems: ecological change and conservation,* Proceedings of 4th SCAR Biology Symposium, Springer Verlag, Berlin: 347–53.

Anon (1971) 'Sovereignty over the Antarctic continent', in DP O'Connell and Ann Riordan, *Opinions on imperial constitutional law,* Law Book, Sydney: 316–28.

______(1978) Tourist flight record 1976–77, 1977–78 summers, *Aurora* Spring, 121–22.

Antarctic and Southern Ocean Coalition (1988) *Some solutions to problems with the draft Antarctic minerals convention MR17/Revision IV,* ASOC Information Paper 1988-2.

______(2002) 'CITES/CCAMLR Frequently Asked Questions'.

Antarctic Science Advisory Committee (1991) *Antarctic research priorities for the 1990s: a review.* Antarctic Science Advisory Committee, Department of the Arts,

Sport, the Environment, Tourism and Territories, Canberra.

______(1997) *Australia's Antarctic program beyond 2000: a framework for the future,* ASAC/Australian Antarctic Division, Kingston.

Antarctic Treaty (1991) *Final Report of the Eleventh Antarctic Treaty Special Consultative Meeting, Madrid,* Ministerio de Asuntos Exteriors, Madrid.

______(1992) *Final Report of the Seventeenth Antarctic Treaty Consultative Meeting, Venice, 11–20 November 1992.*

______(1998) *Final Report of the Twenty-second Antarctic Treaty Consultative Meeting, Tromso, Norway, 25 May – 5 June 1998.*

______(2001) *Final Report of the Twenty-fourth Antarctic Treaty Consultative Meeting, St Petersburg, 9–20 July 2001.*

Argentina (1962) *Report of the Second Consultative Meeting of the Antarctic Treaty,* Buenos Aires <www .ats/aq/e/ats_meetings_atcm.htm>.

______(1969) *Antarctic Treaty and Final Reports of the First, Second, Third, Fourth and Fifth Consultative Meetings,* Buenos Aires.

Auburn FM (1982) *Antarctic law and politics,* C Hurst & Co, London.

Australia (1961a) *Antarctic Treaty First Consultative Meeting: Brief for the Australian Delegation,* Department of External Affairs, Canberra.

______(1961b) *Report of the First Consultative Meeting,* Commonwealth Government Printer, Canberra. Also at <www.ats/aq/e/ats_meetings_atc m.htm>.

______(1961c) *Delegation Report on the First Consultative Meeting,* (unpublished).

______(1966) *Antarctic Treaty Fourth Consultative Meeting: Brief for the Australian Delegation,* Department of External Affairs, Canberra (unpublished).

______(1968) *Antarctic Treaty Fifth Consultative Meeting: Brief for the Australian Delegation,* Department of External Affairs, Canberra (unpublished).

______(1978) Joint Committee on Foreign Affairs and Defence, *Australia, Antarctica and the Law of the Sea: Interim Report,* Parliament of the Commonwealth of Australia, Canberra.

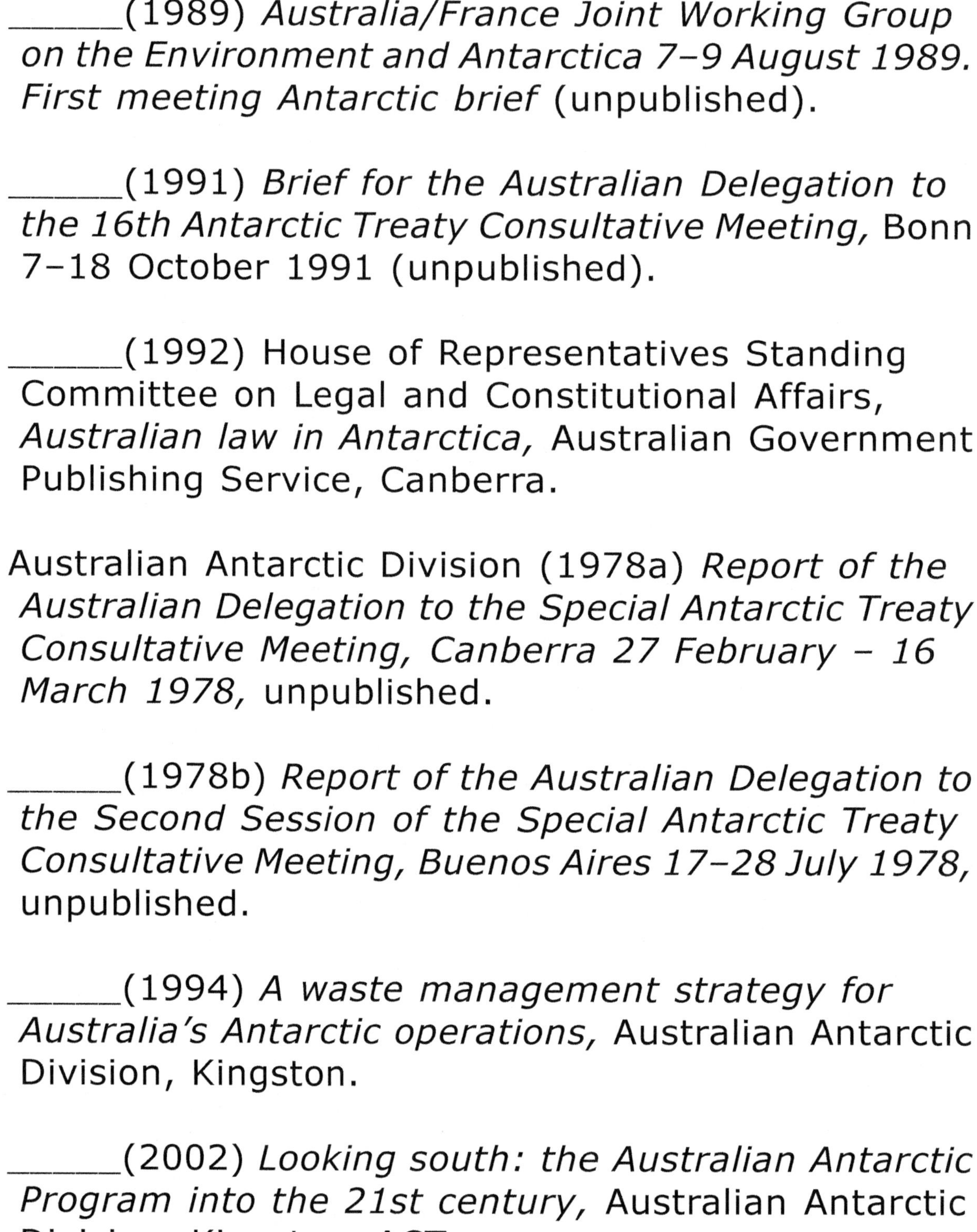

_______(1989) *Australia/France Joint Working Group on the Environment and Antarctica 7–9 August 1989. First meeting Antarctic brief* (unpublished).

_______(1991) *Brief for the Australian Delegation to the 16th Antarctic Treaty Consultative Meeting,* Bonn 7–18 October 1991 (unpublished).

_______(1992) House of Representatives Standing Committee on Legal and Constitutional Affairs, *Australian law in Antarctica,* Australian Government Publishing Service, Canberra.

Australian Antarctic Division (1978a) *Report of the Australian Delegation to the Special Antarctic Treaty Consultative Meeting, Canberra 27 February – 16 March 1978,* unpublished.

_______(1978b) *Report of the Australian Delegation to the Second Session of the Special Antarctic Treaty Consultative Meeting, Buenos Aires 17–28 July 1978,* unpublished.

_______(1994) *A waste management strategy for Australia's Antarctic operations,* Australian Antarctic Division, Kingston.

_______(2002) *Looking south: the Australian Antarctic Program into the 21st century,* Australian Antarctic Division, Kingston, ACT.

______(2005) *Background to the TAP for the incidental catch (or by-catch of seabirds during oceanic longline fishing operations: a key threatening process listed under the EPBC Act,* Australian Antarctic Division, Kingston.

______(2009) Australia's contribution to the International Polar Year, *Australian Antarctic Magazine* 16, 9–13.

Australian Government (1981) Antarctica in the 1980s, *Australian Foreign Affairs Record* 52(1) January 1981: 4–13.

______(1984) *Antarctica: Australian contribution in response to the request from the Secretary-General of the United Nations* (unpublished).

______(1998) 'Our Antarctic future: Australia's Antarctic Program beyond 2000', Department of the Environment.

______(2009) *Defending Australia in the Asia Pacific century: Force 2030,* Department of Defence.

Australian Parliament (1981) *Minutes of evidence relating to the redevelopment of Australian Antarctic bases,* Parliamentary Standing Committee on Public Works, Commonwealth Government Printer, 113–114.

Ayres, Philip (1999) *Mawson: a life,* Miegunyah Press, Melbourne.

Barnes JN (1982) 'The emerging Convention on the Conservation of Antarctic Marine Living Resources: an attempt to meet the new realities of resource exploitation in the Southern Ocean', in JI Charney (ed) *The new nationalism and the use of common spaces,* Allanheld, Totowa, NJ: 239–28.

Barrett, Noel D (2009) Norway and the 'winning' of Australian Antarctica, *Polar Record* 45 (235): 360–67.

Baughman TH (1990) 'British contributions to Antarctic exploration, 1891–1900', PhD thesis, College of Arts and Sciences, Florida State University.

Bayliss EP and JS Cumpston (1939) *Handbook and index to accompany a map of Antarctica,* Commonwealth Government Printer, Canberra.

Beaglehole, John Cawte (1974) *The life of Captain James Cook,* Adam & Charles Black, London.

Beale, Bob (1988) Antarctica is a goldmine of minerals, scientists believe, *Sydney Morning Herald* 8 March.

Béchervaise, John (1963) *Blizzard and fire: a year at Mawson, Antarctica,* Angus & Robertson, Sydney.

_____(1981) Davis, John King (1884–1967), *Australian dictionary of biography,* vol8, Melbourne University Press, Melbourne.

_____(1988) Rymill, John Riddoch (1905–1968), *Australian dictionary of biography,* vol11, Melbourne University Press, Melbourne.

Beck, Peter J (1983a) British Antarctic policy in the early 20th century, *Polar Record* 21 (134): 475–83.

_____(1983b) Securing the dominant 'place in the wan Antarctic sun' for the British Empire: the policy of extending British control over Antarctica, *Australian Journal of Politics and History* 29 (3): 448–61.

_____(1986a) *The international politics of Antarctica,* Croom Helm, London.

_____(1986b) Antarctica and the United Nations, 1985: the end of consensus? *Polar Record* 23 (143): 159–66.

_____(1988) Another sterile annual ritual? The United Nations and Antarctica 1987, *Polar Record* 24 (150): 207–12.

_____(1989) Antarctica at the UN 1988: seeking a bridge to understanding, *Polar Record* 25 (155): 329–34.

Beddington JR and WK de la Mare (1985) Marine mammal fishery interactions: modelling and the Southern Ocean, *SC-CCAMLR Selected Scientific Papers 1982–1984* Pt 2: 155–78.

Belgium (1964) *Report of the Third Antarctic Treaty Consultative Meeting,* Brussels <www.ats/aq/e/ats_meetings_atcm.htm>.

Belsky MH (1985) Management of large marine ecosystems: developing a new rule of customary international law, *San Diego Law Review* 22: 733–763.

Berger AA (2010) 'Selling the adventure of a lifetime: an ethnographic report on cruising in the Antarctic,' in M Lück, PT Maher and EJ Stewart (eds) *Cruise tourism in polar regions: promoting environmental and social sustainability?* Earthscan, Washington, DC, 43–54.

Bergin, Anthony (1991) The politics of Antarctic minerals – the greening of white Australia, *Australian Journal of Political Science* 26: 216.

______and M Haward (1995) Australia's approach to high seas fishing, *International Journal of Ocean and Coastal Law,* 10 (3), 349–367.

________and M Haward (2007) Frozen assets: securing Australia's Antarctic future. *Strategic insights 34.* Australian Strategic Policy Institute.

Bergsager E (1983) 'Basic conditions for the exploration and exploitation of mineral resources in Antarctica: options and precedents', in FO Vicuña (ed) *Antarctic resources policy: scientific, legal and political issues,* Cambridge University Press, Cambridge, 167–184.

Bernacchi, Louis (1901) *To the south polar regions: expedition of 1898–1900,* Hurst & Blackett, London.

Bowden, T (1997) *The silence calling – Australians in Antarctica 1947–97,* Allen & Unwin, Sydney.

Boyer, Peter (ed) (1988) *Antarctic journey: three artists in Antarctica,* Australian Antarctic Division, Kingston.

Branagan, David (2005) *TW Edgeworth David: a life,* National Library of Australia, Canberra.

Brook J (1984) 'Australia's policies towards Antarctica', in Stuart Harris (ed) *Australia's Antarctic policy options,* CRES Monograph 11, Australian National University, Canberra, 255–64.

574

Brown, Paul (1990) UK still wants to mine the Antarctic, *The Sunday Age,* 28 October: 12.

Budd WF (1986) 'The Antarctic Treaty as a scientific mechanism (Post-IGY) – contributions of Antarctic scientific research', in *Antarctic Treaty System: an assessment,* US National Academy Press, Washington, DC, 103–51.

Burke WT (1994) *The new international law of fisheries,* Clarendon Press, Oxford.

Burn Murdoch, WG (1984) *From Edinburgh to the Antarctic: an artist's notes and sketches during the Dundee Antarctic Expedition, 1892–93,* The Paradigm Press, Bluntisham Books, Norfolk.

Burns, Robin (2005) *Women in Antarctica: sharing this life-changing experience,* Fourth Annual Phillip Law Lecture, Antarctic Tasmania.

Bush WM (1982) *Antarctica and international law,* 2 vols, Oceana, London.

______(1997) *Antarctica and international law – a collection of inter-state and national documents,* part 10: Australia.

______(1988) *Antarctica and international law: a collection of inter-state and national documents,* Oceana, London.

Bush, William (2000) 'Australian implementation of the Environmental Protocol', in Davor Vidas (ed) *Implementing the Environmental Protection Regime for the Antarctic,* Kluwer, Dordrecht: 309–35.

Casey, Richard (1959) *Current notes on international affairs,* 30 (12), Department of External Affairs, Canberra.

CCAMLR (1985) *Report of the Fourth Meeting of the Commission, 2–13 September,* Hobart.

______(1989) *Report of the Eighth Meeting of the Commission, 6–17 November,* Hobart.

______(1990) *Report of the Ninth Meeting of the Commission, 22 October – 2 November,* Hobart.

______(1996) *Report of the Fifteenth Meeting of the Commission,* 21 October – 1 November, Hobart.

______(1997) *Report of the Sixteenth Meeting of the Commission,* 27 October – 7 November, Hobart.

576

______(2002) *Report of the Twenty-First Meeting of the Commission, 21 October – 1 November,* Hobart.

______(2006) *Report of the Twenty-fifth Meeting of the Commission, 23 October – 3 November,* Hobart.

Chaturvedi, Sanjay (1996) *The polar regions: a political geography,* John Wiley, Chichester.

Chile (1990) *Interim Report of the Eleventh Antarctic Treaty Special Consultative Meeting, Viña del Mar, 19 November – 6 December 1990,* 114–55 <www.ats/aq/e/ats_meetings_atcm.htm>.

Chipman, Elizabeth (1986) *Women on the ice: a history of women in the far south,* Melbourne University Press, Melbourne.

Chittleborough, G (1984) 'Nature, extent and management of Antarctic living resources', in S Harris (ed) *Australia's Antarctic policy options,* Australian National University, Canberra.

Christie EWH (1951) *The Antarctic problem,* George Allen & Unwin, London.

Clark, Pitta (1989) Richardson wavers on Antarctic Treaty, *Sydney Morning Herald* 16 May: 4.

Cole, Lynette (1990) *Proposals for the first Australian Antarctic Expedition,* Monash Publications in Geography no 39.

Collis, Christy (2000) Mawson's hut: emptying post-colonial Antarctica, *Journal of Australian Studies* 63: 22–29.

______(2004) The Proclamation Island moment: making Antarctica Australian, *Law Text Culture,* 8: 39–56.

______and Quentin Stevens (2007) Cold colonies: Antarctic spatialities at Mawson and McMurdo stations, *Cultural Geographies,* 14: 234–54.

Constable, AJ (2001) 'The status of Antarctic fisheries research', in J Jabour-Green and M Haward (eds) *The Antarctic: past, present and future,* Research Report no 28, Antarctic CRC, Hobart.

Constable AJ and WK de la Mare (1996) A generalised yield model for evaluating yield and the long-term status of fish stocks under conditions of uncertainty, *CCAMLR Science* 3: 31–54.

Constable AJ and WK de la Mare, DJ Agnew, I Everson and D Miller (2000) Managing fisheries to conserve the Antarctic marine ecosystem: practical

578

implementation of the Convention on the Conservation of Antarctic Marine Living Resources (CCAMLR), *ICES Journal of Marine Science* 57: 778–91.

Cook, Frederick (1900) *Through the first Antarctic night, 1898–1899, a narrative of the Belgica,* Heinemann, London.

Crawford, Janet (1998) *That first Antarctic winter: the story of the Southern Cross Expedition of 1898–1900 as told in the diaries of Louis Charles Bernacchi,* South Latitude Research, Christchurch.

d'Alpuget B (2010) *Hawke: the prime minister,* Melbourne University Press, Melbourne.

Dastidar PG and O Persson (2005) Mapping the global structure of Antarctic science vis-à-vis the Antarctic Treaty System, *Current Science* 89(9): 1552–54.

Dastidar PG and S Ramachandran (2008) Intellectual structure of Antarctic science: a 25-year analysis, *Scientometrics* 77: 389–414.

Davis JK (1915) 'The ship's story', chapter XVIII in Douglas Mawson, *The home of the blizzard,* vol2, William Heinemann, London.

de la Mare WK (1987) Some principles for fisheries regulation from an ecosystem perspective, *SC-CCAMLR Selected Scientific Papers* Pt 3: 323–40.

Dewart, Gilbert (1989) *Antarctic comrades: an American with the Russians in Antarctica,* Ohio State University Press, Columbus.

Division of National Mapping (Australia) (1961) *Standard symbols for use on topographic maps of Antarctica (compiled on behalf of SCAR),* Division of National Mapping, Canberra.

Dodds K (1997) *Geopolitics in Antarctica: views from the southern oceanic rim,* Wiley, New York.

Dodds K and AD Hemmings (2009) Frontier vigilantism? Australia and contemporary representations of Australian Antarctic Territory, *Australian Journal of Politics and History* 55(4): 513–29.

______(2010) Stenographers of power: reply to Haward and Bergin, *Australian Journal of Politics and History* 56(4) December: 617–19.

Dodds, Klaus J (2006) Post-colonial Antarctica: an emerging engagement, *Polar Record* 42 (220): 59–70.

580

Downer, Alexander, Philip Ruddock and Ian Macfarlane (2004) Australia Lodges Continental Shelf Submission (joint media release, 16 November) at <www.foreignminister.gov.au/releases/2004/joint_continental_shelf_submission> (accessed 29 April 2005).

Edeson W (1999) Closing the gap: the role of 'soft' international instruments to control fishing, *Australian Yearbook of International Law,* 20, [incl p 94].

Edwards DM and JA Heap (1981) Convention on the Conservation of Antarctic Marine Living Resources: a commentary, *Polar Record* 20: 353–362.

Edwards PJ (1983) *Prime ministers and diplomats: the making of Australian foreign policy, 1901–1949,* Oxford University Press, Melbourne.

Evans, Hugh B and AGE Jones (1975) A forgotten explorer: Carsten Egeberg Borchgrevink, *Polar Record* 17(108): 221–35.

Fogg, GE (1992) *A history of Antarctic science,* Cambridge University Press, Cambridge.

Foster J, S Nicol and S Kawaguchi (2009) 'The use of patent databases to detect trends in the krill fishery', paper submitted by the Government of

Australia to the Scientific Committee of the Commission for the Conservation of Antarctic Marine Living Resources, SC-CAMLR-XXVIII.

Fowler, Alfred N (2000) *COMNAP: the national managers in Antarctica,* American Literary Press Inc, Baltimore.

Fox, William L (2005) *Terra Antarctica: looking into the emptiest continent,* Trinity University Press, San Antonio.

France (1968) *Final Report of the Fifth Antarctic Treaty Consultative Meeting, Paris*<www.ats/aq/e/a ts_meetings_atcm.htm>.

Frenot Y, SL Chown, J Whinam, PM Selkirk, P Convey, M Skotnicki and DM Bergstrom (2005) Biological invasions in the Antarctic: extent, impacts and implications, *Biological Reviews* 80: 45–72.

Gardam, JG (1985) Management regimes for Antarctic marine living resources: an Australian perspective, *Melbourne University Law Review* 15: 279–312.

Giese M (1996) Effects of human activity on Adelie penguin *(Pygoscelis adeliae)* breeding success, *Biological Conservation* 75(2): 157–64.

______(1997) Guidelines for people approaching breeding groups of Adelie penguins *(Pygoscelis adeliae),Polar Record* 34: 287–92.

______and Riddle, M (1999) Disturbance of emperor penguin *(Aptenodytes forsteri)* chicks by helicopters, *Polar Biology* 22: 366–71.

Gibbs WJ (1975) *The origins of Australian meteorology,* Australian Government Publishing Service, Canberra.

Gjelsvik T (1983) 'The mineral resources of Antarctica: progress in their identification', in FO Vicuña (ed) *Antarctic resources policy: scientific, legal and political issues,* Cambridge University Press, Cambridge, 61–76.

Goldsworthy L (1990) 'World Park Antarctica, an environmentalist's vision', in RA Herr, HR Hall and MG Haward, *Antarctica's future: continuity or change?* AIIA, Hobart.

González-Ferrán O (1983) 'The mineral resources of Antarctica: progress in their identification', in FO Vicuña (ed) *Antarctic resources policy: scientific, legal and political issues,* Cambridge University Press, Cambridge, 159–166.

Green, Bill (1995) *Water, ice and stone: science and memory on the Antarctic lakes,* Harmony Books, New York.

Green, Sir Guy (2002) 'Antarctic Treaty – science under scrutiny', Inaugural Phillip Law lecture, Hobart, *Australian Antarctic Magazine* 4, <www.aad.gov.au/default.asp?casid=4379>.

Green, Marshall (1974) Diary of Antarctic Trip [23–28 December 1974], NAA A1838, 1495/18/1 Annex.

Greenwood, Gordon and Charles Grimshaw (eds) (1977) *Documents on Australian international affairs 1901–1918,* Thomas Nelson (Australia), Melbourne.

Griffiths, Tom (2007) *Slicing the silence: voyaging to Antarctica,* UNSW Press, Sydney.

______(2010) 'A humanist on thin ice', *Griffith Review* 29: 67–88.

Hains, Brigid (2002a) 'The graveyard of a century', in Tim Bonyhady and Tom Griffiths (eds) *Words for country: landscape and language in Australia,* UNSW Press, Sydney: 124–39.

584

______(2002b) *The ice and the inland: Mawson, Flynn, and the myth of the frontier,* Melbourne University Press, Melbourne.

Hall HR (1989) The open door into Antarctica: an explanation of the Hughes doctrine, *Polar Record* 25 (153): 137–40.

______and M Haward (2001) Enhancing compliance with international legislation and agreements mitigating seabird mortality on longlines, *Marine Ornithology* 28: 183–90.

Hall R (2007) 'Saving seabirds', in L Kriwoken, J Jabour and AD Hemmings (eds) *Looking south: Australia's Antarctic agenda,* Federation Press, Sydney, 117–32.

Hamzah BA (2010) Malaysia and the Southern Ocean: revisiting the question of Antarctica, *Ocean Development and International Law* 41: 186–95.

Hanessian J (1960) The Antarctic Treaty 1959, *International and Comparative Law Quarterly* 9: 436–80.

______(1965) 'National interests in Antarctica', in T Hatherton (ed) *Antarctica,* Methuen, London.

Harris Stuart (ed) (1984) *Australia's Antarctic policy options,* CRES, Monograph 11, Australian National University, Canberra.

Hassall, Anthony (1988) 'Quests', *Australian Literary Studies* 13(4): 390–408.

Hattersley-Smith G (1989) Guest editorial – Antarctic place-names, *Antarctic Science* 1(4): 299.

Haward M (2004) 'IUU fishing: contemporary practice', in AG Oude Elferink and DR Rothwell (eds) *Oceans management in the 21st century: institutional frameworks and responses,* Martinus Nijhoff Publishers, Leiden, 87–106.

_______and Anthony Bergin (2010) 'Vision not vigilantism: reply to Dodds and Hemmings', *Australian Journal of Politics and History* 56(4) December: 612–16.

_______and J Vince (2008) *Oceans governance in the twenty-first century: managing the blue planet,* Edward Elgar Publishing Ltd, Cheltenham UK and Northampton MA.

_______Rob Hall and Aynsley Kellow (2007) 'Settling and implementing the agenda: Australian Antarctic policy', in L Kriwoken, J Jabour and AD Hemmings (eds) *Looking south: Australia's Antarctic agenda,* Federation Press, Sydney, 21–37.

______DR Rothwell, J Jabour, R Hall, A Kellow, L Kriwoken, G Luyten and A Hemming (2006) Australia's Antarctic agenda, *Australian Journal of International Affairs* 60(3): 439–456. Hawke RJ (1994) *The Hawke memoirs,* William Heinemann, Melbourne.

Hayes, J Gordon (1928) *Antarctica: a treatise on the southern continent,* Richards Press, London.

Headland RK (1994a) First on the Antarctic continent? *Antarctic* 13(8): 346–48.

______(1994b) Historical development of Antarctic tourism, *Annals of Tourism Research,* 21(2): 269–80.

Hemmings, AD and LK Kriwoken (2010) High level Antarctic EIA under the Madrid Protocol: state practice and the effectiveness of the comprehensive environmental evaluation process, *International Environmental Agreements* 10(3): 187–208.

Herr RA (2001) 'The international regulation of Patagonian toothfish: CCAMLR and high seas management', in OS Stokke (ed) *Governing high seas fisheries: the interplay of global and regional regimes,* Oxford University Press, Oxford, 303–28.

_______and HR Hall (1989) 'Science as currency and the currency of science', in J Handmer (ed) *Antarctica: policies and policy development,* Centre for Resources and Environmental Studies, Australian National University, Canberra, 13–23.

_______HR Hall and MG Haward (eds) (1990) *Antarctica's future: continuity or change?,* Government Printer for AIIA, Hobart.

Hince, Bernadette (2000) *The Antarctic dictionary: a complete guide to Antarctic English,* CSIRO Publishing and Museum Victoria, Melbourne.

_______(2005) 'The teeth of the wind: an environmental history of subantarctic islands', PhD thesis, Australian National University.

Holmes N, M Giese, H Achurch, S Robinson and LK Kriwoken (2006) Behaviour and breeding success of gentoo penguins *Pygoscelis papua* in areas of low and high human activity, *Polar Biology* 29(4): 399–412.

Holmes N, M Giese and LK Kriwoken (2005) Testing the minimum approach distance guidelines for

588

incubating royal penguins *Eudyptes schlegeli, Biological Conservation* 126(3): 339–50.

______(2008) Linking variation in penguin responses to pedestrian activity for best practice management on Macquarie Island, *Polarforschung* 77(1), 7–15, 2007 (Erschienen 2008).

Howard M (1989) The Convention on the Conservation of Antarctic Marine Living Resources: a five year review, *International and Comparative Law Quarterly* 38: 104–49.

Houwelling, Suzanne (1989) Cabinet to say no to Antarctic mining treaty, *Australian* 22 May: 1.

Hudson WJ (1986) *Casey,* Oxford University Press, Melbourne.

______(1993) 'Casey, Richard Gavin Gardiner [Baron Casey] (1890–1976)', *Australian dictionary of biography,* vol13, Melbourne University Press, 1993.

______and Jane North (eds) (1980) *My Dear P.M.: R.G. Casey's Letters to S.M. Bruce 1924–1929,* Australian Government Publishing Service, Canberra.

Huntford, Roland (1986) *Shackleton,* Atheneum, New York.

Hussain, Rajamah (1990) 'The Antarctic: common heritage of mankind?' Paper presented at the Symposium on the Antarctic and the Environment: Future Prospects, Brussels, 9–10 October 1990, 1–7.

Hyde, Charles Cheney (1933) The case concerning the legal status of eastern Greenland, *American Journal of International Law* 27(4): 732–38.

Jabour, Julia (2006) High latitude diplomacy: Australia's Antarctic extended continental shelf, *Marine Policy* 30: 197.

______(2008) The Australian continental shelf: has Australia's high latitude diplomacy paid off? *Marine Policy* 33, 429–31.

______(2010) Biological prospecting: the ethics of exclusive reward from Antarctic activities, *Ethics in Science and Environmental Politics,* 10: 19–29.

Jabour-Green J and D Nicol (2003) Bioprospecting in areas outside national jurisdiction: Antarctica and the Southern Ocean, *Melbourne Journal of International Law* 4(1) 76–111.

Jacka FJ (1986) 'Mawson, Sir Douglas (1882–1958)', *Australian dictionary of biography,* vol10, Melbourne University Press, Melbourne.

590

Jacka, Fred and Eleanor Jacka (eds) (1988) *Mawson's Antarctic diaries,* Allen & Unwin, Sydney.

Jackson, Andrew (1989) Australia calls for an Antarctic wilderness reserve, *ANARE News,* September 1989, 6.

______(ed) (1995) *On the Antarctic horizon,* Proceedings of the International Symposium on the Future of the Antarctic Treaty System, Ushuaia, Argentina.

Jacobsson M (2007) 'The Antarctic Treaty System: future challenges', in G Triggs and A Riddell (eds) *Antarctica: legal and environmental challenges for the future,* British Institute of International and Comparative Law, London.

James, Rodney (2006) *Sidney Nolan: Antarctic journey,* Mornington Peninsula Regional Gallery, Mornington.

Japan (1970) *Antarctic Treaty: Report of Sixth Consultative Meeting, Tokyo.*

Johanson JM (1998) 'The CCAMLR ecosystem approach to the management of marine harvesting', PhD thesis, University of Tasmania.

Johnson, Murray P and Lorne Kriwoken (2007) 'Emerging issues of Australian Antarctic tourism: legal and policy directions', in L Kriwoken, J Jabour and AD Hemmings (eds) *Looking south: Australia's Antarctic agenda,* Federation Press, Sydney.

Joyner CC (1985) The Southern Ocean and marine pollution: problems and prospects, *Case Western Reserve Journal of International Law* 17.

______(1992) *Antarctica and the Law of the Sea,* Martinus Nijhoff, Dordrecht.

______(1998) *Governing the frozen commons,* University of South Carolina Press, Columbia.

Kawaja, Marie (2010) 'Politics and diplomacy of the Australian Antarctic, 1901–1945', PhD thesis, Australian National University, Canberra.

Kaye SB (2004) Territorial sea baselines along ice covered coasts: international practice and the limits of the Laws of the Sea, *Ocean Development and International Law* 35: 75–102.

______DR Rothwell S and Dando (1999) *The laws of the Australian Antarctic Territory,* Antarctic and Southern Ocean Law and Policy Occasional Papers 8.

592

_______DR Rothwell and M Haward (2001) 'Ecosystem management in the Southern Ocean', in M Haward (ed) *Integrated ocean management: issues in implementing Australia's oceans policy,* Antarctic CRC Research Report 26, 41–54.

Kerr A (2009) *A federation in these seas: an account of the acquisition by Australia of its external territories, with selected documents,*Attorney-General's Department, Canberra.

Khoo BT (1995) *Paradoxes of Mahathirism: an intellectual biography of Mahathir Mohamad,* Oxford University Press, Kuala Lumpur.

Kirkby, Syd (1993) Sledge dogs to satellites: some personal recollections of the exploration and mapping of Australian Antarctica, *Queensland Geographical Journal* 8: 11–22.

Kock K-H (1992) *Antarctic fish and fisheries,* Cambridge University Press, Cambridge.

Kovalskis S (1993) Tourism report: the Government responds, *ANARE News* 73: 5.

Kriwoken LK (1991) Antarctic environmental planning and management: conclusions from Casey Station, Australian Antarctic Territory, *Polar Record* 27(160): 1–8.

Kriwoken, Lorne, Julia Jabour and Alan Hemmings (eds) (2007) *Looking south: Australia's Antarctic agenda,* Federation Press, Sydney.

Lambert BP (1971) Secretary to the Working Group on Geodesy and Cartography, *Geodetic surveying in Antarctica, 1967–1970.* Report to the Fifteenth General Assembly of the International Union of Geodesy and Geophysics, Moscow, 2–13 August 1971.

Lambert BP and G Laclavère (1961) 'Foreword', in SCAR Working Group on Geodesy and Cartography, *Standard symbols for use on topographic maps of Antarctica,* Division of National Mapping, Canberra.

Law PG (1964) *Antarctica –1984,* Sir John Morris Memorial Lecture 1964, Adult Education Board, Hobart.

Law, Phillip (1983) *Antarctic odyssey,* Heinemann, Melbourne.

______(1990) 'The Antarctic wilderness – a wild idea!' in RA Hall, HR Hall and MG Haward (eds) (1990) *Antarctica's future,* Government Printer for AIIA, Hobart, 71-90.

______(2002) 'Developing ANARE research programs', in HJ Marchant, DJ Lugg and PG Quilty (eds) (2002) *Australian Antarctic science: the first 50 years of*

ANARE, Australian Antarctic Division, Kingston, 15–19.

Laws, Richard (1991) Unacceptable threats to Antarctic science, *New Scientist* 30 March: 4.

Leane, Elizabeth (2007) 'A place of ideals in conflict': images of Antarctica in Australian literature', in CA Cranston and Robert Zeller (eds) *The littoral zone: Australian contexts and their writers,* Rodopi, Amsterdam.

Lopez, Barry (1998) *About this life: journeys on the threshold of memory,* The Harvill Press, London.

Lovering JF and JRV Prescott (1979) *Last of lands ... Antarctica,* Melbourne University Press.

Mahathir bin Mohamad (1982) Statement by the Prime Minister of Malaysia at the 37th Session of the United Nations General Assembly in New York, 29th September 1982, *Foreign Affairs Malaysia* 15: 173–84.

______(1986) Statement by the Prime Minister at the 41st Session in New York on September 29, 1986, *Foreign Affairs Malaysia* 19(3): 55–65.

Malaysia (1983) 'Antarctica: Common Heritage of Mankind', Malaysian statement on Antarctica to the Non-Governmental Organisations at the United Nations delivered on November 17, 1983, *Foreign Affairs Malaysia* 16(4): 437–39.

Manning, John (2002) Australian National Antarctic Research Expeditions (ANARE): mapping and geodesy 1947–1997, in HJ Marchant, DJ Lugg and PG Quilty (eds) *Australian Antarctic science: the first 50 years of ANARE,* Australian Antarctic Division, Kingston, 54–72.

______(2010) The 1939 Australian map of Antarctica, *The Globe: Journal of the Australian and New Zealand Map Society* 65, 19–27.

Marchal A (1989) Convention for the Conservation of Antarctic Seals: 1988 review of operations, *Polar Record* 25: 142–43.

Marchant HJ, DJ Lugg and PG Quilty (eds) (2002) *Australian Antarctic science: the first 50 years of ANARE,* Australian Antarctic Division, Kingston.

Mawer, Granville Allen (2006) *South by northwest: the magnetic crusade and the contest for Antarctica,* Wakefield Press, Adelaide.

Mawson, Douglas (1911) *Australasian Association for the Advancement of Science Report* 13: 398.

______(1915) *The home of the blizzard: the story of the Australasian Antarctic Expedition, 1911–1914,* 2 vols, William Heinemann, London.

McCarthy, Michael (1991) Major adds weight to Antarctic mining ban, *Australian* 15 May: 10.

McElrea, Richard and David Harrowfield (2004) *Polar castaways,* Canterbury University Press, Canterbury (NZ).

McIntyre D (1996) *Two below zero: a year alone in Antarctica,* Australian Geographic, Sydney.

Millar TB (ed) (1972) *Australian Foreign Minister: the diaries of RG Casey 1951–1960,* Collins, London.

______(1978) *Australia in peace and war,* Australian National University Press, Canberra.

Molenaar EJ (2000) The concept of 'real interest' and other aspects of co-operation through regional fisheries management mechanisms, *International Journal of Marine and Coastal Law* 15(4): 475–531.

Montgomery, Bruce (1990) US likely to back ban on Antarctic mining – Hawke. *The Australian* 26 February.

Moonie, Patrick (1991) The Mawson huskies – the case for retention, *Aurora [ANARE Club Magazine]* 12(1): 1–3.

Morgan J (1996) 'Australia's Antarctic policy: theory and practice', Graduate Diploma of Antarctic and Southern Ocean Studies with Honours thesis, Institute of Antarctic and Southern Ocean Studies, University of Tasmania.

Mortimer, Greg (2006) Third Annual Phillip Law lecture, *Antarctic tourism – past, present and future,* Antarctic Tasmania, Hobart.

Mosley, Geoff (2007) *Antarctica: securing its heritage for the whole world,* Envirobook, Sydney.

______(2009) *Saving the Antarctic wilderness,* Envirobook, Sydney.

Mossop, Joanna (2005) When is a whale sanctuary not a whale sanctuary? Japanese whaling in Australian Antarctic maritime zones, *Victoria University of Wellington Law Review* 36: 757–73.

Murray, Carl and Julia Jabour (2004) Independent expeditions and Antarctic tourism policy, *Polar Record* 40 (215): 309–17.

Murray-Smith, Stephen (1988) *Sitting on penguins: people and politics in Australian Antarctica,* Hutchinson Australia, Sydney.

Nasht, Simon (2005) *The last explorer: Hubert Wilkins: Australia's unknown hero,* Hodder Australia, Sydney.

New Zealand (1989) White paper on Antarctic environment. House of Representatives, August, Government Printer, Wellington.

Nicol S and Y Endo (1997) *Krill fisheries of the world,* Food and Agriculture Organization, Rome, FAO Fisheries Technical Paper no 367.

Orheim O, A Press and N Gilbert (2011) 'Managing the Antarctic environment – the evolving role of the Committee for Environmental Protection', in *Science diplomacy: Antarctica, science, and the governance of international spaces,* Smithsonian Institution Scholarly Press, Washington, DC.

Orrego Vicuña F (1988) 'The Law of the Sea and the Antarctic Treaty System: new approaches to offshore jurisdiction', in CC Joyner and SK Chopra (eds), *The*

Antarctic legal regime, Martinus Nijhoff, Dordrecht, 97–127.

______(1991) 'The effectiveness of the decision-making machinery of CCAMLR: an Assessment', in A Jørgensen-Dahl and W østreng (eds) *The Antarctic Treaty System in world politics,* Macmillan, London.

Parliament of Australia (1989) *Tourism in Antarctica – Report of the House of Representatives Standing Committee on Environment, Recreation and the Arts,* Australian Government Publishing Service, Canberra.

______(1992) 'Australia's Antarctic policy objectives' in *Australian Law in Antarctica, The report of the second phase of an inquiry into the legal regimes of Australia's external Territories and the Jervis Bay Territory, House of Representatives Standing Committee on Legal and Constitutional Affairs,* Australian Government Publishing Service, Canberra.

Peake, Ross (1990) Ban on mining unlikely in Antarctic pact, *The Age* 5 December.

______and Caroline Milburn (1989) Cabinet likely to veto Antarctic mining, *The Age* 17 May: 5.

Potter S (2003) 'Approaches to Antarctic solid waste management logistics: past, present, potential',

Master of Environmental Management thesis, Centre for Environmental Studies, University of Tasmania.

Powell D (1990) 'Antarctic marine living resources and CCAMLR', in RA Herr, HR Hall and MG Haward (eds) *Antarctica's future: continuity or change?* AIIA/TGPO, Hobart, 61–70.

Powell, Stephen and Andrew Jackson (2007) 'Australian influence in the Antarctic Treaty System: an end or a means?', in L Kriwoken, J Jabour and AD Hemmings (eds) *Looking south: Australia's Antarctic agenda,* Federation Press, Sydney, 38–53.

Priestley, Raymond (1914) *Antarctic adventure: Scott's northern party,* T Fisher Unwin, London.

Press AJ (2001) 'Antarctica and the future', in J Jabour-Green and M Haward (eds) *The Antarctic: past, present and future,* Antarctic CRC, Hobart, 153-154.

Prescott, Victor and Gillian D Triggs (2008) *International frontiers and boundaries: law, politics and geography,* Martinus Nijhoff, Leiden.

Price, A Grenfell (1962) *The winning of Australian Antarctica,* Angus & Robertson, Sydney.

Pyne, Stephen J (1986) *The ice: a journey to Antarctica,* University of Washington Press, Seattle.

Richards P (2010) 'The Antarctic Treaty today', in *Australia and the Antarctic Treaty – then and now,* Occasional Publication no 1, Institute for Marine and Antarctic Studies, University of Tasmania, July 2010.

Riddle MJ and PM Goldsworthy (2002) 'Environmental science and the environmental ethos of ANARE', in HJ Marchant, DJ Lugg, and P Quilty (eds) *Australian Antarctic science: the first 50 years of ANARE,* Australian Antarctic Division, Kingston, 561–70.

Roberts, Brian (1964) Antarctic gazetteers, *Polar Record* 12(76) 84–86.

Rolf P (1979) *The journalistic javelin: an illustrated history of The Bulletin,* Wildcat Press, Sydney.

Roots EF (1986) 'The role of science in the Antarctic Treaty System', in *Antarctic Treaty System: an assessment,* US National Academy Press, Washington, DC, 169–84.

Rothblum, Esther D, Jacqueline S Weinstock and Jessica F Morris (eds) (1998) *Women in the Antarctic,* The Haworth Press, New York.

602

Rothwell DR (1995) 'Environmental regulation in the Southern Ocean', in J Crawford and DR Rothwell, *The Law of the Sea in the Asian Pacific region,* Martinus Nijhoff, Dordrecht: 102–03.

______(1996) *The polar regions and the development of international law,* Cambridge University Press.

Rothwell, Donald R and Hitoshi Nasu (2008) 'Antarctica and international security discourse: a primer', *New Zealand Yearbook of International Law* 6: 3.

______and Shirley V Scott (2007) 'Flexing Australian sovereignty in Antarctica: pushing Antarctic Treaty limits in the national interests', in L Kriwoken, J Jabour and AD Hemmings (eds) *Looking south: Australia's Antarctic agenda,* Federation Press, Sydney, 7–20.

Scientific Committee on Antarctic Research (1989) *Waste disposal in the Antarctic,* Australian Antarctic Division, Kingston.

Scott, Keith (1989) Antarctica in delay basket, *Canberra Times* 3 May: 3.

Schreuder DM and S Ward (eds) (2008) *Australia's empire,* Oxford University Press, Oxford.

Seccombe, Mike (1988) Keating warns against signing Antarctic treaty, *Sydney Morning Herald,* 21 November: 2.

______(1991) Nations agree to protect Antarctica, *Sydney Morning Herald,* 1 May: 9.

Serdy, Andrew (2005) Toward certainty of seabed jurisdiction beyond 200 nautical miles from the territorial sea baseline: Australia's submission to the Commission on the Limits of the Continental Shelf, *Ocean Development and International Law* 36: 201.

Shackleton EH (1909) *The heart of the Antarctic: being the story of the British Antarctic Expedition 1907–1909,* 2 vols, William Heinemann, London.

Shackleton, Sir Ernest (1919) *South: the story of Shackleton's last expedition 1914–1917,* William Heinemann, London.

Somov, Mikhail Mikhailovich (1966) Cooperation of scientists in the Antarctic, *Vestnik [Herald] of the Academy of Sciences, USSR,* January: 73–80, translated into English, typescript, AAD Library.

Snape I, MJ Riddle, JS Stark, CM Cole, CK King, S Duquesne and DB Gore (2001) Management and remediation of contaminated sites at Casey Station, East Antarctica, *Polar Record* 37(202): 199–214.

Sprent, Chas P (1887) Antarctic exploration, in *Royal Society of Tasmania, Papers and Proceedings for 1886.*

Spufford, Francis (1996) *I may be some time,* Faber & Faber, London.

Stark JS, I Snape and MJ Riddle (2003) The effects of petroleum hydrocarbon and heavy metal contamination of marine sediments on recruitment of Antarctic soft-sediment assemblages: a field experimental investigation, *Journal of Experimental Marine Biology and Ecology* 283: 21–50.

Stephens T and B Boer (2007) 'Enforcement and compliance in the Australian Antarctic Territory: legal and policy dilemmas', in L Kriwoken, J Jabour and AD Hemmings (eds) *Looking south: Australia's Antarctic agenda,* Federation Press, Sydney, 54–70.

Stoddart DM (ed) (2008) *Australia's contribution to Antarctic climate science,* Department of the Environment, Water, Heritage and the Arts, Australian Antarctic Division, Hobart.

Stokke OS (1996) 'The effectiveness of CCAMLR', in OS Stokke and D Vidas (eds) *Governing the*

Antarctic: the effectiveness and legitimacy of the Antarctic Treaty System, Cambridge University Press, Cambridge, 120–51.

Strange, Carolyn and Alison Bashford (2008) *Griffith Taylor: visionary, environmentalist, explorer,* National Library of Australia, Canberra.

Sulong ZA (1983a) 'Antarctica: heritage of mankind': Statement by Malaysia's Permanent Representative to the United Nations, Tan Sri Zainal Abidin Sulong, in the General Committee on the inclusion of supplementary item on 'question of Antarctica' as Agenda of the 38th UNGA on 21st September, 1983, *Foreign Affairs Malaysia* 16(3): 329–33.

______(1983b) 'Question of Antarctica': Address by Permanent Representative to the United Nations Tan Sri Zainal Abidin Sulong on the 'Question of Antarctica' on November 28th, 1983, *Foreign Affairs Malaysia* 16(4): 446.

Sulzberger PH (1975) *Views on Australian involvement in Antarctica,* Antarctic Division, Department of Science (unpublished).

Swan RA (1961) *Australia in the Antarctic: interest, activity and endeavour,* Melbourne University Press, Melbourne.

______(1990) 'Wilkins, Sir George Hubert (1888–1958)', *Australian dictionary of biography,* vol12, Melbourne University Press, Melbourne.

Swithinbank, Charles (1997) *An alien in Antarctica: reflections upon forty years of exploration and research on the frozen continent,* The McDonald & Woodward Publishing Company, Blacksburg, VA.

Talboys BE (1978) New Zealand and the Antarctic Treaty, *New Zealand Foreign Affairs Review* 28(3&4): 33.

Taylor, Griffith (1930) *Antarctic adventure and research,* D Appleton & Company, New York.

Tepper, Rohan and Marcus Haward (2005) The development of Malaysia's position on Antarctica: 1982–2004, *Polar Record* 41 (217): 113–24.

Thompson, Janet (1997) Antarctic mapping: a bleak future? *Antarctic Science* 9(4): 371–72.

Triggs GD (1984) Antarctica: a conflict of interest, *Current Affairs Bulletin* 63(6): 13–24.

Triggs, Gillian D (1986) *International law and Australian sovereignty in Antarctica,* Legal Books, Sydney.

Trombetta-Panigadi F (1996) 'The exploitation of Antarctic icebergs in international law', in F Francioni and T Scovazzi (eds) *International law for Antarctica,* 2nd edn, 225–57.

Tyler-Lewis, Kelly (2006) *The lost men,* Bloomsbury, London.

United States of America (1984) 'Assessment and avoidance of incidental mortality of Antarctic marine living resources', in CCAMLR, *Report of the Third Meeting of the Commission 3 September – 14 September,* Hobart.

United States Government (1960) *The Conference on Antarctica, Washington, October 15 – December 1, 1959. Conference Documents, The Antarctic Treaty and Related Papers,* Department of State Publication 7060, International Organization and Conference Series 13, Historical Office, Bureau of Public Affairs, Washington, DC.

US Department of State (2002) *Antarctic Treaty handbook,* 9th edn.

van Ommen TD and V Morgan (2010) Snowfall increase in coastal East Antarctica linked with southwest Western Australian drought, *Nature Geoscience,*doi:10.1038/NGEO761.

Vidas D (1993) The Antarctic Treaty System and the Law of the Sea: a new dimension introduced by the Madrid Protocol, 1 *International Antarctic Research Project,* 7–9.

Vidas, Davor (1996a) 'The Antarctic Treaty System in the international community: an overview', in OS Stokke and D Vidas (eds) *Governing the Antarctic: the effectiveness and legitimacy of the Antarctic Treaty System,* Cambridge University Press, Cambridge.

______(1996b) 'The Antarctic Treaty System and the Law of the Sea: a new dimension introduced by the protocol', in OS Stokke and D Vidas (eds) *Governing the Antarctic: the effectiveness and legitimacy of the Antarctic Treaty System,* Cambridge University Press, Cambridge, 73–74.

Watt, Alan (1967) *The evolution of Australian foreign policy, 1938–1965,* Cambridge University Press, London.

Weeks WF (1980) Iceberg water: an assessment, *Annals of Glaciology* 1: 5–10.

Weber M (2011) 'The strength to continue: a case study approach to examining the robustness of polar governance in the era of environmental and energy security', PhD thesis, University of Tasmania.

Wheeler, Sara (1997) *Terra Incognita: travels in Antarctica,* Vintage, London.

Wolfrum R (1995) 'Possible challenges and the future development of the Antarctic Treaty System', in A Jackson (ed) *On the Antarctic horizon,* Consejo Argentino para las Relaciones Internacionales, Buenos Aires, 85–91.

Woolcott, Richard (2003) *The hot seat: reflections on diplomacy from Stalin's death to the Bali bombings,* Harper Collins, Sydney.

Zainuddin Y (2002) Statement by the Deputy Permanent Representative of Malaysia to The United Nations on Agenda Item 59: 'Question of Antarctica' at the First Committee of the 57th Session of the United Nations General Assembly, New York. Ministry of Foreign Affairs, Malaysia.

A

Books For ALL Kinds of Readers

At ReadHowYouWant we understand that one size does not fit all types of readers. Our innovative, patent pending technology allows us to design new formats to make reading easier and more enjoyable for you. This helps improve your speed of reading and your comprehension. Our EasyRead printed books have been optimized to improve word recognition, ease eye tracking by adjusting word and line spacing as well as minimizing hyphenation. Our EasyRead SuperLarge editions have been developed to make reading easier and more accessible for vision-impaired readers. We offer Braille and DAISY formats of our books and all popular E-Book formats.

We are continually introducing new formats based upon research and reader preferences. Visit our web-site to see all of our formats and learn how you can Personalize our books for yourself or as gifts. Sign up to Become A RHYW Registered Reader.

www.readhowyouwant.com

Printed in Great Britain
by Amazon

Praise for THE BRIDGE and HAVOC

'*The Bridge* is a captivating tale of friendship
and loyalty.' *Australian Women's Weekly*

'Taut adventure, high stakes, big emotion, individual
heroism and no less than the possible end of the world.
A fantastic read.' *ABC Brisbane*

'Brilliant. Every sentence is skillfully crafted,
with just enough left unsaid that the reader is always
hungry for more…A breathtaking first novel.'
Junior Bookseller+Publisher

'If you loved Suzanne Collins' *The Hunger Games* series and
John Marsden's Tomorrow series, chances are you'll love
this'. *Girlfriend NZ*

'A powerful dystopian adventure about questioning
authority, the complexities of war and enduring bonds.'
Sydney Morning Herald

'*Havoc* is urgent, moving and believable.'
New Zealand Listener

'Complex and thought-provoking.'
New Zealand Book Council

'An outstanding teenage novel…World class.' Nine to Noon

'A thought-provoking story of friendship, loyalty, betrayal
and the desire for power at any cost.' *Kids Book Review*

'*Havoc* is a brilliantly wrought story, the characterisation
is subtle and nuanced, the moral underpinnings of the
story are really something else…So moving…I burst
into tears while I was reading it.' Kate de Goldi